EMERGENCY MANAGEMENT

for Sport and Physical Activity

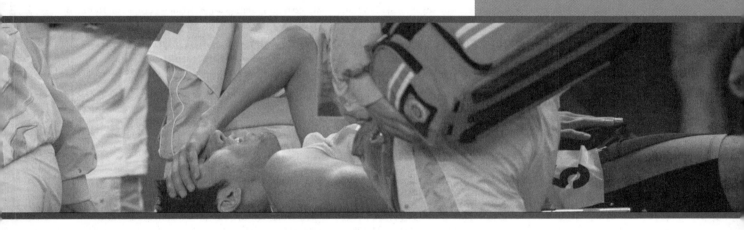

Edited by

Douglas J. Casa, PhD, ATC, FACSM, FNATA

Professor, Department of Kinesiology
Chief Operating Officer, Korey Stringer Institute
Director, Athletic Training Education
University of Connecticut
Storrs, CT

Rebecca L. Stearns, PhD, ATC

Vice President of Operations and Director of Education, Korey Stringer Institute
Department of Kinesiology
University of Connecticut
Storrs, CT

JONES & BARTLETT
LEARNING

World Headquarters
Jones & Bartlett Learning
5 Wall Street
Burlington, MA 01803
978-443-5000
info@jblearning.com
www.jblearning.com

Jones & Bartlett Learning books and products are available through most bookstores and online booksellers. To contact Jones & Bartlett Learning directly, call 800-832-0034, fax 978-443-8000, or visit our website, www.jblearning.com.

Substantial discounts on bulk quantities of Jones & Bartlett Learning publications are available to corporations, professional associations, and other qualified organizations. For details and specific discount information, contact the special sales department at Jones & Bartlett Learning via the above contact information or send an email to specialsales@jblearning.com.

Production Credits

Publisher: Cathy L. Esperti
Acquisitions Editor: Ryan Angel
Associate Editor: Kayla Dos Santos
Associate Director of Production: Julie C. Bolduc
Production Editor: Keith Henry
Senior Marketing Manager: Andrea DeFronzo
VP, Manufacturing and Inventory Control: Therese Connell

Photo Research and Permissions Coordinator: Joe Veiga
Cover Design: Kristin E. Parker
Composition: Cenveo Publisher Services
Cover and Title Page Image: © PETER PARKS/AFP/Getty Images
Printing and Binding: Edwards Brothers Malloy
Cover Printing: Edwards Brothers Malloy

Library of Congress Cataloging-in-Publication Data

Emergency management for sport and physical activity / [edited by] Douglas J. Casa and Rebecca L. Stearns.
    p. ; cm.
Includes bibliographical references and index.
ISBN 978-1-284-02216-2 (pbk.)
I. Casa, Douglas J., editor of compilation. II. Stearns, Rebecca L., editor of compilation.
[DNLM: 1. Athletic Injuries—prevention & control. 2. Death, Sudden, Cardiac. 3. Emergency Treatment. QT 261]
RD97
617.1'027—dc23
                          2014000902
6048

Printed in the United States of America
18 17 16 15 14   10 9 8 7 6 5 4 3 2 1

DEDICATION

We would like to dedicate this text to those left behind. After the death of an athlete, parents, grandparents, spouses, children, brothers, sisters, friends, boyfriends, girlfriends, coaches, teachers, school personnel, and medical providers are left with a grief that is incomprehensible to those who have not experienced it. This text honors those loved ones who live with this constant struggle. We hope that with our efforts, together we can prevent future tragedies.

We would also like to dedicate the text to the staff at the Korey Stringer Institute (KSI). They give tirelessly, working toward the ultimate goal of making sports and physical activity safer for all those involved. The passion and energy at KSI are contagious, and we are very thankful to all of those who have served, who currently serve, and who will serve in the future. A special note of thanks to the KSI Founders Council, the amazing University of Connecticut students, employees, and friends who helped us create KSI in the fall of 2009 and winter of 2010: Julie DeMartini, Kerri Gavin, James Gould, Rachel Karslo, Carl Maresh, Jessica Martschinske, Kelly Pagnotta, Geryl Rose, Kelci Stringer, Sandra Tierney, and Megan VanSumeren.

BRIEF CONTENTS

CONTENTS

CHAPTER 1 Developing Safety Policies for Organized Sports 1

Michael S. Ferrara, PhD, ATC, FNATA
Ralph Swearngin, PhD
William M. Adams, MS, ATC
Douglas J. Casa, PhD, ATC, FACSM, FNATA

CHAPTER 2 Fatal and Catastrophic Injuries in Athletics: Epidemiologic
Data and Challenging Circumstances 17

Zachary Y. Kerr, PhD, MPH
Karen Roos, MSPT, ATC
Frederick O. Mueller, PhD, FACSM
Douglas J. Casa, PhD, ATC, FACSM, FNATA

CHAPTER 3 **Prevention of Sudden Cardiac Death in Young Athletes**   31
Brett G. Toresdahl, MD
Jonathan A. Drezner, MD

CHAPTER 4 **Prevention of Sudden Cardiac Death in Older Athletes**   43
Shishir Mathur, MD
Paul D. Thompson, MD, FACC, FACSM

CHAPTER 5 **Prevention of Sudden Cardiac Death: Commotio Cordis**   53
John A. Kalin, MD
Christopher Madias, MD
Mark S. Link, MD, FACC

CHAPTER 6 **Exertional Heat Stroke** 61

Rebecca L. Stearns, PhD, ATC
Francis G. O'Connor, MD, MPH, FACSM
Douglas J. Casa, PhD, ATC, FACSM, FNATA
Glen P. Kenny, PhD

CHAPTER 7 **Brain Injuries** 83

Jason P. Mihalik, PhD, CAT(C), ATC
Kevin M. Guskiewicz, PhD, ATC, FACSM, FNATA

FOREWORD

A Chance to Lead

Roger S. Goodell, Commissioner, National Football League

Times have changed. The culture of sports has shifted in recent years to a more progressive approach that emphasizes safety along with competitive success.

This can be an extremely challenging tightrope to walk, but it is a path we must take to ensure the success of the sports we love. The culture of change is a result of the tremendous advances made in the field of sports medicine. We now have more certainty about what can be done to decrease or eliminate the risk of several serious medical conditions. Those of us who appreciate the tremendous value of organized sports must make sure that this information is broadly shared and that we challenge those around us to do everything possible to protect the health and safety of athletes.

Take, for example, heat stroke. We lost a member of the NFL family when Korey Stringer died very suddenly in August 2001 as a result of heat stroke. Current medical recommendations regarding heat stroke offer a wealth of information on how to prevent the condition from occurring in the first place and, if it does occur, the treatment course to follow in order to maximize chances for survival. Other examples include head injuries and cardiac conditions. This text offers the best cutting-edge information on these and other potentially serious medical issues facing athletes at all levels.

Dr. Casa and Dr. Stearns have compiled information from national experts that is presented in terms that can be used by sports professionals without medical training to enhance the safety of all athletes. It was a project developed at the Korey Stringer Institute at the University of Connecticut, a place close to our hearts because of Korey Stringer. Korey's wife Kelci and the Korey Stringer Institute provide a guiding light for how we can better serve athletes in sports at every level.

Sports medicine has evolved dramatically in recent years. The decade from 2000 to 2010 may be remembered as a pivotal period when sports medicine met sports policies to effect a significant change toward a culture of safety. While some are resistant to change and fear it may compromise the integrity of the sport they love, we cannot go back. The science and medicine tell us we can do better. This is our chance to lead. Whether you are a parent, leader of a state athletic organization, coach, youth league administrator, athlete, medical staff member, or commissioner of the NFL, we all must move forward with safety as our first priority.

Sports will thrive because we are acting courageously to protect our athletes. In the end, everyone wins.

© Giorgio Micheletti/ShutterStock, Inc.

Emergency Management for Sport and Physical Activity is an important contribution to the sports safety literature. It is the first text of its type that has individual topic chapters written by content area experts. The text was carefully designed to offer a blend of clinical, scientific, and research expertise regarding each medical condition that can cause sudden death during sport and physical activity. The chapter authors actively work in clinical settings to prevent and treat the conditions described and perform research to further their understanding of the conditions. The text is geared toward those who supervise activities in which the participating athletes/soldiers/laborers are at risk for sustaining emergency medical conditions. Specifically, coaches, athletic directors, league administrators, parents, drill sergeants, supervisors, strength and conditioning coaches, and athletes themselves can benefit from the information.

Key Features

This text presents several unique and significant offerings that bolster a reader's clinical competence and educational opportunities. These include, but are not limited to, the following:

- A detailed overview of the 10 most common causes of death in sport and physical activity
- Coverage of epidemiology, emergency action plans, and legal issues, showing how the infrastructure of preventing sudden death during sport and activity are influenced

Instructor Resources

Instructors who use the text will have access to a number of resources, including:

- PROBLEM-BASED LEARNING SCENARIOS (PBLS) that give instructors the opportunity to push students' critical thinking further by having students apply the information gained in the chapters to fictional scenarios. The PBLs also come with a suggested grading matrix to help instructors assess their students' work.
- A TEST BANK FOR EACH CHAPTER, which includes a variety of multiple choice, matching, true or false, and short-answer questions.
- POWERPOINT LECTURE OUTLINES to help guide discussion in the classroom.

Ultimately, the greatest asset readers of this text gain is an in-depth understanding of the conditions and issues being discussed as imparted by content area experts who have been on the front lines. This connection with cutting-edge information will afford supervisors with the best opportunity to prevent sudden death during sport and physical activity.

In December 2010, Douglas Casa had the opportunity to speak with numerous parents and spouses who had either lost a loved one or had a loved one experience a near-death episode (some with long-term and lasting complications), and he was struck with a powerful thought: Nearly every death in sport (or event with a long-term medical consequence) is preventable. Imagine the crushing grip of sadness when a parent or spouse comes to realize that the tragedy could have been averted, often with minimal effort and cost. Although not all deaths or serious medical outcomes in sport are preventable, a close examination of them makes us realize that most are. Doug's mantra has always been, "Do whatever you can *before* they die." Changes that are made after a death (as they usually are) leave us wondering "What if?" That is a burden none of us wants to bear.

ACKNOWLEDGMENTS

We have numerous people to thank. The staff at Jones & Bartlett Learning have made a challenging project relatively painless: Bill Brottmiller, Ed Moura, Megan Turner, Kayla Dos Santos, Agnes Burt, Ryan Angel, Cathy Esperti, and Keith Henry. A huge thank you also to the world-class authors who were willing to give so much of their time to contribute the chapters in this text. We are very grateful to have had such high caliber authors come together for such an important cause.

Finally, thanks to the following external reviewers, who gave valuable insights and suggestions to enhance the final product.

Lois A. Butcher-Poffley, PhD, CC-AASP
Temple University
Philadelphia, PA

Kathleen A. English, MS, ATC
University of Nebraska at Kearney
Kearney, NV

Betty Etier, BS, MS
Huston-Tillotson University
Austin, TX

Matthew Garrett, MD
Loras College
Dubuque, IA

JoAnne Graf, PhD
Florida State University
Tallahassee, FL

Kris Ring, MS, ATC, LAT
Texas Women's University
Denton, TX

Dr. Douglas J. Casa

Douglas J. Casa earned his bachelor's degree in biology from Allegheny College in 1990, his master's degree in athletic training from the University of Florida in 1993, and his doctorate in exercise physiology from the University of Connecticut in 1997. For the past 15 years, Dr. Casa has worked toward his goal of preventing sudden death in sport at the Department of Kinesiology, University of Connecticut. During this time he has published more than 150 peer-reviewed publications and presented more than 350 times on subjects related to exertional heat stroke, heat-related illnesses, preventing sudden death in sport, and hydration. Dr. Casa has successfully treated more than 170 cases of exertional heat stroke (with zero fatalities).

In April 2010, Kelci Stringer (Korey Stringer's widow) and James Gould (Korey's agent) asked Dr. Casa to develop and run the Korey Stringer Institute (KSI) at the University of Connecticut. Korey was an All-Pro offensive tackle for the Minnesota Vikings in the NFL. He died from exertional heat stroke in August 2001. KSI (ksi.uconn.edu) serves the public by working toward preventing sudden death in sport by means of education, advocacy, public policy, research, media outreach, and publications.

Dr. Casa was named full professor at the University of Connecticut in August 2010. In 2008, he was the recipient of the Medal for Distinguished Athletic Training Research from the National Athletic Trainers' Association (NATA). He was named a fellow of NATA in 2008. He received the Sayers "Bud" Miller Distinguished Educator Award from NATA in 2007 and has been a fellow of the American College of Sports Medicine (ACSM) since 2001. He has been a lead author or coauthor on numerous sports medicine (ACSM, NATA) position statements related to heat illness and hydration. He is an associate editor of the *Journal of Athletic Training* and *Journal of Science and Medicine in Sport* and is on the editorial board of *Current Sports Medicine Reports*, *Journal of Sport Rehabilitation*, and the *Journal of Strength and Conditioning Research*. Dr. Casa has worked with numerous media outlets across the country in discussing his research, including NBC's *Today Show*, *Good Morning America*, ESPN's *Outside the Lines*, CNN, PBS's *Frontline*, *Sports Illustrated*, *USA Today*, *Runners' World*, *National Geographic*, *The Wall Street Journal*, and *The New York Times*.

Dr. Casa has been happily married to his wife, Tutita Casa, PhD, for 18 years; they have three children.

Dr. Rebecca L. Stearns

Rebecca L. Stearns earned her bachelor's degree in athletic training from Duquesne University in 2006, her master's degree in exercise science from the University of Connecticut in 2008, and her doctorate in exercise science from the University of Connecticut in 2012. Dr. Stearns currently works at the KSI within the Department of Kinesiology at the University of Connecticut. During her time at the university, Dr. Stearns has published more than 20 peer-reviewed publications and given over 35 local or national presentations on subjects related to exertional heat stroke, heat-related illnesses, enhancing athletic performance in the heat, preventing sudden death in sport, and hydration.

In April 2010, Dr. Stearns was one of the founding members of KSI and continues to work toward the KSI mission, serving the public in preventing sudden death in sport by means of education, advocacy, public policy, research, media outreach, and publications.

Dr. Stearns has been a coauthor of numerous sports medicine interassociation task forces and position statements pertaining to sudden death in exercise including: The National Athletic Trainers' Association position statement, *Preventing Sudden Death in Sports*; the Inter-Association Task Force for Preventing Sudden Death in Collegiate Conditioning Sessions, *Best Practices Recommendations*; and The Inter-Association Task Force for Preventing Sudden Death in Secondary School Athletics Programs, *Best Practices Recommendations*.

Dr. Stearns is joyfully married to her husband, Jacob E. Earp, PhD.

CONTRIBUTORS

William M. Adams, MS, ATC
Director of Sport Safety Policy Initiatives, Korey
Stringer Institute
Department of Kinesiology
University of Connecticut
Storrs, CT

Scott Anderson, ATC
Head Athletic Trainer
University of Oklahoma
Norman, OK

Lawrence E. Armstrong, PhD, FACSM
Human Performance Laboratory
Professor, Department of Kinesiology
University of Connecticut
Storrs, CT
Member, Korey Stringer Institute Medical and
Science Advisory Board

**Robert J. Baker, MD, PhD, ATC,
FACSM, FAAFP**
Professor, Family and Community Medicine
Program Director, Sports Medicine Fellowship
Western Michigan University School
of Medicine

Douglas J. Casa, PhD, ATC, FACSM, FNATA
Professor, Department of Kinesiology
Chief Operating Officer, Korey Stringer Institute
Director, Athletic Training Education
University of Connecticut
Storrs, CT

Ron Courson, ATC, PT, NREMT-I, CSCS
Senior Associate Athletic Director, Sports
Medicine
University of Georgia
Athens, GA
Member, Korey Stringer Institute Medical and
Science Advisory Board

Jonathan A. Drezner, MD
Professor, Department of Family Medicine
Director, Center for Sports Cardiology
Team Physician, Seattle Seahawks and
University of Washington Athletics
Seattle, WA
Member, Korey Stringer Institute Medical and
Science Advisory Board

E. Randy Eichner, MD, FACSM
Emeritus Professor of Medicine
University of Oklahoma Health Sciences Center
Oklahoma City, OK

Michael S. Ferrara, PhD, ATC
Dean, College of Health and Human Services
University of New Hampshire
Durham, NH
Member, Korey Stringer Institute Medical and
Science Advisory Board

Katie Walsh Flanagan, EdD, ATC
Director of Sports Medicine and
Athletic Training
Professor, Department of Health Education
and Promotion
East Carolina University
Greenville, NC

Gil Fried, JD
Chair and Professor,
Sport Management Department
College of Business
University of New Haven
New Haven, CT

Kevin M. Guskiewicz, PhD, ATC, FACSM, FNATA
Senior Associate Dean, College of Arts and Sciences
Professor, Department of Exercise and Sport Science
University of North Carolina at Chapel Hill
Chapel Hill, NC
Member, Korey Stringer Institute Medical and Science Advisory Board

John A. Kalin, MD
The Cardiac Arrhythmia Center
Tufts Medical Center
Boston, MA

Glen P. Kenny, PhD
Professor, School of Human Kinetics
Human and Environmental Physiology Research Unit
University of Ottawa
Ottawa, Ontario, Canada
Member, Korey Stringer Institute Medical and Science Advisory Board

Zachary Y. Kerr, PhD, MPH
Department of Epidemiology
University of North Carolina
Chapel Hill, NC

Mark S. Link, MD, FACC
The Cardiac Arrhythmia Center
Tufts Medical Center
Boston, MA

Christopher Madias, MD
The Cardiac Arrhythmia Center
Tufts Medical Center
Boston, MA

Shishir Mathur, MD
Preventive Cardiology Fellow
Hartford Hospital
Hartford, CT

Brendon P. McDermott, PhD, ATC
Assistant Professor of Kinesiology
Clinical Coordinator of Athletic Training Education
Health, Human Performance and Recreation
University of Arkansas
Fayetteville, AR
Member, Korey Stringer Institute Medical and Science Advisory Board

Jason P. Mihalik, PhD, CAT(C), ATC
Assistant Professor, Department of Exercise and Co-Director, Matthew Gfeller Sport-Related Traumatic Brain Injury Research Center
University of North Carolina at Chapel Hill
Chapel Hill, NC

Michael G. Miller, PhD, EdD, ATC, CSCS, FNATA
Director of Graduate Athletic Training Education
Professor, Department of Human Performance and Health Education
Western Michigan University
Kalamazoo, MI

Frederick O. Mueller, PhD, FACSM
Professor, Department of Exercise and Sport Science
University of North Carolina at Chapel Hill
Chapel Hill, NC

Francis G. O'Connor, MD, MPH, COL, MC, USA
Professor and Chair, Military and Emergency Medicine
Uniformed Services University for the Health Sciences (USUHS)
Bethesda, MD
Member, Korey Stringer Institute Medical and Science Advisory Board

Margot Putukian, MD, FACSM
Director of Athletic Medicine, Princeton
University
Associate Clinical Professor, Robert Wood
Johnson Medical School
University of Medicine and Dentistry of
New Jersey
Princeton, NJ
Member, Korey Stringer Institute Medical and
Science Advisory Board

Karen Roos, MSPT, ATC
Department of Exercise and Sport Science
University of North Carolina
Chapel Hill, NC

Rebecca L. Stearns, PhD, ATC
Vice President of Operations and Director of
Education, Korey Stringer Institute
Department of Kinesiology
University of Connecticut
Storrs, CT

Erik E. Swartz, PhD, ATC, FNATA
Professor, Department of Kinesiology
University of New Hampshire
Durham, NH
Member, Korey Stringer Institute Medical and
Science Advisory Board

Ralph Swearngin, PhD
Executive Director, Georgia High School
Association
Thomaston, GA

Charlie Thompson, MS, ATC
Head Athletic Trainer
Princeton University
Princeton, NJ

Paul D. Thompson, MD, FACC, FACSM
Director of Cardiology
Hartford Hospital
Hartford, CT

Brett G. Toresdahl, MD
Department of Family Medicine
University of Washington
Seattle, WA

Lesley W. Vandermark, MS, ATC, PES
Assistant Director of Research, Korey Stringer
Institute
University of Connecticut
Storrs, CT

Susan W. Yeargin, PhD, ATC
Assistant Professor, Department of Physical
Education and Athletic Training
College of Education
University of South Carolina
Columbia, SC
Member, Korey Stringer Institute Medical and
Science Advisory Board

PAST CONTRIBUTORS

Jeffrey M. Anderson, MD, FACSM
Team Physician
University of Connecticut
Storrs, CT

Tutita M. Casa, PhD
Assistant Professor, Department of Educational
Psychology
Neag School of Education
University of Connecticut
Storrs, CT

Mary Ann Cooper, MD
Professor Emerita, Department of Emergency
Medicine
University of Illinois at Chicago
Chicago, IL

Julie DeMartini, PhD, ATC
Director of Research, Korey Stringer Institute
Assistant Professor and Athletic Training
Program Director
Westfield State University
Westfield, MA

Fawad A. Kazi, MD
Cardiology Fellow
Hartford Hospital
Hartford, CT

Rebecca M. Lopez, PhD, ATC, CSCS
Assistant Professor, Department of Orthopaedics
and Sports Medicine
University of South Florida
Tampa, FL
Member, Korey Stringer Institute Medical and
Science Advisory Board

Stephanie M. Mazerolle, PhD, ATC
Assistant Professor, Department of Kinesiology
Neag School of Education
University of Connecticut
Member, Korey Stringer Institute Medical
and Science Advisory Board
Storrs, CT

Kelly Pagnotta, MA, ATC, PES
Chief Information Officer, Korey Stringer
Institute
Department of Kinesiology
Neag School of Education
University of Connecticut
Storrs, CT

William O. Roberts, MD, MS, FACSM
Professor, Family Medicine and
Community Health
Director, St. John's Hospital Family Medicine
Residency Sports Medicine Fellowship
University of Minnesota
Minneapolis, MN

Kevin R. Ronneberg, MD
Medical Director
Fairview Sports and Orthopedic Care
Minneapolis, MN

Brad Yeargin, ATC
Athletic Training Coordinator
Drayer Physical Therapy Institute
Columbia, SC

© Giorgio Micheletti/ShutterStock, Inc.

Founding of the Korey Stringer Institute

In August 2001, Korey Stringer, a Minnesota Vikings NFL offensive lineman who had earned Pro Bowl
honors during his 5-year tenure with the team, died from exertional heat stroke. Since the time of Korey's
death, Korey's wife, Kelci Stringer, and his agent, James Gould, have worked tirelessly to develop a sport
safety institute to honor Korey's legacy. To that end, in 2009, they joined forces with exertional heat stroke
expert Douglas J. Casa from the University of Connecticut, to make this dream a reality. The Korey
Stringer Institute (KSI) officially opened on April 23, 2010.

Korey Stringer Institute's Mission Statement and Goals

The mission of KSI is to provide first-rate information, research, resources, assistance, education, and
advocacy for the prevention of sudden death in sport.

KSI is housed in the Department of Kinesiology at the University of Connecticut. The University
of Connecticut has a strong tradition and reputation as one of the leading institutions studying heat and
hydration issues related to athletes and the physically active. In 2010, the university's Department of
Kinesiology was ranked the number one doctoral program in the country by the National Academy
of Kinesiology and number one for research productivity by the National Research Council.

KSI serves the needs of active people and athletes at all levels—youth, high school, college, and professional and recreational athletes—and those who supervise and care for these individuals. Components
of these services include consultations, advocacy, education, research, and mass-market outreach. KSI's
founding partners are Gatorade and the NFL. KSI's other corporate partners include CamelBak, Kestrel,
and One Beat CPR.

Accomplishments of the Korey Stringer Institute

Since the inception of KSI, the institute's members have been hard at work assisting numerous organizations
and individuals with education, policies, advocacy, research, and information. A sampling of these include
the U.S. Army, Army Rangers, American Football Coaches Association, National Collegiate Athletic
Association, National Athletic Trainers' Association, National Strength and Conditioning Association,
American College of Sports Medicine, American Medical Society of Sports Medicine, Centers for Disease

Control and Prevention, Safe Kids, Advocates for Injured Athletes, International Tennis Federation, NFL, NFL Players Association, PBS, NBC, ABC, *USA Today*, *The Washington Post*, *The New York Times*, Human Rights Watch, Youth Sports Safety Alliance, the National Air and Space Administration, United States Tennis Association, Women's Tennis Association, USA Football, USA Cycling, *Runners' World*, Marine Corps Marathon, Falmouth Road Race, Rock 'n' Roll Marathon, the Boston Marathon, numerous state organizations, among many others. The efforts of KSI have helped 12 states pass heat acclimatization guidelines for high school football since May 2011, as well as other safety-related policies.

KSI is very proud that 15 individuals involved with this text are affiliated with the institute.

For more information, visit the website (ksi.uconn.edu).

The KSI logo is used courtesy of University of Connecticut Foundation.

Developing Safety Policies for Organized Sports

Michael S. Ferrara, PhD, ATC, FNATA

Ralph Swearngin, PhD

William M. Adams, MS, ATC

Douglas J. Casa, PhD, ATC, FACSM, FNATA

Introduction

The goal of every high school administrator, coach, and sports medicine team is to facilitate their athletes' safe and injury-free participation in sports. Sports provide an opportunity to experience competition, teamwork, success and adversity, and most importantly, athletes develop a framework for future successes as they move into adulthood. Many of the life lessons learned in sports are building blocks for successful careers and the development of lifetime sports achievements.

It has been reported that approximately 42%[1] of interscholastic programs have access to an athletic trainer. More recent data suggest that this number has risen in the last 10 years to closer to 70%. Athletic trainers are essential healthcare professionals who provide a safe playing environment, evaluate injuries, implement rehabilitation programs for the return to activity following injury, and lastly, provide expertise in developing policies and procedures for safe sports participation.

Trends in Policy Development

There are several medical conditions that lead to death, disability, or permanent injury. It is important to be aware of them in today's environment and litigious society. Many of these conditions are preventable with proper rules and regulations that are designed to prevent injury or at least mitigate the risk of these injuries. Among others, these medical conditions include:

- Heat stroke
- Brain trauma and concussion
- Sickle cell trait
- Heart abnormalities

This text will describe each of these conditions in much greater detail with criteria for the cause, treatment, return to play, and prevention considerations. The purpose of this chapter is to describe how various interest groups can work together to develop policies to reduce the risk of injury and allow for safe athletic participation.

Using a Data-Based Approach

With sports participation, there is an inherent risk of injury. Over the past several years, there has been an increased emphasis on collecting data to mitigate risk, to reduce severe or **catastrophic injuries**, and to develop injury/illness prevention programs based on empirical data. This is clearly evidenced by some of the recent rule changes regarding concussion and preseason acclimatization that used data as part of the policymaking process. When making policy decisions or changing rules, it is extremely important for decision makers to rely on data rather than casual observation or intuition about what they think is happening. VanMechelen[2] et al. suggested an excellent model for thinking about policy or rules changes for sports:

1. Describe the injury or condition related to the policy or condition.
2. Establish the etiology and injury mechanism based on the available data.
3. Identify preventive measures based on the injury data analysis.
4. Assess the effectiveness of the new policy and intervention program and make any revisions to the policy based on the data.

How to Develop a Policy

Once an injury has been identified or a question developed to prevent an injury, a comprehensive team approach to finding a solution that decreases the incidence of the injury should be implemented. First, all parties and stakeholders who have an interest in the process and could provide input must be identified from the outset. This will allow all parties to have a voice in the development of the policy rather than coming in at a later point in the process. This will prevent rehashing and delays caused by bringing other parties up to speed while the larger group has been moving together in developing the solution.

All concerned groups should be involved in data analysis and identifying potential solutions to an injury. This should be done in a way that is not laden with statistical jargon but rather identifies trends and patterns for the injury while honoring those findings that are statistically and practically significant. For example, the Georgia High School Heat Illness project discovered there was an increased trend in the first week for exertional heat stroke (EHS) cases when practices lasted longer than 2 hours. For those practices that went beyond 2 hours, the injury rate increased 4.8 times. However, in the second week, participants demonstrated a 30-minute **acclimation** time and the injury rate did not increase until 2.5 hours of practice. Using these data, a policy was implemented to limit practice to 2 hours for the first week, then increasing the practice time for the second week onward during the preseason period, up to a maximum of 3 hours.

Once trends and patterns are identified in the data, all parties must be involved in developing a subsequent rule change or modification. The change should take a commonsense approach that does not drastically alter the sport, but rather provides the safest playing environment possible with rules in place to mitigate risk. All aspects of the existing and proposed rules should be discussed in detail to identify the intended and unintended consequences. Many times when new rules are implemented, there are unanticipated effects that were not considered when they were being developed. New rules should be vetted by as many people and professionals as possible, discussing the implications of the rule change and how it may be interpreted and implemented by those who were not involved in deciding on the change but who now have to apply it.

Lastly, the governing structure of an organization should be adhered to during policy change. All members of the governing body should have a voice in policy development and implementation. This will facilitate "buy-in" to the policy and allow affected parties to voice concern or identify potential areas of concern. Further, a rule change should be made publically available for comment within the important committees, such as the state athletic association or state medical advisory committee, for review and comment.

Examples of Rule Changes

As mentioned previously, providing a safe sports environment is a common goal as demonstrated by recent publications on heat.[3] However, many of today's injury prevention policies are not based on data, but rather on observation, educated guesses, and common sense. For example, face shields were introduced to girls lacrosse to reduce eye injuries. Although there were limited data to support that the number of eye injuries were increasing because of lack of protective equipment or that such injuries were resulting in permanent injury, a decision was made to require the equipment. This was a commonsense approach to prevent injury; the simple piece of equipment did not have an effect on how the sport was played or any of the historical contexts of that sport. This has not been the case with soccer. Some have suggested that a headband be worn to prevent concussion and head injuries. Again, there were no data to support or refute the claim. However, in this case it was clear from the pathomechanics of concussion that a headband would not prevent a concussion, and thus wearing this piece of equipment during participation did not become a requirement.

The sport of football has been proactive in trying to reduce injuries for years by changing rules and modifying techniques at all levels (National Football League [NFL], National Collegiate Athletic Association [NCAA], and National Federation of State High School Associations [NFHS]). However, the NCAA data suggest that while there has been improvement in sports techniques and coaching and training of athletes, the injury rate for games has remained relatively flat for the past 20 years. Unless the fundamentals of the sport are changed (e.g., blocking, tackling, etc.), the injury rates will not change significantly.[4]

Nonetheless, there have been several rule changes that have had a positive impact on reducing the number of injuries. Recently, the NFL moved the kickoff 5 yards closer to the 35 yard line and only allowed a 5-yard run up, which has reduced the number of collisions and thus reduced the number of concussions. The NCAA enacted modifications for the preseason football **acclimatization** period in 2003 by setting regulations for the duration and frequency of practice. This has reduced the number of heat-related illnesses. These are just two examples of recent changes that have been utilized to reduce injury.

> **acclimatization** A complex series of adaptive responses that demonstrate improved homeostatic balance in multiple organs; usually requires 10 to 14 days for responses to develop adequately. The body can acclimatize (to varying degrees) to hot, cold, high altitude, and underwater environments.

Education About Rule Changes

Once a rule change or modification has been made, a comprehensive approach to educating coaches must be developed and implemented. The education should use as many forms of media as possible to educate those involved about the change. Some obvious educational formats include use of the Internet for webinar and educational materials. There are numerous successful examples, such as the Centers for Disease Control and Prevention's (CDC) approach to education on concussion. The CDC has developed numerous materials geared to different audiences such as coaches, parents, student-athletes, and medical personnel. Similarly, the NFHS developed a webinar for the prevention, recognition, and treatment of heat illnesses.

For rule changes or modifications that are technique based, a video can be used to demonstrate proper and improved techniques. This was particularly important for the spearing mechanism in tackling. When the head is bent (flexion) about 15–20 degrees, the spine is placed in a segmented column or an axial loaded position. The National Athletic Trainers' Association (NATA) created a video that showed a reenactment of the spine and the forces that crush the spinal column when it is in an axial loaded position. This demonstration showed in a clear and concise format the position of the forces and how the cervical spine (C-spine) buckles under those forces. NATA also used a drinking straw to illustrate the effect of force on the C-spine. When force is applied to both ends of the straw, the straw breaks or bends at the midpoint of the forces, which is the same as the C-spine.

Protecting the health and safety of athletes has become a major focus at all levels of sports. While professional associations such as the NFL and the NCAA have made great strides in implementing policy changes to protect the health and safety of their athletes, policies protecting high school student-athletes are still in their infancy. In regard to concussion management, states have done a good job passing legislation to protect young student-athletes, but for injuries such as heat illness, state high school associations are just now beginning to make policies to help prevent these injuries from occurring. Implementing health and safety policies at the high school level requires each state's high school athletic association to adopt health and safety policies because the NFHS has no power to mandate policy changes nationwide. The following section of this chapter outlines 10 policy initiatives that high schools and state high school athletic associations should adopt to further protect their student-athletes. Many of these ideas or initiatives are discussed in greater detail or reinforced in later chapters.

Ten Policy Initiatives to Be Considered in Organized Sport

First Initiative

High schools and state high school athletics associations should adopt the 2009 *NATA Heat Acclimatization Guidelines for Preseason Practices*.

Components

One of the most effective ways to prevent EHS is to implement appropriate heat acclimatization guidelines for preseason practices, particularly in August. Heat acclimatization is the physiologic adaptation to exercise in the heat that occurs over a period of 10 to 14 days, which ultimately results in adaptations that improve an athlete's ability to cope with heat stress. During exercise in the heat, internal body temperature rises and is affected by the following six factors:

- Intensity/duration of exercise
- Hydration level of athletes
- Protective equipment worn
- Fitness level of the athlete
- Environmental conditions
- Individual differences (weight/body fat, medications, illness)

Heat acclimatization guidelines gradually phase in an increase in exercise intensity/duration and the use of protective equipment in sports such as football over a period of about 14 days. **Table 1.1** depicts

---

TABLE 1.1   National Athletic Trainers' Association's Preseason Heat Acclimatization Guidelines for Secondary School Athletics[3]

Area of Practice Modification	Practice Days 1–5		Practice Days 6–14
	Days 1–2	Days 3–5	
Number of practices permitted per day	1		2, only every other day (1 all other days)
Equipment (if applicable)	Helmets only	Helmets and shoulder pads	Full equipment
Maximum duration of single practice session	3 hours*		3 hours (a total maximum of 5 hours on double session days)
Permitted walkthrough time	1 hour (but must be separated from practice for 3 continuous hours)		
Contact	No contact	Contact only with blocking sleds/dummies	Full, 100% live contact drills

*Based on data gathered by Ferrara and Casa, the risk of heat illness increased after the 2-hour mark during the first five days of practice, so limiting practice to 2 hours during the first five days may increase player safety (Personal Communication: Douglas J. Casa, PhD, ATC, August 2013).

the components of an appropriate heat acclimatization protocol recommended for secondary school student athletes.[3]

Successes

In 2003, the NCAA mandated that every school follow specific heat acclimatization guidelines for pre-season practice in response to a series of EHS deaths that occurred in the years prior. Since 2003, there has been only one EHS-related death during an August practice at the NCAA level. In 2009, NATA published a similar document, closely following the NCAA guidelines but specific to secondary school student-athletes. These guidelines, although recommended by NFHS, are not mandatory at the secondary school level nationwide. In order for secondary schools to mandate the use of appropriate heat acclimatization guidelines, each state's high school athletic association must adopt these guidelines and mandate their use. Since 2011, 11 states (see **Figure 1.1**) have adopted heat acclimatization guidelines that meet the recommendations made by both the NATA and NFHS. The state of Georgia for example, mandated heat acclimatization guidelines that are taken word-for-word from the NATA recommendations. Georgia also added requirements in coaching education for first aid and CPR, as well as training on specific emergency conditions likely in sport.

In addition, the states of Illinois, Pennsylvania, and South Carolina have passed heat acclimatization guidelines at the secondary school setting. Although these four states have made improvements and have passed heat acclimatization guidelines, they do not fully meet the recommendations previously published.[3] In order to protect the health and safety of secondary school athletes as they relate to the prevention of EHS, all states must mandate the use of appropriate heat acclimatization guidelines.

Second Initiative

Adopt policies that promote the creation and use of environmental monitoring measures (such as wet-bulb globe temperature) for practice and game modifications or cancellations.

Components

Wet bulb globe temperature (WBGT) is an environmental measure that is used to calculate the heat stress index. WBGT is used in athletic, military, and industrial settings to control the

> **wet bulb globe temperature (WBGT)** The most widely used heat stress index in industry and sports; may be used to assess the severity of hot environments. It is derived from a formula that incorporates the dry bulb, wet bulb, and black globe temperature.

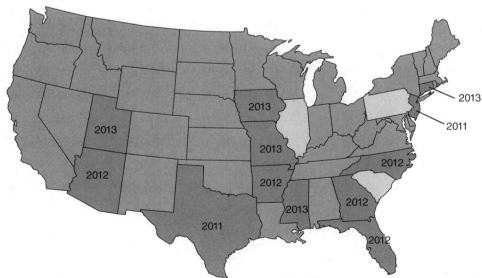

Figure 1.1   The states in dark green depict states that have passed heat acclimatization guidelines to meet the minimum standard set in place by the National Athletic Trainers' Association. The states in light green show the states that have passed improved heat acclimatization guidelines, although insufficient from the 2009 guidelines. The states colored in gray have insufficient heat acclimatization guidelines.

Data from Korey Stringer Institute. Heat Acclimatization Guidelines by State. 2013. Available at: http://ksi.uconn.edu/prevention-strategies/high-school-state-policies/heat-acclimatization-state-policies/. Accessed September 28, 2013.

number of heat casualties and to set limits for physical exertion in the heat. Temperature, humidity, wind, and solar radiation are taken into account when calculating the particular WBGT value.[3]

The risk of EHS increases when factors such as temperature, humidity, or heavy protective equipment are present during exercise.[5] The incidence of EHS can be reduced by establishing activity modification and rest break guidelines for exercise in the heat according to environmental measures, such as WBGT. The essential components of implementing effective environmental monitoring policies include:

- State athletic associations should require all schools to have a heat modification policy that is based on WBGT measures.
- The WBGT temperature guidelines should be based on epidemiologic data specific to the state/ region (e.g., the temperature guidelines for New England may be different than those needed in the Southeast).
- The heat policy should have at least a four-step progression of modifications dependent on environmental conditions (ranging from no modifications to cancellation of practice/games).
- The heat policy should include modifications of equipment (if applicable to the sport), work-to-rest ratios, total practice time, number of water breaks, and mention the use of shaded areas for rest breaks.

These guidelines should be detailed in each state's athletics handbook so they are strictly enforced. **Table 1.2** outlines the WBGT guidelines established by the Georgia High School Association that every secondary school in the state of Georgia must follow for practices and games at the secondary school setting.

Successes

As mentioned, the state of Georgia has been successful in incorporating WBGT guidelines into its policies for secondary school. All secondary schools are required to monitor environmental conditions during practices and make any necessary activity modifications to protect the health and safety of the student-athletes. WBGT guidelines have also been used successfully to monitor environmental conditions in the military and industrial settings. The military has been using WBGT for a number of years to protect soldiers against the risk of EHS. Industrial settings such as steel mills also use environmental monitoring measures such as WBGT to protect workers against the extreme conditions in which they are required to work.

TABLE 1.2	WBGT Guidelines Established by the Georgia State High School Association
WBGT Reading(°F)	**Activity Guidelines and Rest Break Guidelines**
Under 82.0	Normal activities: provide at least three separate rest breaks each hour lasting a minimum of 3 minutes each during a workout
82.0–86.9	Use discretion for intense or prolonged exercise; watch at-risk players carefully; provide at least three separate rest breaks each hour lasting a minimum of 4 minutes each
87.0–89.9	Maximum practice time is 2 hours. For football: players restricted to helmet, shoulder pads, and shorts during practice. All protective equipment must be removed for conditioning activities. For all sports: provide at least four separate rest breaks each hour lasting a minimum of 4 minutes each
90.0–92.0	Maximum length of practice is 1 hour, no protective equipment may be worn during practice, and there may be no conditioning activities. There must be 20 minutes of rest breaks provided during the hour of practice
Over 92.1	No outdoor workouts; cancel exercise; delay practices until a cooler WBGT reading occurs

Source: Data from Georgia High School Association. GHSA Constitution and By-Laws for 2013-2014. 2013. Available at: http://www.ghsa.net/sites/default/files/documents/Constitution/Constitution2013-14Complete.pdf. Accessed September 28, 2013.

Third Initiative

Adopt policies that promote the creation and maintenance of optimal emergency action plans that cover all potential emergency scenarios.

Components

In order to appropriately and adequately respond to emergency situations such as natural disasters or serious illnesses and injuries, it is essential that an **emergency action plan (EAP)** be in place. The purpose of an EAP is to reduce the incidence of catastrophic injuries and sudden death during sports. An EAP should be a written, site-specific document that ensures that medical personnel have access to a venue in the event of a catastrophic injury occurring.[6] The components of what should be included in an EAP to allow for a prompt response to an emergency situation are shown in **Table 1.3**. The people involved in the development of these policies should include the on-site medical staff (e.g., the athletic trainer), local emergency medical services (EMS), school safety officials, coaches, on-site first responders, and school administrators.

> **emergency action plan**
> **(EAP)** A written document that defines the standard of care for the management of emergencies in athletics.

Successes

Some states have taken action to require EAPs for all secondary school athletic departments. Twelve of the 50 states require secondary schools to have an EAP for their athletics programs (see **Table 1.4**). Arkansas, for example, passed legislation in 2011 requiring that every public secondary school develop and implement an EAP relevant for its athletics program.[7] This is the first state in the United States to pass legislation requiring the use of a written EAP to help protect the health and safety of its student-athletes. It is imperative that every state's athletics association mandates its member schools develop and implement a school-specific EAP in the event of a catastrophic sports-related injury.

Fourth Initiative

Adopt policies that promote hiring on-site medical care, such as athletic trainers, who are trained in the prevention, diagnosis, and treatment of emergency medical conditions.

Components

Athletic trainers are licensed medical professionals who specialize in the recognition, assessment, prevention, and treatment of sports-related injuries. They also have the knowledge to prevent, recognize,

---

TABLE 1.3 Components of an EAP

- Every school or organization that sponsors an athletic program should develop an EAP for managing serious and/or life-threatening injuries.
- Schools should have a written EAP document that is distributed to all staff members.
- The EAP should be specific to each venue and include maps and/or directions for access to the venue.
- On-site equipment that may be needed in an emergency situation should be listed in the written EAP.
- The EAP should identify personnel and their responsibilities for carrying out the plan of action with a designated chain of command.
- Facility address, location, contact information (for both the school and EMS), etc. should be identified in the EAP.
- The EAP should specify actions that need to be taken after an emergency.
- The EAP should be reviewed and rehearsed annually by all parties involved.
- Healthcare professionals who will provide medical coverage during games, practices, or other events should be included in the EAP.

TABLE 1.4	States Requiring Secondary Schools to Have an EAP for Their Athletics Program

- Arkansas
- California
- Colorado
- Georgia
- Kentucky
- Maryland
- Massachusetts
- New Hampshire
- New Jersey
- North Carolina
- Ohio
- Virginia

diagnose, and treat life-threatening emergency situations in sports to reduce the incidence of sudden death. It is essential to have appropriate medical staff at all school-sanctioned athletics events to ensure the safety of young athletes. Policies to promote the hiring of on-site medical care workers who are trained in the diagnosis and treatment of emergency medical conditions should contain the following components:

- All schools that sponsor a sanctioned athletics program should hire appropriate on-site medical care for its student athletes. Hiring an athletic trainer is recommended, because they are trained in the prevention, recognition, assessment, and treatment of sports-related injuries (including life-threatening injuries).
- The hired on-site medical care should be in charge of the development and implementation of the school's EAP and the policies and procedures to follow in the event of an emergency situation occurring during participation in sports.
- On-site medical care should be available for all sanctioned practices and games, and coverage decisions should be based on scientific evidence related to sports with the highest incidence of catastrophic events.
- The on-site medical care should collaborate with a state licensed sports medicine trained physician (medical doctor or osteopath).

Successes

Access to on-site medical care, especially at the secondary school setting, has increased over the past decade. Previous research has shown that approximately 42% of secondary schools employ an athletic trainer for their athletics program.[1] More recent data, from a study to be published by the Korey Stringer Institute in 2014, puts the number of all secondary schools that have access to an athletic trainer for their athletics program closer to 70%. This represents a huge improvement. As secondary schools continue to recognize the value of and need for appropriate medical staff on site for school-sponsored athletics programs, the number of athletes that have access to medical care will continue to increase.

Recently, numerous medical organizations endorsed a report titled "The Inter-Association Task Force for Preventing Sudden Death in Secondary School Athletics Programs: Best-Practices Recommendations." This document covers how to prevent sudden death in sports, including having appropriate medical staff and an athletic trainer employed at secondary schools. This document clearly identifies the roles and responsibilities that the athletic trainer should have in the secondary school setting in regard to handling emergency situations.[8]

Fifth Initiative

Adopt policies that implement standards for coaching education, continuing education, and certification in first aid, cardiopulmonary resuscitation (CPR), and recognition of emergency conditions.

Components

Roughly 70% of high school student-athletes have access to appropriate medical care during participation in high school sports. Because this leaves ~30% of high school student-athletes without access to appropriate medical care, it is imperative that coaches are required to undergo regular continuing education focused on the health and safety of athletes. Educating coaches on signs and symptoms of emergency situations, such as EHS or traumatic brain injury, is pertinent to the athlete's survival in life-and-death situations. Policies that require coaches to obtain continuing education for emergency and medical conditions should encompass the following components:

- Should require all coaches on staff to be CPR/AED and first aid certified
- Should require all coaches to attend annual continuing education courses focused on emergency and medical conditions in sports
- Continuing education courses should focus on the prevention, identification, and treatment of causes of sudden death in sports

Successes

Currently, 37 of the states in the United States require coaches to obtain at least first aid certification. Of those 37 states, 18 require coaches to obtain both first aid and CPR/ **automated external defibrillator (AED)** certification in order to coach at the high school level.[9] In light of recent changes in legislation related to concussions, some states require coaches to undergo regular education on concussion.[10] The state of Connecticut, for example, requires all coaches to undergo an initial training session prior to receiving coaching certification on signs and symptoms of concussion and protocols they must follow if they suspect one of their athletes has sustained a concussion. Once they have their coaching certification, coaches must undergo a yearly refresher course on concussion management in order to maintain their coaching credential.[11] State high school athletics associations need to continue to implement coaching education standards as they relate to emergency and medical conditions to ensure proper safety of student-athletes.

> **automated external defibrillator (AED)** A computerized device that analyzes the heart rhythm, determines whether a shock is needed to restart a normal rhythm, charges to an appropriate shock dose, shocks a patient's heart, and uses audio and visual instructions to guide the rescuer.

Sixth Initiative

Adopt policies for the creation and implementation of supervision policies and exercise acclimatization policies, specifically for strength and conditioning sessions.

Components

Strength and conditioning sessions, especially at the collegiate level, have become a cause for concern in relation to the health and safety of the participating student-athletes. Since 2000, at the NCAA level, 21 collegiate football players have died during strength and conditioning sessions. The top three causes of death of these athletes were sickle cell trait, EHS, and cardiac arrest. The issues surrounding these deaths were implementing exercise programs that were novel or too intense too soon, using exercise as punishment, and not having appropriate medical coverage during these sessions. Implementing policies that focus on supervision and exercise acclimatization during strength and conditioning sessions will assist in reducing the risk of sudden death during these activities. **Table 1.5** outlines the key points for promoting the health and safety of athletes during strength and conditioning sessions.

TABLE 1.5	Components for Best Practices During Strength and Conditioning Sessions

- Acclimatize progressively by phasing in exercise gradually (in terms of volume and intensity)
- Introduce new conditioning activities gradually
- Do not use exercise and conditioning activities as punishment
- Ensure proper education, experience, and credentialing of strength and conditioning coaches
- Provide appropriate medical coverage
- Develop and practice EAPs
- Be cognizant of medical conditions
- Administer strength and conditioning programs
- Partner with recognized professional organizations
- Provide adequate continuing education for the entire coaching and medical team

Source: Data from State of Arkansas, Act 496. *An act to create "the antony hobbs iii act" and to create school-based automated external defibrillator and cardiopulmonary resuscitation programs.*; 2009. Available at: http://www.statescape.com/TextArchive/BillTextArchive/SSBillText2009/AR2009/AR_2009_SB_000312_Current_2896.pdf.

Successes

In 2012, "The Inter-Association Task Force for Preventing Sudden Death in Collegiate Conditioning Sessions: Best Practices Recommendations," which is endorsed by numerous medical organizations, was published by the NATA. It outlines specific ways to reduce the incidence of sudden death during strength and conditioning sessions at the collegiate level.[12] In addition to this document, the NATA document regarding preventing sudden death in the secondary school setting also outlines how sudden death can be prevented during strength and conditioning sessions using recommended best practices.[8] These documents are instrumental in providing athletics programs, in both collegiate and secondary school settings, the information needed to implement changes to strength and conditioning sessions to make them safer for athletes and reduce the risk of sudden death.

Seventh Initiative

Adopt policies promoting the installation of AEDs that can be accessed within 1 minute of any athletic venue.

Components

Sudden cardiac death is the leading cause of death in sports, especially in young athletes. In 78% of cases involving sudden cardiac death, the first symptom is death. An AED is a device that is used to deliver an electric shock in the event of a person collapsing from cardiac arrest. Research has shown that for every minute after collapse as a result of cardiac arrest without the application of an AED, the chance of survival decreases about 10%. Utilizing the following guidelines helps to ensure that proper care is used in the event of a cardiac arrest in terms of accessing an AED.

- AEDs are to be used under the advice and consent of a physician by individuals with proper training and certification.
- The AED should be kept in a safe place and should be easily accessible; all athletic trainers, coaches, administrators, school nurses, and physical education teachers should have access to an AED on school property and at all school-sanctioned athletic events/activities.
- Institutions sponsoring athletic events should have an AED on site or access to one at each athletic venue for practices, games, or other athletic events. Ideally, an AED should be accessible within 1 minute at every athletic venue.
- Individuals should be provided annual training and certification in CPR and AED use.

- The location of the AED should be well marked, publicized, and known among trained staff.
- The AED should be used only after activating the EMS system.
- AEDs should be inspected frequently to ensure proper working order (batteries charged, electrodes and wires are in good condition).

Successes

Implementing AEDs in public venues has become commonplace in today's society. Most public venues (e.g., airports, shopping malls, schools) have an AED on site for use in the event of an emergency. When looking specifically at secondary schools, almost all have an AED within their walls. In Arkansas, legislation was passed in 2009 to create AED and CPR programs in secondary schools. This requires schools to have an AED on site in the event of an emergency situation involving cardiac arrest.[13] In 2013, Arkansas passed Act 1016, which, starting in the 2014–2015 school year, will require all public school students to become trained in both CPR and AED use.[14]

It is important for schools that have an AED (or more than one) to make them accessible in the event of an emergency and to store them in a location that is central to athletics venues. For schools in which the athletics venues are not adjacent to one another or some venues are off campus, it is important to have an AED at each venue or close to multiple venues so that they can be accessed from any location within 1 minute. Having quick access to an AED increases the chance of survival in the event of a cardiac arrest.

Eighth Initiative

Adopt policies that promote the creation and use of preparticipation exams that utilize specific screening questions to target the top reasons why athletes die in sports.

Components

Preparticipation exams (PPEs) are an important screening tool to be administered prior to participation in sports. PPEs are used to identify underlying medical conditions that can be detrimental to the health of a participating athlete or put him or her at greater risk for an emergency medical event. It is imperative that PPEs contain specific screening questions that target the top reasons why athletes die in sports. These screening questions should be system specific (e.g., cardiovascular, central nervous system, pulmonary, general medical) and ask about previous history, existing medical conditions, family history, and signs/symptoms during exercise. In addition to screening questions, the PPE should also include a thorough physical examination in order to identify any present pathology that would warrant exclusion from participation. A team physician or a physician familiar with the demands and risks associated with sport should always perform PPEs.

preparticipation exams (PPEs) A formal requirement prior to participation in sports. PPEs must be conducted by a qualified health professional. They are usually performed once a year with the goal of identifying medical problems that may place an athlete at risk for injury or illness.

Successes

The NATA document addressing the prevention of sudden death in secondary school athletics programs recommends using best practices as they relate to the leading causes of death during sports. Along with recommending that all secondary schools have appropriate medical staff on site, NATA also recommends using minimum standards set forth by the American Academy of Family Pediatrics for cardiac screening (comprehensive personal history, family history, and physical examination) during the athlete's PPE. It is also recommended that the PPE includes obtaining the athlete's sickle cell trait status before allowing participation in sports.[8] Following recommendations such as these during an athlete's PPE is critical in reducing the risk of sudden death during sport.

Ninth Initiative

Adopt concussion and head injury policies that are in line with leading sports health organization recommendations.

Components

The CDC estimates that sports-related concussions affect 1.6 to 3.8 million athletes annually.[15] A concussion is a traumatic brain injury that, if not treated appropriately, can have long-lasting effects. Recent media attention about the severity of concussions and their relationship to chronic traumatic encephalopathy has raised awareness of this injury, especially in young athletes who may not have access to appropriate medical care at the time of injury. An appropriate concussion and head injury policy includes the following components:

- Preseason education should be provided for personnel, coaches, athletes, and parents on the basics of concussion (signs/symptoms, treatment, return to play, that helmets do not prevent concussions).
- High school athletes suspected of sustaining a concussion should not be permitted to return to a practice, game, or activity involving exertional activity on the same day.
- Athletes suspected of a concussion should not be permitted to return to participation until written release from a licensed physician or athletic trainer is received.
- No child/adolescent should return to sports/activity unless he or she has managed to return to school.
- There should be implementation of a graduated return to participation protocol (see **Table 1.6**), with at least five steps and no more than two in one day.[16]
- There should be a comprehensive medical management plan for acute care of a potential head or cervical spine injury.

Successes

Between 2009 and 2013, 47 of the 50 states, including the District of Columbia, enacted legislation that requires each state to mandate policies regarding concussions, specifically sports-related concussions

TABLE 1.6	**Graduated Return to Play Protocol**[15]	
Rehabilitation Stage	Functional Exercise at Each Stage of Rehabilitation	Objective of Each Stage
1. No activity	Symptom-limited physical and cognitive rest.	Recovery
2. Light aerobic exercise	Walking, swimming, or stationary cycling, keeping intensity < 70% maximum permitted heart rate. No resistance training.	Increase heart rate
3. Sport-specific exercise	Skating drills in ice hockey, running drills in soccer. No head impact activities.	Add movement
4. Noncontact training drills	Progression to more complex training drills (e.g., passing drills in football and ice hockey). May start progressive resistance training.	Exercise, coordination, and cognitive load
5. Full-contact practice	Following medical clearance, participate in normal training activities.	Restore confidence and assess functional skills by coaching staff
6. Return to play	Normal game play	

Source: From: McCrory P, Meeuwisse WH, Aubry M, et al. Consensus statement on concussion in sport: the 4th International Conference on Concussion in Sport held in Zurich, November 2012. *J Am Coll Surg.* 2013;216(5):e55–71. doi:10.1016/j.jamcollsurg.2013.02.020.

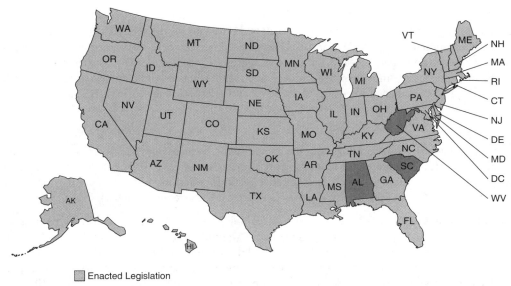

☐ Enacted Legislation

Figure 1.2 Map of the United States indicating states that have enacted legislation regarding sport concussion.

Source: Traumatic Brain Injury Legislation. National Conference of State Legislatures; 2013. Available at: http://www.ncsl.org/issues-research/health/traumatic-brain-injury-legislation.aspx. Accessed July 1, 2013.

(see **Figure 1.2**). The concussion legislation is specific to the appropriate management of a concussion (evaluation by a licensed medical professional; clearance to return to play by a licensed medical professional, athlete, parent, and coaching education on the signs and symptoms of concussion; etc.).

Tenth Initiative

Adopt policies for the creation and implementation of policies for the appropriate management of exertional heat stroke.

Components

EHS is 100% survivable if it is promptly recognized and treated using cold water immersion. The goal of treatment is to aggressively cool an athlete so that his or her core temperature reaches 102°F (38.9°C) as quickly as possible to reduce the risk of morbidity and mortality.[6] Using the concept of "cool first, transport second" maximizes the chance of survival because it limits the amount of time that the person is above the critical threshold temperature of 104.5°F (40.3°C). Implementing policies for the appropriate management of EHS is essential for the health and safety of athletes, and such policies should contain the following recommendations:

- Any athlete suspected of suffering from EHS should have an accurate temperature taken (rectal temperature) by a licensed healthcare professional.
- Athletes suffering from EHS should be cooled first via cold water immersion prior to being transported to the hospital. In cases where an athletic trainer is present, the athletic trainer is responsible for managing the situation (take the rectal temp, instruct coaches to activate EMS, and direct the cooling of the athlete).
- In situations in which an athletic trainer is not present, coaches should immediately activate EMS and attempt to cool the athlete until licensed medical professionals arrive to take over.
- Once the body temperature reaches 102°F, cooling should be ceased and the athlete should be transported to a hospital.

Successes

In 2012, the Arkansas Department of Health developed protocols for the state's EMS section. Within the protocols is a section dedicated to EHS and exertional heat illnesses where responding emergency personnel must take a rectal temperature and, if indicated, aggressively cool the patient prior to transport to the receiving medical facility. Implementing protocols such as these ensures that athletes suffering from EHS will be appropriately managed to protect their health and safety and maximize their chance of survival.

Summary

In summary, coaches, administrators, and the sports medicine team play an integral role in protecting the health and safety of athletes. Coaches can play a proactive role in ensuring the health and safety of athletes through education, following best practice recommendations and policy changes at the local, regional, and state levels.[7] Specifically, coaches can increase the safety of athletes by:

- Advocating for policy changes at the local, regional, and state levels, such as implementing heat acclimatization policies, WBGT policies, and EAP policies at all secondary schools.
- Advocating for policy changes at the state level that require coaches to undergo annual continuing education as it relates to emergency conditions and preventing sudden death during sports.
- Coaches should follow the best practices for preventing sudden death in sports, as outlined in the report, "Inter-Association Task Force for Preventing Sudden Death in Secondary School Athletics Programs: Best-Practice Recommendations."

Key Terms

Acclimation

Acclimatization

Automated external defibrillator (AED)

Catastrophic injury

Emergency action plan (EAP)

Preparticipation exams (PPEs)

Wet bulb globe temperature (WBGT)

References

1. Lyznicki JM, Riggs JA, Champion HC. Certified athletic trainers in secondary schools: report of the Council on Scientific Affairs, American Medical Association. *J Athl Train.* 1999;34(3):272–276.
2. Van Mechelen W, Hlobil H, Kemper HC. Incidence, severity, aetiology and prevention of sports injuries: a review of concepts. *Sports Med.* 1992;14:82–99.
3. Casa DJ, Csillan D, Armstrong LE, et al. Preseason heat-acclimatization guidelines for secondary school athletics. *J Athl Train.* 2009;44(3):332–333. doi:10.4085/1062-6050-44.3.332.
4. Hootman JM, Dick R, Agel J. Epidemiology of collegiate injuries for 15 sports: summary and recommendations for injury prevention initiatives. *J Athl Train.* 2007;42(2):311–319.
5. Bergeron MF, McKeag DB, Casa DJ, et al. Youth football: heat stress and injury risk. *Med Sci Sports Exerc.* 2005;37(8): 1421–1430.
6. Casa DJ, Guskiewicz KM, Anderson SA, et al. National Athletic Trainers' Association position statement: preventing sudden death in sports. *J Athl Train.* 2012;47(1):96–118.
7. State of Arkansas, Act 1214. *An Act to Promote the Health and Safety of Students in Public School Athletic Activities Through the Use of Athletic Trainers and Professional Development for Coaches; and Other Purposes.* 2011. http://www.arkleg.state.ar.us /assembly/2011/2011R/Acts/Act1214.pdf. Accessed July 2, 2013.
8. Casa DJ, Almquist J, Anderson SA, et al. The Inter-Association Task Force for Preventing Sudden Death in Secondary School Athletics Programs: best-practices recommendations. *J Athl Train.* 2013. doi:10.4085/1062-6050-48.4.12.

9. National Federation of State High School Associations. *2009-2010 High School Coaching State Requirements.* 2011. http://www.nfhslearn.com/StatePricingRegs.aspx. Accessed April 15, 2011.

10. *Traumatic Brain Injury Legislation.* National Conference of State Legislatures. 2013. http://www.ncsl.org/issues-research/health/traumatic-brain-injury-legislation.aspx. Accessed July 1, 2013.

11. State of Connecticut. *Public Act No. 10–62.* 2010.

12. Casa DJ, Anderson SA, Baker L, et al. The Inter-Association Task Force for Preventing Sudden Death in Collegiate Conditioning Sessions: best practices recommendations. *J Athl Train.* 2012;47(4):477–480. doi:10.4085/1062-6050-47.4.08.

13. State of Arkansas, Act 496. *An Act to Create "The Antony Hobbs III Act" and to Create School-Based Automated External Defibrillator and Cardiopulmonary Resuscitation Programs.* 2009. http://www.statescape.com/TextArchive/BillTextArchive/SSBillText2009/AR2009/AR_2009_SB_000312_Current_2896.pdf.

14. State of Arkansas, Act 1016. *An Act to Require Cardiopulmonary Resuscitation Instruction in Public School Health and Safety Classes; and for Other Purposes.* 2013. http://www.arkleg.state.ar.us/assembly/2013/2013R/Acts/Act1016.pdf.

15. Langlois JA, Rutland-Brown W, Wald MM. The epidemiology and impact of traumatic brain injury: a brief overview. *J Head Trauma Rehabil.* 2006;21(5):375–378.

16. McCrory P, Meeuwisse WH, Aubry M, et al. Consensus statement on concussion in sport: the 4th International Conference on Concussion in Sport held in Zurich, November 2012. *J Am Coll Surg.* 2013;216(5):e55–e71.

Fatal and Catastrophic Injuries in Athletics: Epidemiologic Data and Challenging Circumstances

Zachary Y. Kerr, PhD, MPH

Karen Roos, MSPT, ATC

Frederick O. Mueller, PhD, FACSM

Douglas J. Casa, PhD, ATC, FACSM, FNATA

Introduction

In the scope of public health, sports injury epidemiology—the study of the patterns, causes, and effects of death and disability during sports participation—is a relatively new field. Nevertheless, the need to examine trends in sports-related injuries has been warranted as far back as the 1930s. In 1931, the American Football Coaches Association (AFCA) became concerned over the great number of fatalities and catastrophic injuries occurring in football. Consequently, the AFCA initiated the first annual survey of football fatalities to track injury data. Even prior to 1931 football was in a state of crisis, when President Roosevelt considered eliminating the game in 1905, which led to the creation of what we know today as the National Collegiate Athletic Association (NCAA).[1]

In 1982, a grant from the NCAA expanded this research to include male and female high school and collegiate sports. The expansion aimed to better develop rules and policies that increase safety in all sports. This expansion was also the beginning of the National Center for Catastrophic Sport Injury Research at the University of North Carolina at Chapel Hill.

It is important to summarize surveillance data in order for all facets of a sports organization, including coaches and their players, to understand the rationale behind rule and policy development and apply research findings to their practice. Insight into factors that increase sports injury risk will also improve quality of life for athletes and optimize athletic performance. This chapter summarizes the catastrophic injury data that the National Center for Catastrophic Sport Injury Research collected over a 27-year time period and discusses the causes of death most prevalent in sports, as well as the prevention strategies that can be implemented to reduce these deaths.

Data Collection and Definitions

Data were collected from high school and collegiate sports that were associated with fatalities and/or catastrophic injuries, which are defined as "sport injuries resulting in a brain or spinal cord injury or skull or spinal fracture." Catastrophic injuries in professional (National Football League) and semiprofessional football were included, as were those in youth football. Other youth and professional sports were excluded, as were nonschool sports, club sports, and intramural sports.

indirect fatality A fatality caused by body system failure as a result of exertion while participating in a sports activity or by a complication that was secondary to a nonfatal injury; examples include cardiac failure and an asthma attack.

direct fatality A fatality resulting directly from participation in the fundamental skills of a sport.

Collected information included athletes' demographic data, accident information, immediate and postinjury medical care, type of injury, and equipment involved. Athletic fatalities were considered **direct fatalities** when the injury resulted directly from participation in the fundamental skills of the sport. Examples of direct fatalities are brain trauma caused by spearing in football or getting impaled by a javelin. Athletic fatalities were considered **indirect fatalities** when they were caused by body system failure as a result of exertion while participating in a sports activity or by a complication that was secondary to a nonfatal injury. Examples of indirect fatalities are cardiac failure or an asthma attack.

Data were compiled with the assistance of coaches, athletic trainers, athletic directors, team physicians, executive officers of state and national organizations, online news reports, and professional associates of the researchers. Autopsy reports were used when available.

Data collection would have been impossible without the support of the AFCA, the NCAA, and the National Federation of State High School Associations. In addition, a joint endeavor was initiated with the Section on Sports Medicine of the American Association of Neurological Surgeons. The continued effort of tracking catastrophic injuries in sport is aided in part by notification of these incidents by the public. To aid or report an incident, please see the National Consortium for Catastrophic Sport Injury Research website (www.unc.edu/depts/nccsi).

Football

During the 1931 through 2009 football seasons, there were 1016 fatalities directly caused by football: 674 in high school football, 178 in recreational play, 86 at the college level, and 78 in professional football.[2,3] Early versions of the AFCA's annual survey of football fatalities helped to quell initial concerns about football safety, but in 1968 there was a second crisis when 36 football head and neck fatalities occurred (26 high school, five college, four recreational, and one professional). Football, during this period of time, was associated with a large occurrence of initial head contact while tackling and blocking and resulted in major litigation cases against coaches, schools, and helmet manufacturers.

Steps were taken to reduce these risks in the late 1970s, which resulted in a dramatic decrease in the number of fatalities. In 1976, a major rule change eliminated initial head contact while tackling and blocking. In 1978, a National Operating Committee on Standards in Athletic Equipment helmet standard went into effect. In addition, there was improved medical care of athletes and better teaching of the fundamentals by coaches. In 1990, for the first time ever, there were no direct football fatalities at any level. Since 1990, direct football fatalities have been in the single digits, with a high of nine in 2001.[2]

Figure 2.1 illustrates the history of direct football fatalities at all levels of play by decades, starting with the period from 1931 to 1940 and ending with the period from 2001 to 2009. Direct football fatalities declined steadily through the decade from 1951 to 1960, but they dramatically increased in the decade from 1961 to 1970. Every decade following this dramatic increase shows a steady decline. Approximately half of the injuries were caused by tackling and being tackled, followed by blocking, being blocked, collisions, and kick-off and punt activity. It is important to mention that one third of the activities involved in direct football deaths were unknown because of early data collection methods. A majority of the football deaths occurred during games. The data also show that playing defensive football is much more dangerous than being on the offensive side of the ball.[2]

In addition to the direct fatalities, there were 737 indirect fatalities, as shown in **Figure 2.2**. Indirect fatalities included exertional heat stroke (EHS) deaths, heart attacks, asthma attacks, and other medical problems that were not the direct result of a football-related activity. In the early years, direct fatalities outnumbered indirect fatalities, but Figure 2.2 illustrates that trend has been reversed.[3]

A major concern in football has been the number of heat stroke deaths associated with the sport. The first recorded EHS death in football took place in 1955; it is unknown why none were recorded prior, although it is possible that they were left unrecorded, or that football organizations lacked the knowledge to recognize EHS at that time. Since 1955 there have been an additional 127 EHS deaths. The greatest number was eight in 1970. However, the 5-year period 2005 to 2009 had more EHS-related deaths in organized sports than any other 5-year period over the past 35 years.

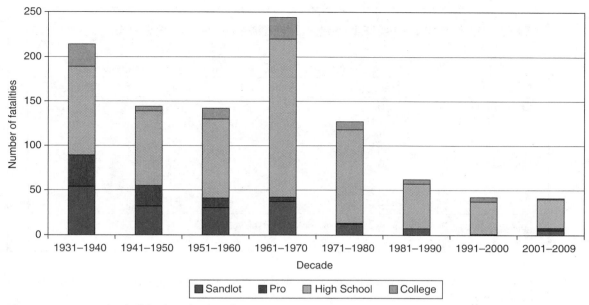

Figure 2.1 Direct football fatalities by decade.

Data from The National Center for Catastrophic Sport Injury Research.

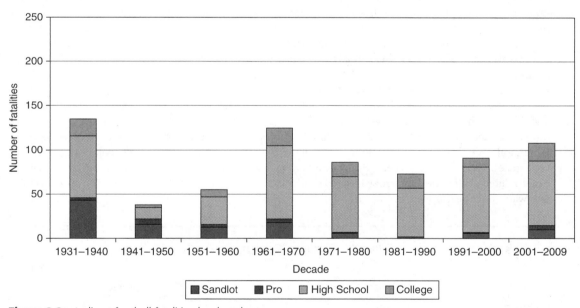

Figure 2.2 Indirect football fatalities by decade.

Data from The National Center for Catastrophic Sport Injury Research.

Fall Sports

High school fall sports were associated with 118 direct fatalities in the 27-year period studied (academic years 1982/83 through 2008/09), with 111 in football and seven in soccer (see **Table 2.1**). All of the direct fatalities involved male athletes. The data related to football were discussed in the previous section. In soccer, of the seven direct fatalities, six occurred in games and one in a practice session. Three of the fatalities

TABLE 2.1 High School Fall Sports Fatalities, Academic Years 1982/83 Through 2008/09

Sport	Direct		Indirect	
	Male	Female	Male	Female
Cross-country	0	0	16	9
Football	111	0	184	0
Soccer	7	0	28	6
Field hockey	0	0	0	1
Water polo	0	0	3	1
Total	118	0	231	17

Source: Data from The National Center for Catastrophic Sport Injury Research

were caused by brain trauma, one a fractured cervical vertebra, two internal injuries, and one a lacerated heart. Three of the fatalities were to goalkeepers, and four were related to collisions in the field of play.

The number of indirect fatalities is almost twice as large as the number of direct fatalities in high school fall sports. Football was associated with the greatest number of indirect fatalities (184 males), followed by soccer (28 males and six females), cross-country (16 males and nine females), water polo (three males and one female), and field hockey (one female). In cross-country, 13 of the indirect fatalities took place in meets and 12 in practice. Twenty-four were heart related, and one was associated with a seizure. All of the soccer indirect fatalities and the one field hockey indirect fatality were also heart related. Three of the water polo deaths were heart related, and one was seizure related. Seventy percent of the football indirect deaths were heart and heat related. Other and unknown causes accounted for the remainder. An interesting fact is that EHS deaths were almost 100% associated with the sport of football.

As illustrated in **Table 2.2**, direct fatalities in collegiate fall sports were all associated with football and followed the same pattern as the high school injuries. Indirect fatalities for the same period of time far outnumbered the direct fatalities (51 to nine). Football again led the list, with 44 indirect fatalities (all male), followed by soccer (two male and three female athletes), cross-country (one male), and water polo (one male). The two male soccer indirect deaths were heart related; the female soccer deaths included one heart-related death, one heat stroke–related death, and one athlete struck by lightning. The cross-country and water polo deaths were both heart related.

TABLE 2.2 College Fall Sports Fatalities, Academic Years 1982/83 Through 2008/09

Sport	Direct		Indirect	
	Male	Female	Male	Female
Cross-country	0	0	1	0
Football	9	0	44	0
Soccer	0	0	2	3
Water polo	0	0	1	0
Total	9	0	48	3

Source: Data from The National Center for Catastrophic Sport Injury Research

Winter Sports

High school winter sports were associated with seven direct fatal injuries during the academic years 1982/83 through 2008/09, with two in basketball, one in gymnastics, two in ice hockey, and two in wrestling (see **Table 2.3**). All of the direct fatalities involved male participants. In basketball, both direct fatalities involved brain injuries, which occurred during games. One of these injuries also included a fractured skull, which happened when the player was hit in the head by the elbow of an opponent, while the other brain injury was associated with a fall (head to floor). The gymnastics direct fatality took place in a practice session when the athlete fell from the parallel bars and suffered a severe brain injury. The two ice hockey direct fatalities took place during games, and both were caused by commotio cordis, a fatal disruption of the heartbeat, which occurs as a result of an impact to the chest, usually directly over the heart. One player was checked to the chest by an opponent, and the second player was hit in the chest by the puck. The wrestling direct fatalities both happened in a match, and both involved takedowns from a standing position. One of the athletes suffered a fractured cervical vertebra; the second athlete suffered a severe brain injury.

As shown in Table 2.3, indirect fatalities outnumbered direct fatalities, with basketball leading the list at 123 indirect fatalities (108 males and 15 females). Sixty of the basketball indirect fatalities occurred in practice, 57 in games, and six at other times from unknown causes. All of these deaths, with the exception of the six unknowns, were heart related. Males accounted for all four ice hockey indirect fatalities; three took place in games and one in practice. All four of these deaths were heart related. Swimming was the only sport in which there were more indirect fatalities for females than males. Four of the deaths happened in practice, three in meets, and one at an unspecified time. With the exception of two unknowns, all of these deaths were heart related. Wrestling was associated with 19 indirect fatalities, with 14 taking place in matches and five in practice sessions. Seventeen of the deaths were heart related, and the cause of two was unknown. Volleyball accounted for one indirect death, which took place in practice and was heart related. Of the 155 indirect deaths for high school winter sports, males accounted for 132 and females for 23.

Collegiate winter sports were associated with two direct fatalities and 47 indirect fatal injuries for the same span of years discussed previously (see **Table 2.4**). The direct fatalities occurred to one male in basketball and one female in skiing. The basketball injury took place in practice while running sprints: the athlete ran into the wall at the end of the court, fractured his cervical vertebra, and died. The female athlete was participating in a skiing practice and ran off the course into a tree, suffering a massive brain injury.

TABLE 2.3   High School Winter Sports Fatalities, Academic Years 1982/83 Through 2008/09

	Direct		Indirect	
Sport	Male	Female	Male	Female
Basketball	2	0	108	15
Gymnastics	1	0	0	0
Ice hockey	2	0	4	0
Swimming	0	0	1	7
Wrestling	2	0	19	0
Volleyball	0	0	0	1
Total	7	0	132	23

Source: Data from The National Center for Catastrophic Sport Injury Research

TABLE 2.4 College Winter Sports Fatalities, Academic Years 1982/83 Through 2008/09

Sport	Direct		Indirect	
	Male	Female	Male	Female
Basketball	1	0	27	4
Gymnastics	0	0	0	1
Ice hockey	0	0	1	0
Swimming	0	0	6	2
Wrestling	0	0	3	0
Skiing	0	1	1	0
Volleyball	0	0	0	2
Total	1	1	38	9

Source: Data from The National Center for Catastrophic Sport Injury Research

College athletes also accounted for 47 indirect fatalities (38 males and nine females). As shown in Table 2.4, basketball led the list of indirect fatalities (27 males and four females). Nineteen took place in practice, nine in games, and three at unknown times. Twenty-nine were heart related, one was the result of a brain aneurysm, and the cause of one was unknown. Gymnastics had one indirect fatality: a lung embolism in a female athlete. Ice hockey also had one indirect death that was heart related: a male participating in a practice session. Swimming was associated with eight indirect fatalities (six males and two females). Six occurred in practice and two in meets. Seven were heart related, and one was an asthma attack. Wrestling had three indirect fatalities, all of which were EHS deaths that occurred while athletes were trying to make weight for a match. All three athletes were wearing sweat suits and exercising in a hot environment with a coach present. These were the only known EHS deaths related to wrestlers trying to make weight. Skiing had one indirect male fatality; the circumstance was unknown. Volleyball was associated with two female indirect fatalities, of which one took place in a game; both were heart related.

Spring Sports

High school spring sports from 1982/83 through 2008/09 were associated with 36 direct fatalities, with 11 in baseball, two in lacrosse, 21 in track (20 males and one female), and two in softball (one male and one female) (see **Table 2.5**).

The baseball direct fatalities constituted four athletes hit by a batted ball, one hit by a ball from a pitching machine, two hit by a thrown ball, two involved in a collision, one injured diving for a ball, and one hit by a pitch. Six injuries took place in games and five in practice. Of these injuries, four were to the brain, three were commotio cordis, one a ruptured carotid artery, two internal injuries, and one a crushed larynx. In lacrosse, there were two male direct fatalities during competition. One was a result of a fractured cervical vertebra from head-down contact, and one was the result of commotio cordis after being hit in the chest by a shot ball. In softball, the two direct fatalities involved a male athlete who died after being hit in the chest with a pitched ball during a game and a female who was struck in the head unintentionally while pitching a baseball to a male baseball player. The cause of death for the male athlete was not available at this time, but it was most likely commotio cordis.

Track had 21 direct fatalities during this time period. Seventeen of the deaths involved pole vaulting, three involved being hit by a thrown discus (two males and one female), and one involved an athlete who ran into an unpadded goalpost. All of the pole vaulting fatalities involved the athlete rebounding out of the landing pit, missing the pit and landing on a hard surface, or falling into the pole plant area. All were head or neck injuries.

TABLE 2.5   High School Spring Sports Fatalities, Academic Years 1982/83 Through 2008/09

Sport	Direct		Indirect	
	Male	Female	Male	Female
Baseball	11	0	15	0
Lacrosse	2	0	7	0
Track	20	1	31	6
Tennis	0	0	3	0
Softball	1	1	0	0
Golf	0	0	1	0
Total	34	2	57	6

Source: Data from The National Center for Catastrophic Sport Injury Research

High school spring sports were also associated with 63 indirect fatalities during the time period illustrated in Table 2.5. Baseball was associated with 15 indirect fatalities, of which nine happened in practice, three in games, and three at unknown times. Thirteen were heart related, and the causes of two were unknown. In lacrosse, all seven indirect fatalities involved males, with two occurring in practice and five in games. Four were heart related, two were caused by aneurysms, and the cause of one was unknown. In tennis, all three tennis fatalities involved males and were heart related; two occurred in practice and one in a match. The one golf indirect fatality involved the heart; additional information was unknown. Track was associated with the greatest number of indirect fatalities, with 37 (31 males and six females). Nineteen took place in practice, 12 in games, and six at unknown times. Thirty were heart related, one was due to unknown causes, and six involved other causes.

As illustrated in **Table 2.6**, collegiate spring sports had 11 direct fatalities (10 males and one female), with four in lacrosse, three in baseball, three in track, and one in equestrian sports (the one female). Two of the lacrosse direct fatalities occurred in practice and two in games. All four were the result of being hit

TABLE 2.6   College Spring Sports Fatalities, Academic Years 1982/83 Through 2008/09

Sport	Direct		Indirect	
	Male	Female	Male	Female
Baseball	3	0	2	0
Lacrosse	4	0	2	0
Track	3	0	1	0
Softball	0	0	0	0
Equestrian	0	1	0	0
Tennis	0	0	1	1
Rowing	0	0	3	0
Total	10	1	9	1

Source: Data from The National Center for Catastrophic Sport Injury Research

by the ball. Three involved balls to the chest (two of which were shots and one that was thrown) with the common cause of death of commotio cordis. The fourth death was caused by a thrown ball impacting the neck that ruptured the carotid artery.

Of the three collegiate baseball direct fatalities, two occurred in practice and one during a game. One involved being hit in the chest with a ball, resulting in commotio cordis; one involved two outfielders colliding, resulting in a brain injury; and one involved a pitcher being hit in the head by a batted ball, causing a subdural hematoma. All three of the track-associated direct fatalities involved the pole vault and were brain injuries. One of the participants rebounded out of the landing pit onto a hard surface, one missed the landing mat completely and landed on a hard surface, and one landed head first onto the pole plant area. The direct fatality in equestrian sports involved a horse falling on a female rider during a practice ride.

As illustrated in Table 2.6, collegiate spring sports were also involved in 10 indirect fatalities (nine males and one female), with three in rowing, two in baseball, two in lacrosse, two in tennis (one male and one female), and one in track. In rowing, two of the indirect fatalities happened in practice and one in a meet; two were heart related and one was heat related. The two baseball, two lacrosse, and one track indirect fatalities were all heart related. In tennis, one indirect fatality was related to a cerebral hemorrhage, and one was related to a brain aneurysm.

Summary of Epidemiologic Data

From the fall of 1982 through the spring of 2009, there were a total of 183 direct sports-related fatalities in high school and college, 161 of which involved high school athletes (159 males and two females) (see **Figure 2.3**). In collegiate sports, there were 22 direct fatalities (20 males and two females). For this 27-year time period, high schools averaged 5.9 direct deaths each year and colleges averaged 0.8 a year.

Based on these counts, it appears that high school sports may place athletes at greater risk of death because of catastrophic injury than collegiate sports. However, participation in high school sports generally exceeds that of collegiate sports. In the 27-year time period, high school participation in the sports with catastrophic injury numbered 161,885,409 (104,926,117 males and 56,959,292 females). College participation in the sports with catastrophic injury numbered 8,887,421 (5,753,902 males and 3,133,519 females). As a result, the rate at which direct fatalities occurred in collegiate sports (0.24 per 100,000

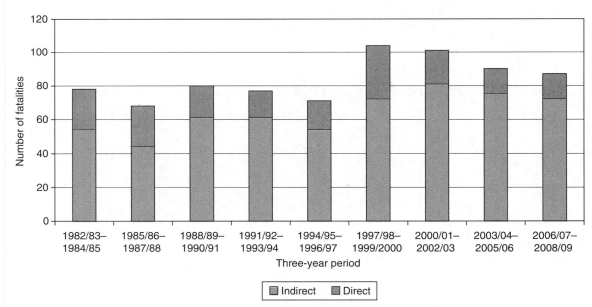

Figure 2.3 Sports fatalities in high school and college sports by three-year period, 1982/83 to 2008/09.

Data from The National Center for Catastrophic Sport Injury Research.

participants) exceeded that of high school sports (0.09 per 100,000 participants). The rate at which indirect fatalities occurred in collegiate sports (1.21 per 100,000 participants) exceeded that of high school sports (0.28 per 100,000 participants).

In addition to the fatalities in high school and collegiate sports, there were a number of catastrophic injuries that resulted in permanent disability and an additional number of catastrophic injuries that eventually resulted in recovery. High school sports for the dates under discussion were associated with 425 permanent disability injuries and 398 catastrophic injuries with full recovery (all head and neck injuries). Collegiate sports for this same time period were associated with 65 permanent disability injuries and 133 catastrophic injuries with full recovery.

Challenging Circumstances

The causes of death described in the first part of this chapter indicate that numerous medical conditions must be addressed.[4–6] The data indicate that the most common causes of death in organized sports are the following (although this ordering does not necessarily reflect the rate at which these causes occur):

- Cardiac
- Head injuries
- EHS
- Exertional sickling
- Asthma
- Trauma (not to head/neck)
- Neck injuries
- Other (lightning, diabetes, etc.)

In many cases, it is possible that sports staff may not even be aware of the number of these conditions or consider them to be pertinent risk factors associated with sports injury. Also, knowledge may vary by playing level. For example, preparticipation screening for athletes with sickle cell trait (the condition associated with exertional sickling) may not regularly occur in recreational leagues or the high school level, as opposed to the college level.

The matter is further complicated by the fact that similar signs and symptoms are found in many of the life-threatening conditions in question (**Table 2.7**), and any delay in appropriate care will increase the risk of severe outcomes such as disability and death. The benefit of being aware of the different potential causes of death is that appropriate emergency action plans can be developed to specify prevention, recognition, treatment, and return to play guidelines for each of the individual medical conditions.[4–7] Additional information on recognizing and preventing causes of sudden death in sports can be found in **Table 2.8** and in a recent position statement by the National Athletic Trainers' Association.[5] These items pertain mostly to on-site sports medicine professionals but nevertheless should be known by coaches in case they are needed to assist.

Many schools may not have policies in place to follow; thus, coaches and their sports organizations should work with a supervising physician as well as their local and state high school athletics associations to develop and implement emergency action plans and return to play guidelines following an injury. Also, in many organized sports settings (e.g., in approximately 30% of high schools), medical staff is not present on site to implement the policies related to the conditions noted previously. In these circumstances, until medical staff arrive on site, coaches may have to act as first responders. Nearly all of the life-threatening medical conditions in sports need to be properly dealt with in the first few minutes. In nearly all circumstances, it is what happens before the ambulance arrives that dictates whether the outcome is life or death. It is clear that no parent would want a coach to be completely responsible for the life-saving recognition of the problem and the treatment of their child. Nor, in defense of coaches, would coaches want to have the pressure of this responsibility on their shoulders.

Thus, it is essential that coaches, in addition to all persons involved with organized sports (administrators, strength coaches, medical professionals, etc.), have a basic understanding of the prevention,

TABLE 2.7 Preventing Sudden Death in Sports: A Potentially Complex Overlap of Signs and Symptoms of Common Causes of Death[a]

	Exertional Heat Stroke	Heat Cramp[b]	Heat Syncope[b]	Exercise Heat Exhaustion[b]	Exertional Hyponatremia	Exertional Sickling	Head Injury	Cardiac[c]	Respiratory[d]	Shock
CNS dysfunction[e]	X		X	X	X	X	X	X	X	X
Dizziness	X		X	X	X		X	X	X	
Drowsiness	X				X		X			X
Fatigue	X	X	X	X	X	X	X	X	X	X
Headache	X			X	X		X			
Light-headedness			X	X	X		X	X		X
Staggering	X			X	X	X	X	X	X	
Syncope	X		X	X				X	X	
Tunnel vision			X					X		
Personality changes[f]	X			X	X		X			
Lethargy		X	X	X	X	X	X	X	X	X
Core body temperature usually < 40°C		X		X	X		X	X	X	X
Core body temperature > 40°C	X									
Cool, clammy skin				X				X		X
Hot and wet or dry skin	X	X	X	X	X	X				
Pale skin			X	X				X		X
Cerebral edema				X	X		X			
Chills			X					X	X	X
Decreased pulse									X	X

Sign/Symptom	1	2	3	4	5	6	7
Decreased urine output	X	X					
Dehydration	X	X		X			
Diarrhea	X	X					
Hyperventillation	X	X			X	X	X
Hypotension					X	X	X
Low blood-sodium levels ($<130\ \text{mEq Na}^+\text{L}^{-1}$)		X					
Nausea/vomiting	X	X	X		X		X
Muscle cramps/pain				X			
Pulmonary edema		X				X	
Seizures	X	X					
Swelling of hands and feet		X					
Tachycardia (100–120 bpm)	X				X	X	X

Abbreviations: bpm, beats per minute; CNS, central nervous system.

a This table is not meant to be inclusive of all signs and symptoms of the conditions listed or of all conditions that could cause sudden death in sports. Nor is the table implying that all the signs and symptoms indicated for a particular condition would be present on each occasion.

b Heat cramps, heat syncope, and heat exhaustion are not life threatening but are included due to the similarity of these conditions to other conditions that could cause sudden death and the potential for confusion with acute recognition.

c Cardiac conditions could be commotio cordis, heart attack, hyperthrophic cardiomyopathy, etc.

d Respiratory could be asthma, pneumothorax, pulmonary edema, etc.

e CNS dysfunction could include altered consciousness, coma, confusion, disorientation, collapse, etc.

f Personality changes could include hysteria, irrational behavior, combativeness, aggressiveness, irritability, apathy, decreased mental acuity, etc.

Source: Casa DJ, Pagnotta KD, Pinkus DE, Mazerolle SM. Should coaches be in charge of medical care for emergencies in high school sport? *Athl Train Sports Health Care.* 2009;1 (4):144– 146. Reproduced with permission of SLACK Incorporated.

TABLE 2.8   How to Prevent, Recognize, and Treat Sudden Death in Sports

Condition	Prevention[a]	Recognition[b]	Treatment
Exertional heat stroke	Heat acclimatization[c] Proper hydration Adequate work-to-rest ratios Practice modifications for WBGT over 28°C Phasing in of practice and equipment[c] Proper hydration	CNS dysfunction Core body temperature above 104.5°F when taken rectally	Aggressively cool via cold water immersion or whole-body cold water dousing Cool first, transport second if AT is on site (cool down to 102°F before transport)
Heat exhaustion[d]	Same as EHS	Core body temperature below 104.5°F when taken rectally Paleness, fatigue, headache, and dizziness	Remove from the heat Rest with feet elevation Cool via cold/wet towels Monitor vitals and core body temperature
Exertional sickling	Testing for sickle cell trait Conditioning modification for sickle cell trait–positive athletes	Collapse without intense cramping or pain Complaints of cramping/tightness/pain feeling in the legs (without muscle contraction)	Immediately remove from activity Activate EMS Supplemental O_2
Heat cramps[d]	Proper hydration Nutritional considerations (i.e., adequate salt in the diet)	Intense painful cramping, typically in lower legs Muscles in obvious contracture when felt	Cease activity Rehydrate with electrolyte beverage Mild stretching
Cardiac arrest	Proper PPE AED on site CPR and AED training for all coaches	Collapse Lack of breathing Loss of pulse	Activate EMS Initiate CPR and AED
Head injury	Proper technique Proper equipment (properly fit and maintained) Baseline testing (cognitive and balance)	CNS dysfunction Cognitive examination Balance assessment Signs and symptoms questionnaire Cranial nerve assessment	Remove from play Monitor symptoms and vitals Refer if symptoms worsen or cranial nerves are disrupted
Asthma	Patient education Adherence to treatment plan Warm-up and cool-down	Wheezing after activity Chest tightness Shortness of breath and coughing Dizziness or light-headedness	Activate EAP Administer rescuer inhaler Reassure the athlete

Abbreviations: AED, automated external defibrillator; AT, athletic trainer; CNS, central nervous system; CPR, cardiopulmonary resuscitation; EAP, emergency action plan; EHS, exertional heat stroke; EMS, emergency medical services; PPE, preparticipation examination; WBGT, wet bulb globe temperature.

[a] Preexisting conditions and/or previous history of condition should be known.
[b] Not all signs or symptoms will be present in all cases.
[c] For an in-depth discussion of the appropriate measures for acclimatization, see the National Athletic Trainers' Association statement on preseason heat acclimatization guidelines for secondary school athletics.
[d] Heat cramps and heat exhaustion are included because they are often confused for exertional sickling and EHS, respectively. Casa DJ, Csillan D, Armstrong LE, et al. Preseason heat-acclimatization guidelines for secondary school athletics. *J Athl Train*. 2009;44(3):332–333.

Source: Pagnotta KD, Mazerolle SM, Casa DJ. Exertional heat stroke and emergency issues in high school sport. *J Strength Conditioning Res*. 2010;24(7):1707–1709. Reprinted with permission from National Strength and Conditioning Association, Colorado Springs, CO.

recognition, and initial treatment of injury, and are trained to implement emergency policies outlined by their institutions. We recommend that coaches are trained in first aid, cardiopulmonary resuscitation, and the use of an automated external defibrillator so that they can provide immediate care. Coaches should also advocate for the presence of an on-site certified athletic trainer who can assume responsibility within minutes of the incident. (Colleges and professional teams already typically have certified athletic trainers present.) A certified athletic trainer is a licensed medical professional specifically trained to prevent, recognize, and treat health emergencies related to physically active individuals.

Furthermore, numerous youth sporting events exist outside the confines of organized high school sports, such as summer sports camps, youth sports festivals (e.g., weekend soccer tournaments), competitive travel team events, and more. We strongly support all sporting events having a certified athletic trainer present to properly handle potential emergencies should they arise.

Summary

The bottom line is that every organized sports program needs to develop an emergency action plan that specifically addresses the following areas:

- The education, training, and expectations of the sport coaches, strength and conditioning coaches, athletics director, and athletes
- Designation of medical staff who will provide medical coverage for practices and games and who will oversee the general implementation of the policies and procedures related to medical care
- Specific prevention strategies for each of the most common causes of death in sports (at a minimum, the eight causes of death noted earlier in this chapter)
- Specific recognition strategies for each of the most common causes of death in sports (at a minimum, the eight causes of death noted earlier in this chapter)
- Specific treatment strategies for each of the most common causes of death in sports (at a minimum, the eight causes of death noted earlier in this chapter)
- Specific return to play strategies for each of the most common causes of death in sports (at a minimum, the eight causes of death noted earlier in this chapter)

A sports organization that does not have medical supervision present at practices and games and is involved with the medical infrastructure runs the risk of legal liability. Those participating in an organized sports situation have a reasonable expectation of receiving appropriate emergency care, and if they do not, the sports organization will have to explain why participant safety was not properly addressed. We are hopeful that the information contained within this text will assist the relevant staff with the appropriate planning and implementation of a successful healthcare plan so that emergencies can be avoided whenever possible or properly addressed when they do arise.

Key Terms

direct fatality

indirect fatality

References

1. Hawes K. The NCAA century series. Part 1: 1900-39. *NCAA News.* November 8, 1999.
2. Mueller F, Cantu R. *Catastrophic Sports Injury Research: Twenty-Seventh Annual Report, Fall 1982-Spring 2011.* 2012. http://www .unc.edu/depts/nccsi/2011Allsport.pdf. Accessed October 7, 2013.
3. Mueller F, Colgate B. *Annual Survey of Football Injury Research: 1931-2011.* 2012. http://www.unc.edu/depts/nccsi/2011FBAnnual .pdf. Accessed October 7, 2013.

4. Casa D, Pagnotta K, Pinkus D, Mazerolle S. Should coaches be in charge of medical care for emergencies in high school sport? *Athl Train Sports Health Care.* 2009;1(4):144–146.

5. Casa DJ, Guskiewicz KM, Anderson SA, et al. National Athletic Trainers' Association position statement: preventing sudden death in sports. *J Athl Train.* 2012;47(1):96–118.

6. Pagnotta KD, Mazerolle SM, Casa DJ. Exertional heat stroke and emergency issues in high school sport. *J Strength Cond Res.* Jul 2010;24(7):1707–1709.

7. Casa DJ, Guskiewicz KM, Anderson SA, et al. National Athletic Trainers' Association position statement: preventing sudden death in secondary school sports. *J Athl Train.* 2013;48(4):546–553.

Prevention of Sudden Cardiac Death in Young Athletes

Brett G. Toresdahl, MD

Jonathan A. Drezner, MD

From the Field Scenario

The varsity basketball team was playing a game at a cross-city rival school. Near the end of the third quarter, the coach put Ronny back in the game. While on defense, Ronny recovered a loose ball and quickly dribbled down the court, laying it in for 2 points. While jogging back, he stumbled, falling first to his knees and then collapsing face down on the court. Ronny's legs began twitching as he lay there. The athletic trainer ran out to the court and found Ronny unresponsive. She instructed the coach to retrieve the automated external defibrillator (AED) from behind the bench and shouted to an assistant coach to call 911. By the time the coach reached Ronny with the AED, the athletic trainer had determined that he had no pulse. He was turned face up and his jersey was cut off. The coach, familiar with their school's AED, opened the case, dried Ronny's chest, and applied the pads while the athletic trainer started chest compressions. As soon as the AED was ready, chest compressions were halted and the AED analyzed the rhythm. "Shock indicated—charging," the AED spouted. All hands were cleared from Ronny prior to the administration of a shock. The athletic trainer resumed chest compressions immediately after the shock until moments later, when Ronny began to move and tried to speak. Paramedics arrived moments later. Having fully regained consciousness, Ronny was placed on a stretcher and transported to the nearby hospital.

Discussion Questions

1. How do you recognize sudden cardiac arrest in an athlete?
2. What about this case could have misled the athletic trainer and coaches, causing them to overlook the possibility of sudden cardiac arrest?
3. What was the advantage of the visiting team bringing their own AED to the game?
4. How did the coaches and athletic trainer work together to provide the needed care? What is needed to provide life-saving care to an athlete in sudden cardiac arrest?

Introduction

Sudden cardiac arrest occurs when the heart stops beating abruptly. It is the leading cause of death in young athletes on the playing field, and it is typically the result of an underlying structural or electrical heart problem (see **Table 3.1**), although sudden cardiac arrest can also

sudden cardiac arrest Sudden cardiac arrest (SCA) is an abrupt stop of the heart beat, typically caused by an abnormal electrical signal from the bottom half of the heart. This is different from a heart attack (or myocardial infarction).

TABLE 3.1   Causes of Sudden Cardiac Death in Young Athletes

Structural	Electrical	Other
Hypertrophic cardiomyopathy*	Long QT syndrome*	Drugs and stimulants
Coronary artery anomalies	Wolff-Parkinson-White syndrome	Commotio cordis
Aortic rupture/Marfan syndrome*	Brugada syndrome*	Primary pulmonary hypertension*
Dilated cardiomyopathy*	Catecholaminergic polymorphic ventricular tachycardia*	
Myocarditis		
Left ventricular outflow tract obstruction	Short QT syndrome*	
Mitral valve prolapse	Complete heart block	
Coronary artery atherosclerotic disease*		
Arrhythmogenic right ventricular cardiomyopathy*		
Postoperative congenital heart disease		

* Inheritable

heart attack (myocardial infarction)   A heart attack is an injury of the muscle wall of the heart caused by a lack of oxygen, usually due to a blockage of the blood vessels on the surface of the heart. In some cases this can lead to sudden cardiac arrest and death.

sudden cardiac death The sudden death of an individual during or within 1 hour after exercise as a result of a cardiovascular disorder.

occur in athletes with normal hearts in the event of a direct blow to the chest. In the news, sudden cardiac arrest is often mistakenly described as a heart attack. However, a **heart attack (or myocardial infarction)** is a problem with the blood vessels that supply oxygen to the muscle walls of the heart.

When sudden cardiac arrest results in death, it is described as **sudden cardiac death**. Preventing sudden cardiac death requires both identifying athletes with underlying heart problems and being prepared to respond to a sudden cardiac arrest when it happens.

Background and Occurrence of Sudden Cardiac Arrest

Sudden cardiac death is the leading cause of death in young athletes (ages 12 to 35) during exercise.[1,2] Estimates of how often it occurs range from 1 in 25,000 to 1 in 300,000 athletes per year.[3,4] The exact frequency of sudden cardiac death in athletes continues to be debated. Most of the research on this topic identifies cases of sudden cardiac death through searches of newspapers, catastrophic insurance claims, and various other electronic databases. When these methods are used, there is a risk of underestimating the true incidence of sudden cardiac death because many cases may not be identified. However, in certain areas and organizations, mandatory reporting systems have been used to identify cases of sudden cardiac death in young athletes, and these systems likely provide a more accurate estimate of how often it occurs.[2,4]

Young athletes have a three times higher risk of sudden cardiac death than nonathletes.[5] There are two to nine times more cases of sudden cardiac death in males compared to females.[1-3] Additionally, black athletes have an increased risk, with a rate of sudden cardiac death up to three times higher than white athletes.[2] Although it can occur during any sport, sudden cardiac death occurs most frequently in basketball and football in the United States.[1,2]

Mechanism and Causes of Sudden Cardiac Arrest

A heart consists of four chambers, two that sit on top (atria) and two that sit beneath these (ventricles). *Ventricles* pump blood to either the lungs or the body, while the *atria* receive blood traveling back from these destinations. In a normal heart, an electrical signal begins in the top (atria) and travels to the bottom

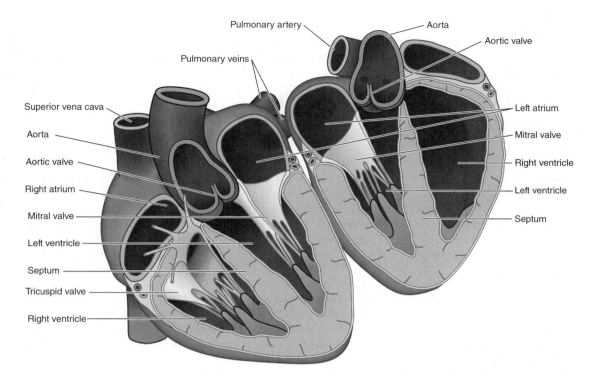

Pulmonary artery

Aorta

Aortic valve

Pulmonary veins

Left atrium

Superior vena cava

Mitral valve

Aorta

Right ventricle

Aortic valve

Left ventricle

Right atrium

Septum

Mitral valve

Left ventricle

Septum

Tricuspid valve

Right ventricle

(ventricles). This produces a coordinated pattern of contractions of the muscle walls of the heart to allow blood to be pumped through it. However, in athletes with an underlying heart problem, vigorous exercise can cause a change in the electrical signals, which can be lethal.[6] How exactly this occurs is different for each type of underlying heart problem. In most cases of sudden cardiac arrest, the electrical signal turns into **ventricular fibrillation**, which is an uncoordinated pattern of electrical signals coming from the bottom of the heart.[7–9] As a result the heart is unable to pump blood effectively. If nothing is done, this electrical signal will soon turn into *asystole* (also called flatline), where there is no measurable electrical activity and consequently no pumping of blood. At this point the chance of survival is very low.[10]

An electrical shock is able to return the dangerous ventricular fibrillation electrical signal back to its normal rhythm. The chance of survival decreases by 7–10% with each minute that goes by until a shock is given.[11] Outside of a hospital, this life-saving electrical shock can be provided by an **automated external defibrillator (AED)**, which is a computerized device about the size of a shoe box. With only a few easy steps, it is able to analyze the electrical signal of the heart and determine if a shock is needed. One study showed that untrained sixth graders were able to operate AEDs almost as well as paramedics.[12]

Cardiopulmonary resuscitation (CPR) is important both before and after using an AED. Chest compressions alone or "hands-only" CPR can effectively provide critical blood flow to the brain and muscle walls of the heart.[13] This increases the likelihood that a shock will return the heart to a normal rhythm.[11] Resuming chest compressions after a shock is also important because there is often a delay in the return of the heart to beating normally and pumping blood.[14]

Specific Causes of Sudden Cardiac Arrest

Hypertrophic Cardiomyopathy

Up to one third of sudden cardiac deaths in young athletes in the United States are a result of hypertrophic cardiomyopathy.[1,15] This is sometimes referred to as an enlarged heart. However, there are a number of heart problems that could fit this description. **Hypertrophic cardiomyopathy**

ventricular fibrillation A lethal irregular heart rhythm characterized by rapid and disorganized contraction of the heart muscle and inability to pump blood effectively.

automated external defibrillator (AED) A computerized device that attaches to a collapsed victim's chest using two adhesive pads, analyzes the heart rhythm, and provides a shock if indicated to try to restart the heart.

hypertrophic cardiomyopathy An asymmetric thickening of the walls of the bottom half of the heart where the heart muscle fibers also become disorganized.

is a thickening of the muscle walls of the lower left chamber of the heart and often in the wall that separates the two lower chambers. The muscle fibers also become disorganized, which changes the way electrical signals pass through the heart.[16] Hypertrophic cardiomyopathy is an inheritable condition that is found in approximately 1 in 500 people in the general population and in about 1 in 1500 athletes.[17,18] The muscle wall does not typically become thick until adolescence, so screening tests are not useful before athletes enter high school.[16]

Coronary Artery Anomalies

About 15% of sudden cardiac deaths in young athletes in the United States are a result of abnormalities in the blood vessels on the surface of the heart that supply the muscle walls.[1,15] These abnormalities as a group are called *coronary artery anomalies*. There are two main coronary arteries on the surface of the heart. They originate from the base of the aorta, which is the large vessel through which all of the oxygen-rich blood flows out of the heart. Problems with the coronary arteries include abnormal locations of where they originate, sharp angles in the path they take, and being buried within the heart muscle instead of on the surface. During exercise, these abnormalities can cause the flow of blood to the muscle walls of the heart to be cut off, which eventually leads to changes in the heart's electrical signal and sudden cardiac arrest.

Myocarditis

Myocarditis is inflammation of the heart muscle that is typically caused by a noncommunicable virus. It accounts for about 7% of sudden cardiac deaths in U.S. athletes.[1,19,20] It can occur in athletes who have no prior underlying heart problem. The inflammation and scar tissue that form in the muscle walls cause a disruption in the electrical signal, which can lead to a sudden cardiac arrest. Often the first symptoms of this are similar to the flu. As the disease worsens, the athlete might develop heart failure, the symptoms of which include worsening athletic performance, shortness of breath, and a cough. This is because the heart can become enlarged. However, unlike hypertrophic cardiomyopathy where the muscle walls become thicker, the enlargement of the heart in myocarditis is caused by the chambers of the heart becoming dilated.

Arrhythmogenic Right Ventricular Cardiomyopathy

arrhythmogenic right ventricular cardiomyopathy (ARVC) Progressive fibro-fatty replacement of the right side of the heart, causing wall thinning.

Another underlying cause of sudden cardiac arrest in athletes is **arrhythmogenic right ventricular cardiomyopathy (ARVC)**. It is found in approximately 1 in 5000 people and suspected to cause about 4% of sudden cardiac deaths in U.S. athletes.[21] Interestingly, Italian researchers found ARVC in 22% of young sudden cardiac death cases, making it the leading cause of sudden cardiac death in young athletes in Italy.[18] In ARVC, the normal heart muscle is replaced by a fibrous and fatty tissue, which causes the walls of the heart to become thin and the lower right chamber of the heart to become dilated. These changes in the heart muscle can interfere with the electrical signal in the heart, which during physical exercise can result in a cardiac arrest.

Aortic Rupture/Marfan Syndrome

Marfan syndrome An inherited disorder of connective tissue that affects multiple organ systems, causing a progressive dilatation and weakness of the aorta that can lead to rupture and sudden death.

Marfan syndrome is an inherited problem with connective tissue that affects 2 to 3 people out of every 10,000.[22] Common characteristics of a person with Marfan syndrome include above average height, long limbs (large "wing span"), long fingers, and increased flexibility.[23] Though many organs are involved, Marfan syndrome specifically causes the walls of the first part of the aorta to become dilated and weak. This puts the vessel walls at risk of tearing, which can cause sudden death. Symptoms of the aorta tearing are sharp chest pain or back pain and/or passing out. Heart valves can be affected as well in people with Marfan syndrome.[22]

Ion Channel Disorders

Electrical problems of the heart without a structural problem are called *ion channel disorders*. This is because they are often caused by mutations in channels through which electrolytes (or ions) pass in and out of cells, which is how the electrical signal is transmitted through the heart. These electrical disorders can cause an abnormal heart rhythm and lead to sudden cardiac arrest. Examples of these disorders include long QT syndrome, short QT syndrome, Brugada syndrome, and familial catecholaminergic polymorphic ventricular tachycardia.[6] In U.S. athletes, confirmed cases of ion channel disorders account for approximately 3% of sudden cardiac deaths.[21] However, researchers suspect that this percentage may actually be higher for the following reason. When an autopsy is done on a young athlete who dies suddenly, the heart sometimes appears normal and no other cause of death is found. Unless specific genetic testing is done, electrical disorders such as these cannot be diagnosed. These cases of sudden unexplained death account for nearly 40% of cases in young people during exertion and may in fact be caused at least in part by ion channel disorders.[15]

Commotio Cordis

While most sudden cardiac arrest in athletes is caused by an underlying heart problem, it can also occur as a result of blunt trauma. **Commotio cordis**, also called cardiac concussion, is a blow to the chest in the area of the heart during a very specific time of the heart rhythm cycle. The blow to the chest does not penetrate the skin or chest wall, and it does not need to be particularly forceful. However, this blow causes a change in the electrical signal and sudden cardiac arrest. Commotio cordis occurs most commonly in adolescent boys (average age 14), which is thought to happen because the chest wall is less thick and not yet fully developed.[24] In 80% of cases that occur in athletes, it is caused by a hard object, such as a baseball, softball, hockey puck, or lacrosse ball. The other 20% of cases are a result of contact with another player.[24] Some companies have attempted to make a chest protector to prevent commotio cordis, but this equipment has not yet been proven effective.[25]

commotio cordis A sudden cardiac arrest caused by a blow to the chest by a hard object (such as a baseball, lacrosse ball, or hockey puck) that interrupts the electrical signal of the heart.

Prevention

Screening for Underlying Heart Problems

The American Heart Association estimates that about 1 in 300 young athletes have an underlying heart problem that puts them at risk for sudden cardiac death.[21] In an effort to identify athletes at risk, most major sporting and medical associations recommend performing heart screenings as part of annual sports physicals.[21,26,27] However, there remains debate about what should be included in heart screenings of athletes. For many years heart screenings included questions about symptoms, heart conditions in family members, and a physical exam. More recently, some physicians have started performing an electrocardiogram (ECG) as part of sports physicals, which is the main subject of this debate.

History and Physical Examination

The standard heart screening has two components. The first includes a detailed questionnaire that the athlete ideally completes with the help of a parent. The athlete is asked if he or she has passed out, experienced chest pain, had a racing or skipped heartbeat, felt lightheaded or more short of breath than expected, had an unexplained seizure, or felt more tired or short of breath more easily than teammates. It asks if the athlete has been diagnosed with a heart problem or has had any testing to look for a heart problem. Additionally, there are questions about family members with specific heart problems, who have died suddenly at a young age or had unexplained fainting, seizures, or near drowning. The second part is a physical exam that includes measuring blood pressure and listening for a heart murmur, which is an extra sound caused by abnormal blood flow through the heart. The doctor will also feel for differences in pulses from side to side and look for signs of Marfan syndrome.[28]

The challenge with this approach to looking for underlying heart problems is that many athletes who suffer a sudden cardiac arrest have no symptoms beforehand and those that do have symptoms often go unrecognized.[29,30] Also, warning symptoms of an underlying heart problem can be caused by many other common conditions, such as asthma. In one study, nearly 70% of high school students reported having at least one of these warning symptoms or a family history that increased their risk for an inheritable heart problem.[31]

Electrocardiogram

An ECG is a recording of the electrical signals of the heart. It is done by placing 10 electrodes in the form of small stickers with wires that connect to a recording device. One electrode is placed on each limb, and six are placed across the left chest. An ECG is simply a snapshot of the electrical signal of the heart, whereas other forms of heart testing record the electrical signals for longer periods of time. The ECG is used by some doctors when screening athletes for underlying heart problems because many heart problems cause a specific pattern of changes in the ECG. In Italy, a mandatory screening program in athletes using ECG resulted in an 89% decrease in the incidence of sudden cardiac death.[4] Using the ECG as a screening tool in athletes is a topic of considerable debate and research.[32,33] Some of the main concerns about using ECGs are related to cost, feasibility, and the false-positive rate.[21,34]

A recent analysis estimated the cost of a history and physical exam to be $111 and an ECG to be $88.[35] However, concern about cost is not simply this added expense. Sometimes an ECG is abnormal when in fact there is no underlying heart problem. This is also called a false-positive result, because it is falsely abnormal. When an ECG is abnormal, other testing is often needed, such as an echocardiogram (ultrasound of the heart) or extended monitoring of the electrical signal of the heart. These additional tests can be expensive and need to be considered carefully when deciding to use an ECG to screen athletes for underlying heart problems.

The concern about feasibility is that not enough doctors are trained to interpret ECGs in athletes. One of the challenges is that there are normal changes in the heart of an athlete as a result of training that can be difficult to distinguish from an underlying heart problem.[36] Part of this challenge is that the criteria used to interpret ECG results in athletes continue to be refined. When a standardized tool is used to assist doctors, untrained doctors are able to achieve an accuracy of over 90%.[37]

In order for ECGs to be used effectively when screening athletes for underlying heart problems, the number of athletes with no underlying heart problem but who have an abnormal ECG must be minimal. This rate of false-positive ECGs was first reported over two decades ago and was 15%.[38] As a result of additional research and refinement of criteria used to interpret ECGs in athletes, the false-positive rate has become as low as 2–3%.[39,40]

Recognizing Sudden Cardiac Arrest

Before an Athlete Collapses

Many athletes who suffer sudden cardiac arrest do not have symptoms before collapsing.[15,30] Once the electrical signal in an athlete's heart changes into ventricular fibrillation (the potentially lethal heart rhythm originating in the bottom of the heart instead of the top), it quickly results in the athlete collapsing because the heart muscle is not working in a coordinated way and blood is not being pumped to the rest of the body. However, if an athlete experiences chest pain, light-headedness, or a racing heartbeat, the athlete should be removed from play and evaluated by the medical staff, because this may be a symptom of an underlying heart problem.

After an Athlete Collapses

Because the chance of survival from a sudden cardiac arrest is dependent on how quickly it is treated with an AED, being able to recognize the signs of sudden cardiac arrest is incredibly important. This is the responsibility of not only the medical staff but also the coaches, referees, other support staff, and even other athletes. A team or venue can be prepared for sudden cardiac arrest by having an emergency plan, trained staff, and an AED. However, these preparations are of no value if no one recognizes sudden cardiac arrest when it happens. It should be suspected anytime an athlete collapses and is unresponsive.[9] It should be also suspected when an athlete is hit in the chest by another player or object, because this could cause commotio cordis.

There are a number of challenges in recognizing a sudden cardiac arrest in athletes. They can be mistakenly presumed to be having a seizure because there may be jerking or shaking movements, which have been reported in up to 50% of cases.[7,41] Seeing these movements should not lessen the suspicion of sudden cardiac arrest, however. Another challenge in recognizing sudden cardiac arrest is correctly assessing for breathing and a pulse. An observer might not suspect a sudden cardiac arrest when the athlete is seen taking gasping breaths. However, occasional gasping breaths can be seen in the first few minutes after an athlete collapses from a sudden cardiac arrest.[42] Additionally, feeling a pulse in a collapsed athlete is very difficult, even for medical professionals. One study found that when attempting to feel the pulse of someone who was known to have one, first responders could identify it only 45% of the time.[43] As a result, the American Heart Association recommends that people without medical training should no longer attempt to feel a pulse before beginning CPR.[44]

Other Considerations

A number of medical problems other than sudden cardiac arrest can cause an athlete to collapse. These include heat exhaustion or heat stroke, electrolyte imbalances, seizure, other heart problems that do not result in cardiac arrest, and pulmonary embolus, which is a clot in the blood vessels of the lungs. These other medical problems should be considered only after an athlete becomes responsive or after the following is confirmed: normal breathing, a definitive pulse, and heart rhythm analysis by an AED.

Management of Sudden Cardiac Arrest

Emergency Planning

Considerable planning and preparations are needed in order to effectively treat a sudden cardiac arrest in an athlete. This is best accomplished by developing a comprehensive emergency action plan (EAP) that is specifically designed for the athletic venue. An EAP should identify potential first responders (such as coaches and athletic trainers) and ensure that all are trained in recognizing sudden cardiac arrest, performing CPR, and using AEDs. The EAP should also outline a communication system, a transportation route for emergency vehicles, and the placement and maintenance of AEDs. An adequate number of AEDs are needed to ensure that a shock can be provided within 3 to 5 minutes from the time of collapse anywhere within the athletic venue. This may include a combination of mounted and portable AEDs. The plan should be coordinated with local emergency medical services and practiced at least once per year (see **Table 3.2**).[9,45,46]

 With proper planning, life-saving treatment can be quickly provided. The American Heart Association's "Chain of Survival" summarizes the treatment of a sudden cardiac arrest in five steps:[44]

1. Immediate recognition of cardiac arrest and activation of the emergency response system
2. Early CPR that emphasizes chest compressions
3. Rapid defibrillation if indicated
4. Effective advanced life support
5. Integrated post–cardiac arrest care

TABLE 3.2   Elements of a Comprehensive Emergency Action Plan for Sudden Cardiac Arrest

Develop a written emergency action plan for each venue

Identify and train likely responders in CPR and AED use

Establish an effective and efficient communication system

Ensure access to early defibrillation through on-site AED(s)

Integrate and register the AED with the local EMS system

Abbreviations: AED, automated external defibrillator; CPR, cardiopulmonary resuscitation; EMS, emergency medical services.

Time-Specific Goals and Objectives

Within 10–15 minutes the following should occur:

- Recognition of sudden cardiac arrest (recall that brief seizure-like activity is common in athletes with sudden cardiac arrest)
- Activation of the emergency medical system by calling 911
- Initiation of CPR ("hands-only" with chest compressions is adequate)
- Retrieval of the AED
- Application of the AED as soon as possible (within the first 3 to 5 minutes) for rhythm analysis and delivery of a shock (if the AED determines a shock is indicated)
- Resumption of CPR if no shock is indicated or after the shock is delivered and continued until the athlete becomes responsive or until the AED analyzes the rhythm again
- Placement of a breathing tube and administration of medications by trained medical professionals if needed

Within 1 hour the following should occur:

- Transportation of the athlete to a hospital with the ability to provide advanced cardiac life support

Within 24 hours the following should occur:

- Continued care of the athlete in the intensive care unit
- Rapid cooling and induced hypothermia if the hospital has the capabilities, because this treatment improves survival and decreases neurologic complications[47]

Beyond 24 hours the following should occur:

- Determining if there is an underlying heart problem that led to the sudden cardiac arrest in the athlete
- Additional management specifically treating the underlying heart problem
- Screening of family members if the underlying heart problem is known to be inheritable (see Table 3.1)
- Genetic testing in the case of an athlete who does not survive and in whom no underlying heart problem is found

Chance of Survival

The most important factor affecting survival from sudden cardiac arrest is the time between collapse and when a shock is given.[48] Historically in the United States, less than 5% of people survived a sudden cardiac arrest if it occurred outside of a hospital. Fortunately, advances in emergency medical care with use of AEDs have increased the survival rate to nearly 50% in some communities.[49] In certain settings such as casinos, airlines, and airports, the use of AEDs has led to survival rates ranging from 41% to 74% when bystanders perform CPR and a shock is given within the goal time frame of 3 to 5 minutes.[50-52]

Only recently has there been more research made available on the rates of survival from sudden cardiac arrests in athletes. In U.S. high schools equipped with at least one AED, 78% of student athletes survived.[9] However, a study of sports-related sudden cardiac arrest in France that included people of all ages found the survival rate to be only 16%.[53]

Recovery

Expected Time Course

Recovery time is variable and dependent on the degree of injury to the athlete's heart, brain, and other organs as a result of the sudden cardiac arrest. For young athletes who survive a sudden cardiac arrest, this is a life-changing event not only for them, but also for their families, team, and community. Every effort must be made to educate athletes and families about their cardiac disorder. The psychological and emotional well-being of the athlete also must be carefully monitored as he or she transitions out of competitive athletics and adjusts to having activity limitations that may be necessary to avoid a repeat cardiac arrest.

Return to Play After Cardiac Arrest

Under the care of a cardiologist, an athlete who has suffered a sudden cardiac arrest will temporarily or permanently be restricted from certain activities or sports depending on the underlying heart problem. Such limitations help reduce the risk of a repeat sudden cardiac arrest.[4] Specific recommendations have been established by the 36th Bethesda Conference sponsored by the American College of Cardiology regarding which sports an athlete can be cleared to play for each underlying heart problem.[54] The recommendations take into account the severity of the underlying problem, the risk of sudden death or worsening of the underlying problem, and the type and intensity of exercise involved in a particular sport.[54]

Some structural heart problems can be treated with surgery. Similarly, some electrical heart problems can be treated with a procedure called catheter ablation. This works by threading an electrode through blood vessels to reach the heart, where the electrode is able to destroy the tissue that is causing the abnormal electrical signal. At other times, an athlete might have a pacemaker and/or a defibrillator implanted. This is a small device inserted under the skin in the left chest and has wires that run to the heart. It is able to force the heart into a normal rhythm or provide a shock in the event of a cardiac arrest. These treatments may allow an athlete to have less restrictions in activities and sports. If disqualified from competitive athletics, the athlete should be provided with clear exercise recommendations after careful consideration of national guidelines by his or her doctor.[55]

Summary

Sudden cardiac death is the leading cause of death in young athletes on the playing field. Preventing such tragedies requires both screening athletes for underlying heart problems and making the necessary preparations to quickly respond to a sudden cardiac arrest.

The traditional screening for underlying heart problems includes a thorough review of an athlete's medical history, symptoms, and family history in addition to a physical exam. However, this strategy is not very effective for detecting athletes at risk for sudden cardiac death. When ECGs are added to a history and physical exam, doctors are better able to identify underlying heart problems and can decrease the number of athletes who die from sudden cardiac arrest. Improvements in the criteria used by doctors to interpret ECGs have minimized unnecessary follow-up tests. There are still challenges with screening large populations of athletes using ECGs in the United States in terms of infrastructure and educating doctors.

Emergency response planning can greatly improve the chances of survival after sudden cardiac arrest. The most important factors affecting survival after sudden cardiac arrest are being able to quickly provide high-quality CPR and a life-saving shock with use of an on-site AED. The athletic community is able to accomplish this by training coaches, athletic trainers, and sports medicine doctors to immediately recognize and respond to a sudden cardiac arrest. Sudden cardiac arrest must always be suspected when an athlete collapses and is unresponsive despite gasping breaths or seizure-like movements. A high rate of survival following sudden cardiac arrest is possible when there is a coordinated emergency response plan that ensures that the necessary treatment is provided as soon as possible.

Clinical Case Scenarios

1. A 17-year-old male high school basketball player complained of chest pain and light-headedness during practice. The light-headedness was severe enough that he thought he might pass out. He has no known medical conditions, and this is the first time he has complained of these symptoms. He

was removed from practice and allowed to rest, and his symptoms then resolved. The player is asking to return for the end of practice.

    a. Should the player be allowed to return to practice?

    b. What are some underlying heart problems that may be responsible for his symptoms and need to be ruled out before he can return to play?

2. A 13-year-old boy is playing lacrosse and is struck in the chest by the lacrosse ball. He takes a few steps after being hit in the chest and then collapses to the ground and stops moving. Rescuers respond to his side and find him to be unresponsive and not breathing.

    a. What condition has likely occurred?

    b. Name three things the first responder should do as part of the emergency response to this athlete.

    c. The rescuers call for an AED. What should be provided while waiting for the AED?

3. A 20-year-old male college soccer player is playing in a game and collapses. After he is on the ground for a few seconds, his arms and legs begin to move in an uncontrolled manner and it appears as if he is having a seizure. He has no history of a seizure disorder, and there was no head trauma prior to his collapse.

    a. As the first responder, what condition do you think is most likely?

    b. Should CPR be started?

    c. When should the AED be applied?

    d. Describe the ideal emergency response to this athlete.

Key Terms

Arrhythmogenic right ventricular cardiomyopathy (ARVC)

Automated external defibrillator (AED)

Commotio cordis

Heart attack (myocardial infarction)

Hypertrophic cardiomyopathy

Marfan syndrome

Sudden cardiac arrest

Sudden cardiac death

Ventricular fibrillation

References

1. Maron BJ, Doerer JJ, Haas TS, Tierney DM, Mueller FO. Sudden deaths in young competitive athletes: analysis of 1866 deaths in the United States, 1980-2006. *Circulation*. 2009;119(8):1085–1092.
2. Harmon KG, Asif IM, Klossner D, Drezner JA. Incidence of sudden cardiac death in national collegiate athletic association athletes. *Circulation*. 2011;123(15):1594–1600.
3. Van Camp SP, Bloor CM, Mueller FO, Cantu RC, Olson HG. Nontraumatic sports death in high school and college athletes. *Med Sci Sports Exerc*. 1995;27(5):641–647.
4. Corrado D, Basso C, Pavei A, et al. Trends in sudden cardiovascular death in young competitive athletes after implementation of a preparticipation screening program. *JAMA*. 2006;296(13):1593–1601.
5. Corrado D, Basso C, Rizzoli G, Schiavon M, Thiene G. Does sports activity enhance the risk of sudden death in adolescents and young adults? *J Am Coll Cardiol*. 2003;42(11):1959–1963.
6. Maron BJ. Sudden death in young athletes. *N Engl J Med*. 2003;349(11):1064–1075.
7. Drezner J, Harmon K, Heistand J, Cramer M, Rao A. Effectiveness of emergency response planning for sudden cardiac arrest in United States high schools with automated external defibrillators. *Br J Sports Med*. 2008;42:515.
8. Drezner JA, Rao AL, Heistand J, Bloomingdale MK, Harmon KG. Effectiveness of emergency response planning for sudden cardiac arrest in United States high schools with automated external defibrillators. *Circulation*. 2009;120(6):518–525.
9. Toresdahl BG, Drezner JD, Rao AL, Harmon KG. Outcomes of sudden cardiac arrest in U.S. high schools: a prospective study from the National Registry for AED Use in Sports. *Clin J Sport Med*. 2011;20(2):137.

10. Morrison LJ, Deakin CD, Morley PT, et al. Part 8: Advanced life support: 2010 International Consensus on Cardiopulmonary Resuscitation and Emergency Cardiovascular Care Science with Treatment Recommendations. *Circulation.* 2010;122(16) (suppl 2):S345–S421.

11. Larsen MP, Eisenberg MS, Cummins RO, Hallstrom AP. Predicting survival from out-of-hospital cardiac arrest: A graphic model. *Ann Emerg Med.* 1993;22(11):1652–1658.

12. Gundry JW, Comess KA, DeRook FA, Jorgenson D, Bardy GH. Comparison of naive sixth-grade children with trained professionals in the use of an automated external defibrillator. *Circulation.* 1999;100(16):1703–1707.

13. Rea TD, Fahrenbruch C, Culley L, et al. CPR with chest compression alone or with rescue breathing. *N Engl J Med.* 2010;363(5):423–433.

14. Berg MD, Clark LL, Valenzuela TD, Kern KB, Berg RA. Post-shock chest compression delays with automated external defibrillator use. *Resuscitation.* 2005;64(3):287–291.

15. Eckart RE, Shry EA, Burke AP, et al. Sudden death in young adults: an autopsy-based series of a population undergoing active surveillance. *J Am Coll Cardiol.* 2011;58(12):1254–1261.

16. Maron BJ. Hypertrophic cardiomyopathy: a systematic review. *JAMA.* 2002;287(10):1308–1320.

17. Maron BJ, Gardin JM, Flack JM, et al. Prevalence of hypertrophic cardiomyopathy in a general population of young adults. Echocardiographic analysis of 4111 subjects in the CARDIA Study. Coronary Artery Risk Development in (Young) Adults. *Circulation.* 1995;92(4):785–789.

18. Corrado D, Basso C, Schiavon M, Thiene G. Screening for hypertrophic cardiomyopathy in young athletes. *N Engl J Med.* 1998;339(6):364–369.

19. Basso C, Corrado D, Thiene G. Cardiovascular causes of sudden death in young individuals including athletes. *Cardiol Rev.* 1999;7(3):127–135.

20. Eckart RE, Scoville SL, Campbell CL, et al. Sudden death in young adults: a 25-year review of autopsies in military recruits. *Ann Intern Med.* 2004;141(11):829–834.

21. Maron BJ, Thompson PD, Ackerman MJ, et al. Recommendations and considerations related to preparticipation screening for cardiovascular abnormalities in competitive athletes: 2007 update: a scientific statement from the American Heart Association Council on Nutrition, Physical Activity, and Metabolism: endorsed by the American College of Cardiology Foundation. *Circulation.* 2007;115(12):1643–1455.

22. Ammash NM, Sundt TM, Connolly HM. Marfan syndrome-diagnosis and management. *Curr Probl Cardiol.* 2008;33(1):7–39.

23. De Paepe A, Devereux RB, Dietz HC, Hennekam RC, Pyeritz RE. Revised diagnostic criteria for the Marfan syndrome. *Am J Med Genet.* 1996;62(4):417–426.

24. Maron BJ, Gohman TE, Kyle SB, Estes NA, 3rd, Link MS. Clinical profile and spectrum of commotio cordis. *JAMA.* 2002;287(9):1142–1146.

25. Weinstock J, Maron BJ, Song C, et al. Failure of commercially available chest wall protectors to prevent sudden cardiac death induced by chest wall blows in an experimental model of commotio cordis. *Pediatrics.* 2006;117(4):e656–e662.

26. Corrado D, Pelliccia A, Bjornstad HH, et al. Cardiovascular pre-participation screening of young competitive athletes for prevention of sudden death: proposal for a common European protocol. Consensus Statement of the Study Group of Sport Cardiology of the Working Group of Cardiac Rehabilitation and Exercise Physiology and the Working Group of Myocardial and Pericardial Diseases of the European Society of Cardiology. *Eur Heart J.* 2005;26(5):516–524.

27. Ljungqvist A, Jenoure P, Engebretsen L, et al. The International Olympic Committee (IOC) consensus statement on periodic health evaluation of elite athletes, March 2009. *Br J Sports Med.* 2009;43(9):631–643.

28. Seto CK. The preparticipation physical examination: an update. *Clin Sports Med.* 2011;30(3):491–501.

29. de Noronha SV, Sharma S, Papadakis M, Desai S, Whyte G, Sheppard MN. Aetiology of sudden cardiac death in athletes in the United Kingdom: a pathological study. *Heart.* 2009;95(17):1409–1414.

30. Drezner JA, Fudge J, Harmon KG, et al. Warning symptoms and family history in children and young adults with sudden cardiac arrest. *J Am Board Fam Med.* 2012;25(4):408–415.

31. Fudge J, Drezner J, Harmon K, et al. Cardiovascular screening in young athletes: a prospective study comparing the PPE monograph 4th edition and electrocardiogram. *Clin J Sports Med.* 2012;22(2):173.

32. Chaitman BR. An electrocardiogram should not be included in routine preparticipation screening of young athletes. *Circulation.* 2007;116(22):2610–2614; discussion 2615.

33. Myerburg RJ, Vetter VL. Electrocardiograms should be included in preparticipation screening of athletes. *Circulation.* 2007;116(22):2616–2626; discussion 2626.

34. Schoenbaum M, Denchev P, Vitiello B, Kaltman JR. Economic evaluation of strategies to reduce sudden cardiac death in young athletes. *Pediatrics.* 2012;130(2):e380–e389.

35. Wheeler MT, Heidenreich PA, Froelicher VF, Hlatky MA, Ashley EA. Cost-effectiveness of preparticipation screening for prevention of sudden cardiac death in young athletes. *Ann Intern Med.* 2010;152(5):276–286.

36. Corrado D, Biffi A, Basso C, Pelliccia A, Thiene G. 12-lead ECG in the athlete: physiological versus pathological abnormalities. *Br J Sports Med.* 2009;43(9):669–676.

37. Drezner JA, Asif IM, Owens DS, et al. Accuracy of ECG interpretation in competitive athletes: the impact of using standised ECG criteria. *Br J Sports Med.* 2012;46(5):335–340.

38. Maron BJ, Bodison SA, Wesley YE, Tucker E, Green KJ. Results of screening a large group of intercollegiate competitive athletes for cardiovascular disease. *J Am Coll Cardiol.* 1987;10(6):1214–1221.

39. Marek J, Bufalino V, Davis J, et al. Feasibility and findings of large-scale electrocardiographic screening in young adults: data from 32,561 subjects. *Heart Rhythm*. 2011;8(10):1555–1559.

40. Wilson MG, Basavarajaiah S, Whyte GP, et al. Efficacy of personal symptom and family history questionnaires when screening for inherited cardiac pathologies: the role of electrocardiography. *Br J Sports Med*. 2008;42(3):207–211.

41. Drezner JA, Rogers KJ. Sudden cardiac arrest in intercollegiate athletes: detailed analysis and outcomes of resuscitation in nine cases. *Heart Rhythm*. 2006;3(7):755–759.

42. Ruppert M, Reith MW, Widmann JH, et al. Checking for breathing: evaluation of the diagnostic capability of emergency medical services personnel, physicians, medical students, and medical laypersons. *Ann Emerg Med*. 1999;34(6):720–729.

43. Eberle B, Dick WF, Schneider T, et al. Checking the carotid pulse check: Diagnostic accuracy of first responders in patients with and without a pulse. *Resuscitation*. 1996;33(2):107–116.

44. Berg RA, Hemphill R, Abella BS, et al. Part 5: adult basic life support: 2010 American Heart Association guidelines for cardiopulmonary resuscitation and emergency cardiovascular care. *Circulation*. 2010;122(18) (suppl 3):S685–S705.

45. Drezner JA, Courson RW, Roberts WO, et al. Inter-association task force recommendations on emergency preparedness and management of sudden cardiac arrest in high school and college athletic programs: a consensus statement. *Heart Rhythm*. 2007;4(4):549–565.

46. Hazinski MF, Markenson D, Neish S, et al. Response to cardiac arrest and selected life-threatening medical emergencies: The medical emergency response plan for schools: a statement for healthcare providers, policymakers, school administrators, and community leaders. *Circulation*. 2004;109(2):278–291.

47. Kim F, Carlbom D. Therapeutic hypothermia for cardiac arrest: yes, we can. *Rev Esp Cardiol*. 2009;62(7):726–728.

48. The American Heart Association in collaboration with the International Liaison Committee on Resuscitation. Guidelines 2000 for cardiopulmonary resuscitation and emergency cardiovascular care. Part 4: The automated external defibrillator: key link in the chain of survival. *Circulation*. 2000;102(8) (suppl):I60–I76.

49. Neumar RW, Barnhart JM, Berg RA, et al. Implementation strategies for improving survival after out-of-hospital cardiac arrest in the United States: consensus recommendations from the 2009 American Heart Association Cardiac Arrest Survival Summit. *Circulation*. 2011;123(24):2898–2910.

50. Caffrey SL, Willoughby PJ, Pepe PE, Becker LB. Public use of automated external defibrillators. *N Engl J Med*. 2002;347(16):1242–1247.

51. Hallstrom AP, Ornato JP, Weisfeldt M, et al. Public-access defibrillation and survival after out-of-hospital cardiac arrest. *N Engl J Med*. 2004;351(7):637–646.

52. Valenzuela TD, Roe DJ, Nichol G, et al. Outcomes of rapid defibrillation by security officers after cardiac arrest in casinos. *N Engl J Med*. 2000;343(17):1206–1209.

53. Marijon E, Tafflet M, Celermajer DS, et al. Sports-related sudden death in the general population. *Circulation*. 2011;124(6):672–681.

54. Maron BJ, Zipes DP. 36th Bethesda Conference: Eligibility recommendations for competitive athletes with cardiovascular abnormalities. *J Am Coll Cardiol*. 2005;45(8):1312–1377.

55. Maron BJ, Chaitman BR, Ackerman MJ, et al. Recommendations for physical activity and recreational sports participation for young patients with genetic cardiovascular diseases. *Circulation*. 2004;109(22):2807–2816.

Prevention of Sudden Cardiac Death in Older Athletes

Shishir Mathur, MD

Paul D. Thompson, MD, FACC, FACSM

From the Field Scenario

Gary was the head coach for the men's cross-country team, but he had been suffering from flulike symptoms for the last few days. He was going to participate in a marathon this weekend and had been training very hard so he could win his age group (men 50–54 years old). He discussed this with his assistant coach, who began to query him about his other symptoms. It appeared that Gary had also begun to feel fatigued and had had some heartburn/gastrointestinal upset during his training runs. Knowing that Gary has also been taking medication for his high blood pressure, his assistant coach suggested that he see the athletic trainer. Gary reluctantly went to the athletic trainer, hoping that he could get some advice to help his upset stomach, but as soon as the athletic trainer heard his symptoms he immediately referred him to a physician for suspected cardiac involvement. It was later revealed that Gary had some large cholesterol deposits and was subsequently diagnosed with coronary artery disease.

Discussion Questions

1. What common prodromal symptoms do you recognize in this coach?
2. What about this case could have misled the athletic trainer and coaches, causing them to overlook the possibility of severe coronary artery disease?
3. What education/policies were likely in place that helped the assistant coach recognize the seriousness of Gary's symptoms?

Introduction

Studies of exercise-related **sudden cardiac death (SCD)** in adults have defined "adults" as individuals older than 35 to 40 years.[1,2] This age distinction is based on the observation that the causes of exercise-related SCD are different in young and old individuals. **Coronary artery disease (CAD)** is the most frequent cause of exercise-related SCD in adults, whereas congenital or inherited cardiac conditions are the most frequent causes of exercise-related SCD in the young.[1,2] This chapter focuses on exercise-related SCD in adult athletes.

sudden cardiac death (SCD) Sudden death occurring during or within 1 hour after exercise because of a cardiovascular disorder.

coronary artery disease (CAD) A condition in which plaque builds up inside the coronary arteries.

A competitive athlete has been described as "one who participates in an organized team or individual sport requiring systematic training and regular competition against others while placing a high premium on athletic excellence and achievement."[3] Compared with young individuals, fewer adults participate in such organized training and competition. In addition, although exercise-related SCD occurs more frequently in adults, it is still relatively rare. The combination of fewer athletes and fewer events necessitates that any discussion of SCD in adult athletes be based on exercise-related cardiac events in the general adult population and not be restricted to individuals meeting the definition of an athlete.

Exercise-related cardiac events are defined as those occurring during or within 1 hour of vigorous physical exertion.[4,5] Vigorous exercise generally refers to exercise intensity at least equal to that of jogging, although relative intensity depends on the individual's fitness.

Background and Occurrence of Cardiac Death in Older Athletes

The incidence of exercise-related SCD is higher in adults than in young athletes because cholesterol deposits resulting in CAD increase with age. There are few studies examining the incidence of exercise-related SCD in adults. Among the most cited are the Rhode Island[6] and Seattle[7] studies. However, both studies suffer from being over 25 years old and from including only 10 and nine SCDs, respectively. Nevertheless, both report a similar incidence of SCD among previously healthy individuals.

The Rhode Island study collected data on all individuals dying during jogging.[6] There were 10 cardiac deaths during jogging, but half of these victims had a history or prior evidence of CAD. If these individuals were eliminated, the exercise-related SCD rate for healthy men over age 30 was only one death per year for every 15,240 men, or an hourly death rate of one death per 792,000 hours of jogging.[6] There were no jogging deaths in women. The Seattle study examined cardiac arrests during vigorous physical activity in previously healthy men. The incidence of SCD during vigorous exertion was one death per year for every 18,000 physically active men, or an hourly death rate of one death per 4.76 million person-hours.

In a study that followed the cardiovascular health of 84,888 women for 1.93 million person-years, there were only nine SCDs during moderate to vigorous physical exercise, yielding an incidence of one death per 36.5 million hours of moderate to vigorous exertion.[8] This difference between men[7] and women[8] can be explained in part by the lower CAD prevalence in women compared with men of similar age and the probability that older adult women, who are more likely to have CAD and therefore be at risk, are less likely to participate in vigorous exercise compared to younger women. Nevertheless, there is also evidence that nonathletic women have a lower risk of CAD-related SCD than men, suggesting that female gender protects against SCD.[9,10]

myocardial infarction (MI)
The sudden loss of blood supply to heart muscle because of blockage in one or more coronary artery.

Both the Rhode Island and Seattle studies demonstrated that exercise increases the risk of SCD. This appears somewhat paradoxical because overall regular physical exertion reduces CAD events,[11] but the risk of SCD is momentarily increased during the exercise period. Exercise also briefly increases the risk of **myocardial infarction (MI)**, also known as a heart attack, by the mechanisms discussed later in this chapter.[12–14]

The CAD event rates reported in these studies, obtained from healthy individuals in the general population, are likely lower in athletes because regular exercise not only decreases the incidence of acute cardiac events but also decreases the risk that such events will occur during exercise. In the Seattle study the risk of a cardiac arrest during vigorous exercise relative to less strenuous activities was 56-fold higher in habitually sedentary men, but only five-fold higher in active men.[7] Similarly, the relative risk of having a heart attack during exercise compared with rest is highest in the most physically inactive men and lowest in those who are most physically active.[12,13,15] More direct measures of exercise-related SCDs in adult athletes estimate that the risk of SCD during a marathon is approximately one death per 125,000 participants, or one death per 500,000 hours of participation.[16]

Because CAD is the primary cause of exercise-related SCD, it should be apparent that the risk of such events increases in individuals with underlying diagnosed or undiagnosed CAD. The most powerful predictor of an exercise-related cardiac event has been demonstrated to be prior history of cardiovascular disease.[17]

Mechanism and Causes of Sudden Cardiac Death in Older Athletes

CAD accounts for approximately 80% of sudden deaths during physical exertion in exercising adults and in adult athletes.[1] Rupture of cholesterol plaques within the heart's arteries leads to clot formation, and sudden complete occlusion of these arteries is the most common mechanism of heart attack and subsequent SCD in previously nonsymptomatic adults during exertion.[18,19]

How exercise initiates plaque disruption is not clear, but it can cause clot formation and blockage of arteries in the heart. The increase in circulating hormones such as epinephrine during exercise could also make these cells more likely to form clots.[20,21] It is likely that all or some combination of these processes contribute to SCD and heart attacks in adults during exercise. Consequently, plaque disruption can ultimately result in a heart attack or SCD in previously healthy adult exercisers and athletes. These changes in the blood vessels cause the heart muscle to become electrically unstable, leading to a fatal electrical irregular heart beat (arrhythmia) such as ventricular fibrillation (severely abnormal heart rhythm), which is the final cause of death.

In addition to the described mechanism, patients who have had an MI in the past have scar tissue in their heart muscle, which can also give rise to similar fatal electrical abnormalities that result in SCD during exercise.

Prevention of Sudden Cardiac Death in Older Athletes

There are no proven strategies to reduce acute cardiovascular events during vigorous physical exercise in adult athletes. The strategies described in this section appear to be potentially beneficial, although none has been thoroughly examined in well-designed research studies.

Preparticipation Screening

A medical history and physical examination seeking increased CAD risk factors and evidence of cardiac abnormalities are routinely recommended prior to vigorous physical exertion. Even low CAD risk factors and a normal physical examination do not guarantee against sudden cardiovascular events during physical exertion and should not provide a false sense of security.

Exercise stress testing is performed by having an individual walk or run on a treadmill to determine the presence of cardiac symptoms such as chest pain while simultaneously analyzing the electrical signaling of the heart for any abnormalities. This test is often recommended as a screening procedure prior to vigorous exercise. A "positive" exercise stress test indicates a significant blockage in coronary arteries but cannot detect nonobstructing yet still vulnerable, **atherosclerotic plaques** (thickening of artery walls because of plaque), the likely cause of most exercise-related cardiac events in adult athletes.

atherosclerotic plaque Deposits of cholesterol and other cells in the walls of the arteries that cause blockages in the arteries.

Consequently, a negative exercise test does not rule out the presence of vulnerable plaques and the risk of an exercise-related cardiac event. On the other hand, exercise testing is prudent in individuals with known CAD (i.e., patients with history of chest pain, previous heart surgery) to ensure that they do not have significant blockages in their arteries that could compromise the blood flow to their heart muscle with the stress of exercise.

There are consensus recommendations for exercise stress testing in healthy adults without symptoms from the American College of Cardiology (ACC)/American Heart Association (AHA), the American College of Sports Medicine (ACSM), and the U.S. Preventive Services Task Force (USPSTF) (see **Table 4.1**). Both the ACC/AHA and ACSM recommend routine exercise testing prior to vigorous exercise training in individuals at increased risk of having underlying CAD, including those with diabetes, asymptomatic men older than 45 years and women older than 55 years, and those with two or more risk factors (other than age and gender) for CAD (see **Table 4.2**). In contrast, the USPSTF recommends against routine exercise stress testing in healthy individuals because of insufficient evidence of any benefits of exercise stress testing prior to starting an exercise training program.[22] Furthermore, a 2009 decision analysis recommended against exercise testing in asymptomatic individuals at all levels of risk because the exercise deaths

TABLE 4.1 Recommendations for Exercise Testing Before Exercise Training in Subjects with No Known Coronary Artery Disease

ACC/AHA	ACSM	USPSTF
Recommended for symptomatic persons with diabetes mellitus who plan to start vigorous exercise (class IIa[a])	Recommended for symptomatic persons with diabetes mellitus (or other metabolic disease) who plan to start moderate (40% to 50% Vo_2 reserve) to vigorous (> 60% Vo_2 reserve) exercise	Recommends against routine exercise testing of low-risk adults in general and finds insufficient evidence for exercise testing before exercise training
Recommended for symptomatic men > 45 years and women > 55 years who plan to start vigorous exercise (class IIb[a])	Recommended for asymptomatic men > 45 years and women > 55 years or those who meet the threshold for more than two risk factors who plan to start vigorous exercise	

Abbreviations: ACC, American College of Cardiology; AHA, American Heart Association; ACSM, American College of Sports Medicine; USPSTF, United States Preventive Services Task Force; Vo_2, maximal exercise oxygen uptake capacity (maximum capacity of an individual's body to transport and utilize oxygen during incremental exercise, which reflects the physical fitness of the individual).
[a] ACC/AHA class IIa indicates that the weight of evidence or opinion is in favor of usefulness or efficacy; class IIb indicates that the usefulness or efficacy is less well established by evidence or opinion.
Source: From Thompson PD, Franklin BA, Balady GJ, et al. Exercise and acute cardiovascular events - placing the risks into perspective: a scientific statement from the American Heart Association Council on Nutrition, Physical Activity, and Metabolism and the Council on Clinical Cardiology. *Circulation.* 2007;115:2358–2368. Reprinted with permission. Copyright © 2007, American Heart Association, Inc.

prevented by exercise testing were fewer than the deaths produced by medical intervention undertaken as a consequence of abnormal results of stress testing.[23] There is general consensus that patients with known CAD should undergo assessment of heart function by ultrasound and maximal exercise treadmill testing for risk assessment before participation in athletic activities (see **Table 4.3**).[24–26]

Education and Awareness

Educating athletes, coaches, exercise attendants, physicians, and other healthcare providers about warning symptoms for CAD events may lead to early recognition of athletes at high risk for cardiac events. Between 50% and 80% of adult athletes who suffered SCD during an athletic event had probable cardiac symptoms and warning signs before death (see **Table 4.4**).[27] Because these symptoms were often not typical and assumed to be stomach upset, individuals either did not seek medical attention or received inappropriate medical advice. Nonspecific symptoms such as fatigue and flulike symptoms are associated with a 12% greater likelihood of exercise-related acute cardiac events.[17] The specificity of such complaints is poor, but athletes should seek medical advice if they develop new symptoms, especially if these are associated with exercise.

Preparing Athletic Facilities for Handling Cardiac Emergencies

The AHA and ACSM have recommended that fitness facility staff be trained in cardiopulmonary resuscitation (CPR), that fitness facilities have automated external defibrillators available, and that fitness facilities screen participants using the questionnaire developed by AHA/ACSM to identify individuals at risk from exercise.[28,29] AHA/ACSM also recommend that fitness centers establish protocols (such as an emergency action plan) and a hotline to summon emergency medical services. These protocols and skills should be practiced during regularly scheduled emergency drills. These recommendations are reasonable, although there is no evidence that questionnaires are effective in preventing exercise-related cardiac events. Emergency medical services should be available during sporting events where a large number of

TABLE 4.2 Atherosclerotic Cardiovascular Disease Risk Factor Thresholds for Use with ACSM Risk Stratification

Positive Risk Factors	Defining Criteria
Age	Men ≥ 45 yr; women ≥ 55 yr
Family history	Myocardial infarction, coronary artery stenting or bypass operation, or sudden death before 55 yr of age in father or other male first-degree relative, or before 65 yr in mother or other female first-degree relative
Cigarette smoking	Current cigarette smoker or those who quit within previous 6 months or have exposure to environmental tobacco smoke
Sedentary lifestyle	Not participating in at least 30 min of moderate intensity physical activity on at least three days of week for at least 3 months
Obesity	Body Mass Index ≥ 30 kg/m_2 or waist girth > 102 cm (> 40 inches) for men and > 88 cm (35 inches) for women
Hypertension	Systolic blood pressure ≥ 140 mm Hg and/or diastolic blood pressure ≥ 90 mm Hg, confirmed by measurements on at least two separate occasions or on anti-hypertensive medication
Abnormal cholesterol levels	Low-density lipoprotein cholesterol (LDL-C) ≥ 130 mg/dl (3.37 mmol/L) or high-density lipoprotein cholesterol (HDL-C) < 40 mg/dl (1.04 mmol/L) or on lipid-lowering medication. If total serum cholesterol is all that is available use ≥ 200 mg/dl (5.18 mmol/L)
Prediabetes (risk of developing future diabetes)	Impaired fasting glucose (IFG) = fasting plasma glucose ≥ 100 mg/dl (5.50 mmol/L) but < 126 mg/dl (6.93 mmol/L) or impaired glucose tolerance = 2-hour values in oral glucose tolerance test (OGTT) > 140 mg/dl (7.70 mmol/L) but < 200 mg/dl (11.00 mmol/L) confirmed by measurements on at least two separate occasions
Negative risk factor	
HDL-C	>/ = 60 mg/dl
HDL-C	≥ 60 mg/dl (1.55 mmol/L)

Source: American College of Sports Medicine's Guidelines for Exercise Testing and Prescription; Ninth Edition. Lippincott Williams & Wilkins; 2013, Box 2.1, p. 30. http://lww.com. Reprinted with permission.

people are participating. These services should include on-site paramedical staff trained in performing CPR and fully equipped ambulances for prompt transfer of patients to hospitals.

Management of Sudden Cardiac Death in Older Athletes

Because the highest rate of cardiac events occurs in individuals unaccustomed to physical exercise,[7,12–15] it is possible that a gradually progressive exercise training program will reduce the likelihood of exercise-related cardiac events. Also, some healthy adults initiate an exercise program because they are concerned that new symptoms may be CAD. Consequently, seemingly healthy adults seeking advice on initiating an exercise program should be questioned about new symptoms, and those experiencing symptoms suggestive of CAD should undergo appropriate evaluation prior to exercise training.

Individuals with known CAD should undergo risk assessment using heart function evaluation with ultrasound and maximal exercise treadmill testing based on recommendations from the 36th Bethesda Conference (see **Table 4.3**). Athletes who have mildly increased risk can participate in low-intensity dynamic and low- to moderate-intensity static competitive sports but should avoid intensely

TABLE 4.3 Risk Stratification and Recommendations for Subjects with Known Coronary Artery Disease[a] Prior to Exercise Training, Based on 36th Bethesda Conference Task Force

Low Risk	High Risk
• Normal LV function (EF > 50%) • Normal exercise tolerance for age[b] • No exercise-induced reduction in blood flow or complex abnormal heart rhythms • Absence of hemodynamically significant coronary narrowing (> 50%) in any major coronary artery (if angiogram performed) • Successful re-establishment of blood flow to the heart muscle (if performed)	• Abnormal LV function (EF < 50%) • Evidence of exercise-induced reduction in blood flow to the heart muscle or complex abnormal heart rhythms • Hemodynamically significant coronary artery narrowing (> 50%) (if angiography performed)

Exercise Recommendations

• Participate in low-intensity dynamic and low- to moderate-intensity static competitive sports • Avoid intensely competitive situations • Aggressive treatment of atherosclerotic risk factors	• Participate in low-intensity competitive sports only • Restricted from moderate- and high-intensity sports • Aggressive treatment of atherosclerotic risk factors

Abbreviations: EF, ejection fraction (measure of the heart's effectiveness in pumping the blood out of its chambers); LV, left ventricle.

[a] Known coronary artery disease is identified as any one of the following: (1) history of myocardial infarction; (2) history suggestive of chest pain with objective evidence of reproducible reduction in blood flow to the heart; (3) coronary atherosclerosis (CAD) of any degree.

[b] Metabolic equivalents (METs) > 10 or maximal exercise oxygen uptake capacity (Vo_2max) > 35 mL O_2/kg-min for age < 50 years; METs > 9 or Vo_2max > 31 mL O_2/kg-min for ages 50–59 years; METs > 8 or Vo_2max > 28 mL O_2/kg-min for ages 60–69 years; METs > 7 or Vo_2max > 24 mL O_2/kg-min for age > 70 years.

Source: Data from Thompson PD, Balady GJ, Chaitman BR, et al. Task Force 6: coronary artery disease. *J Am Coll Cardiol*. 2005;45(8):1348–1353.

competitive situations. Athletes with known CAD who are high risk should generally be restricted to low-intensity competitive sports.[26,30] These recommendations are not rigid, however, and some athletes can be allowed to return to more vigorous and even very competitive activities depending on their risk profile. All athletes with atherosclerotic CAD should receive aggressive treatment for atherosclerotic risk factors. Patients with known advanced CAD should be advised to perform at least 5 minutes of warm-up and cool-down before and after exercise training sessions. A warm-up will reduce the likelihood of sudden lack of blood supply to the heart muscle with sudden intense physical effort, and a cool-down will improve blood flow return to the rest of the body that can be drastically reduced with sudden termination of physical activity.[31,32] Environmental factors such as extreme cold conditions have been associated with rapid onset of cardiovascular events.[33–36] Physically inactive individuals with known CAD should therefore avoid unaccustomed strenuous physical exercise under extreme environmental conditions. Increased altitude places individuals at greater risk. Individuals exercising at altitudes higher than 1500 meters should gradually increase their exercise training at new altitudes to allow acclimatization.[25,37]

TABLE 4.4	Early Symptoms Reported by Forty-Five Individuals Within One Week of Their Sudden Death
Symptom	Number of Reports
Chest pain/angina	15
Increasing fatigue	12
Indigestion, heartburn, or gastrointestinal symptoms	10
Excessive breathlessness	6
Ear or neck pain	5
Vague malaise	5
Upper respiratory tract infection	4
Dizziness/palpitations (heart skipping beats)	3
Severe headache	2

Source: From Thompson PD, Franklin BA, Balady GJ, et al. Exercise and acute cardiovascular events - placing the risks into perspective: a scientific statement from the American Heart Association Council on Nutrition, Physical Activity, and Metabolism and the Council on Clinical Cardiology. *Circulation*. 2007;115:2358–2368. Reprinted with permission. Copyright © 2007, American Heart Association, Inc.

Summary

The benefits of physical exercise outweigh the risk of exercise-related cardiac events. Nevertheless, exercise briefly and suddenly increases the risk of cardiac events, especially in those performing unaccustomed physical exercise and those with underlying CAD. This chapter summarizes prevention strategies that seem prudent (see **Table 4.5**) while recognizing that none has been tested by well-designed research studies.

Clinical Case Scenarios

1. A 40-year-old man wants to start intensive training for running a marathon. He does not report any symptoms suggestive of heart disease such as chest pain or shortness of breath during mild to moderate exercise. He does not have any cardiovascular risk factors by history, and his physical examination is completely normal.

   a. What screening recommendations would you expect in this scenario?

   b. What exercise recommendations would you expect in this scenario?

   c. What main factors should be taken into consideration when these decisions are made?

2. A 56-year-old man wants to start an intensive aerobic exercise program and wants to run a marathon in 6 to 12 months' time. He has been physically active doing mild to moderate aerobic exercise for at least 2 years. He has a past history of MI approximately 3 years ago. His other risk factors for CAD are hypercholesterolemia and family history of CAD in his father at age 48.

   a. What kind of screening would you expect this athlete to undergo to determine exercise recommendations?

   b. What restrictions would you expect to be put on his exercise habits?

   c. What type of exercise is probably best for this athlete?

TABLE 4.5   Strategies to Prevent Sudden Cardiac Death in Adult Athletes

---

1. Perform preparticipation screening history and physical examination (or AHA/ACSM screening questionnaires at fitness facilities).

2. Perform exercise stress testing and other appropriate cardiac investigations in selected healthy individuals based on risk factors and physical exam findings.

3. Individuals with known CAD should have their heart function assessed and an exercise stress test performed followed with appropriate exercise restrictions based on the resulting risk assessment in these individuals.

4. Educate athletes, coaches, and strength coaches on reporting possible early symptoms suggestive of CAD.

5. Prepare fitness centers with external cardiac defibrillators and staff trained in CPR.

6. Gradually increase the physical training program for individuals who are relatively physically inactive, rather than using a sudden or strenuous onset.

7. Avoid unaccustomed physical activity, especially in extreme environmental conditions such as heat, cold, and high altitude.

Abbreviations: ACSM, American College of Sports Medicine; AHA, American Heart Association; CAD, coronary artery disease; CPR, cardiopulmonary resuscitation.

Key Terms

atherosclerotic plaques

coronary artery disease (CAD)

myocardial infarction (MI)

sudden cardiac death (SCD)

References

1. Maron BJ, Epstein SE, Roberts WC. Causes of sudden death in competitive athletes. *J Am Coll Cardiol*. 1986;7:204–214.
2. Maron BJ, Thompson PD, Ackerman MJ, et al. Recommendations and considerations related to preparticipation screening for cardiovascular abnormalities in competitive athletes—2007 update: a scientific statement from the American Heart Association Council on Nutrition, Physical Activity, and Metabolism. *Circulation*. 2007;115(12):1643–1645.
3. Maron BJ, Mitchell JH. Revised eligibility recommendations for competitive athletes with cardiovascular abnormalities. *J Am Coll Cardiol*. 1994;24(4):848–850.
4. Rai M, Thompson PD. The definition of exertion-related cardiac events [published online ahead of print April 19, 2010]. *Br J Sports Med*. doi:10.1136/bjsm.2009.057653.
5. Thompson PD, Franklin BA, Balady GJ, et al. Exercise and acute cardiovascular events - placing the risks into perspective: a scientific statement from the American Heart Association Council on Nutrition, Physical Activity, and Metabolism and the Council on Clinical Cardiology. *Circulation*. 2007;115:2358–2368.
6. Thompson PD, Funk EJ, Carleton RA, Sturner WQ. Incidence of death during jogging in Rhode Island from 1975 through 1980. *JAMA*. 1982;247(18):2535–2538.
7. Siscovick DS, Weiss NS, Fletcher RH, Lasky T. The incidence of primary cardiac arrest during vigorous exercise. *N Engl J Med*. 1984;311(14):874–877.
8. Whang W, Manson JE, Hu FB, et al. Physical exertion, exercise, and sudden cardiac death in women. *JAMA*. 2006;295:1399–1403.
9. Kaikkonen KS, Kortelainen ML, Huikuri HV. Comparison of risk profiles between survivors and victims of sudden cardiac death from an acute coronary event. *Ann Med*. 2009;41(2):120–127.

10. Ni H, Coady S, Rosamond W, et al. Trends from 1987 to 2004 in sudden death due to coronary heart disease: the Atherosclerosis Risk in Communities (ARIC) study. *Am Heart J.* 2009;157(1):46–52.

11. Thompson PD, Buchner D, Pina IL, et al. Exercise and physical activity in the prevention and treatment of atherosclerotic cardiovascular disease: a statement from the Council on Clinical Cardiology (Subcommittee on Exercise, Rehabilitation, and Prevention) and the Council on Nutrition, Physical Activity, and Metabolism (Subcommittee on Physical Activity). *Circulation.* 2003;107(24):3109–3116.

12. Mittleman MA, Maclure M, Tofler GH, et al. Triggering of acute myocardial infarction by heavy physical exertion. Protection against triggering by regular exertion. Determinants of Myocardial Infarction Onset Study Investigators. *N Engl J Med.* 1993;329:1677–1683.

13. Hallqvist J, Möller J, Ahlbom A, et al. Does heavy physical exertion trigger myocardial infarction? A case-crossover analysis nested in a population-based case-referent study. *Am J Epidemiol.* 2000;151(5):459–467.

14. Giri S, Thompson PD, Kiernan FJ, et al. Clinical and angiographic characteristics of exertion-related acute myocardial infarction. *JAMA.* 1999;282:1731–1736.

15. Willich SN, Lewis M, Löwel H, et al. Physical exertion as a trigger of acute myocardial infarction. Triggers and Mechanisms of Myocardial Infarction Study Group. *N Engl J Med.* 1993;329(23):1684–1690.

16. Redelmeier DA, Greenwald JA. Competing risks of mortality with marathons: retrospective analysis. *BMJ.* 2007;335(7633):1275–1277.

17. van Teeffelen WM, de Beus MF, Mosterd A, et al. Risk factors for exercise-related acute cardiac events. A case-control study. *Br J Sports Med.* 2009;43(9):722–725.

18. Burke AP, Farb A, Malcom GT, et al. Plaque rupture and sudden death related to exertion in men with coronary artery disease. *JAMA.* 1999;281(10):921–926.

19. Black A, Black MM, Gensini G. Exertion and acute coronary artery injury. *Angiology.* 1975;26(11):759–783.

20. Ikarugi H, Taka T, Nakajima S, et al. Norepinephrine, but not epinephrine, enhances platelet reactivity and coagulation after exercise in humans. *J Appl Physiol.* 1999;86(1):133–138.

21. Ikarugi H, Shibata M, Shibata S, et al. High intensity exercise enhances platelet reactivity to shear stress and coagulation during and after exercise. *Pathophysiol Haemost Thromb.* 2003;33(3):127–133.

22. U.S. Preventive Services Task Force. Screening for coronary heart disease: recommendation statement. *Ann Intern Med.* 2004;140:569–572.

23. Lahav D, Leshno M, Brezis M. Is an exercise tolerance test indicated before beginning regular exercise? A decision analysis. *J Gen Intern Med.* 2009;24(8):934–938.

24. Gibbons RJ, Balady GJ, Bricker JT, et al. ACC/AHA 2002 guideline update for exercise testing: a report of the American College of Cardiology/American Heart Association Task Force on Practice Guidelines. *Circulation.* 2002;106:1883–1892.

25. American College of Sports Medicine. *Guidelines for Exercise Testing and Prescription.* 7th ed. Baltimore, MD: Lippincott Williams & Wilkins; 2005.

26. Thompson PD, Balady GJ, Chaitman BR, et al. Task Force 6: coronary artery disease. *J Am Coll Cardiol.* 2005;45(8):1348–1353.

27. Northcote RJ, Flannigan C, Ballantyne D. Sudden death and vigorous exercise—a study of 60 deaths associated with squash. *Br Heart J.* 1986;55:198–203.

28. Balady GJ, Chaitman B, Foster C, et al. Automated external defibrillators in health/fitness facilities: supplement to the AHA/ACSM recommendations for cardiovascular screening, staffing, and emergency policies at health/fitness facilities. *Circulation.* 2002;105(9):1147–1150.

29. Balady GJ, Chaitman B, Driscoll D, et al. Recommendations for cardiovascular screening, staffing, and emergency policies at health/fitness facilities. *Circulation.* 1998;97(22):2283–2293.

30. Maron BJ, Zipes DJ. Eligibility recommendations for competitive athletes with cardiovascular abnormalities—general considerations. *J Am Coll Cardiol.* 2005;45(8):1318–1321.

31. Barnard RJ, MacAlpin R, Kattus AA, Buckberg GD. Ischemic response to sudden strenuous exercise in healthy men. *Circulation.* 1973;48(5):936–942.

32. Barnard RJ, Gardner GW, Diaco NV, MacAlpin RN, Kattus AA. Cardiovascular responses to sudden strenuous exercise—heart rate, blood pressure, and ECG. *J Appl Physiol.* 1973;34(6):833–837.

33. Faich G, Rose R. Blizzard morbidity and mortality: Rhode Island, 1978. *Am J Public Health.* 1979;69:1050–1052.

34. Hammoudeh AJ, Haft JI. Coronary-plaque rupture in acute coronary syndromes triggered by snow shoveling. *N Engl J Med.* 1996;335:2001.

35. Glass RI, Zack MM Jr. Increase in deaths from ischaemic heart disease after blizzards. *Lancet.* 1979;1:485–487.

36. Pandolf KB, Cafarelli E, Noble BJ, Metz KF. Hyperthermia: effect on exercise prescription. *Arch Phys Med Rehabil.* 1975;56:524–526.

37. Levine BD, Zuckerman JH, deFilippi CR. Effect of high-altitude exposure in the elderly: the Tenth Mountain Division study. *Circulation.* 1997;96:1224–1232.

Prevention of Sudden Cardiac Death: Commotio Cordis

John A. Kalin, MD

Christopher Madias, MD

Mark S. Link, MD, FACC

From the Field Scenario

The Springfield youth boys baseball team was playing on the local middle school fields. Jack was an assistant coach for the middle school team. He also had a child on the youth team and so he was at the game. When one of the boys went up to bat, a wild pitch was thrown, and the boy took the hit on his chest. He took a moment to collect himself, and then he tried to return to the plate, but he suddenly slumped over and collapsed. Jack immediately rushed over to the boy. He was unconscious, had no pulse, and was not responsive. Recalling the emergency action plan for the middle school, Jack remembered that there was a public automated external defibrillator (AED) located just inside the entrance to the middle school. He instructed the coach to run and retrieve the AED from the school and shouted to an assistant coach to call 911. Jack initiated cardiopulmonary resuscitation (CPR). Within 2 minutes the coach returned with the AED, and they cut off the boy's shirt. Jack, familiar with their school's AED, opened the case, dried the boy's chest, applied the pads, and followed the AED's instructions. The AED analyzed the boy's heart rhythm. "Shock indicated—charging," the AED commanded. All hands were cleared from the boy prior to the administration of a shock. Jack resumed chest compressions immediately after the shock, until moments later when the boy began to move and tried to speak. Paramedics arrived minutes later. The boy was placed on a stretcher and transported to the nearby hospital.

Discussion Questions

1. How do you recognize commotio cordis in an athlete?
2. What about this case could have misled Jack and coaches, causing them to overlook the possibility of a sudden cardiac arrest?
3. What were the advantages of the game being held at a location that has public AEDs that are easily accessible?
4. How did the coaches and Jack work together to provide the necessary care? What was vital in providing life-saving care to the athlete in sudden cardiac arrest?

Introduction

Sudden death in athletes is uncommon.[1,2] Although many high-profile deaths in competitive sports have been associated with underlying structural heart disease, a number of deaths have resulted from chest wall impacts in individuals with normal hearts.[3–5] Sudden arrhythmic (abnormal heart beat) death from low-energy chest wall impact is known as **commotio cordis**. Commotio cordis is uncommon, occurring with a reported incidence of 5 to 20 events per year in the United States.[4,5] These events most commonly have been reported in young athletes between 8 and 18 years of age. Victims are most often struck by projectiles that are regarded as standard implements of the sport, such as baseballs or hockey pucks. Sudden death occurs within seconds, and the event carries a grim prognosis unless resuscitation and defibrillation are performed.[3,6]

Background and Occurrence of Commotio Cordis

The term *commotio cordis* is derived from the Latin for concussion of the heart. More specifically, commotio cordis refers to sudden death as a result of a seemingly innocent chest wall impact that occurs without any significant chest or cardiac trauma.[7,8] Commotio cordis is distinct from *contusio cordis*, in which high-energy chest wall impacts result in direct injury to the heart and chest. *Contusio cordis* is most commonly seen in motor vehicle accidents and can result in profuse bleeding of the heart, disruption of heart artery function, and rib fractures.

Commotio cordis was reported as early as 1763,[8] but Dim Mak, a sudden death from a judo blow to the chest, was described in ancient China. In the 19th century, sudden death after falls or industrial accidents prompted experimental work with rabbits in an attempt to explain the cause.[9] A 2010 review of deaths occurring in the United States during baseball games in the early 20th century revealed 18 deaths that were likely attributable to commotio cordis.[10] In the 1930s, Georg Schlomka at Bonn University was the first to describe a number of arrhythmic events induced by chest impacts in small animals.[11] Over the subsequent decades, commotio cordis was largely forgotten, represented in medical literature only by sporadic case reports. The first fully documented case in the United States occurred in 1978 during a T-ball game.[12] In 1995, a series of 25 cases of sudden death from blunt chest impact in children and young adults engaged in competitive sports was reported.[3] Through the identification of these cases, a profile of commotio cordis began to be defined, resulting in the creation of a national registry. Development of a contemporary animal model has led to further insight into the underlying causes of commotio cordis.

Mechanism, Causes, and Recognition of Commotio Cordis

A 2003 review of sudden deaths in young athletes revealed commotio cordis to be the second leading cause of death, behind only hypertrophic cardiomyopathy.[2] Since the creation of the National Commotio Cordis Registry in 1996, more than 220 cases of sudden death from chest impact have been documented.[4] Approximately 75% of these cases occurred in the setting of sports: 50% during competitive sporting events and 25% during recreational sports. In most cases victims were struck by projectiles normally implemented in the game, such as balls and pucks (see **Figure 5.1**). The majority of cases occurred in sports that involve a small projectile with a dense core that tends to be propelled at a high velocity, such as baseball, lacrosse, and hockey. All impacts were sustained over the surface of the body over the left side of the heart. Half of the subjects in the registry collapsed instantaneously, whereas others experienced brief light-headedness before losing consciousness. The initial heart rhythm seen in the majority of patients with attempted resuscitation was **ventricular fibrillation** (VF) or uncoordinated contractions of the lower portions of the heart. However, in those victims undergoing prolonged resuscitation, asystole (no measurable heart beat) has also been reported.[13]

Commotio cordis is not exclusive to sports, with approximately 25% of cases in the National Commotio Cordis Registry occurring during nonsporting activities such as playful fighting between individuals or

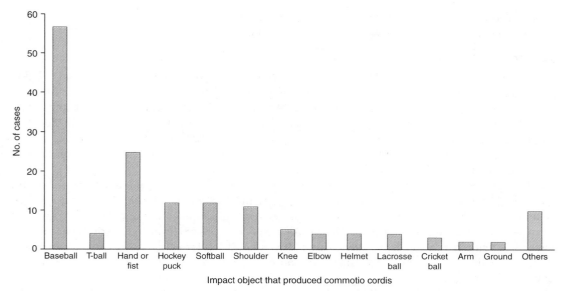

Figure 5.1 Distribution of projectiles implicated in commotio cordis, including a number of common balls and projectiles seen in youth sports.

Source: Link MS, Estes III NAM, Maron BJ. Sudden death caused by chest wall trauma (commotio cordis). In Kohl P, Sachs F, Franz MR, eds. *Cardiac Mechano-Electric Feedback and Arrhythmias: From Pipette to Patient.* Philadelphia: Elsevier Saunders; 2005:270–276. Reprinted by permission of the author.

child discipline.[4] Some of these cases of fist or hand strikes have resulted in criminal charges.[14] Notable cases in the registry include a young boy who died after being hit in the chest by a sled and a young girl who died suddenly after the head of her family dog struck her in the chest.

A review of the spectrum of cases within the national registry reveals that commotio cordis is most commonly seen in the young, with a peak incidence between the ages of 13 and 19 years (median age 14 years; see **Figure 5.2**). Males account for 95% of cases for unclear reasons, but theories have included disproportionate participation in implicated sports and possibly increased chest wall flexibility. The predominance of young subjects in the registry likely relates to the high level of participation in youth

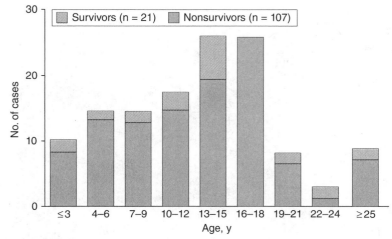

Figure 5.2 Age distribution at the time of impact of cases in the commotio cordis registry, showing a similar distribution of survivors and nonsurvivors. Median age is 14 years, with 80% of cases occurring in individuals 18 years or younger.

Source: Reprinted from *Heart Rhythm*, 4(4), Link MS, Estes III NAM. Mechanically induced ventricular fibrillation (commotio cordis), Pages 529–532, Copyright 2007, with permission from Elsevier.

sports in American culture. Furthermore, young individuals might also be at higher risk because of an increased flexibility of the chest wall as compared with adults.

Experimental Model

In 1998, a reliable, contemporary experimental model of commotio cordis was first described.[15] Using the model described here, VF can be consistently and reproducibly induced by chest wall impact if a combination of several factors is achieved (see **Figure 5.3**).[5] Initial experiments revealed that the timing of impact is among the most crucial of variables for VF induction and therefore commotion cordis.[15] Impacts must occur during a narrow window of vulnerability, specifically when the heart is recharging. Impacts at other time periods of the heart cycle did not result in VF but were noted to cause other arrhythmic events, such as premature contractions.

Impact velocity has also proven to be an important variable for induction of commotio cordis. Faster, higher-energy impacts more consistently resulted in VF as compared with low-velocity impacts. In animals weighing between 10 and 25 kilograms, chest impacts induced VF over 50% of the time at speeds between 40 and 50 mph.[16] These data are of particular relevance for youth baseball, in which ball velocity is typically between 30 and 50 mph. At impacts faster than 50 mph, an increased incidence of direct chest and heart damage was observed; at these velocities the model becomes one of cardiac contusion.

Consistent with the clinical profile of commotio cordis in humans, impact location directly over the heart is necessary for VF induction in the animal model. Examination of impact location using ultrasound revealed that impacts over the center of the lower left heart (left ventricle) most frequently induced VF.[17] Impacts at the top or bottom of the heart were less likely to result in VF. Impacts that occurred outside the borders of the cardiac silhouette never resulted in VF induction.

Object hardness and shape proved to be other important variables for VF induction. Softer projectiles were associated with a lower incidence of VF.[15,18] In a series of experiments, a dense wooden object, similar in size but harder than a regulation baseball, was noted to result in the highest incidence of VF. The lowest incidence of VF was seen with a safety baseball commonly known as a "T-ball." Smaller, more compact objects, such as those shaped like a golf ball, produced VF more frequently than objects with a larger surface that distributed the energy of impact over a wider area.[19]

There may be an individual susceptibility to commotio cordis. In the experimental model only a small percentage of animals were uniquely susceptible to VF with chest impact, while a higher number of animals were resistant to chest wall impact VF.[20]

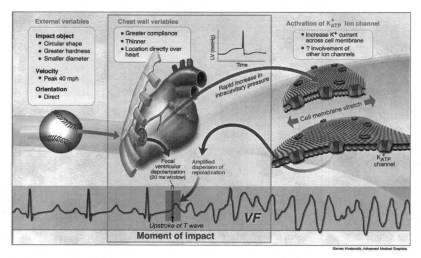

Figure 5.3 Confluence of variables necessary to cause commotio cordis.

Source: Link MS, Estes NA. Athletes and arrhythmias. *J. Cardiovasc Electrophysiol*. 2010;21:1184-9.1. Reproduced with permission of BLACKWELL PUBLISHING, INC. in the format reprint in a book via Copyright Clearance Center.

The variables of velocity, hardness, shape, and location all likely relate to the creation of a critical threshold pressure in the heart that is necessary for VF induction. It is theorized that the true manifestations of commotio cordis are a result of the instantaneous rise in peak left ventricular pressure seen with chest wall impact. In the experimental animal model, impact velocity correlated with the peak left ventricular pressure created by chest impacts. Similarly, higher peak left ventricular pressures were more likely to result in VF.

Prevention of Commotio Cordis

Of the 125 events that occurred during competitive sports noted in the National Commotio Cordis Registry, 32% involved individuals who were wearing some sort of chest protection at the time of impact.[4,21] Despite the use of chest protectors, sudden death was not prevented in these individuals. In some cases, it appears the chest protector moved during play and was not overlying the cardiac silhouette at the time of impact. In other cases, however, impact occurred directly over the chest protector, but commotio cordis was not prevented. Standard chest protectors are not currently designed to prevent commotio cordis. In fact, in experiments using the animal model of commotio cordis, seven commercially available lacrosse chest protectors and nine baseball chest protectors proved ineffective at preventing VF induction (see **Figure 5.4**). Chest protectors still provide protection from highly traumatic injury. However, their utility in preventing commotio cordis remains under debate. These findings support the need for further

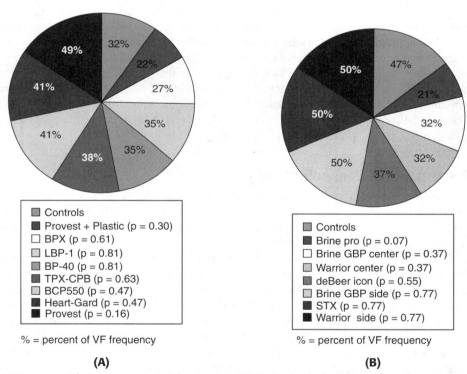

Figure 5.4 (A) Commercial chest protectors did not prevent VF induction by lacrosse balls in the experimental model. Numbers in box are P values calculated for chest protectors versus controls. Corresponding P values using McNemar's test are as follows: Provest+Plastic, 0.35; BPX, 0.95; LBP-1, 1.00; BP-40, 1.00; TPX-CPB, 0.75; BCP550, 0.45; Heart-Gard, 0.45; and Provest, 0.18. (B) Commercial chest protectors did not prevent VF induction by lacrosse balls in the experimental model. Numbers in box are P values calculated for chest protectors versus controls. Corresponding P values using McNemar's test are as follows: Brine Pro, 0.07; Brine GBP Center, 0.45; Warrior Center, 0.45; deBeer Icon, 0.69; Brine GBP Side, 1.00; STX, 1.00; and Warrior Side, 1.00.

Source: Data from Weinstock J, Maron BJ, Song C, et al. Failure of commercially available chest wall protectors to prevent sudden cardiac death induced by chest wall blows in an experimental model of commotio cordis. *Pediatrics.* 2006;117(4):e656–662.

TABLE 5.1	Strategies to Reduce Commotio Cordis in Sports		
	Lacrosse	Baseball	Hockey and Other Sports
Avoidance of chest wall impact	Coaching, rule changes	Coaching, rule changes	Coaching
Chest protectors	Modification of current lacrosse chest protectors	Appropriately sized and age appropriate	Appropriately sized and age appropriate
Safety equipment	Automated external defibrillators (AEDs)	AEDs, safety baseballs	AEDs
Projectile/ball	Possible safety lacrosse ball	Safety baseballs	

research in the development of adequate chest protectors designed for the prevention of commotio cordis in youth sports.

The use of safety baseballs might also decrease the risk of commotio cordis. In the animal model, safety baseballs significantly reduced the incidence of VF induction by chest impacts.[15,18] Data from this model and other clinical data from the U.S. Consumer Protection Agency have led to calls for the utilization of age-appropriate safety baseballs in sports.[22] Safety baseballs are similar in weight and feel during competitive play and represent an inexpensive and effective preventive measure.

Age-appropriate coaching and rule changes might also be instrumental in preventing commotio cordis. Avoidance of chest wall impact with the ball would lower the risk of commotion cordis. Although unpredictable motion of a projectile cannot be prevented, coaching athletes to turn away (by turning their back to the ball) can provide a measure of preparedness and understanding that might allow participants to avoid unnecessary chest wall impact (see **Table 5.1**).

Management of Commotio Cordis

Reported outcomes of commotio cordis events were initially quite grim, with an overall survival rate of less than 5% in the national registry.[3] However, more recent data from the registry have shown that survival is increasing and now approaches 60%[6] (see **Figure 5.5**). It is clear that early resuscitation and AED application are the keys to survival.

With broader visibility and understanding, commotio cordis is now recognized with increasing frequency. This improved awareness, along with the recent increased distribution of AEDs at many sports facilities, has correlated with an improved survival rate of approximately 35% over the last decade in the registry.[6] The importance of readily available AEDs on the field of play cannot be stressed enough. AEDs provide a potentially highly effective life-saving therapy for commotio cordis and other cardiac death events. Survival of commotio cordis is most likely to occur when defibrillation with an AED is done as soon as possible. Coaches, strength coaches, and athletic trainers involved in youth athletics should be made aware of the clinical scenario of commotio cordis and become familiar with CPR and the use of AEDs. Commotio cordis should be suspected if an athlete collapses suddenly (or after several seconds) following a chest impact and remains unarousable. Emergency medical services should be contacted immediately, and an AED should be placed on the victim as soon as possible. CPR should be performed as guided by standard out-of-hospital cardiac arrest protocols.

Survivors of commotio cordis often wish to return to competitive sports in which chest impact is possible.[23] There are limited data to guide clinical decision making in this regard. The guidelines issued by

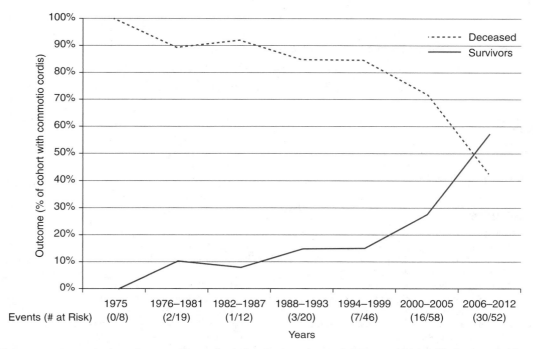

Figure 5.5 Rescusitation of commotio cordis victims has continuously improved. This is likely a result of improved recognition of commotio, improved CPR, and readily available AEDs.

Source: Reprinted from Heart Rhythm 10(2), Maron BJ, Haas TS, Ahluwalia A, Garberich RF, Estes NA 3rd, Link MS., Increasing survival rate from commotio cordis, pp. 219–23, Copyright 2013, with permission from Elsevier.

the 36th Bethesda Conference recommend decisions based on individual cases and clinical judgment.[24] There have been no recurrences of commotio cordis events reported by survivors in the national registry. However, recent data from the animal model of commotio cordis suggest that individual susceptibility might play a role in this phenomenon.[20] Survivors should have a thorough cardiac evaluation. After review of clinical data and careful weighing of the risks and benefits of sports participation, a return to play should be an individual decision between the survivor, his or her family, and his or her clinician.

Summary

Commotio cordis is a rare but tragic event that typically occurs in young men and boys in the setting of organized sports. Through the development of a comprehensive registry and the creation of a reliable animal model, our understanding of the clinical profile and the underlying mechanisms has evolved considerably over the last 10 to 15 years. Whereas the earliest experimental and observational findings pointed to the basic requirements for VF induction by chest impact, more recent work has been directed at more specific scenarios and parameters, such as the possibility of individual susceptibility to commotio cordis. Research in the areas of chest wall protection and the use of safety baseballs is directed at prevention. The safety of young athletes would be further advanced by increased awareness of commotio cordis, coaching athletes (specifically baseball athletes) how to turn their backs to a pitched ball directed at their chest, quick and easy access to AEDs, and more widespread education on AED/CPR use.

Clinical Case Scenario

1. A 13-year-old boy participating in youth baseball is struck in the chest by a pitch. He is not wearing a chest protector, which is typical for the sport. He collapses several seconds after recoiling

from the pain of impact. The umpire finds him unarousable and quickly determines that he is pulseless and is not breathing.

a. What potential life-saving steps should be performed immediately?

b. What are the most important factors in surviving a commotio cordis event?

c. If the boy survives, should he be allowed to return to the field of play?

Key Terms

commotio cordis

ventricular fibrillation (VF)

References

1. Link MS, Estes NA. Athletes and arrhythmias. *J Cardiovasc Electrophysiol.* 2010;21:1184–1189.
2. Maron BJ. Sudden death in young athletes. *N J Med.* 2003;349:1064–1075.
3. Maron BJ, Poliac LC, Kaplan JA, Mueller FO. Blunt impact to the chest leading to sudden death from cardiac arrest during sports activities. *N Engl J Med.* 1995;333:337–342.
4. Maron BJ, Estes NA, 3rd. Commotio cordis. *N Engl J Med.* 2010;362:917–927.
5. Link MS. Commotio cordis: ventricular fibrillation triggered by chest impact-induced abnormalities in repolarization. *Circ Arrhythm Electrophysiol.* 2012;5:425–432.
6. Maron BJ, Haas TS, Ahluwalia A, et al. Increasing survival rate from commotio cordis. *Heart Rhythm.* 2013;10(2):219–223.
7. Geddes LA, Roeder RA. Evolution of our knowledge of sudden death due to commotio cordis. *Am J of Emerg Med.* 2005;23:67–75.
8. Nesbitt AD, Cooper PJ, Kohl P. Rediscovering commotio cordis. *Lancet.* 2001;357:1195–1197.
9. Meola F. La commozione toracica. *Gior Internaz Sci Med.* 1879;1:923–937.
10. Maron BJ, Boren SD, Estes NA, 3rd. Early descriptions of sudden cardiac death due to commotio cordis occurring in baseball. *Heart Rhythm.* 2010;7:992–993.
11. Schlomka G. Commotio cordis und ihre folgen. Die einwirkung stumpfer brustwandtraumen auf das herz. *Ergebn Inn Med Kinderheilk.* 1934;47:1–91.
12. Dickman GL, Hassan A, Luckstead EF. Ventricular fibrillation following baseball injury. *Phys and Sport Med.* 1978;6:85–86.
13. Maron BJ, Gohman TE, Kyle SB, Estes NA, 3rd, Link MS. Clinical profile and spectrum of commotio cordis. *JAMA.* 2002;287:1142–1146.
14. Froede RC, Lindsey D, Steinbronn K. Sudden unexpected death from cardiac concussion (commotio cordis) with unusual legal complications. *J Forensic Sciences.* 1979;24:752–756.
15. Link MS, Wang PJ, Pandian NG, et al. An experimental model of sudden death due to low-energy chest-wall impact (commotio cordis). *N Engl J Med.* 1998;338:1805–1811.
16. Link MS, Maron BJ, Wang PJ, et al. Upper and lower limits of vulnerability to sudden arrhythmic death with chest-wall impact (commotio cordis). *J Am Coll Cardiol.* 2003;41:99–104.
17. Link MS, Maron BJ, VanderBrink BA, et al. Impact directly over the cardiac silhouette is necessary to produce ventricular fibrillation in an experimental model of commotio cordis. *J Am Coll Cardiol.* 2001;37:649–654.
18. Link MS, Maron BJ, Wang PJ, et al. Reduced risk of sudden death from chest wall blows (commotio cordis) with safety baseballs. *Pediatrics.* 2002;109:873–877.
19. Kalin J, Madias C, Alsheikh-Ali AA, Link MS. Reduced diameter spheres increases the risk of chest blow-induced ventricular fibrillation (commotio cordis). *Heart Rhythm.* 2011;8:1578–1581.
20. Alsheikh-Ali AA, Madias C, Supran S, Link MS. Marked variability in susceptibility to ventricular fibrillation in an experimental commotio cordis model. *Circulation.* 2010;122:2499–2504.
21. Drewniak EI, Spenciner DB, Crisco JJ. Mechanical properties of chest protectors and the likelihood of ventricular fibrillation due to commotio cordis. *J Appl Biomech.* 2007;23:282–288.
22. Kyle SB. *Youth Baseball Protective Equipment Project Final Report.* Washington, DC: United States Consumer Product Safety Commission; 1996.
23. Link MS. Prevention of sudden cardiac death: return to sport considerations in athletes with identified cardiovascular abnormalities. *Br J Sports Med.* 2009;43:685–689.
24. Maron BJ, Estes NA, 3rd, Link MS. Task Force 11: Commotio cordis: 36th Bethesda Conference: eligibility recommendations for competitive athletes with cardiovascular abnormalities. *J Am Coll Cardiol.* 2005;45:1371–1373.

Exertional Heat Stroke

Rebecca L. Stearns, PhD, ATC

Francis G. O'Connor, MD, MPH, FACSM

Douglas J. Casa, PhD, ATC, FACSM, FNATA

Glen P. Kenny, PhD

From the Field Scenario

Joe had been the head football coach for Capital Prep High School for 8 years. Today was the third day of preseason practice for the team, and they had not started full contact practices yet. The temperature was 87°F with 75% humidity. The team was just finishing some conditioning drills at the end of practice. One team member, Steve, had struggled but was able to finish the conditioning drills. However, as he was walking back to the sideline, he collapsed. He tried to get up but was too weak, and he collapsed again. Joe noticed that Steve was struggling and immediately walked over to him. Steve made his way over to the sideline with the help of a teammate. Joe noticed that Steve seemed slow and confused, but he was breathing and conscious. He just looked extremely exhausted and confused. Joe gave Steve some water, but after 5 minutes Steve continued to seem confused and could not clearly communicate. Joe called the athletic trainer over to the sideline during this time, and as the athletic trainer did his evaluation he began to suspect heat stroke. Joe helped the athletic trainer move Steve to the athletic training room where the athletic trainer obtained a rectal temperature (confirming it was heat stroke with a temperature of 107°F) and with the help of some assistant coaches, they moved Steve into the cold water immersion tub and began cooling him. During this time, Joe called emergency medical services (EMS) and provided them with clear instructions on the location. While EMS was on the way, the coaches continued to immerse Steve for the next 15 minutes. By the time the ambulance arrived, Steve's rectal temperature had lowered to 102°F. Steve was transported to the hospital for observation. Given the immediate recognition, relay of this information on the part of Joe to the athletic trainer, and Joe's knowledge of the protocols to treat a heat stroke victim, Steve survived his heat stroke without any complications.

Discussion Questions

1. What items/policies were in place that helped Joe (the coach) recognize the seriousness of this situation? (What knowledge do you expect he had? What policies were in place to appropriately handle this situation?)
2. What steps did the coach take that played an important role in the positive outcome for this athlete?
3. How did the coach and athletic trainer work together to provide the necessary care?

The opinions herein reflect personal opinion and do not represent opinions of the U.S. Army, Uniformed Services University, or the Department of Defense at large.

4. If you were the athletic director, what follow-up steps would you take after this incident to evaluate how it was handled and improve future cases?

Introduction

Any participation in sports or physical activity is associated with inherent risks. Among those of greatest concern are conditions that present risks associated with long-term morbidity and the possibility of death, such as exertional heat stroke (EHS), the second leading cause of death in sports after cardiac conditions.[1] Although there have been many advances in knowledge and research in the area of heat illnesses, the incidence of EHS deaths continues to rise.[1] Unlike some other potentially fatal conditions, however, death from EHS can be prevented if the condition is promptly recognized in combination with swift and effective treatment.

exertional heat stroke (EHS) A medical emergency involving life-threatening hyperthermia (rectal temperature > 40.5°C [105°F]) with concomitant central nervous system dysfunction; treatment involves cooling the body.

Definition of Condition

Exertional heat stroke (EHS) occurs when core body temperature reaches a dangerous level (usually ≥ 40.5°C [105°F]), with signs of organ failure related to this high body temperature.[2-7] This condition occurs when the body's temperature regulation system is overwhelmed because of excessive heat production and/or inadequate heat loss. Both of these factors can contribute and lead to temperature regulation system (thermoregulatory) failure. The first marker of EHS is often collapse or alterations in a person's brain functioning (cognitive dysfunction). EHS is survivable, but if not treated immediately and effectively, it can lead to death.[2-7]

Background and Occurrence of Exertional Heat Stroke

EHS is one of the top three leading causes of sudden death in athletes, although when the variation in incidence across seasons is adjusted for, EHS may actually only be the primary cause of sudden death in athletes during summer months.[1] In the 5-year period from 2005 to 2009, there were twice as many deaths from EHS than the average 5-year block for the 35-year time span since 1975.[1] (See **Table 6.1**.) Based on the years 2010, 2011, and 2012, it is likely that the next 5-year period will have almost 33% more deaths than the previous record-breaking period from 2005 to 2009. The incidence of fatal EHS in American

TABLE 6.1	Number of Football Deaths from Exertional Heat Stroke from 1975 to 2009
Years	**Number of Deaths**
1975–1979	8
1980–1984	9
1985–1989	5
1990–1994	2
1995–1999	13
2000–2004	11
2005–2009	18
5-year average	9

Source: Data from Mueller F, Colgate B. ANNUAL SURVEY OF FOOTBALL INJURY RESEARCH 1931– 2008. Copyright 2009 by The American Football Coaches Association, The National Collegiate Athletic Association, and the National Federation of State High School Associations.

football players was about 1 in 350,000 participants from 1995 to 2002.[1] In the period from 1980 to 2009, there were 58 recorded EHS deaths of American football players.[8] Popular road races have reported as many as 1 to 2 EHS cases per 1000 entrants.[4] There are no clear reasons for the increase in the number of EHS deaths, although many athletic activities are becoming more intense/competitive, the environment has tended to have record high temperatures, increased childhood obesity, and the overall fitness level of the population has dropped. All of these factors could potentially contribute to the higher incidence of heat illness.

Mechanisms and Causes of Exertional Heat Stroke

EHS occurs when the body's cooling mechanisms are unable to dissipate the heat being gained and produced by the body during exercise. There are two main mechanisms by which a body may gain heat during exercise, either internally (working muscles producing heat) or externally (high air temperature), although it should be noted that this does not account for medications or drugs that can contribute to heat load (e.g., amphetamines). Having a fever caused by an illness also may contribute to heat load; however, fever-based increases in body temperature work in different pathways than exercise-induced heat gains, which is an important consideration when treating these two scenarios (see **Box 6.1**). There are also many mechanisms by which cooling (heat loss) may occur (air flow or sweat evaporation).[9]

The extent of heat loss depends on the temperature difference that exists between the surfaces receiving and producing the heat as well as the heat transfer method. Water, for example, has a great ability to transfer heat. It is approximately 40 times more effective than air at removing or releasing heat to or from the body.[10] This is an extremely important consideration when determining the course of treatment for an EHS victim. Conversely, conduction makes up a small amount of the total heat exchange (approximately 1%) and does not contribute greatly to cooling of the body.[10]

During exercise, however, sweat evaporation is the main method the body relies on for cooling in high ambient temperatures. Humidity becomes a major factor because once air temperature rises above skin temperature, cooling by radiation and convection can no longer occur and these processes then contribute to heat gain as opposed to loss. This leaves only evaporation as a means of cooling. Unfortunately, the rate at which the body can cool through this last method decreases as humidity rises. Sweat that cannot evaporate will drip off the body. Without evaporation, sweat does not contribute to cooling the body and only leads to further **dehydration** via fluid loss.[10]

> **dehydration** The process of water loss leading to hypohydration. Usually measured by body mass loss, urine color, urine osmolality, urine specific gravity, or serum osmolality (the gold standard).

> **body temperature** The temperature of the internal organs or thermal core as measured by a valid device (i.e., rectal thermometer, gastrointestinal thermistor).

Box 6.1

Fever Versus Exercise-Induced Body Temperature Changes

The mechanism by which a fever causes an increase in **body temperature** is quite different from what occurs during exercise. When a virus or bacteria attacks the body, the initial response is to release chemical substances that cause the body to "reset" to a higher temperature than normal.[10] The body then responds by trying to reduce heat loss and maintain or increase heat gain. This response is believed to help the body fight the attack, but it will also result in the symptom of chills until the body reaches the new set temperature.[10,11]

During exercise, the rise in body temperature is a result of the heat produced by the exercising or working muscle. Heat is a product of the use of carbohydrates, fats, and proteins by the muscle. During high-intensity exercise or exercise that incorporates a large amount of muscle mass, a high demand for energy is created; consequently, the body produces a large amount of heat. It is important to differentiate between these two mechanisms (fever-based vs. exercise-induced body temperature rises) for the purpose of treating the condition. In a febrile individual, aspirin-like drugs will block the chemical response to the illness and prevent the individual's body temperature from increasing. Because the increase in temperature during exercise is caused by muscular activation and not a chemical response, providing an athlete with aspirin-like drugs will not have the same effect on temperature regulation.

Heat Gain

Body heat storage may be exacerbated during exercise by hot and humid environments, eventually leading to an accumulation of heat within the body at a rate at which the body is unable to dissipate it. During maximal exercise, heat production can be increased by a factor of 10 or more.[12] This process may be compounded by drugs and heat-producing supplements, which can drive heat production as well as deter a sense of fatigue in athletes, potentially placing them at higher risk.[4]

To cope with these stressors, the body will increase blood output from the heart, causing increased blood flow to the muscles and skin, which in turn causes a decrease in blood returning to the heart. This cycle ultimately fuels competing demands for blood flow between the heart system, abdominal organs, muscles, and skin.[11] The body is providing the skin with additional blood in order to aid in cooling via sweat and evaporation; however, the working muscles also demand blood for oxygen and nutrient requirements. When intense exercise in the heat is maintained, muscle blood flow eventually takes precedence over skin blood flow, and the current rate of cooling cannot be maintained. Ultimately, muscle blood flow is prioritized second so that the body can maintain blood pressure (and avoid collapse) above all else. Signs of this stress on the body are seen through increases in heart rate, decreased performance, and increased heat storage; eventually dangerously high body temperatures can occur, increasing the risk for EHS.

Heat Loss

Combining all the heat loss/gain factors previously mentioned, there are numerous methods by which the body can gain heat. Ironically, as the environmental risks for heat illness increase, the options for cooling the body decrease. As discussed, the three main cooling methods that the body uses are radiation, convection, and evaporation. Radiation and convection work as methods of heat loss when air temperature is low, or at least lower than skin temperature. However, when air temperature is greater than skin temperature, these forms of heat transfer become factors of heat gain. Similarly, evaporation is the most effective and heavily relied upon form of heat loss in the body and is the only avenue of heat loss when air temperature is greater than skin temperature. It is possible that children handle heat differently than adults, although the evidence for this is still emerging. In conditions of high humidity sweating is severely limited, as sweat will increasingly drip off the skin, thereby providing no cooling to the body and leaving the body with few effective cooling options. This causes the core body temperature to start to rise; without a cessation of exercise or the application of external cooling methods, it will continue to do so. It is at this point that modification of activity and/or clothing and equipment becomes important to lower the risk of EHS.

Specific Factors Affecting the Heat Stress Response

Although the body has methods of heat gain and loss as well as factors influencing how intense heat stress exposure is, understanding the underlying physiologic changes that occur as well as other factors that may be trained or adjusted to help expand exercise capacity and heat tolerance may also help explain the occurrence of EHS in the athletic population. The factors that likely influence an individual's exercise heat tolerance are extensive, but the five most important are as follows:

1. Body temperature and skin blood flow (sweating response)
2. Heat acclimation/acclimatization
3. Hydration status
4. Wet bulb globe temperature (WBGT)
5. Equipment load

Physiologic Changes in Response to Heat Stress

Multiple factors can contribute to exhaustion and cessation of exercise in the heat.[13–19] Many times the body temperature upon cessation of exercise is coincidentally also similar to the limit used to diagnose heat stroke (i.e., 40.5°C [105°F]). However, in many instances athletes are able to override this signal and continue to exercise past the 40.5°C/105°F mark (most of the time with no ill effects). Overall, this leads us to conclude that the explanation for cessation of exercise in the heat is multifaceted but largely based on the perceived stress on the individual, body temperature, and skin temperature.

Heat Acclimation/Acclimatization

It has been known since the 1940s that heat acclimation (or an individual's readiness to exercise in a warm to hot environment) plays a large part in the body's physiologic responses, adaptations, and overall ability to cope with heat exposure.[20] Heat **acclimation** is a broad term that can be loosely defined as a complex series of changes or adaptations that occur in a controlled environment over the course of 7 to 14 days, leading to reductions in:

- Heart rate
- Body and skin temperature responses
- Perceived exertion

Acclimation also leads to increases in:

- Sweat rate
- Sweat onset (sweating starts earlier)
- Skin blood flow
- Heart function/blood distribution
- Overall ability to perform in the heat[21,22]

Other physiologic changes include decreased salt losses in sweat and urine[21] as well as an improved blood pressure response.[23] All of these changes improve an athlete's ability to cope with heat stress during exercise. Heat **acclimatization** results in the same physiologic changes; however, it occurs in the natural environment.

It has been shown that factors affecting these changes determine the extent to which adaptations occur. For example, acclimation in hot and dry environments has been shown to be different from that in hot and humid environments (a greater sweat rate increase has been seen in the latter case).[21] It is also highly important for the athlete to train in the heat at an intensity great enough to induce these changes. This intensity is needed to elevate the body temperature, which is the main stimulus behind heat acclimation. Although the evidence specifying the ideal intensity at which to train for acclimation is diverse, acclimation is known to depend on volume of exercise, intensity, and maintenance of an elevated body temperature during exercise.[21,24]

Prior to heat exposure and attempts to acclimatize to the heat, athletes should gain a base level of fitness in a cool environment. Highly fit individuals already have some of the physical advantages that are gained with acclimation—for example, an increased sweat rate. Additionally, athletes should exercise at intensities greater than 50% of their maximal oxygen consumption (Vo_2max), with intensity increasing throughout training to maximize adaptation.[21] After an athlete is acclimatized to the heat, he or she will lose less sodium and potassium during exercise, thereby retaining more water. The athlete will increase his or her sweat rate, which aids in cooling but at the same time increases the demand for water consumption during exercise. This last point is extremely important to note because as athletes gain fitness and become acclimatized to the heat, their water needs increase. Guidelines have been introduced for the high school population for the purpose of gradual heat acclimatization during the preseason.[25] The main recommendations can be seen in **Table 6.2**, starting with the first day of preseason practice.

Recently, state high school athletic associations have started to acknowledge the importance of heat acclimatization and adopted the 2009 guidelines released by the National Athletic Trainers' Association for secondary schools. These were modeled after the 2003 guidelines that the National Collegiate Athletic Association (NCAA) released and implemented. More states are also working toward adopting such guidelines with the assistance of associations such as the Korey Stringer Institute. A timeline of adaptation of heat acclimatization guidelines is shown in **Table 6.3**.

Hydration Status

Hydration status is another important factor in heat tolerance. It is widely known that water is essential for life; however, in terms of daily functioning, it also has a large impact on heat tolerance and exercise performance.[2,26–30] Although the term *dehydration* is used here to indicate

acclimation Adaptive changes that occur in response to experimentally induced changes in particular climatic factors. Used most often in research studies to refer to the artificial process of acclimatization that is induced via climate-controlled chambers.

acclimatization A complex series of adaptive responses that demonstrate improved homeostatic balance in multiple organs; usually requires 10 to 14 days for responses to develop adequately. The body can acclimatize (to varying degrees) to hot, cold, high altitude, and underwater environments.

hydration status Measurement of an individual's body water content (usually done via urine or blood sample) that can be used to indicate if an individual has a healthy, low, or high level of body water content. Either extreme (high or low levels) can have health and performance implications.

TABLE 6.2   Preseason Heat Acclimatization Guidelines

Day(s)	Recommendations
General	• Total practice time should not exceed 3 hours in any 1 day. Warmup, stretching, cool-down, walkthroughs, conditioning, and weight room activities are included as practice time.
1–5	• No more than one practice per day. • A 1-hour maximum walkthrough is permitted; however, it cannot occur immediately prior to or following the general 3-hour practice session.
1–2	• If the sport requires protective equipment (helmets/shoulder pads), a helmet is the only protective equipment permitted. Goalies (e.g., field hockey) should *not* wear full protective equipment.
3–5	• Only helmets and shoulder pads should be worn for protective equipment.
6	• All protective equipment may be worn. • Full contact may begin.
6–14	• Double-practice-session days may begin but must be followed by a single-practice day and separated within practice by at least 3 hours of continuous rest in a cool environment.
Double practices	• On these days neither practice should exceed 3 hours in duration. • Athletes should not participate in more than 5 total hours of practice.

Source: Data from Casa DJ, Csillan D, et al. Preseason heat-acclimatization guidelines for secondary school athletics. *J Athl Train.* 2009;44(3):332–333.[25]

TABLE 6.3   Adaptation Timeline for Heat Acclimatization Guidelines Meeting Best Practice Recommendations[25] for Various States and Organizations

State	Date Guidelines Adopted
NCAA	May, 2003
New Jersey	May, 2011
National Football League	July, 2011
Texas	October, 2011
North Carolina	February, 2012
Georgia	March, 2012
Arkansas	June, 2012
Florida	June, 2012
Arizona	June, 2012
Connecticut	March, 2013
Iowa	April, 2013
Missouri	May, 2013

Source: Korey Stringer Institute. *Real Time Registry of Sudden Death in Sport and Physical Activity.* Available at http://ksi.uconn.edu/research/real-time-registry-of-sudden-death-in-sport/. Accessed March 15, 2013. Reprinted by permission of Korey Stringer Institute.

water deficit, it should be clarified that dehydration by definition is the process of water loss, whereas *hypohydration* is a steady state of fluid deficit.[27] The term *dehydration* will be used for the purpose of this chapter.

Although hydration status may receive the most attention in the public eye, it should be clearly noted that EHS results from a combination of multiple factors. Therefore, an athlete may have a normal hydration status, but with high-intensity exercise he or she can still succumb to EHS. However, dehydration alone can place such a large stress on the body that it can negate the positive effects of heat acclimatization. Dehydration has been proven to delay sweat onset and volume,[28] increase core temperature to a greater extent than that seen in a nonacclimatized and normally hydrated individual,[29] and even impair neuromuscular function and balance.[31] Research studies have found about a 0.4°F to 0.5°F body temperature increase for every additional 1% body mass loss during intense exercise in the heat.[28–30] Therefore, while dehydration can place athletes at greater risk, the alternative of an optimal hydration status can be protective in high-risk scenarios. It is recommended that athletes take routine water breaks, during which they may replace fluids as needed.[3,4,6] They should also understand the importance of hydration during exercise.[32]

Once an athlete is acclimatized, he or she will require more fluid during exercise because of the increase in sweat rate.[26] It is recommended that athletes attempt to consume fluids at the same rate as their individual sweat rate, but not a greater amount than their sweat rate.[33] Consuming enough fluid can be challenging because the high **intensity of exercise**, the rules/structure of the particular sport, equipment, high humidity, and other factors can cause sweat rate to increase more than normal.[26]

intensity of exercise The relative workload during a bout of exercise. This is largely individual, varying between athletes, and will change with exercise training.

Wet Bulb Globe Temperature

Wet bulb globe temperature (WBGT) is also an important factor in the body's response to the environment. WBGT is a widely used indicator of heat stress that incorporates the dry bulb temperature, wet bulb temperature, and black globe (solar) temperature. It is calculated by the following formula: WBGT = 0.7 (Wet Bulb Temperature) + 0.2 (Black Globe Temperature) + 0.1 (Dry Bulb Temperature). When indoors, the globe temperature cannot be incorporated and the new WBGT = 0.7 (Wet Bulb Temperature) + 0.3 (Dry Bulb Temperature).[4] This highlights the large impact (and relative contribution) a change in the WBGT (reflecting humidity in the air) plays on heat stress. This consequently also mirrors the risk for exertional heat illness as WBGT increases, because of the reduced ability to utilize the evaporation of sweat to dissipate heat, as discussed earlier.

wet bulb globe temperature (WBGT) The most widely used heat stress index in industry and sports; may be used to assess the severity of hot environments. It is derived from a formula that incorporates the dry bulb, wet bulb, and black globe temperature.

WBGT has been used in the past as a guide for practice and equipment modification guidelines.[34] While WBGT helps to provide standards by which to alter practices and equipment use, it should be stressed that appropriate guidelines will vary based on region. The recommendations provided here should be used as a guide for the progression of practice modification in conjunction with medical opinion, practice duration and intensity, and the previous week of environmental conditions during practice sessions (see earlier discussion of the heat acclimatization response). There should be a designated individual who is responsible and knowledgeable regarding practice modification and who can determine if it is needed for the day's practice sessions (preferably an athletic trainer, team physician, or other medical professional).[35] Coaches should not be responsible for this decision, because their primary role as a coach could potentially cloud this decision process. **Table 6.4** is an example of WBGT guidelines that the Georgia State Athletic Association passed in March 2012. These guidelines were based on heat illness data collected from this state and may not be applicable to areas with differing environmental patterns.

equipment load Amount of equipment that an athlete wears during practice or competition (protective or uniform motivated). In the case of exertional heat illnesses, increases in the amount of clothing or gear that an athlete wears will increase heat load and potentially the ability for an athlete to dissipate heat.

Equipment Load

Equipment or additional clothing is another factor that can alter exercise capacity in the heat. Extra clothing in warm environments creates a barrier to sweat evaporation and consequently to cooling. This causes greater physiologic strain, increases the sweat rate, and increases the potential for a greater level of dehydration (the athlete must now be more vigilant to ensure

TABLE 6.4	Georgia State High School Association Exercise Modification Guidelines
WBGT Reading	**Activity and Rest Break Guidelines**
Under 82.0	Normal activities: provide at least three separate rest breaks each hour, lasting a minimum duration of 3 minutes each, during workout.
	Use discretion for intense or prolonged exercise; watch at-risk players carefully.
82.0–86.9	Provide at least three separate rest breaks each hour, lasting a minimum of 4 minutes duration each.
87.0–89.9	Maximum practice time is 2 hours. For football: players restricted to helmet, shoulder pads, and shorts during practice. All protective equipment must be removed for conditioning activities. For all sports: provide at least four separate rest breaks each hour, lasting a minimum of 4 minutes each.
90.0–92.0	Maximum length of practice is 1 hour, no protective equipment may be worn during practice, and there may be no conditioning activities. There must be 20 minutes of rest breaks provided during the hour of practice.
Over 92.1	No outdoor workouts; cancel exercise; delay practices until a cooler WBGT reading occurs.

Source: Georgia High School Association, Thomaston, Georgia 30286. Minutes from State Executive Committee, 3/19/2012, page 3. Reprinted by permission of Georgia High School Association.

he or she drinks sufficient fluids to replace the amount of fluid being lost). The added stress is the main reason why acclimatization guidelines are put into place for preseason practices, as discussed earlier.

Exercise Intensity

Finally, intensity of exercise, which is based on individual physical fitness, has been demonstrated to be the greatest influence on the rate of body temperature increase.[36-38] When risk factors that are outside the control of the athlete are not in play, intensity of exercise will largely determine the extent of body temperature rise (the harder or more intense the physical effort, the greater the rate of heat production). This is most evident when pressure to succeed or perform is high, such as new football players trying to make the team, or marathon runners trying to obtain a qualifying time. Therefore, it is important during high-risk scenarios to modify rest-to-work ratios, among other modifiable factors (if possible), to allow recovery and to minimize rises in core body temperature.

Prevention

Certain precautions may be taken to help avoid EHS. In particular, recognizing and understanding predisposing risk factors can aid in prevention strategies. Although some extrinsic factors are outside the control of the exercising individual, there are also intrinsic factors, which the exercising individual can (in most cases) control (see **Table 6.5**). Efforts can also be made to minimize extrinsic factors, such as exercising at a cooler time of day.

A study by Rav-Acha et al.[39] examined the prevalence of predisposing factors for EHS in six fatal cases. In total, the authors looked at 134 cases of EHS (6 fatal, 128 nonfatal) and attempted to isolate the factors that were more likely to cause death. Many of the fatal cases had variables that could be reduced or controlled to lower the risk of EHS, and certainly death from EHS (see **Figure 6.1**). Poor physical fitness, sleep deprivation, a high heat load (WBGT ≥ 27°C [80.6°F]), high solar radiation, and training during the hottest hours of the day were each present in 83% of the fatal cases. Physical effort unmatched to physical fitness and absence of proper medical triage were present in 100% of the fatal cases.[39] Because these last two factors were present in 100% of these fatal cases, it is important to examine them closer.

TABLE 6.5	Extrinsic and Intrinsic Risk Factors for Exertional Heat Stroke

Extrinsic Risk Factors	Intrinsic Risk Factors
High ambient temperature, solar radiation, and humidity	High intensity of exercise and/or poor physical conditioning
Athletic gear or uniforms	Sleep loss
Peer or organizational pressure	Dehydration or inadequate water intake
Inappropriate work-to-rest ratios based on intensity, WBGT, clothing, equipment, fitness, and athlete's medical condition	Use of diuretics or certain medications (e.g., antihistamines, antihypertensives, attention deficit hyperactivity disorder drugs)
Predisposing medical conditions (e.g., malignant hyperthermia, cystic fibrosis)	Overzealousness or reluctance to report problems, issues, or illness
Lack of education and awareness of heat illnesses among coaches, athletes, and medical staff	Inadequate heat acclimation
No emergency plan to identify and treat EHS	High muscle mass-to-body fat ratio
Minimal access to fluids before and during practice and rest breaks	Presence of a fever
Delay in recognition of early warning signs	Skin disorder (e.g., *miliaria rubra* [heat rash] or sunburn)

Source: Adapted from Binkley HM, Beckett J, Casa DJ, Kleiner DM, Plummer PE. National Athletic Trainers' Association position statement: exertional heat illnesses. *J Athl Train.* 2002;37(3):329–343.

Effort unmatched to physical fitness is a common scenario in sporting venues, where athletes are pressured by others or feel internal pressure to perform well. In many distance running and cycling events, athletes are motivated by others vying for position. This causes many to push beyond the normal limits at which they would volitionally cease exercise. Working at this intensity only drives the athlete's

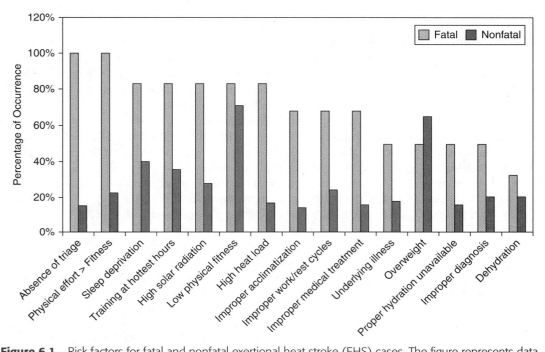

Figure 6.1 Risk factors for fatal and nonfatal exertional heat stroke (EHS) cases. The figure represents data in which there were 6 fatal and 128 nonfatal EHS cases.

Source: McDermott BP, Casa DJ, Yeargin SW, et al. Recovery and return to activity following exertional heat stroke: considerations for the sports medicine staff. *J Sport Rehabil.* 2007;16:163–181.

body temperature higher. A recent military study found that military recruits with a high body mass index had a higher incidence of exertional heat illnesses, likely a result of universal exercise regimes and the need for military recruits with more body fat to work harder to keep up with smaller counterparts.[40]

The absence of proper medical triage is a large problem, which, in most cases of organized sport, can be prevented. Although almost all college and professional teams hire physicians or athletic trainers, high schools represent the largest athletic population that still lacks proper medical personnel. Only about half of America's high schools have an employed athletic trainer.[6]

Efforts should be made to control factors that help lower the risk of EHS. With respect to extrinsic factors, adjustments can be made such as exercising during the cooler times of the day, practicing without the use of protective equipment, having proper medical care on site, and preparing and planning ahead of time (e.g., having appropriate equipment and protocols in place) in the event that there is an instance of EHS.

Preventive steps can be categorized into setting-specific and athlete-specific measures.

Setting-Specific Preventive Measures

- Employ on-site medical personnel (i.e., athletic trainers or sports medicine physicians) who have the authority to restrict the athlete from participating because of any associated risk factors (medical, environmental, or other).[2]
- Ensure that appropriate medical treatment equipment (e.g., immersion tub, accurate temperature measurement device, water/ice) is available and ready for use in the event that an athlete has EHS.[2]
- When possible, adjust starting times and practice times to avoid the hottest part of the day (usually between 10 AM and 5 PM).[2] If unable to do so, adjust work-to-rest ratios.
- Implement heat acclimatization guidelines.[2,3] Updated guidelines were introduced in 2009 specifically for secondary school athletes (see Table 6.2).[25] These guidelines help the athlete to adjust to physical stressors in combination with the environment without overwhelming the body's system. New guidelines released for the collegiate level have also introduced the idea of exercise acclimatization, which recommends an overall gradual introduction of exercise in both duration and intensity.[41]

Athlete-Specific Preventive Measures

- Those directly involved with the sporting team should be familiar with the prevention, recognition, and treatment of heat illnesses and the risks associated with exercising in hot, humid environmental conditions.[42] Every year there should be a coach's meeting at which the medical staff can address these concerns along with other pertinent medical topics.
- Athletes should not participate in exercise if they are ill and have a fever.
- Athletes should discuss any supplements or medications they are taking with a medical professional (i.e., their physician, athletic trainer, or team physician) to ensure that they will not place the athlete at increased risk during exercise and competitions.
- Athletes should have a preparticipation physical exam that includes medical history questions specific to heat illnesses.[42] The following questions should be included:
  - Have you ever had a heat illness? If so, when? What was your final diagnosis?
  - Do you find it hard or have you ever had trouble exercising in the heat?
  - How much sleep do you get per night on average? In the last week?
  - Do you sleep in an air-conditioned room?
  - In the last 2 weeks have you been exercising in the heat? On average, how long each day did you perform aerobic conditioning?
  - In the past 3 months, on average, how many days per week did you perform some sort of aerobic workout?
  - For how many years have you been participating in sports? Do you participate year-round? If not, how many months of the year are you active?

These questions will help gain insight into whether an athlete is fit, has a history that might indicate a predisposition to a heat illness, and is acclimatized to exercising in the heat.

- Ensure that athletes have access to water and are allowed water breaks throughout practice.[2,3] Athletes should be encouraged to drink fluids throughout practice, and at no point should an athlete be refused fluids. Water should be accessible, bountiful, and chilled, and athletes should have plenty of time to consume it. If athletes become dehydrated, this can completely negate the advantages gained with heat acclimatization.[29]
- Monitor body weight changes during multiple practice days or at the end of practice to ensure proper rehydration.[2] Although weight is not a good indicator of hydration status globally, it can reflect and account for water loss during a practice session. This means that while the precise level of dehydration is not known, the amount lost during a session can be calculated and replenished at the end of practice. An important caveat, however, is that if an athlete starts exercise in fluid deficit, his or her body weight change will not reflect this. If the athlete replaces only the fluids lost during that session, but started the session dehydrated, the athlete will only return to his or her prepractice level of dehydration.
- On hot days, limit the use of protective equipment and athletic equipment that act as barriers to evaporation.[2,3] A sudden increase in environmental temperature can increase the physical strain on the body, even in an individual who is acclimatized.
- Ensure that athletes have proper fitness leading into preseason/practice and get proper sleep every night.[2,36] Research has found that sleep deprivation has been a common factor reported in multiple EHS cases.[39]

Recognition of Exertional Heat Stroke

EHS may or may not arise slowly, but in most cases athletes are not aware of how close they are to this serious condition. EHS is more common in bouts of intense exercise lasting in the range of 30 to 90 minutes, such as the Falmouth road race. As exercise duration increases, relative intensity of the exercise must decrease, which is why EHS in the marathon occurs but is not as prevalent as it is in shorter duration races. On the other side of this, EHS in running events such as a 5-kilometer race is rare because the athletes usually are not running long enough to reach a dangerous body temperature. Precollapse symptoms may include fatigue, irritability, dizziness, inability to run or continue on, and irrational thought. Collapse will soon follow and in most cases is the first indication to medical personnel that something is wrong.

Immediate postcollapse symptoms include the following:

- Rectal temperature usually higher than 40.5°C (105°F) if taken within a few minutes after collapse or suspicion of EHS
- Central nervous system dysfunction (disorientation, confusion, dizziness, irrational or unusual behavior, inappropriate comments, irritability, headache, inability to walk, loss of balance or muscle function, vomiting, diarrhea, loss of consciousness)

These symptoms are the main two criteria for diagnosing EHS.[2,3,42–44] It is important to note that the athlete may have a lucid interval during which he or she may appear normal but then experience rapidly deteriorating symptoms. This is misleading and often delays proper treatment. One very common misconception of EHS victims is that they will have dry skin. This misconception comes from the diagnosis of a condition called classical heat stroke, which occurs in elderly persons who get stuck in small rooms with no ventilation during heat waves and young infants who are left in hot, unventilated cars.[6] In these cases, the victims have hot, dry skin because they have not been exercising. However, EHS victims who have been exercising will have skin that is still wet from sweat. For a full list of EHS signs and symptoms, see **Table 6.6**. EHS should be considered in any collapsed athlete who has been exercising intensely in a warm environment until it is ruled out.

TABLE 6.6	Signs and Symptoms of Exertional Heat Stroke

Diagnostic Signs and Symptoms	Other Potential Signs and Symptoms
Rectal temperature ≥ 40.5°C (105°F)	Hot, wet skin
	Dehydration
	Tachycardia
	Hyperventilation
	Hypotension
	Vomiting
	Diarrhea
Central nervous system dysfunction such as:	
Dizziness	
Collapse	
Confusion	
Irrational behavior	
Hysteria	
Aggressiveness	
Disorientation	
Seizures	
Coma	

Sources: Adapted from Binkley H, Beckett J, Casa D, Kleiner D, Plummer P. National Athletic Trainers' Association position statement: exertional heat illnesses. *J Athl Train.* 2002;37:329–343; Armstrong L, Casa D, Millard-Strafford D, et al. American College of Sports Medicine position stand. Exertional heat illnesses during training and competition. *Med Sci Sports Exerc.* 2007;39(3):556–572.

Other possibilities include the following:

- Heat exhaustion
- Exertional hyponatremia
    - Exertional sickling
    - Diabetic emergency
    - Concussion
    - Heat syncope

If an athlete has both a severely elevated body temperature (≥ 40.5°C [105°F]) and is exhibiting central nervous system dysfunction, he or she should be treated immediately as an EHS victim. Hyperthermia should be diagnosed only via a rectal thermometer by a trained professional because all other temperature measurement devices or methods have been found to be invalid in exercising individuals.[3,44–48] Simply obtaining a **rectal temperature** soon after collapse can rule out a concussion or head injury, heat exhaustion, cardiac events, heat syncope, postural hypotension, and shock.

Management of Exertional Heat Stroke

Within the first 5 minutes of collapse or onset, the athlete should have his or her rectal temperature assessed and upon confirmation of EHS, the athlete should be immersed in ice water (see **Figure 6.2**). Ice water immersion is the gold standard of treatment for EHS. Of 252 cases of EHS that occurred between 1975 and 1990 that were treated by immersion in cold water, no deaths occurred.[49] Such a statement cannot be made for any other treatment method.[49] While many myths exist regarding EHS (see **Box 6.2**) it is important to understand the most current evidence-based recommendations.

Figure 6.2 An example of cold water immersion setup and treatment, including the use of a rectal thermometer, towels for the head, and holding the athlete above water.

It is extremely important to minimize the length of time at which body temperature remains at or above 40.5°C (105°F). The heat stress incurred by either the magnitude by which a person's temperature exceeds 40.5°C (105°F), the length of time that it remains over this temperature, or a combination of both factors determines the extent of long-term injury and risk of death.[49–53] The goal in any EHS case should be to cool the athlete down to 39°C (102°F) within the first 30 minutes after collapse. Coordinating with EMS so that treatment for EHS takes place on site, prior to transport, is also recommended.

EHS is an emergency medical condition and should be diagnosed by a medical professional. If no medical professional is immediately available, and a coach, parent, or other staff person believes that an athlete is suffering from EHS, these steps should be followed:

1. A cardiac emergency needs to be immediately ruled out via a lay responder with automated external defibrillator and cardiopulmonary resuscitation training.
2. Once a cardiac emergency has been ruled out, the victim should be aggressively cooled while awaiting EMS arrival. This is vital to save an EHS victim. Even if the athlete is suffering from heat exhaustion, exertional sickling, or some other condition, cooling is very unlikely to cause complications.
3. Cool the athlete until EMS arrives and takes over care (via cold water immersion, cold water dousing, rotating wet ice towels, etc.). Even if EMS arrival takes 10 to 15 minutes, this is an appropriate amount of time to cool an EHS victim, even with the most effective cooling modality.

It must be stressed that appropriate care includes on-site medical staff; therefore, these recommendations regarding the care of a suspected EHS victim in the absence of on-site EMS care are provided as a last resort option only. Any institution that holds intense athletic practices without medical coverage has the potential for great legal liability.

Cold Water Immersion: A Powerful Cooling Modality

Cold water immersion (CWI) (< 10°C) is considered a highly effective treatment for EHS,[40] with circulated ice water immersion (2°C) providing some of the highest average (0.35°C/minute) and peak (0.5°C/minute for second-degree drop) in body temperature cooling rates. At these rates, core body temperature can be reestablished to near normal values as quickly as 9 minutes from the start of immersion, thus dramatically reducing the time an EHS victim is severely hyperthermic, which dictates the individual's health outcome.[54] These rates are two- to 17-fold greater than other cooling modalities such as regional or whole-body application of wet towels

cold water immersion (CWI) Cooling via immersion in a tub of water with temperatures ranging from approximately 2° to 13°C (35°–55°F), with faster cooling occurring at lower temperatures and when the water is circulated. Often referred to as *ice-water immersion*.

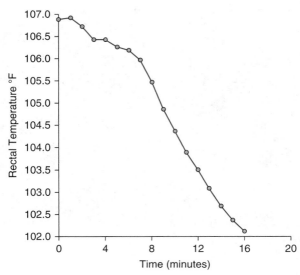

Figure 6.3 Hypothetical cooling curve via cold water dousing. Note: cooling rate = 0.29°F/min or 0.16°C/min.

and ice or cold packs, evaporative cooling (i.e., spraying water over the patient and facilitating evaporation and convection with use of fans), and temperate or tap water immersion (≥ 15°C or 59°F).[53,55–57]

Despite concerns raised by some experts that CWI may elicit potentially lethal cold shock responses (i.e., sudden immersion in cold water inducing an initial gasp, hypertension, hyperventilation, and tachycardia),[58]

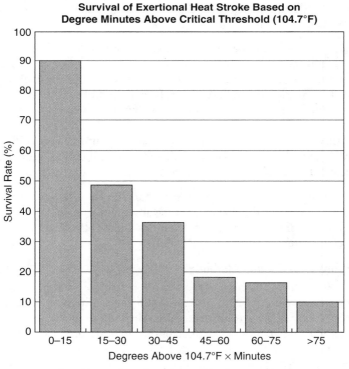

Figure 6.4 Relationship between severity of hyperthermia measured in degree-minutes and rate of survivability. Thermal area (degrees × minutes) = ∑ Time interval (min) × ½[°C above 40.4°C at start of interval + °C above 40.4°C at end of interval].

Source: Casa DJ, Kenny GP, Taylor NA. Immersion treatment for exertional hyperthermia: cold or temperate water? *Med Sci Sports Exerc.* 2010;42(7):1246–1252. Reprinted with permission.

Figure 6.5 A 150-gallon tub for cold water immersion treatment.

the superior cooling rate of CWI has been shown to provide an important advantage in reducing the likelihood of death or long-term complications associated with the condition (see **Figure 6.3** and **Figure 6.4**). Evidence of the powerful influence of cold water on cooling of actual EHS patients has been well documented in the athletic field, mass medical tents, and military training centers. For example, in the over three-decade-long history of the Falmouth Road Race in Falmouth, Massachusetts, CWI treatment provided a 100% survival rate for the more than 400 EHS victims.[59] Similar evidence of success has been reported when using ice water at other athletic events, such as the Marine Corps Marathon, and at military bases such as Fort Benning, Quantico, Parris Island, and others. While the authors agree that CWI is the most powerful treatment for EHS, it is also recognized that in some scenarios it may not always be practical or available (e.g., in remote hiking areas). In these cases the recommendation is to aggressively and continuously douse the patient with water (cold water is best). This is the best option if it is not possible to fully immerse the athlete. Other options include rotation of wet ice towels. While these options are available in the absence of CWI availability, they do not release responsible medical and associated staff from the responsibility of planning for such an event and having the best treatment materials (e.g., immersion tub) ready at athletic venues. (See **Figure 6.5**.)

Keeping It Safe: Managing the Power of Cold Water Immersion

Although CWI is a safe and powerful cooling modality for the treatment of EHS, extreme care should be taken when considering when to remove individuals from a water bath. One potential danger associated with this treatment is the risk of causing hypothermia (a lower than normal body temperature) as a result of too much cooling. From a clinical standpoint, however, the dangers associated with hyperthermia far outweigh those associated with overcooling. Therefore, cooling of the hyperthermic individual should be undertaken as quickly as possible even if a measurement of core temperature is not readily available. Immersion time will depend on the water temperature employed. As water temperature increases, immersion times will increase. On average, immersion of the EHS victim should not exceed 9, 14, 17, and 18 minutes for a water bath temperature of 2°C, 8°C, 14°C, or 20°C respectively.[54] However, if the measurement of body core temperature is possible, an exit rectal temperature of 38.6°C is a safe cooling

---

Box 6.2

Common Misconceptions

A multitude of misconceptions exist regarding all facets of EHS. The following list addresses these misconceptions.

- *Heat stroke has to occur in the heat.* Because of the name of the condition, many fail to recognize EHS if an affected athlete is not participating in hot conditions. However, as mentioned previously, environmental conditions are not the only factor that can contribute to EHS, and many times they are not the primary factors. There have been reports of EHS in temperatures of 9.4°C (49°F) and 62% humidity.[60]

(continues)

Common Misconceptions (*continued*)

- *Nutritional supplements cause EHS deaths.* Many supplements have been implicated in deaths occurring from EHS. Among them are creatine and ephedra. The evidence that creatine decreases heat tolerance is lacking or demonstrates no effect.[61,62] Much less research has been done on ephedra. While these and some other supplements or drugs may contribute to the heat load experienced by the athlete and place him or her at more risk for an incident of EHS, there is no evidence that with immediate proper treatment these athletes would not survive.

- *Axillary, oral, tympanic, aural canal, and temporal artery thermometers and temperature stickers are all valid methods of temperature assessment for EHS.* The only temperature assessment method that has been validated for use in EHS victims is rectal and gastrointestinal thermometry.[3,45–48] It is recommended that rectal temperatures be used in EHS scenarios because they provide an immediate and accurate body temperature. It is *not* recommended that an inaccurate temperature device be used in the absence of an accurate device, because this can lead to an incorrect medical diagnosis. In this situation, it is much better to base the diagnosis on history and presenting signs and symptoms.

- *Rectal temperature must be over 40.5°C (105°F).* Although this is the defining temperature for EHS, it is quite possible that temperature assessment may be delayed and may not accurately reflect the heat stress incurred. In this case, it is safer to err on the side of caution and cool the athlete, because it is rare that cooling would ever cause another potential medical condition to worsen.

- *The athlete must be severely dehydrated to experience EHS.* Although body temperature does increase with dehydration,[29,63,64] intensity of exercise and environmental temperature are also important factors that can contribute to an increase in core body temperature. It is certainly possible for EHS to occur without severe dehydration, as evidenced by some past cases.

- *The athlete with EHS will become unconscious.* Although an athlete with EHS *may* become unconscious, this is not *always* the case. Central nervous system dysfunction may present in other fashions, often as irritability or confusion. It is also very important to note that the athlete may have a lucid interval during which central nervous system functions may appear normal, followed by quickly deteriorating symptoms.[43]

- *Cooling an athlete with EHS via CWI will cause peripheral vasoconstriction that will inhibit cooling or can cause cardiovascular shock.* No other cooling modality has ever proved faster than CWI.[43,53,65] It is believed that in a normal, healthy, individual the risk of cardiovascular shock is extremely low, and without proper treatment for EHS the risk of death is very high; therefore, treatment should commence with CWI. There may be slight vasoconstriction, even in a hyperthermic individual. However, the power of the CWI will override this, and it may even help provide an immediate shift of blood, which can protect the heart. If a cardiovascular event occurs, the athlete should be removed from the water and treated accordingly.[43]

limit during the treatment of hyperthermic individuals. This temperature provides a good balance between sufficient cooling to treat the potential dangers associated with heat stroke and providing protection against overcooling and any subsequent core temperature afterdrop. Medical providers should also place a towel or other device under the athlete's arms to ensure that the athlete's head remains above water during treatment, especially in obtunded or comatose patients who are unable to protect their own airway.

Recovery

Within 1 hour of collapse, the athlete should have been cooled and then monitored for approximately 15 minutes to observe for hypothermia. (This is in the absence of other emergency medical issues that could potentially arise.) At this point the athlete should be transported to the hospital for follow-up blood work. The athlete should *not* be transported to the hospital until a safe body temperature has been attained. Only in the event that there is no effective cooling modality and a lack of appropriate on-site medical care should an EHS victim be immediately transported to the hospital.

Long-term prognosis and recovery from EHS is improved if the initial treatment includes rapid whole-body cooling. A person with a core body temperature of 41°C (106°F) for an hour could be at much greater risk for mortality and morbidity than one who has a body temperature of 42.8°C (109°F) and is cooled within 15 minutes. In the majority of EHS cases where the athlete is not cooled immediately but survives, there is an extended recovery time (often lasting up to 1 year after the event) with likely organ function complications. In contrast, Individuals treated immediately on site are usually released and return home the same day.

Return to Play After Exertional Heat Stroke

At the 2000 American College of Sports Medicine's (ACSM) Team Physician conference, the core concepts of athlete medical management were described and published as a consensus statement.[66] The return-to-play (RTP) process, defined as deciding when an injured or ill athlete may safely return to practice or competition, is arguably the most challenging component of athlete injury management. The final decision for safe and timely return to practice or competition is the desired result of an integrated process of evaluation, treatment, and rehabilitation coordinated by the sports medicine team (i.e., the athletic trainer, team physician, and physical therapist).[67]

RTP decision making can be a complex and demanding process. Although the final decision is most commonly left in the hands of the providing physician, the assessments frequently require the incorporation of information from and execution by the athletic trainer, physical therapist, coach, and family members, as well as the athlete. EHS RTP is especially challenging because we have an incomplete understanding of the pathophysiologic processes involved in the development of and recovery from this disorder.[43,68]

Despite the frequency of EHS, current civilian and military RTP guidelines are largely based on anecdotal observation and caution.[68,69] At this time, no evidence-based guidelines or recommendations exist for returning athletes or warfighters to play or duty. Most guidelines are commonsense recommendations that require a normal state and normal laboratory parameters, coupled with a cautious reintroduction of activity and gradual heat acclimatization. Current suggestions for a return of EHS victims to full activity range from 7 days to 15 months.[70] This lack of consistency and clinical agreement can negatively affect athletes and soldiers and force medical providers to guess about the best solution for each individual; the inconsistencies also can directly affect military force readiness. Additionally, whereas current guidance states that EHS casualties may return to practice and competition when they have reestablished heat tolerance, no evidence-based tools are available to assess when the body's thermoregulatory system has returned to normal.[68]

RTP after EHS should, however, like return from any other injury, involve a carefully planned and incrementally increased physical challenge that is closely supervised by an athletic trainer and physician, as previously identified in the ACSM conference statement. Current research indicates that most individuals will eventually recover fully from EHS (with some exceptions[71,72]); indeed, this occurs in the vast majority of cases when the athlete is treated promptly with aggressive cooling strategies (i.e., ice-water immersion).[43,51,73,74] Although definitive, evidence-based guidelines regarding RTP do not presently exist, the current recommendations are summarized in the following sections.

Current Recommendations for Return to Play

In the authors' opinion, the consensus RTP guidelines set forth by the ACSM are clear, succinct, and provide a rational process for guiding athletes who have experienced EHS. Current recommendations from the ACSM for returning an athlete to training and competition are as follows:[70,74]

1. Refrain from exercise for at least 7 days following release from medical care.
2. Follow up about 1 week post incident for a physical examination and lab testing or diagnostic imaging of the affected organs, based on the clinical course of the heat stroke incident.
3. When cleared for return to activity, begin exercise in a cool environment and gradually increase the duration, intensity, and heat exposure over 2 weeks to demonstrate heat tolerance and to initiate acclimatization. This should be performed under medical supervision to observe for any complications during this progression.
4. If return to vigorous activity is not accomplished over 4 weeks, a laboratory exercise heat tolerance test should be considered.
5. Clear the athlete for full competition if heat tolerant between 2 and 4 weeks of full training.

Summary

EHS is a medical emergency that, if not promptly recognized and treated immediately, can result in death. Many factors either independently or in combination, such as exercise intensity, hydration status, environmental conditions, and use of protective equipment, can cause an overwhelming of the thermoregulatory system. This accumulation of heat within the body causes a dangerously high body temperature, with concomitant central nervous system dysfunction. Although there are preventive steps that should be taken, there is no method to fully protect athletes from EHS. EHS is unfortunately not always preventable, but death from heat stroke is. Cooling an athlete via CWI is the only treatment, if performed immediately, that has a 100% survival rate. If prevention strategies are followed, emergency action plans incorporate accurate temperature measurement (via rectal thermometry), and CWI is utilized for treatment of EHS, the incidence of and death from this condition can be dramatically reduced.

Clinical Case Scenarios

1. James is a 6-foot, 240-pound lineman. He had just graduated from high school and was trying to make the starting line for a Division I college in the northeast. It was preseason and the first day of practice in full pads. James had struggled the day before with an intense conditioning bout the team had performed, but he was determined to prove his ability to be a starter. Over the past few days the air temperature had been much higher than usual. The second practice of the day started at 3:00 PM and ended at 5:00 PM with more conditioning. James collapsed during the end of some sprinting drills. He tried to get up and was able to stagger across the line. His coaches came to his side and noted that he was unable to talk coherently or answer simple questions. James's skin was hot and sweaty, and there were salt stains all over his clothes. The coaches quickly called the athletic trainer, who took his core temperature, which read 42.8°C (109°F). The athletic trainer was able to douse James with cold water and lower his body temperature to 39.4°C (103°F) before transporting him to the hospital. Because of the prompt recognition and care James received, he was able to recover and return to football the next week.

    a. What other medical conditions could present with similar signs and symptoms?

    b. What materials would you need to treat an athlete with EHS?

    c. What is your ideal cooling modality for this situation?

2. Ann is a 23-year-old former Division I collegiate runner. She has been a runner since high school, and in her postcollegiate years she was working on her goal of qualifying for the Boston marathon. She trained all summer and entered her first marathon in the fall. She had a friend who ran the last 10 miles with her to help pace her and push her to finish. Toward the end of the race, the air temperature had reached 15.6°C (60°F). With the help of her friend, Ann made it to the finish and barely made the qualifying time. However, right after she crossed the finish line, she collapsed and could not regain her ability to walk. She was immediately carried to a nearby medical tent while her friend screamed orders at the medical staff. As the medical staff began to diagnose her, they decided to obtain a rectal body temperature. At this point she became combative and tried to refuse treatment. Her initial rectal temperature was 42°C (107.5°F). She was immediately moved to the immersion tub; however, she started to shout obscenities and thrash violently. The medical team restrained her during the cooling treatment. Over the course of the next 15 minutes, her temperature lowered under 40.6°C (105°F), at which point she quickly became lucid and returned to a compliant state. She was removed from cooling once her temperature reached 39.4°C (103°F) and transferred to the hospital for follow-up care.

    a. How would you organize a mass medical tent to accommodate this scenario?

    b. What other conditions would you want to rule out that might present with symptoms similar to this athlete's central nervous system disorder?

    c. What steps or considerations should you take before this athlete returns to play?

Key Terms

acclimation

acclimatization

body temperature

cold water immersion (CWI)

dehydration

equipment load

exertional heat stroke (EHS)

hydration status

intensity of exercise

rectal temperature

wet bulb globe temperature (WBGT)

References

1. Mueller F, Cantu R. *Twenty Sixth Annual Report of the National Center for Catastrophic Sports Injury Research: Catastrophic Football Injuries.* Chapel Hill, NC: National Center for Catastrophic Sports Injury Research; 2009.
2. Binkley H, Beckett J, Casa D, Kleiner D, Plummer P. National Athletic Trainers' Association position statement: exertional heat illnesses. *J Athl Train.* 2002;37:329–343.
3. Casa D, Armstrong L. Exertional heatstroke: a medical emergency. In: Armstrong LE, ed. *Exertional Heat Illnesses.* Champaign, IL: Human Kinetics; 2003:29–56.
4. Armstrong L, Casa D, Millard-Strafford D, et al. American College of Sports Medicine position stand. Exertional heat illnesses during training and competition. *Med Sci Sports Exerc.* 2007;39(3):556–572.
5. Casa DJ, Armstrong LE, Kenny GP, O'Connor FG, Huggins RA. Exertional heat stroke: new concepts regarding cause and care. *Curr Sports Med Rep.* 2012;11(3):115–123.
6. Casa DJ, Guskiewicz KM, Anderson SA, et al. National Athletic Trainers' Association position statement: preventing sudden death in sports. *J Athl Train.* 2012;47(1):96–118.
7. Casa DJ, Guskiewicz KM, Anderson SA, et al. National Athletic Trainers' Association position statement: preventing sudden death in secondary school sports. *J Athl Train.* 2013;48(4):546–553.
8. Grundstein AJ, Ramseyer C, Zhao F, et al. A retrospective analysis of American football hyperthermia deaths in the United States. *Int J Biometeorol.* 2012;56(1):11–20.
9. Santee W, Gonzalez R. Characteristics of the thermal environment. In: Pandolf KB, Sawka MN, Gonzalez RR, eds. *Human Performance Physiology and Environmental Medicine at Terrestrial Extremes.* Indianapolis, IL: Benchmark Press; 1988:1–44.
10. Stitt J. Central regulation of body temperature. In: Gisolfi CV, Lamb DR, Nadel ER, eds. *Exercise, Heat and Thermoregulation.* Traverse City, MI: Cooper Publishing Group; 2001.
11. Castellani J. Physiology of heat stress. In: Armstrong LE, ed. *Exertional Heat Illnesses.* Champaign, IL: Human Kinetics; 2003.
12. Neilsen M. Die regulation der korper temperatur bei muskelarbiet. *Skan Arch Physiol.* 1938;79:193–230.
13. Booth J, Marino F, Ward J. Improved running performance in hot humid conditions following whole body precooling. *Med Sci Sports Exerc.* 1997;29:943–949.
14. Cheung S, Sleivert G. Multiple triggers for hyperthermic fatigue and exhaustion. *Exerc Sport Sci Rev.* 2004;32(3):100–106.
15. Marino F. Anticipatory regulation and avoidance of catastrophe during exercise-induced hyperthermia. *Comp Biochem Physiol B Biochem Mol Biol.* 2004;139:561–569.
16. Tucker R, Marle T, Lambert EV, Noakes T. The rate of heat storage mediates an anticipatory reduction in exercise intensity during cycling at a fixed rating of perceived exertion. *J Physiol.* 2006;574(3):905–915.
17. Tucker R, Rauch L, Harley Y, Noakes T. Impaired exercise performance in the heat is associated with an anticipatory reduction in skeletal muscle recruitment. *Pflügers Archiv.* 2004;448:422–430.
18. Cheung S. Hyperthermia and voluntary exhaustion: integrating models and future challenges. *Appl Physiol Nutr Metab.* 2007;32(4):808–817.
19. Ely B, Cheuvront S, Kenefick R, Sawka M. Aerobic performance is degraded, despite modest hyperthermia, in hot environments. *Med Sci Sports Exerc.* 2010;42(1):135–141.
20. Pandolf K. Time course of heat acclimation and its decay. *Int J Sports Med.* 1998;19:S157–S160.
21. Armstrong L, Maresh C. The induction and decay of heat acclimatisation in trained athletes. *Sports Med.* 1991;12(5):302–312.
22. Pawelczyk J. Neural control of skin and muscle blood flow during exercise and thermal stress. In: Gisolfi CV, Lamb DR, Nadel ER, eds. *Exercise, Heat and Thermoregulation.* Traverse City, MI: Cooper Publishing Group; 2001.
23. Poh PYS, Armstrong Le, Casa DJ, et al. Orthostatic hypotension after 10 days of exercise-heat acclimation and 28 hours of sleep loss. *Aviat Space Environ Med.* 2012;83:403–411.
24. Pandolf K. Effects of physical training and cardiorespiratory physical fitness on exercise-heat tolerance: recent observations. *Med Sci Sports Exerc.* 1979;11:60–65.
25. Casa D, Csillan D. Preseason heat-acclimatization guidelines for secondary school athletics. *J Athl Train.* 2009;44(3):332–333.

26. Casa D, Armstrong L, Hillman S, et al. National Athletic Trainers' Association position statement: fluid replacement for athletes. *J Athl Train*. 2000;35(2):212–224.

27. Sawka M, Pandolf K. Effects of body water loss on physiological function and exercise performance. In: Gisolfi CV, Lamb DR, eds. *Fluid Homeostasis During Exercise*. Traverse MI: Cooper Publishing Group; 2001.

28. Armstrong L, Maresh C, Gabaree C, et al. Thermal and circulatory responses during exercise: effects of hypohydration, dehydration, and water intake. *J Appl Physiol*. 1997;82:2028–2035.

29. Sawka M, Latzka W, Matott R, Montain S. Hydration effects on temperature regulation. *Int J Sports Med*. 1998;19:S108–S110.

30. Casa DJ, Stearns RL, Lopez RM, et al. Influence of hydration on physiological function and performance during trail running in the heat. *J Athl Train*. 2010;45(2):147–156.

31. Distefano LJ, Casa DJ, Vansumeren MM, et al. Hypohydration and hyperthermia impair neuromuscular control after exercise. *Med Sci Sports Exerc*. 2013;45(6):1166–1173.

32. Mazerolle SM, Casa TM, Casa DJ. Heat and hydration curriculum issues: part 1 of 4, hydration and exercise. *Athl Ther Today*. 2009;14(2):39–44.

33. Ganio M, Casa D, Armstrong L, Maresh C. Evidence-based approach to lingering hydration questions. *Clinics Sports Med*. 2007;26:1–16.

34. Kolka MA, Latzka WA, Montain SJ, Sawka MN. Current U.S. Military Fluid Replacement Guidelines. RTO-MP-HFM-086.

35. Mazerolle SM, Yeargin SW, Casa TM, Casa DJ. Heat and hydration curriculum issues: part 2 of 4, exercising in the heat. *Athl Ther Today*. 2009;14(3):42–47.

36. Saltin B, Hermansen L. Esophageal, rectal and muscle temperature during exercise. *J Appl Physiol*. 1966;21(6):1757–1762.

37. Noakes TD, Myburgh KH, du Plessis J, et al. Metabolic rate, not percent dehydration, predicts rectal temperature in marathon runners. *Med Sci Sports Exerc*. 1991;23(4):443–449.

38. Davies CT. Influence of skin temperature on sweating and aerobic performance during severe work. *J Appl Physiol*. 1979;47(4):770–777.

39. Rav-Acha M, Hadad E, Epstein Y, Heled Y, Moran D. Fatal exertional heat stroke: a case series. *Am J Med Sci*. 2004;328:84–87.

40. Bedno SA, Han W, Cowan DN, et al. Exertional heat illness among army recruits. *Aviat Space Environ Med*. 2010;81(2):107–111.

41. Casa DJ, Anderson SA, Baker L, et al. The inter-association task force for preventing sudden death in collegiate conditioning sessions: best practices recommendations. *J Athl Train*. 2012;47(4):477–480.

42. Casa D, Almquist J, Anderson SEA. Inter-Association Task Force on Exertional Heat Illnesses consensus statement. *NATA News*. June 2003:24–29.

43. Casa D, Armstrong L, Ganio M, Yeargin S. Exertional heat stroke in competitive athletes. *Curr Sports Med Rep*. 2005;4:309–317.

44. Mazerolle SM, Yeargin SW, Casa TM, Casa DJ. Heat and hydration curriculum issues: part 3 of 4, rectal thermometry. *Athl Ther Today*. 2009;14(4):25–31.

45. Low D, Vu A, Brown M, et al. Temporal thermometry fails to track body core temperature during heat stress. *Med Sci Sports Exerc*. 2007;39(7):1029–1035.

46. Casa D, Becker S, Ganio M, et al. Validity of devices that assess body temperature during outdoor exercise in the heat. *J Athl Train*. 2007;42(3):333–342.

47. Ganio MS, Brown CM, Casa DJ, et al. Validity and reliability of devices that assess body temperature during indoor exercise in the heat. *J Athl Train*. 2009;44(2):124–135.

48. Moran D, Mendal L. Core temperature measurement methods and current insights. *Sports Med*. 2002;32:879–885.

49. Costrini A. Emergency treatment of exertional heatstroke and comparison of whole body cooling techniques. *Med Sci Sports Exerc*. 1990;22(1):15–18.

50. Casa DJ, Kenny GP, Taylor NA. Immersion treatment for exertional hyperthermia: cold or temperate water? *Med Sci Sports Exerc*. 2010;42(7):1246–1252.

51. Armstrong L, Maresh C. Can humans avoid and recover from exertional heat stroke? In: Pandolf KB, Takeda N, Singal PK, eds. *Adaptation Biology and Medicine*. Vol. 2. New Delhi, India: Narosa Publishing; 1999:344–351.

52. Shibolet S, Lancaster M, Danon Y. Heatstroke: a review. *Aviation Space Environ Med*. 1976;47:280–301.

53. Casa D, McDermott B, Lee E, et al. Cold water immersion: the gold standard for exertional heatstroke treatment. *Exerc Sport Sci Rev*. 2007;35(3):141–149.

54. Proulx CI, Ducharme MB, Kenny GP. Safe cooling limits from exercise-induced hyperthermia. *Eur J Appl Physiol*. 2006;96:434–445.

55. McDermott BP, Casa DJ, Ganio MS, et al. Acute whole-body cooling for exercise-induced hyperthermia: a systematic review. *J Athl Train*. 2009;44:84–93.

56. DeMartini JK, Ranalli GF, Casa DJ, et al. Comparison of body cooling methods on physiological and perceptual measures of mildly hyperthermic athletes. *J Strength Cond Res*. 2011;25(8):2065–2074.

57. Mazerolle SM, Casa TM, Casa DJ, Lopez RL. Heat and hydration curriculum issues: part 4 of 4, cold water immersion. *Athl Ther Today*. 2009;14(5):15–20.

58. Taylor NA, Caldwell JN, Van den Heuvel AM, Patterson MJ. To cool, but not too cool: that is the question—immersion cooling for hyperthermia. *Med Sci Sports Exerc*. 2008;40(11):1962–1969.

59. O'Malley D. Hyperthermia on a short race course: the Falmouth road race experience. Paper presented at: American Medical Athletic Association's 37th Annual Sport Medicine Symposium at the Boston Marathon; April 19, 2008; Boston, MA.

60. Roberts W. Exertional heat stroke during a cool weather marathon: a case study. *Med Sci Sports Exerc*. 2006;38(7):1197–1203.

61. Kilduff L, Georgiades E, James N, et al. Effects of creatine supplementation on cardiovascular, metabolic and thermoregulatory responses during exercise in the heat in endurance trained humans. *Int J Sport Nutr Exerc Metab*. 2004;14(4):443–460.
62. Watson G, Casa D, Fiala K, et al. Creatine use and exercise heat tolerance in dehydrated men. *J Athl Train*. 2006;41(1):18–29.
63. Montain S, Coyle E. Influence of graded dehydration on hyperthermia and cardiovascular drift during exercise. *J Appl Physiol*. 1992;73:1340–1350.
64. Adolph E. *Physiology of Man in the Desert: Survival in an Arid Land*. New York, NY: Interscience Publishers; 1947:172–196, 208–221.
65. McDermott B, Casa D, O'Connor F, et al. Cold-water dousing with ice massage to treat exertional heat stroke: a case series. *Aviation Space Environ Med*. 2009;80(8):720–722.
66. American College of Sports Medicine. Team physician consensus statement. *Med Sci Sports Exerc*. 2000;32(4):877–878.
67. American College of Sports Medicine. The team physician and return-to-play issues: a consensus statement. *Med Sci Sports Exerc*. 2002;34(7):1212–1214.
68. McDermott BP, Casa DJ, Yeargin SW, et al. Recovery and return to activity following exertional heat stroke: considerations for the sports medicine staff. *J Sport Rehabil*. 2007;16:163–181.
69. O'Connor FG, Williams AD, Blivin S, et al. Guidelines for return to duty (play) after heat illness: a military perspective. *J Sport Rehabil*. 2007(16):227–237.
70. Armstrong LE, Casa DJ, Millard-Stafford M, et al. Exertional heat illness during training and competition. *Med Sci Sports Exerc*. 2007;39(3):556–572.
71. Mehta AC, Baker RN. Persistent neurological deficits in heat stroke. *Neurology*. 1970;20:336–340.
72. Royburt M, Epstein Y, Solomon Z, Shemer J. Long term psychosocial and physiological effects of heat stroke. *Physiol Behav*. 1993;54:265–267.
73. Roberts WO. Death in the heat: can football heat stroke be prevented? *Curr Sports Med Rep*. 2004;3(1):1–3.
74. O'Connor FG, Casa DJ, Bergeron MF, et al. American College of Sports Medicine Roundtable on Exertional Heat Stroke— Return to duty/return to play: Conference proceedings. *Curr Sports Med Rep*. 2010;9(5):314–321.

Brain Injuries

Jason P. Mihalik, PhD, CAT(C), ATC

Kevin M. Guskiewicz, PhD, ATC, FACSM, FNATA

© Giorgio Micheletti/ShutterStock, Inc.

From the Field Scenario

During a particularly intense and physical game, several players on the State High School football team had already been injured. The team's athletic trainer, Mike, was helping another injured athlete off the field while the team's head coach, Andy, was calling in the next play. In one of Andy's favorite plays, State's all-state senior captain and right guard Tyler was called upon to quickly move to his left and attempt to block an opponent. When Tyler lunged forward to engage the block, an opposing linebacker attempted to split between him and another lineman, catching the side of Tyler's helmet with his knee. As Mike was busy attending to his latest injury on the sideline, he had no view or knowledge of the play. Andy, however, immediately saw the knee-to-helmet impact and noticed Tyler was slow to get up. Andy also noted that as Tyler began to stand, he appeared slightly dizzy and did not immediately go to the huddle, but instead seemed to look to each sideline briefly as if to establish his bearings. After finally reaching the huddle, Andy noticed that Tyler did not stand in his usual assigned spot. Upon concluding this behavior was very abnormal, especially for a captain and team leader, Andy decided to call a timeout. He immediately approached Tyler and asked the senior how he was feeling. The sluggish look on Tyler's face coupled with his slow and unsteady response of "I feel fine" triggered Andy to remove him from the game and seek the athletic trainer's opinion. Mike sat Tyler down on the bench and conducted a brief—but thorough—clinical examination. Mike also administered a symptom checklist, balance assessment, and short neurocognitive exam. Although Tyler had no abnormal findings on his clinical exam, because of a reported increase in symptoms along with noticeable balance and neurocognitive deficits, Mike made the decision to remove him from the game. Thanks to Andy's quick action and attention to detail during the game, Tyler was appropriately diagnosed with a concussion and provided the necessary care to ensure a safe return to activity.

Discussion Questions

1. Tyler reported to his coach that he felt fine. Was Andy justified in removing him from the game? Why or why not?
2. What signs exhibited by Tyler did Andy base his decision on and what other things may he have been looking for?

3. What steps—including those not discussed in this example—helped Andy make a decision? What steps can be taken to ensure all coaches have the ability to make this kind of judgment call?

Introduction

No other sports injury has generated as much public interest in recent years as brain injury. Brain injuries vary by name, type, and severity in the athletic setting. It should be noted, however, that these injuries do not occur only in the athletic arena. Brain injuries also occur in recreational and workplace/industrial settings, and they are also common following motor vehicle accidents.

It has been estimated that between 1.6 and 3.8 million traumatic brain injuries (TBIs) result from sports each year in the United States.[1] These injuries cost the American health-care system approximately $56.3 billion in direct and indirect costs[2] and make TBI among the most expensive conditions to treat in children.[3] This chapter defines the various types of brain injury common in sports and describes how frequently they occur, how the brain is affected, how to recognize and manage these injuries, and what to expect as an athlete recovers from such injury. Some return-to-activity considerations for the brain-injured athlete will also be discussed.

Definitions

The most common form of brain injury is a **cerebral concussion**. Although there are many definitions for this injury, it is generally agreed that concussion is a "complex pathophysiological process affecting the brain, induced by biomechanical forces."[4] Cerebral concussions may be caused by direct impacts to the head or, in the example of a body tackle or a rear-end motor vehicle collision, by impulsive forces transmitted to the head through indirect impacts. A key feature of most cerebral concussions is the rapid onset of signs that are observable in the injured athlete and symptoms that an athlete should be encouraged to report. Concussions rarely result in any structural brain injury that can be identified using traditional imaging techniques, including computed tomography (CT) scans or magnetic resonance imaging (MRI).[4]

In more serious concussions, structural **diffuse brain injury** (diffuse axonal injury) results in axonal disruption. Axons are the nerve fibers responsible for conducting impulses by which all of the body's processes are controlled (e.g., thought, memory, balance, movement, etc.). In its most severe form, diffuse axonal injury can disrupt the brainstem centers responsible for breathing, heart rate, and wakefulness.[5,6] Cerebral concussion, the most common sport-related TBI, can best be classified as a mild diffuse axonal injury and is often referred to as mild TBI. The injury usually results in one or more of the following signs and symptoms: headache, nausea, vomiting, dizziness, balance problems, feeling "slowed down," fatigue, trouble sleeping, drowsiness, sensitivity to light or noise, loss of consciousness, blurred vision, difficulty remembering, and difficulty concentrating.[7,8]

Sudden death rarely occurs in athletes who suffer a cerebral concussion. However, cerebral concussions may initiate a process scientists refer to as the *neurometabolic cascade*, during which time the brain is believed to be extremely sensitive to head trauma. It is during the neurometabolic cascade that a large majority of **second impact syndrome** cases have been identified (discussed in more detail later in the chapter). Sudden death in sports because of brain injuries typically results from blood accumulation (hematoma) in confined spaces of the brain. The brain and spinal cord are protected by three layers of the meninges: pia mater (innermost layer that clings to the entire surface of the brain), arachnoid mater (middle layer; spiderweb-like in appearance), and dura mater (outermost layer; translates roughly into "tough mother"). In a **subdural hematoma**, blood accumulates between the dura mater and arachnoid

TABLE 7.1   Traumatic Intracranial Lesions

Type	Mechanism	Injured Structures	Signs and Symptoms	Care/Other
Cerebral contusion	Object impacts skull Skull impacts object	Injured vessels bleed internally Progressive swelling may injure brain tissue not originally harmed	LOC, partial paralysis, hemiplegia, unilateral pupil dilation, altered vital signs	Adequate ventilation, CPR if necessary, proper transport, expert evaluation; May not require surgery
Cerebral hematoma				
Epidural	Severe blow to head Skull fracture	Middle meningeal artery	Neurologic status deteriorates in 10 minutes to 2 hours	Transport and expert evaluation Immediate surgery may be required
Subdural	Force of blow thrusts brain against point of impact	Subdural vessels tear and result in venous bleeding	Neurologic status deteriorates in hours, days, or even weeks	Prolonged observation/monitoring Surgical intervention may be required
Intracerebral	Depressed skull fracture, penetrating wound, acceleration-deceleration injury	Ruptured artery bleeds within brain substance	Rapid deterioration of neurologic status	Immediate transport to emergency department Death may occur before athlete can be transported
Second impact syndrome	Sustains second brain injury before symptoms from first injury fully resolve	Brain loses autoregulation of blood supply; rapidly swells and brainstem herniates	Typically occurs in athletes < 18 years of age within 1 week of previous concussion; pupils rapidly dilate, loss of eye movement, respiratory failure, eventual coma	Rapid intubation; 50% mortality rate; 100% morbidity rate

Abbreviations: CPR, cardiopulmonary resuscitation; LOC, loss of consciousness.

mater. With **epidural hematoma**, blood pools between the dura mater and the skull. In both cases, the risk of death is high if the condition goes unnoticed or is mismanaged. **Table 7.1** identifies and describes a number of conditions that may result in sudden death in athletes and for which immediate transport to an emergency facility is needed for successful recovery.

epidural hematoma   A brain injury characterized by pooling of blood between the dura mater (outermost meningeal layer) and the skull.

Background and Occurrence of Brain Injuries

Since 1945, over 510 fatalities have resulted from brain injuries in football alone.[9] **Table 7.2** presents these data over six decades. The sharp reduction in the number of football fatalities caused by brain injuries beginning in the mid-1970s can likely be attributed to improvements in helmet and equipment design introduced to the game at that time. Also important are the playing regulation changes implemented since then that prohibit spearing and other mechanisms of injury associated with brain injury in football.

TABLE 7.2	Number of Football Brain Injury Fatalities Between 1945–2004

Years	Number of Fatalities
1945–1954	87
1955–1964	115
1965–1974	162
1975–1984	69
1985–1994	33
1995–2004	44
Totals	510

Source: Data from Mueller FO, Colgate B. *Annual Survey of Football Injury Research: 1931–2009.* Chapel Hill, NC: National Center for Catastrophic Sport Injury Research; 2010.

Although there has been a drastic reduction in the number of fatalities compared with their frequency between 1945 and 1974, the number of nonfatal brain injuries has gradually increased over time. In a report on TBI sponsored by the Centers for Disease Control and Prevention in the United States for the period from 1995 to 2001, information reported from emergency departments suggested that at least 1.4 million people sustain a TBI from all causes annually. Of those injured, 1.1 million are treated in and released from emergency departments; as many as 235,000 cases result in hospitalization. As many as 50,000 people die every year in the United States as a result of all forms of TBI. Subdural hematoma is the leading cause of brain-related death among participating athletes in the United States, according to the National Center for Catastrophic Sport Injury Research at the University of North Carolina at Chapel Hill.

Children younger than 15 years represent the majority of all cases of TBI; during the period of time under discussion, they represented as many as 475,000 cases each year. A more interesting, and perhaps speculative, statistic suggests that many more TBIs are sustained annually in the United States for which care is either not sought in emergency departments or not sought at all. Adolescents are at an increased risk for second impact syndrome, in which a catastrophic injury results from returning to activity or full sport participation while still experiencing symptoms from a prior injury. Further, in almost every age group, the rate of TBI in the United States is higher for males than for their female counterparts for reasons that remain unclear to researchers at this time.[2]

Mechanisms and Causes of Brain Injury: From Cause to Protection

As discussed, cerebral concussions are a form of mild TBI that occur when an athlete sustains a direct blow to the head or when an indirect blow to the body causes the transmission of impulsive forces to the brain. The exact mechanisms that cause concussion remain elusive to researchers at this time. Notwithstanding, the human body is equipped to withstand many external forces; the head and brain are no exception to this. The brain has several structures that help protect it from external trauma: eight cranial bones enclose and protect the brain, the meninges are membranous connective tissue coverings that surround the brain and spinal cord, and the cerebrospinal fluid (CSF) provides a buoyant cushion around the brain and its structures. The CSF acts as a buoy for the central nervous system, reducing the damaging effects of brain trauma by spreading the force over a larger area. The CSF reduces the effective mass of the brain by 97%.[10] Leakage of the CSF at the level of the spine or into the middle ear in acute settings should trigger appropriate emergency transport to a medical facility. It has been reported that headaches caused by decreases in intracranial pressure may be a result of spontaneous leaks of CSF.[11]

The degree of complexity in quantifying the biomechanics of sport-related brain injury has led some people to question whether a comprehensive understanding of the dynamics of brain injury can ever be achieved.[12] Brain injury mechanisms all involve a near instant transfer of kinetic energy that requires either an absorption (acceleration) or release (deceleration). Although force is the product of mass and acceleration, little trade-off occurs between the two. For example, a high-velocity bullet may penetrate the skull and brain but not cause a concussion because the mass of the bullet is too small to impart the necessary kinetic energy to the head and brain.[13] In an alternative scenario more realistic to athletics, a larger projectile (e.g., soccer ball, lacrosse stick, or even an opponent) traveling at a lower speed and striking the head may more easily cause concussion. It is important to recognize that the forces imparted on the head cause the brain to be set in motion.

Prevention

A number of preventive measures and predisposing factors have been discussed in the context of athletic cerebral concussions. The obvious method of minimizing impacts transmitted to the brain is to wear properly fitted playing equipment, practice proper techniques, and respect playing rules at all times during athletic participation. A number of organizations have established standards for commercially available playing equipment. These organizations include, but are not limited to, the National Operating Committee for Standards on Athletic Equipment, the Hockey Equipment Certification Council, and the Canadian Standards Association. Because all equipment has a limited lifespan of effective protection, coaches, parents, school or league officials, and the athletes themselves should ensure that young athletes are using adequate equipment.

Player Behaviors and Respect for Playing Regulations

Although the purpose of this chapter is not to speculate about the influence of coaches' and players' aggressive behaviors, it is difficult to ignore this aspect of athletics, and a brief discussion of this subject is warranted in the context of the current topic. Although some amateur athletic associations (e.g., USA Hockey and Hockey Canada) extensively promote sportsmanlike conduct, the culture of sport often predicates a mentality among players to ignore injury and to play recklessly. This behavior encourages unsportsmanlike conduct that may include disrespecting opponents and infracting upon playing regulations.

In a youth hockey study where 100% of coaches responded that sportsmanship was "real important," only 59% of players shared this attitude.[14] Parents and coaches, in this sample, viewed the enforcement of rules as being the most important factor in reducing all injuries, including cerebral concussions. These findings have some very natural extensions to other collision sports because the underlying message of "play within the rules" applies to all levels of competitive and recreational sport.

Previous Injury

The previous number of concussions sustained by an athlete is believed to be a predisposing factor for subsequent brain injuries. Why are athletes with a history of cerebral concussion more likely to sustain a subsequent brain injury? The neuromechanics behind this phenomenon are not yet clearly understood by researchers. Current theories on cause include mismanaged previous injuries, a lowering of the brain structure's injury threshold, and an increased likelihood that a previously injured athlete will recognize and report a subsequent brain injury to medical professionals.

Recognition and Management

The recognition of a cerebral concussion is usually not straightforward, with the exception of the athlete who has an observed bout of loss of consciousness ("getting knocked out") following a collision. Coaches or parents may not witness the injury in many instances. Loss of consciousness or altered central nervous system could occur with other conditions described in this text, making the blanket diagnosis of concussion with all cases of loss of consciousness incorrect. The large majority of concussions (approximately

90–95%) involves no loss of consciousness. The athlete will likely appear dazed, dizzy, and disoriented. In more obvious injurious collisions, the coach, parent, or nonmedical professional may observe an athlete struggling to stand on his or her own, not conforming to plays, or, in a more obvious scenario, not moving from the field following injury. Often, concussions are not identified at the time of injury unless an athlete approaches medical personnel and reports symptoms following a head injury. That said, the first step in recognizing brain injury begins in the preseason with educational interventions with players, coaches, and parents to teach the signs and symptoms of concussion, the importance of reporting them to medical professionals, and the injury management policies employed by the team.

The *signs* of cerebral concussion are those that can be observed by others. These signs may include any of the following: disorientation and momentary confusion, **retrograde amnesia**, **anterograde amnesia** (or posttraumatic amnesia), loss of consciousness (even for seconds), automatic behavior, unequal pupil size, combativeness, slowness to answer questions, loss of balance, and a change in typical behavior or personality.[15–17] *Symptoms* of cerebral concussion are those reported by the athlete. These usually include headache, nausea, balance problems or dizziness, tinnitus ("ringing in the ears"), diplopia (double vision) or blurred vision, changes in sleep patterns, problems with concentration or memory, irritability, sadness, and sensitivity to light or noise.[16]

Coaches should share a **graded symptom checklist** with players and parents, because this may help them identify that a concussion has been sustained in a player when they otherwise would have dismissed those signs and symptoms as a natural consequence of athletic participation. **Table 7.3** provides a sample 18-symptom graded symptom checklist. It should be noted that the graded symptom checklist is used not only for the initial symptom evaluation but also for each subsequent follow-up assessment, which should be periodically repeated until all postconcussion signs and symptoms have cleared at rest and during physical exertion.

There is currently no gold standard imaging technique capable of identifying concussion in athletes who otherwise do not report any symptoms. As was noted earlier in this chapter, concussion is a functional injury, and standard structural imaging techniques are not sensitive to this condition (i.e., they are not able to identify that it is present). In these cases, using the graded symptom checklist will often be the only way for coaches or parents to recognize the injury on the field.

Evaluation

In the past, the field and clinical assessments for brain injuries were often conducted independent of each other. This disjointed approach to managing the injury has been eliminated because the athlete's physician or athletic trainer will require information from the initial assessment conducted by the first responder, who may be a coach or parent. Information from the on-field assessment is quintessential in understanding the natural course of recovery that the athlete may expect to observe in a controlled clinical setting.

There are three primary objectives for the coach or parent dealing with a brain-injured athlete: (1) recognition of the injury and its severity, (2) immediate removal of the athlete from participation, and (3) referral to a physician or other trained medical personnel for follow-up. Performing a thorough initial evaluation can easily address the first of these objectives. As with the other catastrophic injuries presented throughout this text, a well-prepared protocol is the key to the successful initial evaluation of an athlete suspected of sustaining a brain injury or any other type of trauma.

On-Field Assessment

To help recognize a concussion, the following occurrences should be watched for and reported: (1) a forceful bump, blow, or jolt to the head or body that results in rapid movement of the head; and (2) any concussion signs or symptoms, such as a change in an athlete's behavior, thinking, or physical functioning. Unconscious athletes must always be managed by first dealing with life-threatening conditions such as obstructed airways, lack of breathing, excessive bleeding, and the possibility of spinal injuries. The coach's first and immediate actions in any instance of an unconscious athlete are to call 911 or his or her local

TABLE 7.3   Graded Symptom Checklist

	None	Mild		Moderate		Severe	
Headache	0	1	2	3	4	5	6
Nausea	0	1	2	3	4	5	6
Vomiting	0	1	2	3	4	5	6
Dizziness	0	1	2	3	4	5	6
Poor balance	0	1	2	3	4	5	6
Sensitivity to noise	0	1	2	3	4	5	6
Ringing in the ear	0	1	2	3	4	5	6
Sensitivity to light	0	1	2	3	4	5	6
Blurred vision	0	1	2	3	4	5	6
Difficulty concentrating	0	1	2	3	4	5	6
Feeling mentally "foggy"	0	1	2	3	4	5	6
Difficulty remembering	0	1	2	3	4	5	6
Trouble falling asleep	0	1	2	3	4	5	6
Drowsiness	0	1	2	3	4	5	6
Fatigue	0	1	2	3	4	5	6
Sadness	0	1	2	3	4	5	6
Irritability	0	1	2	3	4	5	6
Neck pain	0	1	2	3	4	5	6

Circle the appropriate number for each symptom experienced.

emergency number and ensure that the athlete's cervical spine (i.e., neck) is not permitted to move. The unconscious athlete should be transported from the field or court on a spine board with the head and neck immobilized. All coaches and members of the sports medicine team, if one exists, should rehearse basic life support procedures on a regular basis and remain current in their respective certifications in this area of emergency care. In settings where immediate access to the athletic trainer may be limited or not exist at all, these potentially life-saving procedures should be shared with all supervising personnel of student-athletes, including coaches, athletic directors, student volunteers, and school nurses, at a minimum. Potential red flags (i.e., conditions requiring immediate emergency transportation) include basilar skull fracture, including posterior auricular hematoma (battle sign; bruising behind the ears), otorrhea (CSF draining from the ear canal. CSF fluid may appear as clear fluid), cerebrospinal fluid rhinorrhea (CSF draining from the nose), and periorbital ecchymosis ("raccoon eyes" or bruising around the eyes) secondary to blood leaking from the anterior cavity of the skull. **Table 7.4** highlights the components of the primary and secondary survey involved with the on-field assessment of a brain-injured athlete that should be performed by most medical professionals trained in emergency management.

Once a blow to the head has been identified and there is reason to suspect a concussion, the coach or parent should assess the youth for possible signs (what they see) or symptoms (what the athlete tells them). The coach should attempt to gain as much information as possible about any (1) mental confusion, (2) loss of consciousness, and (3) amnesia. Confusion can be determined rather quickly by noting facial expression (dazed, stunned, glassy-eyed) and any inappropriate behavior such as running the wrong play

TABLE 7.4   On-Field Assessment

Primary Survey	Secondary Survey	
Establish level of consciousness	History	Mental confusion
Ensure open airway		Loss of consciousness
Check respirations (breathing)		Amnesia
Check cardiac status	Observation	Monitor eyes
Control significant hemorrhaging		Graded symptom checklist
Rule out life-threatening condition		Abnormal facial expressions, speech patterns, respirations, extremity movement, palpable deformities
	Palpation	Skull and cervical spine deformities
		Pulse and blood pressures (especially if deteriorating)

or returning to the wrong huddle. Questions of orientation (name, date, time, and place) may be asked; however, research suggests that orientation questions are not good discriminators between injured and noninjured athletes.[18] The coach should use a concussion symptom checklist similar to that found in Table 7.3 to facilitate the follow-up assessment of signs and symptoms.

The deterioration of signs and symptoms—including changing levels of consciousness—will indicate an emergent medical situation requiring immediate transportation to an emergency or neurosurgical department. For these procedures to occur in a timely and efficient manner, it is essential for the coaching staff's emergency action plan to include procedures for managing injury. The presence of trained emergency care providers is essential. Careful and thorough planning with local emergency medical personnel is critical. The first responder is ultimately responsible for identifying deteriorating conditions that would warrant immediate physician referral or transfer to the emergency department. **Table 7.5** presents a physician referral checklist. *Athletes should never be returned to play on the same day as a suspected cerebral concussion.*

TABLE 7.5   Red Flags Requiring Immediate Physician Referral

Day-of-Injury Referral

- Loss of consciousness on the field
- Amnesia lasting longer than 15 minutes
- Deterioration of neurologic function[a]
- Decreasing level of consciousness[a]
- Decrease or irregularity in respirations[a]
- Decrease or irregularity in pulse[a]
- Increase in blood pressure
- Unequal, dilated, or unreactive pupils[a]

TABLE 7.5   Red Flags Requiring Immediate Physician Referral (*Continued*)

Day-of-Injury Referral

- Cranial nerve deficits
- Any signs or symptoms of associated injuries, spine or skull fracture, or bleeding[a]
- Mental status changes: lethargy, difficulty maintaining arousal, confusion, agitation[a]
- Seizure activity[a]
- Vomiting
- Motor deficits subsequent to initial on-field assessment
- Sensory deficits subsequent to initial on-field assessment
- Balance deficits subsequent to initial on-field assessment
- Cranial nerve deficits subsequent to initial on-field assessment
- Postconcussion symptoms that worsen
- Additional postconcussion symptoms as compared with those on the field
- Athlete still symptomatic at the end of the game (especially at high school level)

Delayed Referral (after the day of injury)

- Any of the findings in the day-of-injury referral category
- Postconcussion symptoms worsen or do not improve over time
- Increase in the number of postconcussion symptoms reported
- Postconcussion symptoms begin to interfere with the athlete's daily activities (e.g., sleep disturbances, cognitive difficulties)

[a] Requires the athlete be transported immediately to the nearest emergency department.

Recovery

The majority of concussions sustained in athletics typically resolve in 5 to 7 days for collegiate athletes[8,19] but on average take longer in high school athletes.[20] It is important to clinically evaluate an injured athlete on a regular basis throughout the course of recovery by employing the use of graded symptom checklists and objective measures of postural stability and cognition. Coaches should recognize that approximately 10% of all concussions resolve along a prolonged recovery course, and in some cases it may take weeks or months for symptoms to resolve. Ensuring full recovery is paramount in protecting the athlete from adverse and potentially catastrophic outcomes such as second impact syndrome.

Second Impact Syndrome

As discussed earlier in the chapter, second impact syndrome occurs when an athlete sustains a second injury to the brain before the symptoms associated with the first have fully cleared.[21] Although rare, it is a well-documented cause of delayed catastrophic deterioration resulting in death or persistent vegetative state after a brain injury, caused by transtentorial brainstem herniation.[22] This condition is poorly understood, but it is thought to be a disruption of the brain's blood autoregulatory system that results in brain swelling and rapidly increasing intracranial pressure, leading to cerebral herniation.[23] The time from second impact syndrome to brainstem failure, and ultimately death, is usually 2 to 5 minutes.[21] Brainstem failure causes rapidly dilating pupils, loss of eye movement, respiratory failure, and eventually coma. On-field management of second impact syndrome should include rapid intubation. Unfortunately, the mortality rate of second impact syndrome is 50%, and the morbidity (or long-term complication) rate is 100%. Any athlete suspected of suffering from a concussion should *never* be permitted to return to activity until he or she has been cleared by a medical professional trained in the management of concussion.

Return to Play After Brain Injury

No athlete should resume participation while still symptomatic. Athletes should undergo a stepwise return-to-activity process once they are deemed asymptomatic and free of any postural, stability, or neurocognitive problems (see **Table 7.6**). Each step should typically take 24 hours, which will allow the coach and the sports medicine team ample time to determine whether a particular stage results in exacerbation of symptoms experienced by the athlete. Ultimately, the return-to-activity process should take approximately 5 to 7 days from the time at which the athlete first presents as symptom free to the medical team.[24]

A number of factors should also be considered when making decisions regarding an athlete's readiness to return to play following head injury. These include the athlete's previous history of concussion, the nature of the sport (contact vs. noncontact), and whether there are signs that the athlete's condition is deteriorating. In the event of a more serious brain injury (i.e., epidural or subdural hematoma), proper management should be supervised by a neurosurgeon, and full clearance to begin a graduated return-to-activity protocol should be authorized by the attending neurosurgeon. These cases are often more complicated than concussions, and decisions about whether to disqualify athletes from further competition or return them to play safely should be carried out on an individual basis. It is important for coaches and parents to work with their athletes' medical professional throughout this return-to-activity process.

TABLE 7.6   Graduated Return to Play Protocol

Rehabilitation Stage	Functional Exercise at Each Stage of Rehabilitation	Objective of Each Stage
1. No activity	Symptom-limited physical and cognitive rest	Recovery
2. Light aerobic exercise	Walking, swimming, or stationary cycling keeping intensity <70% maximum permitted heart rate; no resistance training	Increase heart rate
3. Sport-specific exercise	Skating drills in ice hockey, running drills in soccer; no head impact activities	Add movement
4. Noncontact training drills	Progression to more complex training drills (e.g., passing drills in football and ice hockey); may start progressive resistance training	Exercise, coordination, and cognitive load
5. Full contact practice	Following medical clearance, participate in normal training activities	Restore confidence and assess functional skills by coaching staff
6. Return to play	Normal game play	

Source: From McCrory P, Meeuwisse W, Aubry M, et al. Consensus statement on concussion in sport—the 4th International Conference on Concussion in Sport held in Zurich, November 2012. *Clin J Sport Med.* 2013; 23(2):89–117. Reprinted with permission.

Summary

The management of sport-related TBI has evolved considerably over the last 15 years. This evolution has brought technology and objective testing methods to the forefront of concussion management aimed at identifying neurologic deficits and preventing catastrophic outcomes. The increased emphasis on education and awareness has likewise played a major part in helping to prevent these injuries, but there is still a lot of work needed to progress in this area of patient care. The greatest influence that coaches can have on preventing catastrophic brain injuries is to educate parents and athletes about the recognition of concussion, the dangers of playing while symptomatic following a concussion, and how to better protect the brain while participating in contact sports. Instituting a preseason baseline testing program for concussion may be helpful, and a graduated exertional testing program should be included as part of every return-to-activity protocol to ensure the athlete can handle the added physical and cognitive stresses of his or her respective sport and academic responsibilities. Coaches must recognize that recovery and return-to-activity considerations involve many factors and that relying solely on self-report of symptoms can be dangerous. Clearly written documentation of serial evaluations conducted on the athlete is important for managing injury as well as for minimizing the risk of legal action in the event that an apparent mild TBI turns into something more serious.

Beyond improving the assessment and management of concussions, coaches must also recognize that catastrophic brain injuries such as subdural and epidural hematomas occasionally occur in sports, and they must be prepared to properly manage these potentially fatal injuries. In both cases, deterioration of signs and symptoms—including changing levels of consciousness—indicates an emergent medical situation requiring immediate transportation to an emergency or neurosurgical department. In most cases, a CT scan to locate the exact pathology will be conducted, followed by neurosurgical evacuation of the developing hematoma. For these procedures to occur in a timely and efficient manner, it is essential for the coach's emergency action plan to include procedures for managing injury. The presence of trained emergency care providers (e.g., physicians, athletic trainers, emergency medical services) is essential during games, practices, and sports where the incidence of concussions is high. Finally, athletic trainers, team physicians, emergency medical personnel, neurosurgeons, neurologists, and neuropsychologists must work together as a team to establish both an emergency action plan and a sound concussion assessment protocol to prevent brain-related sudden death.

Clinical Case Scenarios

1. Terry is a 16-year-old high school quarterback. In the middle of the second quarter, his offensive line breaks coverage and he is blindsided by the opposing linebacker during a first-and-ten play. He seems stunned on the field but rises to his feet under his own power a few seconds later and assembles the huddle as usual. The offensive coordinator observes that Terry proceeds to make the same play call for the ensuing two plays, and the star quarterback returns to the sideline as the punt team is sent on the field to complete the fourth-down play. One of the offensive linemen approaches the coach and mentions that something "just isn't right" with the quarterback. Upon further evaluation on the sideline, the coach identifies that Terry may have a concussion and informs him that he will not be returning to play on that day and not until he can follow up with a physician. Because of the coach's decision to keep him out of play, Terry was able to recover and return to football after missing only one game.

   a. What, if anything, could the coach have done differently to have better identified this head injury?

   b. If the athlete complained only of a headache and slight confusion, what other medical conditions might you suspect to be present?

2. Josie is a 15-year-old ice hockey player. She has been playing for the past 8 years and has ambitions to work toward a Division I collegiate scholarship. Last week she was involved in a minor

motor vehicle accident, after which she complained of a headache, had difficulty remembering the events leading up to the accident, and was confused. Standard diagnostic CT scans and MRI did not reveal any brain structure abnormalities, and she was promptly released from the emergency department with no real follow-up instructions. You are aware of the accident but think nothing of it because the emergency department discharged her. She returns to the ice 4 days later, where she loses her footing during a tournament and crashes into the end boards. She does not appear to be moving and lies motionless on the playing ice surface. The play is stopped and the on-ice official assists you safely over to her location on the playing surface.

   a. What would be the first things you seek to accomplish in managing this scenario?

   b. A basic primary survey is conducted, after which she is still unresponsive. She is showing signs of rapid deterioration. What condition(s) do you suspect, and what are your immediate actions in response?

   c. How might this scenario have been prevented, and what prevention programs might you implement to limit the chances of these brain injuries occurring?

Key Terms

anterograde amnesia

cerebral concussion

diffuse brain injury

epidural hematoma

graded symptom checklist

retrograde amnesia

second impact syndrome

subdural hematoma

References

1. Langlois JA, Rutland-Brown W, Wald MM. The epidemiology and impact of traumatic brain injury: a brief overview. *J Head Trauma Rehabil*. 2006;21(5):375–378.
2. Langlois JA, Rutland-Brown W, Thomas KE. *Traumatic Brain Injury in the United States: Emergency Department Visits, Hospitalizations, and Deaths*. Atlanta, GA: Centers for Disease Control and Prevention, National Center for Injury Prevention and Control; 2004.
3. Schneier AJ, Shields BJ, Hostetler SG, Xiang H, Smith GA. Incidence of pediatric traumatic brain injury and associated hospital resource utilization in the United States. *Pediatrics*. 2006;118(2):483–492.
4. McCrory P, Meeuwisse W, Johnston K, et al. Consensus statement on concussion in sport: the Third International Conference on Concussion in Sport held in Zurich, November 2008. *Clin J Sport Med*. 2009;19(3):185–200.
5. Gennarelli TA. Mechanisms of brain injury. *J Emerg Med*. 1993;11(suppl 1):5–11.
6. Schneider RC. *Head and Neck Injuries in Football*. Baltimore, MD: Williams & Wilkins; 1973.
7. American Academy of Neurology. Practice parameter: the management of concussion in sports (summary statement). Report of the Quality Standards Subcommittee. *Neurology*. 1997;48(3):581–585.
8. Guskiewicz KM, McCrea M, Marshall SW, et al. Cumulative effects associated with recurrent concussion in collegiate football players: the NCAA Concussion Study. *JAMA*. 2003;290(19):2549–2555.
9. Mueller FO, Colgate B. *Annual Survey of Football Injury Research: 1931–2009*. Chapel Hill, NC: National Center for Catastrophic Sport Injury Research; 2010.
10. Van De Graaff KM, Fox SI. *Concepts of Human Anatomy and Physiology*. 5th ed. Boston, MA: WCB/McGraw-Hill; 1999.
11. Mokri B. Headaches caused by decreased intracranial pressure: diagnosis and management. *Curr Opin Neurol*. 2003;16:319–326.
12. Shetter AG, Demakas JJ. The pathophysiology of concussion: a review. *Adv Neurol*. 1979;22:5–14.
13. Gurdjian ES, Lissner HR, Webster JE, Latimer FR, Haddad BF. Studies on experimental concussion: relation of physiologic effect to time duration of intracranial pressure increase at impact. *Neurology*. 1954;4:674–681.
14. Brust JD, Leonard BJ, Pheley A, Roberts WO. Children's ice hockey injuries. *Am J Dis Child*. 1992;146(6):741–747.
15. Hafen BQ, Karren KJ, Mistovich JJ. *Prehospital Emergency Care*. 5th ed. Upper Saddle River, NJ: Prentice Hall; 1996.

16. Collins MW, Lovell MR, McKeag DB. Current issues in managing sports-related concussion. *J Am Med Assoc.* 1999;282(24):2283–2285.

17. Arnheim DD, Prentice WE. *Principles of Athletic Training.* 9th ed. Boston, MA: WCB/ McGraw-Hill; 1997.

18. Maddocks DL, Dicker GD, Saling MM. The assessment of orientation following concussion in athletes. *Clin J Sport Med.* 1995;5(1):32–35.

19. McCrea M, Guskiewicz KM, Marshall SW, et al. Acute effects and recovery time following concussion in collegiate football players: the NCAA Concussion Study. *JAMA.* 2003;290(19):2556–2563.

20. Field M, Collins MW, Lovell MR, Maroon J. Does age play a role in recovery from sports-related concussion? A comparison of high school and collegiate athletes. *J Pediatr.* 2003;142(5):546–553.

21. Cantu RC, Voy R. Second impact syndrome: a risk in any contact sport. *Physician Sportsmed.* 1995;23(6):27–28.

22. McCrory P. Does second impact syndrome exist? *Clin J Sports Med.* 2001;11(3):144–149.

23. Bruce DA, Alavi A, Bilaniuk L, et al. Diffuse cerebral swelling following head injuries in children: the syndrome of "malignant brain edema." *J Neurosurg.* 1981;54(2):170–178.

24. McCrory P, Meeuwisse W, Aubry M, et al. Consensus statement on concussion in sport—the 4th International Conference on Concussion in Sport held in Zurich, November 2012. *Clin J Sport Med.* 2013;23(2):89–117.

Cervical Spine Injury

Erik E. Swartz, PhD, ATC, FNATA

From the Field Scenario

Karen was in her third year as head coach for the women's ice hockey team when during an afternoon practice a player accidentally collided with a teammate during a drill and fell face down, lying motionless on the ice. Karen and the athletic trainer (AT) assigned to the team hurried out to the ice to assess the situation. The AT's primary survey indicated that the player may have sustained a cervical spine injury, and he informed Karen of this. Because there was an emergency action plan already in place, Karen knew that her role at this point was to first call campus dispatch to report the emergency and then to assist the AT, along with the assistant coach, in log-rolling the player onto her back. The next step of the plan was to then commence removing her helmet and shoulder pads. Karen closely followed the commands of the AT, who was stabilizing the head of the player to prevent excessive movement, and they successfully removed her equipment so they would have direct access to her airway and chest should she be in need of life-saving measures. Karen, her assistant, three other players, and the AT then proceeded to go through previously rehearsed steps to perform a lift-and-slide transfer onto a spine board. An ambulance arrived at the same time the AT, Karen, and her assistant coach finished securing all of the spine board straps and the head immobilization device to the player. Because of the nature of the injury, the AT directed the paramedics to transport the player directly to the area's level I trauma center. As it turned out, the player did have a cervical spine fracture, but it was appropriately stabilized by the attending neurosurgeons within 2 hours of the initial injury. While the player's future playing ice hockey was at that point questionable, she was expected to make a full recovery.

Discussion Questions

1. What was the most important step taken that contributed to the successful management of this catastrophic neck injury?
2. What might have been the implications if the player had been transported to a hospital that was not prepared to handle a serious neurologic injury and then had to be transferred to the level I trauma center?
3. How might the injured player's teammates react to this situation and what strategies could be used to alleviate concerns they might have about sustaining serious injuries themselves?

Introduction

Sudden death in sports and athletics may occur from a serious, or catastrophic, cervical spinal cord injury. The incidence of catastrophic cervical spine injuries in the exercising individual is low,[1,2] yet when these injuries occur they are troubling because of high morbidity and the potential for permanent loss of neural function (i.e., **tetraplegia**). Cervical spine injuries have been reported in most contact sports, as well as in several noncontact sports such as skiing, track and field, cheerleading, diving, surfing, power lifting, and equestrian events. Proper, timely management and accurate diagnosis of acute spinal cord injuries is paramount because of the recognized risk of sudden death and neurologic deterioration during or after the **emergency management** process.[3,4]

Definition of Condition

A **catastrophic cervical spinal cord injury** (SCI) is one in which a structural distortion of the cervical spinal column has occurred and is associated with actual or potential damage to the spinal cord.[5] The neck consists of seven bones that make up what is known as the cervical spine (C1–C7), which serves as the link between the skull and the body. The cervical spine also contains a canal that carries the spinal cord from the brain to all of its branches to the rest of the body. These connections are responsible for the signals that are sent to the brain and received by the brain, referred to as the nervous system. The National Center for Catastrophic Sport Injury Research classifies catastrophic injuries as **direct injuries** (resulting from participation in the skills of a sport) or indirect injuries (resulting from systemic failure secondary to exertion while participating in a sport) and subdivides each classification into three categories: (1) fatal (the injury causes the death of the athlete), (2) nonfatal (the injury causes a permanent neurologic functional disability), and (3) serious (a severe injury, but the athlete has no permanent functional disability; for example, a fractured cervical vertebra that does not cause paralysis).[2]

A catastrophic cervical SCI infrequently results in sudden death, but the risk of death in the athlete increases in cases when the injury involves the C5 level and above, which can inhibit central nervous system control of breathing. Further compounding this condition is the risk of complications resulting from the complex biological reaction that occurs in the injured spinal cord during the 24 to 72 hours following the initial injury.[6,7] Therefore, immediate recognition and timely treatment in the prehospital setting, with close and careful emergency department management focusing on decompression of the spinal cord and controlling the secondary injury process, are critical.

Background and Occurrence of Cervical Spinal Cord Injury

An accurate incidence of sudden death caused by SCI in the United States is challenging to report. The National Spinal Cord Injury Statistical Center (NSCISC) collects and reports data regarding SCI in the United States, but it only collects data on those patients who are transported to one of the system's hospitals and therefore does not include those who die on the scene.[8,9] According to the NSCISC, there are an estimated 12,000 new cases of SCI in the United States each year.[9] Vehicle crashes constitute the most frequent cause of SCI, at 42%.[8] Sports participation constitutes the fourth most common cause (approximately 7.9%) of spinal injuries,[8] and for those younger than 30 years, it is the second most common cause after motor vehicle crashes.[10] Approximately 80% of SCIs occur in males.

Historically, American football has been associated with the highest rates of sudden death caused by catastrophic spinal injuries among all sports.[2] In 1968, 36 documented deaths occurred directly because of participation in American football alone.[2] Death caused by SCI from participation in American football has been dramatically reduced by rule changes enacted in 1976 to prevent head-first contact,[11] and a documented case of sudden death resulting from SCI in American football has not occurred in several years.[2] During the 2011 football season, there were 8 cervical SCIs with incomplete neurologic recovery, 7 of these injuries occurring in games.[1] Of concern is that between 2002 and 2011 there was an average of 9.4 cervical cord injuries with incomplete neurologic recovery, compared with the 10 years prior,

TABLE 8.1   Combined High School and College Catastrophic Injury Data in Select Sports

Sport and Setting	Direct Catastrophic Injuries	Direct Injury Incidence Rates (Nonfatal[a]) per 100,000
American football (M)		
High school	699	0.83
College	147	1.74
Gymnastics		
High school	13	1.98 (M), 0.91 (F)
College	6	19.19 (M), 4.97 (F)
Ice hockey		
High school	21	1.18 (M), 2.47 (F)
College	12	3.85 (M), 0.00 (F)
Track and field		
High school	65	0.11 (M), 0.01 (F)
College	10	0.34 (M), 0.12 (F)
Lacrosse		
High school	13	0.42 (M), 0.00 (F)
College	11	1.86 (M), 1.76 (F)
Wrestling (M)		
High school	58	0.55
College	1	0.54
Cheerleading		
High school	46	N/A
College	23	N.A

Abbreviations: F, female; M, male.
[a] Nonfatal is defined as permanent severe functional disability.

Source: Data adapted from the National Center for Catastrophic Sport Injury Research, fall 1982 through spring 2009.

during which the average was 7.7 annual cervical cord injuries with incomplete recovery.[1] Clearly, the risk of serious SCI, and thus sudden death, associated with participation in American football persists.

It is important to recognize that epidemiologic data have established the risk of catastrophic SCI in other sports as well. Sports such as ice hockey,[12] skiing,[13] rugby,[14] gymnastics,[2] swimming and diving,[11] track and field (e.g., pole vaulting),[2,15] cheerleading,[2,16] and baseball[17] all involve activities that place participants at risk for SCI and sudden death. In fact, the incidence of nonfatal, direct catastrophic injuries in the sports of lacrosse, gymnastics, and men's ice hockey is higher than in American football (see **Table 8.1**).[2]

Mechanisms and Causes of Spinal Cord Injury

The most common mechanism of injury in sports leading to a cervical SCI is an **axial load**,[18,19] in which the neck is flexed and the head serves as a point of contact, such as when diving into a pool or leading with the head during blocking or tackling. Large compressive forces are

axial load   A situation in which the neck is flexed between 20° and 30° and the head serves as a point of contact.

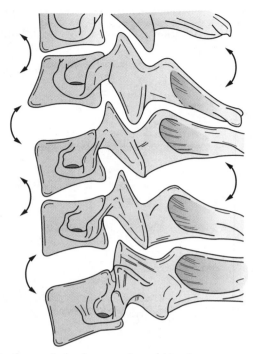

Figure 8.1 Buckling effect in the cervical column under axial load.

Source: Reprinted with permission from Swartz EE, Floyd RT, Cendoma M. Cervical spine functional anatomy and the biomechanics of injury due to compressive loading. *J Athl Train.* 2005;40(3):152–158.

transferred to the cervical spine because contact at the top of the head has stopped its forward motion, but the weight of the torso continues to move in the same direction. This creates a buckling effect in the cervical spine. This buckling releases the additional strain energy that has been produced because of the compression and is the cause of the injury (see **Figure 8.1**).[20,21] The resultant injury may be a cervical fracture, dislocation, disc herniation, torn ligaments, or a combination of these, which invades the space naturally surrounding the spinal cord and physically comes into contact with it, causing acute tissue trauma. The most common level of SCI in sports is at the C4 to C5 level.[22] Even though in most cases the spinal cord will not be torn completely, permanent neurologic dysfunction, paralysis, and even death can still occur.

Prevention

Certain precautions can be taken to help avoid catastrophic cervical spine injury. These precautions include attempting to control or avoid extrinsic and intrinsic predisposing factors of acute cervical spine injury, examples of which are given in **Table 8.2**. Extrinsic factors are generally outside the control of the exercising individual, especially in respect to accidental contact to the crown of the head because of a fall or unintentional contact with another object (e.g., the ground), participant, or piece of equipment (e.g., goalpost). Intrinsic factors (in most cases) can be controlled, and every effort should be made to do so in order to help prevent catastrophic cervical spine injury in athletes. Preventive steps can be categorized into setting-specific and athlete-specific measures.[1,2,23,24]

Setting-Specific Preventive Measures

- Individuals responsible for coordinating the use of facilities for sports and exercise should ensure that the conditions, setup, physical environment, and implementation of the activity are safe and minimize the risk of cervical spine injury.
- Individuals responsible for coordinating athletic events and the use of facilities for sports and exercise that carry a risk of cervical spine injury should ensure that such events are covered by physicians, certified ATs, or emergency service personnel.

TABLE 8.2   Examples of Risk Factors for Cervical Spine Injury

Extrinsic Risk Factors	Intrinsic Risk Factors
No emergency plan to identify and treat cervical spine injury	Improper technique, such as leading with the head into contact
Lack of education and awareness of causes of cervical spine injury among coaches when instructing and training athletes	Poor physical conditioning
	Lack of adherence to rules enacted to protect the participant from cervical spine injury
Faulty athletic gear	Performing skills or stunts without receiving proper training, such as in cheerleading or gymnastics
Improperly placed or secured sporting equipment (e.g., goalposts or gymnastics beams) or lack of signs indicating risk (e.g., poolside indications of depth of water)	Lack of awareness of the athletic environment where unsecured equipment such as goalposts poses a threat of spine injury
Failure to restrict exposure to areas that pose danger, such as throwing areas for javelin and discus or athletic fields with equipment, when no supervision is present	Lack of confirmation of the presence or readiness of spotters in gymnastics or cheerleading prior to performing activities that pose a threat of spine injury
Faulty emergency equipment	
Not fitting protective equipment properly, altering protective equipment against recommendations, or neglecting to maintain or recertify equipment	Not wearing protective equipment properly or altering protective equipment against recommendations
Officials not calling penalties for illegal play known to cause cervical spine injury, such as helmet contact or checking from behind in hockey	Predisposing medical conditions, such as cervical stenosis, spina bifida, or Klippel-Feil syndrome

- Individuals responsible for coordinating and administering organized sports and activities should arrange to have a sports medicine professional, such as an AT, physician, or other qualified emergency medical personnel, present in order to respond to potential SCIs in a timely manner.
- Individuals responsible for teaching, coaching, or training, as well as those responsible for the emergency care of athletes, should be familiar with safety rules enacted for the prevention of cervical spine injuries and should take actions to ensure that such rules are followed.
- Individuals responsible for teaching, coaching, or training, as well as those responsible for the emergency care of athletes, should be familiar with sport-specific causes of catastrophic cervical spine injury and understand the acute physiologic response of the spinal cord to injury.
- Spotters should be used in activities such as cheerleading and gymnastics.
- Individuals responsible for the emergency care of athletes, athletes themselves, coaches, and parents should be familiar with pertinent protective equipment manufacturers' recommendations and specifications relative to fit and maintenance. Maintaining the integrity of protective equipment minimizes the risk of injury.
- Individuals responsible for the emergency care of athletes should educate coaches and athletes about the mechanisms of catastrophic spine injuries, the dangers of head-down contact, and pertinent safety rules enacted for the prevention of cervical spine injuries.
- Planning in advance for events carrying a risk of cervical spine injury should include preparation of a venue-specific emergency action plan. Components of the emergency action plan

immobilization The use of external stabilization devices such as extrication collars and a spine board with straps to secure an injured patient's body so that it will not move during transport or emergency treatment.

include appointing a team leader and acquiring appropriate equipment to facilitate stabilization (see **Table 8.3**), **immobilization**, and removal of treatment barriers, if appropriate (i.e., sporting equipment). The emergency action plan should also incorporate communication with local emergency medical services (EMS) and identification of the most appropriate emergency care facility to receive the injured athlete. These groups should be involved in creating the emergency action plan.

• All individuals responsible for the care of athletes should be involved in regular (at least annual) rehearsals of the emergency action plan, as well as training and practice in the special skills required to manage a cervical spine injury. Skills that require training and regular practice may include manual head and neck stabilization techniques, the multiple methods of transferring injured athletes (e.g., log rolling, lift-and-slide techniques), equipment management (e.g., gaining access to the airway or chest), and immobilization methods (e.g., long spine board, cervical collar application).

Athlete-Specific Preventive Measures

• Participants in sports and exercise should be conditioned and trained to the level necessary to safely participate.
• Participants in sports and exercise should be familiar with sport-specific causes of catastrophic cervical spine injury and avoid behaviors that increase the risk of sustaining acute SCI.
• Participants in sports or activities known to carry risk of SCI should have complete medical examinations that include identifying factors that increase the risk or severity of an SCI (e.g., cervical stenosis) prior to participating.
• Participants in sports and exercise should be familiar with the specific safety rules enacted for the prevention of cervical spine injuries and should take actions to ensure they follow such rules

---

TABLE 8.3   Equipment List for Items That May Be Needed in the Emergency Treatment of a Catastrophic Cervical Spinal Cord Injury

Pocket mask

Artificial airways bag-valve-mask

Cervical collar

Spine board

Straps to secure the athlete to the spine board

Tape to secure head

Head-immobilization device

Wrist straps or tape to secure the patient's hands together on spine board

Various sizes of padding or toweling to fill gaps during immobilization

EMT shears or scissors to cut jerseys, pads, or straps

Reflex hammer with flat handle to detach cheek pads

Cordless, powered screwdriver and face mask removal cutting tools

Automated external defibrillator

Abbreviation: EMT, emergency medical technician.

(e.g., regarding helmet-to-helmet contact or checking from behind) for their own safety and the safety of others.

- Participants in sports and exercise should be familiar with pertinent protective equipment manufacturers' recommendations and specifications relative to fit and maintenance. Maintaining the integrity of protective equipment helps to minimize the risk of injury and enhances treatment by emergency responders in the event of an injury.

Recognition and Management of Spinal Cord Injury

Recognition of a potential catastrophic cervical spine injury occurs in two phases. An initial recognition, or awareness, phase for a potential acute cervical spine injury occurs when a common injury mechanism is witnessed, such as being checked into the boards in ice hockey from behind or striking a player with the top of the helmet in football. The injury mechanism itself is not always witnessed, so the initial recognition may come about by observing that an athlete has remained down, or inactive, following a play. However it comes about, this initial recognition should heighten the awareness of coaches, teammates, parents, or emergency responders that the potential for SCI exists.

The assessment phase, discussed in greater detail in the textbook *Preventing Sudden Death in Sport and Physical Activity*,[25] involves determining the presence of injury and the extent of disability. Coaches, teammates, and parents may perform an initial assessment for an injured athlete suspected of having a potential catastrophic cervical SCI. The first individual on the scene should look for the presence of any or all of the following four "red flags" that warrant activation of EMS or an established spine injury management protocol: (1) unconsciousness or altered level of consciousness (LOC), (2) neurologic findings or complaints on both sides of the body, (3) significant cervical spine pain, and (4) obvious spinal column deformity.[23,26,27] Although neurologic findings or complaints on only one side of the body may not necessarily indicate SCI, activation of EMS is recommended in the event that there is an underlying cervical spine or SCI. The following first two sections (primary survey and survey of the scene) are recommendations for the initial treatment of a suspected cervical spine injury for those who have an emergency first responder or similar certification. The best thing that coaches, parents, teammates, or anyone else who does NOT have any medical training can do in these situations is to activate the emergency response system and ensure the athlete is not moved unless the environment poses a significant threat to safety. The remaining actions should be performed only by a trained medical professional, but assistance from coaches, parents, and teammates may aid in providing optimal care.

Management of Spinal Cord Injury

Primary Survey

Once emergency responders have become aware of a potential cervical SCI, they should approach the situation as they would any emergency and perform a primary survey because at this time little to nothing is known about the extent of the injury. These steps focus on assessing the ABCDEs of standard trauma management: *a*irway, *b*reathing, *c*irculation, *d*isability, and *e*xposure. However, two important steps must first be taken during the primary survey: surveying the scene and applying manual cervical stabilization.

Survey of the Scene

An abbreviated survey of the scene within the immediate area of the injured athlete must be performed to determine whether the scene is safe for patient management. A survey of the scene in the athletic environment ensures that the athlete(s) involved, and those responsible for their treatment, are exposed to no further threat or danger by remaining at the initial area of the injury. An example would be a gymnastics event rescue where a large piece of equipment was not properly secured and now makes it dangerous to continue the treatment in the immediate area. This step should be initiated simultaneously while approaching the injured athlete(s) and in most cases can be completed even before arriving at the athlete's side, wasting no time in continuing with the primary survey.

Manual Cervical Spine Stabilization

When a potential spine injury is suspected, a qualified emergency responder (i.e., AT, paramedic, physician, or emergency medical technician [EMT]) should immediately apply manual cervical spine stabilization.[23,26] The rescuer should position his or her hands so the thumbs are pointed toward the face of the injured athlete. This technique ensures that hand placement does not have to be changed with repositioning of the injured person, unless rolling from a prone (face down) to a supine (face up) position, for which the rescuer's arms should be crossed before rolling. Rescuers should not apply traction to the cervical spine because this may cause distraction at the site of injury.[28] If the rescuer is alone, it may be appropriate to use the knees to maintain spine stabilization, thus freeing the rescuer's hands to assist with ventilation or conduct further tests.

Neutral Alignment

If the spine is not in a neutral position, a qualified emergency responder such as an AT, paramedic, physician, or EMT should realign the cervical spine back to neutral, if possible.[23,26] Neutral alignment of the head and neck is the optimal position for immobilization of an injured cervical spine.[29, 30] **Neutral alignment** of the spine is recommended for airway management procedures and facilitates the application of cervical immobilization devices. More important, the space within the spinal canal, or **space available for the cord (SAC)**, must be maintained for proper functioning of the spinal cord and optimal tissue perfusion, thus reducing spinal cord morbidity.[27,31,32]

However, the presence or development of any of the following, alone or in combination, while moving the head back to neutral is a contraindication for this action: the movement causes increased pain, neurologic symptoms, muscle spasm, or airway compromise; it is physically difficult to reposition the spine; resistance is encountered during the attempt at realignment; or the patient expresses apprehension.[23,27]

It is important to keep in mind that if the airway becomes compromised at any time thereafter, the head and neck will need to be aligned to facilitate airway support. Once the decision has been made that the potential exists for a catastrophic cervical SCI, rescuers should immediately attempt to expose the airway by removing any existing barriers. The airway should be kept open and clear of any obstructions. Potential instability in the cervical spine because of an injury necessitates careful airway management procedures in case rescue breathing or introduction of an artificial airway becomes necessary. If rescue breathing becomes necessary, the individual with the most training and experience should establish an airway and commence rescue breathing using the safest technique.[23,27] During airway management, rescuers should cause as little motion as possible.[27] The jaw-thrust maneuver is recommended over the head-tilt technique, which produces unnecessary motion at the head and in the cervical spine. Advanced airway management techniques (e.g., laryngoscope, endotracheal tube) are recommended in the presence of appropriately trained and certified rescuers; these methods have been shown to allow for rapid airway establishment and cause less motion, and therefore they are less likely to worsen the injury.[27, 33]

Primary Assessment

The injured patient's breathing and circulation should also be assessed. This is done through visual observation of the nose, mouth, and chest and listening (through auscultation if possible) and feeling for normal breathing and pulse. Normal breathing is verified by counting the number of breaths per minute (BPM), which should be between 10 and 30. The exercising individual has likely just been participating in a sporting event that may yield breathing rates closer to 30 BPM. The patient's circulation, and an impression of the patient's blood pressure, is determined through assessing the carotid, femoral, and radial pulses. The patient's pulse should be evaluated for its quality (strong, weak), rate (abnormally fast or slow), and rhythm (normal, abnormal, or asynchronous). Any signs of airway blockage, absence of or irregular breathing, or absence of or diminished circulation should be addressed before any other action is taken.

If it has been concluded that the injured patient's airway, breathing, and circulation are all okay, then an abbreviated assessment of the patient's neurologic status must be performed to determine the extent of disability. The patient's LOC is established by determining his or her ability to respond to verbal or painful stimuli. If there is no response, pinching the skin or firmly rubbing a knuckle into the patient's sternum should elicit a pain response. If the patient is completely unresponsive, even though he or she may be breathing normally, no further evaluation is necessary and the sports medicine team or emergency rescuers should immediately prepare the athlete for immobilization and transport. If the patient is alert and responsive, a general upper and lower extremity sensory test should be performed. Lightly brush the patient's skin bilaterally on both the upper and lower extremities and ask the patient if sensation was felt. While still maintaining stabilization of the head and neck, ask the patient to move his or her fingers and toes. A lack of sensation or inability to move a distal extremity alerts the emergency responder to impending neurologic involvement.

The final step of the primary survey is determining the degree to which one should expose the patient's body for examination. If certain signs (breathing, LOC) indicate a more serious situation, exposure of vital areas for treatment should be established. For example, exposure of the chest by removing equipment or jerseys for the application of an automated external defibrillator or removing the face mask to gain access to the airway may be necessary. If the rescue occurs outdoors or on a cold surface indoors (e.g., figure skating, ice hockey), rescuers should attempt to limit the amount or time of exposure to protect the athlete from becoming hypothermic.

Transfer and Immobilization

At this time or as soon as qualified emergency medical responders arrive on the scene, manual stabilization of the head should be converted to immobilization using a combination of external devices (e.g., cervical collars, foam blocks). Application of a cervical collar in an equipment-intensive sport may be difficult or impossible with the decreased space between helmets and shoulder pads. Regardless, a combination of padding (e.g., foam blocks, towels), rigid collar application, and taping to a backboard or full-body splint is recommended.[29,34] Manual stabilization should be continued whether or not external stabilization devices are applied.[35]

After application of an external cervical immobilization device, the injured individual must be transferred to a full-body immobilization device. To achieve full spinal immobilization during on-field management of an injury, patients are typically transferred to and secured on a long spine board. The task of moving a patient to a spine board can prove challenging, because the head and trunk must be moved as a unit. Spine boarding athletes may present additional challenges, such as the size of the patient, the implications of equipment being worn, and sporting venue barriers or obstacles, such as spine boarding a patient from a swimming pool, a pole vault pit, or a gymnastics foam pit. A variety of techniques exist to move and immobilize the injured patient. Rescuers should use the technique that they have rehearsed and are most comfortable with and, most important, that produces the least amount of spinal movement in the given situation.[23]

Currently, certified ATs or emergency personnel typically perform a log roll onto a traditional spine board to stabilize and prepare a patient for transport.[23] The log-roll maneuver is versatile in that it can be used for a patient who is in a face-down or face-up position. For the patient lying in a face-down position, a prone log-roll transfer onto a full-body immobilization device may be performed. A standard prone log-roll maneuver has the rescuers positioned on the side toward which the injured patient will be rolled. An alternative prone log-roll technique, referred to as the prone log-roll push, has the rescuers positioned on the side opposite to that of the immobilization device, performing a "push" maneuver to position the patient onto the immobilization device.[23] For patients who are lying face up, a supine log roll can be performed. Typically, log rolls are performed in two steps: the first step rolls the patient onto his or her side, either from prone or supine, at which point the immobilization device is positioned; the next step lowers the patient onto the immobilization device. Careful attention should be focused on the patient's position once lowered onto the board. Often the patient is not squarely placed onto the board and an adjustment is required. The person at the head remains in charge and should direct the others in their preferred method for realignment. The number of rescuers required to perform a log roll can range

Figure 8.2 A lift-and-slide transfer technique. The rescuers are performing a lift maneuver on a supine athlete. Observe the path the head travels during the execution of the lift, starting from the upper left image and ending at the lower right. The rescuer normally positioned at the head is removed for illustrative purposes.

Source: Swartz EE, Del Rossi G. *Sports Health* 1(3), pp. 247–252, copyright (c) 2009 by SAGE Publications. Reprinted by permission of SAGE Publications.

between two and seven. Specific protocols for performing log rolls may differ slightly, and step-by-step procedures can be found in many resources.[23]

lift and slide A transfer technique to a spine board for a potential spine-injured victim who is lying supine.

An alternative to the log roll is a lift-and-slide transfer technique, which includes the six-plus-person lift and the straddle **lift and slide**. In contrast to the log roll, in which the patient is rolled to his or her side and the spine board is positioned beneath him or her, with the lift and slide the patient is simply lifted off the ground to allow the spine board to be slid underneath. The premise behind the lift-and-slide technique is that the patient is lifted straight up by four to eight rescuers (see **Figure 8.2**), in contrast to rolling the body during a log roll; the former has been reported to create less motion in injured cervical spine cadaveric research studies.[36] In addition, this technique avoids the difficulty in synchronously rolling the injured patient's head and torso as one unit, as well as rolling the patient over the arm or bulky protective equipment, minimizing misalignment caused by proportional differences between the upper torso and lower body (see **Figure 8.3**).[37] A limitation is that the lift-and-slide technique may be used only for supine patients, whereas a prone patient must be log rolled for transfer to a spine board.

Regardless of the transfer technique used, individuals responsible for the emergency care of patients with cervical spine injuries should immobilize these patients with a long spine board or other full-body immobilization device. Although the traditional spine board represents the most common device used for full-body immobilization, devices such as the full-body vacuum splint are more comfortable for patients, reduce superficial irritation and sores over bony prominences, and may be used in appropriate situations.[38]

The Equipment-Intensive Patient

The treatment described in the previous section for the patient with a potential cervical SCI did not fully address the fact that many exercising individuals wear protective equipment. Exercising individuals wear helmets, face guards, mouth guards, and a variety of padding to shield their head, face, and other body parts from impacts sustained from sporting equipment (e.g., balls, pucks, bats, sticks) and playing surfaces (e.g., court, turf, walls) or from collisions with other participants; this equipment

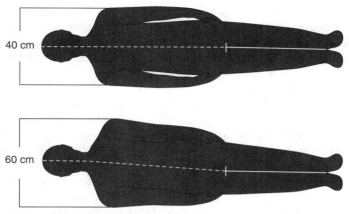

Figure 8.3 Lateral displacement in the log-rolled individual because of proportional differences in the upper torso compared with the lower body. This effect may be exacerbated in an equipment-laden patient.

Source: Swartz EE, Del Rossi G. *Sports Health* 1(3), pp. 247–252, copyright (c) 2009 by SAGE Publications. Reprinted by permission of SAGE Publications.

has been used in a variety of sports for decades. Although the benefit of wearing protective equipment in reducing the number and severity of impact injuries is obvious, sometimes the equipment itself can act as a barrier to full access to the head, face, and chest for emergency life support measures, and in other cases the equipment may not allow for neutral alignment of the spine or adequate stabilization of the head when immobilized to a spine board. Rescuers are faced with making a decision about whether it is appropriate to remove these pieces of protective equipment to facilitate treatment and immobilization in neutral alignment.

Only those with specialized training should remove such equipment, such as a certified AT. The National Athletic Trainers' Association position statement[23] on the acute care of the cervical spine–injured athlete states that regardless of the sport or the equipment being used, two underlying principles should guide management of the equipment-laden athlete with a potential cervical spine injury:

1. Exposure and access to vital life functions (airway, chest for cardiopulmonary resuscitation or use of an automated external defibrillator) must be established or easily achieved in a reasonable and acceptable manner.
2. Neutral alignment of the cervical spine should be maintained while allowing as little motion at the head and neck as possible.[23]

When emergency responders adhere to these guidelines when responding to a cervical SCI in an equipment-intensive activity, their actions regarding what to do with any type of protective equipment will be dictated accordingly. It must be stressed that staying up to date on current evidence-based management recommendations and changes in equipment use or design should remain a priority so that the treatment applied in any given situation can be as effective as possible. Keeping in mind the two underlying principles just listed, the following sections review the evidence from current research pertaining to recommendations that can be made for specific sports or types of equipment. It should be emphasized that equipment-specific and sport-specific recommendations can quickly become outdated as changes in design and technology continue to occur.

Football

In the sport of American football, the protective face mask of the football helmet impedes **airway access** during management of a potentially catastrophic head or neck injury and must be removed if the injured patient needs airway support. However, removal of a football helmet creates alterations in the position of adjacent cervical vertebrae,[39] and removal of a

airway access The ability to expose and maintain breathing through an injured patient's airway.

football helmet without removal of the shoulder pads or placing padding under the head places the cervical spine in a misaligned, hyperextended position.[40–42] Because of the concerns that exist relative to the motion created when removing a football helmet and because the helmet and shoulder pads in football players maintain neutral alignment of the cervical spine, current recommendations state that the helmet and shoulder pads should remain in place and that the face mask be removed in order to access the airway.[23]

There has been some research devoted to investigating the best method of face mask removal.[43–49] A cordless screwdriver has been reported to be faster[43,44] and easier to use[43] and to create less motion[43] at the head than many cutting tools used to remove the face mask. **Table 8.4** shows the results for time, motion, and difficulty for the cordless screwdriver compared with other cutting tools on one style of a football helmet face mask and loop strap.[43] Because of this research, the cordless screwdriver has been recommended for removal of the face mask.[43,45] However, relying solely on a screwdriver is risky because screws can fail to be removed because of problems with the helmet hardware (e.g., screws, T-nuts) such as corrosion and rust, which can cause the screw face to shred or the T-nut to spin with the screw while turning.[46] Studies have reported a failure rate of up to 16% in removing face mask screws with a cordless screwdriver.[46,47]

Because screw failure is a possibility, a combined-tool technique has been recommended.[46] This technique takes advantage of the efficiency found in using a cordless screwdriver, but in the event a screw fails to be removed, it provides the rescuer the added security of a backup cutting tool. This backup cutting tool must be appropriately matched to the helmet and loop strap type being used. Research investigating the success rates of this combined-tool technique found it to be an extremely reliable approach with a high rate of success (97–100%).[45,48]

Helmet, face mask, loop strap fasteners, and tool designs continually evolve. For example, recent changes in the design of some manufacturers' football helmets include a quick-release attachment system

---

TABLE 8.4   Means, Standard Deviations, and Effect Sizes for Time to Complete Task, Rate of Perceived Exertion, and Movement Variables for Tools with the Schutt Helmet and ArmourGuard Loop Strap Configuration

Dependent Variables	Screwdriver Mean ± SD($N = 15$)	FM Extractor Mean ± SD($N = 7$)	Trainer's Angel Mean ± SD($N = 9$)	Effect Size
Time(s)	47 ± 7.8[a, b]	160.6 ± 62.6	131 ± 28.9	0.710
RPE	2.1 ± 2.1[a]	5.9 ± 2.9	3.9 ± 1.1	0.362
Lateral flexion movement (°)	3.4 ± 1.4[a, b]	9.9 ± 4.5	7.8 ± 2.7	0.542
Flexion/extension movement (°)	7.6 ± 2[a, b]	14.6 ± 4.7	13.6 ± 6.1	0.398
Rotation movement (°)	3.2 ± 0.8[a, c]	7.7 ± 2.1[b]	4.7 ± 0.089	0.688

Abbreviations: FM, Face Mask; RPE, rate of perceived exertion; SD, standard deviation.
[a] Significantly different from FM Extractor ($P < 0.01$)
[b] Significantly different from Trainer's Angel ($P < 0.01$)
[c] Significantly different from Trainer's Angel ($P < 0.05$)

Source: Data from Swartz EE, Norkus S, Cappaert T, Decoster LC. Football equipment design affects face mask removal efficiency. *Am J Sports Med.* 2005;33(8):1210–1219.

for the face mask. Researchers have reported that such a device allows for quick and easy face mask removal that minimizes head motion when compared with traditional screw and T-nut–secured loop strap removal with a cordless screwdriver.[49]

There may be situations in which exposure of the head, chest, or body is necessary, and removal of the football helmet and shoulder pads may be required. Removal of the helmet and shoulder pads using four healthcare providers has been shown to be effective in limiting motion in the cervical spine of a healthy volunteer,[42] although other studies have provided conflicting results.[39] Different helmets may require different steps to prepare them for removal, such as deflating air cells within the helmet or removing cheek pads or the chin strap. Familiarity with current available equipment used in football, and in any activity for that matter, is extremely important.

Ice Hockey

In ice hockey, players lying supine with the helmet and shoulder pads left in place have neutral cervical spine alignment, and removing the helmet without padding underneath the head or also removing shoulder pads may alter that alignment.[50,51] Ice hockey helmets were reported to adequately immobilize the head of an athlete when secured on a spine board, provided the helmets were fitted correctly and securely.[52] These findings suggest that when an ice hockey player may have a cervical spine injury, the helmet should be left in place. However, Mihalik et al.[53] investigated head motion created during a prone log roll in hockey players wearing properly fitted helmets, improperly fitted helmets, and no helmets. The smallest amount of head motion occurred when the volunteers wore no helmet at all. With the improperly fitted helmets, the volunteers' heads moved independently within the helmet, suggesting that the rescuers would be unable to obtain appropriate head immobilization during transfer or transport if the helmet were left on. It is also important to note that the face guards used in ice hockey may vary depending on level of play (e.g., full cage, plastic visor) and are not easily removable. These factors suggest that when an ice hockey player is suspected of having a cervical spine injury, the helmet should be carefully removed. Again, individual situations will determine the necessary steps.

Lacrosse

For supine lacrosse players, equipment may not create the same neutral positioning of the cervical spine as that created for football and ice hockey players.[54,55] Whether this misalignment actually affects the critical SAC has been questioned.[54] Lacrosse helmets were previously reported to provide head immobilization when an athlete was immobilized on a spine board, provided the helmet was applied correctly and fitted securely.[52] However, more recent research found that the best immobilization of healthy collegiate lacrosse athletes was in a no-equipment condition compared with conditions in which helmets were both improperly and properly fit.[56] These findings suggest that leaving the equipment in place precludes neutral alignment of the cervical spine and may not provide adequate stabilization of the head. Finally, in many lacrosse helmets the face masks are not easily removed. Based on these factors, the lacrosse helmet may need to be removed on the field in an athlete with a suspected SCI.[23]

Other Equipment-Intensive Activities

Additional data for the many other equipment-laden sports and recreational activities, such as horseback riding, downhill skiing, baseball, softball, field hockey (goalies), and mountain biking, are not available. When dealing with a suspected catastrophic cervical SCI in patients in these sports, adhering to the two underlying principles of managing the equipment-laden athlete dictates the necessary steps in making decisions about **equipment removal** during the management process.[23] For example, participants in several of the sports just listed wear only a helmet. This is likely to take the spine out of neutral alignment, requiring the rescuer to remove the helmet to establish neutral alignment.

> **equipment removal** Skills executed in an emergency injury situation to remove protective equipment that interferes with the ability to effectively treat or immobilize a victim.

In summary, for the equipment-intensive athlete, the rescuer should perform whatever tasks are necessary to comply with the underlying principles for the acute management of the equipment-intensive SCI athlete. If an athlete who is wearing a helmet and shoulder pads has a potential cervical spine injury and the helmet does not provide adequate immobilization or cervical spine alignment, or if face mask removal is not possible, the rescuer may need to remove the helmet. If time and personnel allow, the shoulder pads should also be removed. If time or resources do not allow simultaneous removal of the helmet and shoulder pads, then foam padding or a similar article (e.g., folded towel) should be placed under the head of the patient to maintain neutral alignment in the cervical spine.[23]

Transportation and the Emergency Department

An AT, team physician, coach, or parent should accompany the injured patient to the hospital. This practice increases communication and allows any available sports medicine professionals to assist emergency department personnel during equipment removal. Unfortunately, this may be difficult or impossible in some settings.[23] Communication between sports medicine and emergency department staff during the emergency planning phase is important. Hospital personnel may be unfamiliar with athletic equipment, including helmets, face masks, visors, shoulder pads, and chest protectors. At a minimum, hospital personnel should understand standards of on-field care for the athlete with a potential SCI and should receive training regarding the proper approach to equipment removal. Sports medicine professionals can be a resource for such information, simultaneously increasing communication and improving collegiality. Improved communication between the sports medicine team and hospital personnel can only enhance the care delivered.[23]

As can likely be appreciated from this section on treatment, the acute care of a potentially catastrophic cervical spine–injured athlete can be complicated. It is important to remember that each situation will be unique and that blanket recommendations for all spine-injured patients may not be appropriate. Given that caveat, **Figure 8.4** is a flowchart that illustrates the process of the acute treatment of a cervical SCI from emergency planning through transport to serve merely as a guide for approaching these injuries.

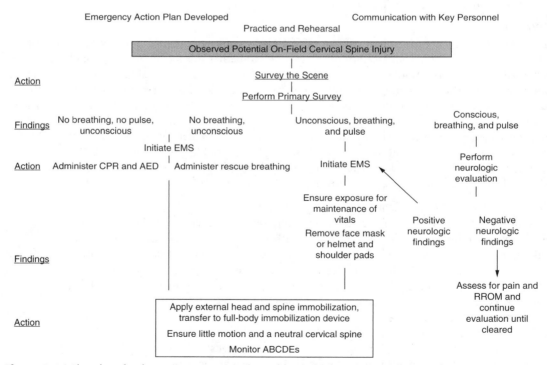

Figure 8.4 Flowchart for the acute treatment of an athlete who has a potential cervical spine injury. AED, automated external defibrillator; CPR, cardiopulmonary resuscitation; EMS, emergency medical services; RROM, resistive range of motion.

Recovery

Animal model research has suggested that recovery from and long-term prognosis after catastrophic cervical spine injury are directly related to the severity, or magnitude, of the initial tissue trauma and the duration of compression to the spinal cord.[32] The less tissue involved and the shorter the duration of compression to the cord, the more favorable the outcome. In addition, retrospective studies have reported that outcomes for SCI become more favorable as the SAC surrounding the level of injury in the spinal canal increases.[57] A systematic review that examined the outcomes of actual SCI patients based on the time of decompression surgery indicates that more favorable outcomes will come with urgent decompression surgery performed in under 72 or even 24 hours.[58]

An individual's recovery from SCI is difficult to predict, considering that the extent of his or her permanent disability, or final degree of injury, may not be determined for up to 72 hours or more following the injury itself. Whenever the extent of injury is determined, the factors that then determine the SCI individual's recovery will include the extent of the primary and secondary injury response, surgical invasiveness and extent of repair, age, previous level of conditioning, current health, and quality of continuing care and rehabilitation support.

Recovery from cervical SCI may be complete, meaning there is no permanent neurologic impairment within 1 year following the injury. The level of recovery for an SCI individual may also be incomplete, meaning there is not a complete resolution of the neurologic complications beyond 1 year following the injury. Incomplete recovery may mean that there is either partial neurologic recovery that has resulted in a paraplegic, or tetraplegic, state or that the injury has had no neurologic recovery and has left the individual quadriplegic.[2]

Return to Play Issues

Athletes should be returned to play only when they are asymptomatic, with full, pain-free range of motion of the cervical spine and a normal neurologic examination, and the athlete does not have a congenital or developmental contraindication to returning to contact or collision sports.[59] The decision to return an athlete to play after a cervical spine injury occurs on a case-by-case basis and should be based on the type of injury, persistence of symptoms, recurrence of injury, sports played, and the amount of risk of future injuries with each sport played. Rule changes in sport and emphasis on proper technique should be addressed when appropriate.

Summary

Although sudden deaths caused by catastrophic cervical spine injuries are relatively rare, the nature of collision sports and the unpredictability of accidental injury in any sport demand that steps be taken to prevent and prepare for them. Time is critical, and the effective execution of the skills necessary to manage a suspected catastrophic cervical spine injury could mean the difference between saving a life or preventing permanent neurologic outcome, and death or permanent neurologic damage for the athlete.

Clinical Case Scenario

1. Jay is a 6-foot, 220-pound defenseman for the local semiprofessional ice hockey team. During the second period an opposing player checks Jay from behind as he approaches his own defensive corner of the ice in pursuit of a loose puck. Jay falls forward and collides into the boards head first. The officials immediately call the penalty, and play is stopped. Jay is lying face down in the corner of the ice against the boards and is not moving. The AT has seen the entire play and immediately suspects that Jay may have suffered a serious head or neck injury.
   a. What are the initial steps that should be taken during the assessment phase?
   b. What challenges is the AT faced with?
   c. What steps must be taken if the assessment reveals that the athlete is not breathing?

Key Terms

airway access

axial load

catastrophic cervical spinal cord injury

direct injury

emergency management

equipment removal

immobilization

indirect injury

lift and slide

neutral alignment

space available for the cord (SAC)

tetraplegia

References

1. Mueller FO, Cantu RC. *Annual Survey of Catastrophic Football Injuries 1977–2011*. Chapel Hill, NC: University of North Carolina; 2010.
2. Mueller FO, Cantu RC. *Twenty-Ninth Annual Report, Fall 1982–Spring 2011*. Chapel Hill, NC: National Center for Catastrophic Sport Injury Research, University of North Carolina; 2010.
3. Masini M, Alencar MR, Neves EG, Alves CF. Spinal cord injury: patients who had an accident, walked but became spinal paralysed. *Paraplegia*. 1994;32:93–97.
4. Toscano J. Prevention of neurological deterioration before admission to a spinal cord injury unit. *Paraplegia*. 1988;26:143–150.
5. Banerjee R, Palumbo MA, Fadale PD. Catastrophic cervical spine injuries in the collision sport athlete, part 1: epidemiology, functional anatomy, and diagnosis. *Am J Sports Med*. 2004;32:1077–1087.
6. Hulsebosch CE. Recent advances in pathophysiology and treatment of spinal cord injury. *Adv Physiol Educ*. 2002;26:238–255.
7. Tator CH. Experimental and clinical studies of the pathophysiology and management of acute spinal cord injury. *J Spinal Cord Med*. 1996;19:206–214.
8. National Spinal Cord Injury Statistical Center. *The 2007 Annual Statistical Report for the Spinal Cord Injury Model Systems*. Birmingham, AL: National Spinal Cord Injury Statistical Center, University of Alabama–Birmingham; 2008.
9. National Spinal Cord Injury Statistical Center. *Spinal Cord Injury: Facts and Figures at a Glance*. Birmingham, AL: National Spinal Cord Injury Statistical Center, University of Alabama–Birmingham; 2008.
10. Nobunaga A, Go B, Karunas R. Recent demographic and injury trends in people served by the model spine cord injury case systems. *Arch Phys Med Rehabil*. 1999;80:1372–1382.
11. Torg JS. Epidemiology, pathomechanics, and prevention of athletic injuries to the cervical spine. *Med Sci Sports Exerc*. 1985;17:295–303.
12. Tator CH, Carson JD, Edmonds VE. Spinal injuries in ice hockey. *Clin Sports Med*. 1998;17:183–194.
13. Hagel BE, Pless B, Platt RW. Trends in emergency department reported head and neck injuries among skiers and snowboarders. *Can J Public Health*. 2003;94:458–462.
14. Scher AT. Rugby injuries to the cervical spine and spinal cord: a 10-year review. *Clin Sports Med*. 1998;17:195–206.
15. Boden BP, Pasquina P, Johnson J, Mueller FO. Catastrophic injuries in pole-vaulters. *Am J Sports Med*. 2001;29:50–54.
16. Boden BP, Tacchetti R, Mueller FO. Catastrophic cheerleading injuries. *Am J Sports Med*. 2003;31:881–888.
17. Boden BP, Tacchetti R, Mueller FO. Catastrophic injuries in high school and college baseball players. *Am J Sports Med*. 2004;32:1189–1196.
18. Cantu RC, Mueller FO. Catastrophic football injuries: 1977–1998. *Neurosurgery*. 2000;47:673-675; discussion 675–677.
19. Torg JS. Epidemiology, pathomechanics, and prevention of football-induced cervical spinal cord trauma. *Exerc Sport Sci Rev*. 1992;20:321–338.
20. Nightingale RW, McElhaney JH, Richardson WJ, Best TM, Myers BS. Experimental impact injury to the cervical spine: relating motion of the head and the mechanism of injury. *J Bone Joint Surg Am*. 1996;78:412–421.
21. Nightingale RW, McElhaney JH, Richardson WJ, Myers BS. Dynamic responses of the head and cervical spine to axial impact loading. *J Biomech*. 1996;29:307–318.
22. Torg JS. Epidemiology, biomechanics, and prevention of cervical spine trauma resulting from athletics and recreational activities. *Operative Tech Sports Med*. 1993;1(3):159–168.

23. Swartz EE, Boden BP, Courson RW, et al. National Athletic Trainers' Association position statement: acute management of the cervical spine-injured athlete. *J Athl Train*. 2009;44:306–331.

24. Andersen J, Courson RW, Kleiner DM, McLoda TA. National Athletic Trainers' Association position statement: emergency planning in athletics. *J Athl Train*. 2002;37:99–104.

25. Casa, D. *Preventing Sudden Death in Sport and Physical Activity*. Burlington, MA: Jones & Bartlett Learning; 2012.

26. Banerjee R, Palumbo MA, Fadale PD. Catastrophic cervical spine injuries in the collision sport athlete, part 2: principles of emergency care. *Am J Sports Med*. 2004;32:1760–1764.

27. Crosby ET. Airway management in adults after cervical spine trauma. *Anesthesiology*. 2006;104:1293–1318.

28. Kaufman HH, Harris JH Jr, Spencer JA, Kopanisky DR. Danger of traction during radiography for cervical trauma. *JAMA*. 1982;247:2369.

29. De Lorenzo RA. A review of spinal immobilization techniques. *J Emerg Med*. 1996;14:603–613.

30. Tierney RT, Maldjian C, Mattacola CG, Straub SJ, Sitler MR. Cervical spine stenosis measures in normal subjects. *J Athl Train*. 2002;37:190–193.

31. Delamarter RB, Sherman J, Carr JB. Pathophysiology of spinal cord injury. Recovery after immediate and delayed decompression. *J Bone Joint Surg Am*. 1995;77:1042–1049.

32. Carlson GD, Gorden CD, Oliff HS, Pillai JJ, LaManna JC. Sustained spinal cord compression, part I: time-dependent effect on long-term pathophysiology. *J Bone Joint Surg Am*. 2003;85A:86–94.

33. Burkey SM, Jeanmonod R, Fedor P, Stromski C, Waninger K. Evaluation of standard endotracheal intubation, assisted laryngoscopy (AirTraq), and laryngeal mask airway in the airway management of the helmeted football player. *Clin J Sport Med*. 2010;20(2):136–137.

34. Hamilton RS, Pons PT. The efficacy and comfort of full-body vacuum splints for cervical-spine immobilization. *J Emerg Med*. 1996;14:553–559.

35. Gerling MC, Davis DP, Hamilton RS, et al. Effects of cervical spine immobilization technique and laryngoscope blade selection on an unstable cervical spine in a cadaver model of intubation. *Ann Emerg Med*. 2000;36:293–300.

36. Del Rossi G, Horodyski MH, Conrad BP, et al. The 6-plus-person lift transfer technique compared with other methods of spine boarding. *J Athl Train*. 2008;43:6–13.

37. Swartz EE, Del Rossi G. Cervical spine alignment during the acute management of potential catastrophic cervical spine injuries in sport. *Health*. 2009;1:242–257.

38. Luscombe MD, Williams JL. Comparison of a long spinal board and vacuum mattress for spinal immobilisation. *Emerg Med J*. 2003;20:476–478.

39. Prinsen RK, Syrotuik DG, Reid DC. Position of the cervical vertebrae during helmet removal and cervical collar application in football and hockey. *Clin J Sport Med*. 1995;5:155–161.

40. Gastel JA, Palumbo MA, Hulstyn MJ, Fadale PD, Lucas P. Emergency removal of football equipment: a cadaveric cervical spine injury model. *Ann Emerg Med*. 1998;32:411–417.

41. Swenson TM, Lauerman WC, Blanc RO, Donaldson WF 3rd, Fu FH. Cervical spine alignment in the immobilized football player. Radiographic analysis before and after helmet removal. *Am J Sports Med*. 1997;25:226–230.

42. Peris MD, Donaldson WW 3rd, Towers J, Blanc R, Muzzonigro TS. Helmet and shoulder pad removal in suspected cervical spine injury: human control model. *Spine*. 2002;27:995–998; discussion 998–999.

43. Swartz EE, Norkus SA, Cappaert T, Decoster L. Football equipment design affects face mask removal efficiency. *Am J Sports Med*. 2005;33:1210–1219.

44. Jenkins HL, Valovich TC, Arnold BL, Gansneder BM. Removal tools are faster and produce less force and torque on the helmet than cutting tools during face-mask retraction. *J Athl Train*. 2002;37:246–251.

45. Copeland AJ, Decoster LC, Swartz EE, Gattie ER, Gale SD. Combined tool approach is 100% successful for emergency football face mask removal. *Clin J Sport Med*. 2007;17:452–457.

46. Swartz EE, Decoster LC, Norkus SA, Cappaert TA. The influence of various factors on high school football helmet face mask removal: a retrospective, cross-sectional analysis. *J Athl Train*. 2007;42:11–19; discussion 20.

47. Decoster LC, Shirley CP, Swartz EE. Football face-mask removal with a cordless screwdriver on helmets used for at least one season of play. *J Athl Train*. 2005;40:169–173.

48. Gale SD, Decoster LC, Swartz EE. The combined tool approach for face mask removal during on-field conditions. *J Athl Train*. 2008;43:14–20.

49. Toler JD, Petschauer MA, Mihalik JP, et al. Comparison of 3 airway access techniques during suspected spine injury management in American football. *Clin J Sport Med*. 2010;20:92–97.

50. Laprade RF, Schnetzler KA, Broxterman RJ, Wentorf F, Gilbert TJ. Cervical spine alignment in the immobilized ice hockey player. A computed tomographic analysis of the effects of helmet removal. *Am J Sports Med*. 2000;28:800–803.

51. Metz CM, Kuhn JE, Greenfield ML. Cervical spine alignment in immobilized hockey players: radiographic analysis with and without helmets and shoulder pads. *Clin J Sport Med*. 1998;8:92–95.

52. Waninger KN, Richards JG, Pan WT, Shay AR, Shindle MK. An evaluation of head movement in backboard-immobilized helmeted football, lacrosse, and ice hockey players. *Clin J Sport Med*. 2001;11:82–86.

53. Mihalik JP, Beard JR, Petschauer MA, Prentice WE, Guskiewicz KM. Effect of ice hockey helmet fit on cervical spine motion during an emergency log roll procedure. *Clin J Sport Med*. 2008;18:394–398.

54. Higgins M, Tierney RT, Driban JB, Edell S, Watkins R. Lacrosse equipment and cervical spinal cord space during immobilization: preliminary analysis. *J Athl Train*. 2010;45:39–43.
55. Sherbondy PS, Hertel JN, Sebastianelli WJ. The effect of protective equipment on cervical spine alignment in collegiate lacrosse players. *Am J Sports Med*. 2006:1675–1679.
56. Petschauer MA, Schmitz R, Gill DL. Helmet fit and cervical spine motion in collegiate men's lacrosse athletes secured to a spine board. *J Athl Train*. 2010;45:215–221.
57. Eismont FJ, Clifford S, Goldberg M, Green B. Cervical sagittal spinal canal size in spine injury. *Spine*. 1984;9:663–666.
58. Fehlings MG, Perrin RG. The timing of surgical intervention in the treatment of spinal cord injury: a systematic review of recent clinical evidence. *Spine (Philadelphia, PA)*. 2006;31:S28–S35; discussion S36.
59. Ellis JL, Gottlieb JE. Return-to-play decisions after cervical spine injuries. *Curr Sports Med Rep*. 2007;6:56–61.

Exertional Sickling

Scott Anderson, ATC

E. Randy Eichner, MD, FACSM

From the Field Scenario

Curtis was an athlete with a great work ethic, but he always seemed to have a problem getting in shape. Because he was an accomplished sprinter in track and a two-way starter in football, several colleges were interested in recruiting him. Football practice ended, as did most, with sideline-to-sideline interval sprinting. Curtis pushed to be sure he won the last sprint, knowing that the coaches had added a couple because of "how slow they performed the previous sprints." Curtis immediately felt weak and wobbly and complained of cramping in his legs. The coaches heard him, but they "always" heard such complaints. It was, after all, the first day, and they had only drills, no contact. It wasn't that hot and there was plenty of water for the players to drink throughout the practice. Curtis sat down. Eventually, a coach stretched Curtis, but he became frustrated because the muscles were soft, not hard and cramping. Curtis could get up and walk only with the help of another person. The coach tried to get him to drink, but he wouldn't. With some help, Curtis was taken to the locker room for more stretching and to put ice on his legs. Curtis was anxious and seemed to be getting worse. The coach called 911. The paramedics administered oxygen as they transported him to the emergency department. Curtis slowly improved. A battery of tests was negative, revealing only that he had sickle cell trait, which his mother knew. However, sickle cell trait status was not part of the preparticipation physical evaluation, and therefore no one at the school was aware of his status.

Discussion Questions

1. How would knowing about Curtis's sickle cell trait status have helped the coach?
2. What steps did the coach take that prevented Curtis from getting worse and this case ending in Curtis's death?
3. What precautions can be taken to prevent recurrent events in the face of sickle cell trait?
4. What points of education should be given to Curtis and the coaching staff?

Introduction

Sickle cell trait (SCT) is considered generally benign and consistent with a long, healthy life. More than three million Americans carry SCT, and almost all live normal lives, no different from Americans without SCT. In other words, SCT is not sickle cell disease. Unlike sickle cell disease, SCT causes no anemia and few clinical problems.

Having the trait does not disqualify an athlete from sports. Athletes can participate at elite levels with the trait because, by and large, SCT poses only four main clinical concerns. Three of these—occasional bouts of gross hematuria (blood in the urine), defects in urine-concentrating ability, and splenic infarction at altitude (cell death occurring in the spleen because of interruption of oxygen and blood flow)—are not life threatening and are covered in more detail in other publications.[1,2] The fourth clinical concern, **exertional sickling** collapse, is the focus of this chapter because it can pose a grave risk for some athletes.

Evidence suggests that, in SCT, sickling can begin within a few minutes of any sustained, intense exertion or successive bouts of maximal exertion with little or no interval of rest. Research suggests how and why sickle red blood cells can accumulate in the bloodstream during intense exercise; red blood cells can "logjam" blood vessels to cause **fulminant ischemic rhabdomyolysis**. The clinical and metabolic consequences of this "explosive" rhabdomyolysis can threaten life. Over the past decade in National Collegiate Athletic Association (NCAA) Division I football, exertional sickling has accounted for 10 (63%) of the 16 deaths from conditioning drills. Exertional sickling also causes deaths in other sports and has been reported in female athletes and in athletes as young as 12 years.[3] These deaths are potentially preventable.

Background and Occurrence of Exertional Sickling Collapse

SCT is a condition, not a disease. It comes from inheriting one gene for normal hemoglobin (A) and one gene for sickle hemoglobin (S). It is useful to think of SCT as "malarial," not racial. The sickle gene is common in people who come from places where malaria is common, for example, parts of Africa. Over the millennia, carrying one sickle gene—SCT—helped prevent early death from malaria, making it more likely that SCT individuals would survive to procreate. As a result, SCT is common in African Americans; it occurs in about 8% of this population. But because SCT is "malarial," the genetics of hemoglobin cannot be predicted by race and skin color. SCT occurs in about 0.5% of Hispanics,[4] and because malaria was also common in the Mediterranean, the Middle East, and parts of India, SCT occurs in about 0.2% of whites.[4,5]

The evidence of occurrence can be grouped into three categories: (1) field studies of athletes in Africa that suggest a pattern regarding SCT and performance; (2) U.S. Army studies of SCT and sudden death in recruits in military basic training, along with accumulating case reports of career military men and women who collapsed during intense physical exertion—usually timed runs—and died from exertional sickling; and (3) the steady accumulation of reports and case studies of college and high school athletes—and even younger athletes—who collapsed in sports training and died from exertional sickling.

Field Studies in Africa

Field studies in Africa suggest that elite SCT runners are limited not in single sprints, but rather in middle-distance, semi-marathon, and altitude racing. A study of all 145 students at a school for elite young athletes in Cameroon found SCT present at the same rate as in the general population, suggesting that SCT is not a barrier to general sports excellence. In the Ivory Coast, 13 SCT runners won 33 titles, but only 1 at 800 meters or more. SCT racers were underrepresented among top finishers in a semi-marathon in the Ivory Coast and underperformed in high-altitude stretches of a distance race in Cameroon. In contrast, a study of 16 French West Indian elite sprinters found that the three sprinters with SCT were winners.[6] Taken together, however, these African field studies suggest that SCT runners may be disadvantaged at altitude or in races of 800 meters and beyond.[6] This pattern seems to hold in training for American college football, where successive sprints that total about 800 meters or beyond seem to pose a sickling hazard.

Army Studies of SCT and Sudden Death in Basic Training

The U.S. military was the first to link SCT to sudden death during the physical training of recruits. In a comprehensive study of all deaths that occurred among two million recruits in military basic training in the U.S. Armed Forces from 1977 to 1981, the risk of unexplained sudden death in black recruits with SCT was 28 times higher than in black recruits without SCT, and 40 times higher than in all other recruits. The numerator, however, was small: there were only 13 sudden deaths among the SCT recruits.[7] In a later analysis, the risk of exercise-related death for black recruits with SCT was 30 times higher than that of black recruits without SCT.[5]

The risk fell sharply for career military people after basic training. This led to speculation that the risk of death related to SCT occurs mainly during intense conditioning (to novel exercise) or during sustained exertion for which the recruit is unprepared. Deaths continue to be reported in military basic training, and case reports are accumulating of career military men (or police academy men) with SCT who suffer fatal or near fatal collapse from exertional sickling, typically when trying to finish a 1.5- to 2-mile fitness run or a longer run.[8–10] It seems that the risk of fatal sickling can perpetuate across a physically demanding career.

Analysis clarified the type of death in SCT military recruits.[5] Most collapses occurred as recruits ran 1 to 3 miles. Of 40 deaths or near deaths from exertional sickling collapse, some had features of heat illness (but not exertional heat stroke [EHS]) and others were sudden cardiac arrhythmias. Most deaths, however, were delayed for hours to a day or two and were from metabolic complications of fulminant rhabdomyolysis and **myoglobinuric renal failure** (renal failure when myoglobin, which is released from muscle damage, saturates the kidneys). Indeed, it is likely that the sudden, fatal **arrhythmias** came from high potassium levels, lactic acidosis, and low calcium levels, all a result of the fulminant rhabdomyolysis. Thus, the main cause of death in exertional sickling is **explosive rhabdomyolysis**. In the Army studies, the risk of fatal rhabdomyolysis in SCT recruits in basic training was increased about 200-fold.[5]

myoglobinuric renal failure Kidney failure from myoglobin (a by-product of muscle breakdown) in the urine.

arrhythmia An abnormal heart rhythm.

explosive rhabdomyolysis A potentially fatal condition involving the breakdown of skeletal muscle fibers, resulting in the release of muscle fiber contents into circulation.

Sickling Collapse in Athletes

The increasing reports of athletes collapsing or dying from exertional sickling are troubling. Most sickling deaths have been in football players, but at least two deaths have been in basketball players, one in a boxer, and one in a runner during a track tryout. For every death reported, there are several nonfatal collapses. These have resulted in compartment syndromes, muscle death within lower back muscles, or acute kidney failure requiring dialysis. An adolescent runner was hospitalized twice for collapse from exertional sickling in two cross-country races a year apart; he survived.[11]

The first well-known exertional sickling collapse tied to SCT in college football was a player at the University of Colorado who was new to the high altitude. He collapsed sprinting on the first day of practice in 1973 and survived. He collapsed again in 1974 on the first day of practice, after sprinting for only 2 minutes or 650 meters. This time, he died from complications of sickling.[12] At least 18 college football players have died from exertional sickling (see **Table 9.1**). Most have not been reported in the medical literature. One who was reported sprinted for only 3 minutes or 800 meters on the first day of practice before he collapsed and soon died from sickling.[13] Another collapsed in the fall, after running 16 successive sprints of 100 yards each. He died about 15 hours later from an elevated concentration of potassium in his blood, which induced a fatal abnormal heart rhythm, a metabolic consequence of fulminant rhabdomyolysis, and acute myoglobinuric kidney failure.[14]

The recent spate of exertional sickling deaths in NCAA Division I football is alarming. In the decade from 2000 to 2010, no death occurred in the play or practice of the game. However, 16 deaths occurred in conditioning for the game: 15 in sprinting or high-speed agility drills, and one in weight lifting. Of the 16 deaths, four were caused by sudden cardiac arrest, one was secondary to asthma, and one was a result of EHS. Ten (63%) of the 16 deaths were tied to complications of sickling. Thus, SCT, carried by an estimated 3% to 4% of all these players, accounts for 63% of the deaths, an excess of 16- to 21-fold. The high intensity of football conditioning seems to play a pivotal role in many of these deaths.

TABLE 9.1 Exertional Sickling Deaths in College Football

Year	State	Setting
1974	CO	Ran 650 meters, new at altitude
1985	AK	Ran 0.75 mile
1986	MS	Ran 1 mile
1987	IN	Ran 1200 meters, first day of practice
1987	UT	Ran 0.75 mile, new at altitude
1990	NM	Ran 800 meters, first day of practice
1992	GA	Ran 1000 meters, first day of off-season practice
1995	AZ	Ran 900 meters, first day of practice
2000	TN	Ran 800 meters, first day of practice
2001	FL	1-hour mat drill
2004	OH	Sprinting, 10 minutes, day 1 of practice
2004	TX	Ran gassers for about 30 minutes
2005	MO	1-hour multistation field drill
2006	TX	Ran 16 sprints, 100 yards each
2008	FL	Station drills, running, just back from break
2008	NC	Ran 15 short uphill sprints
2009	NC	Ran 700 yards, new at modest altitude
2010	MS	Station drills, first day of team conditioning

Mechanisms and Causes of Exertional Sickling Collapse

Exercise physiology research helps explain why strenuous exertion in SCT can cause fulminant rhabdomyolysis. In SCT, in which typically about 40% of the hemoglobin in each red blood cell is hemoglobin S, maximal exertion evokes four forces that lead to sickling (i.e., change in red-cell shape, when the cell releases its oxygen, from round to quarter moon or "sickle"). These four forces are (1) inadequate level of oxygen in the blood (hypoxemia), (2) a buildup of lactic acid (lactic acidosis), (3) hyperthermia of muscles, and (4) dehydration of red cells coursing through muscles. In concert, these forces foster sickling. Sickle cells are "stiff" and "sticky" and so tend to "logjam" the small blood vessels supplying working muscles. This causes fulminant ischemic rhabdomyolysis as the athlete tries to keep going on with muscles that are getting no blood. It seems likely that the harder and faster SCT athletes try to go, the earlier and more severe the sickling and its consequences.

In fact, sickling in athletes going "all out" can be rapid and profound. Multiple research studies demonstrate that maximal exertion can evoke profound lactic acidosis and low oxygen levels in only 1 to 5 minutes.[15–17] Hyperthermia of working muscles and dehydration of red cells complete the sickling foursome.

Just as these adverse forces develop within minutes, so too does sickling. When young men did brief, maximal arm-cranking exercise tests, sickling was seen within 2 to 5 minutes of starting this strenuous exercise.[18] In a follow-up study published only as an abstract, when SCT recruits exercised to near exhaustion via *leg* cycling, sickle cells were seen in venous blood draining the *arm*.[19] This suggests the possibility that as exercise stress increases, sickle cells accumulate in the arterial circulation. Note that here too the exercise was done mainly with the legs, but the sickling was seen in venous blood from the arms, implying that sickle cells may be pumped throughout the entire body.

Research shows that dehydration can increase exertional sickling. Two men with SCT walked briskly for 45 minutes in the heat, once with fluids to offset sweat loss and once without fluids. Without fluids to offset dehydration, core temperature rose slightly higher and sickling (in forearm venous blood) increased steadily to peaks of 3.5% and 5.5%.

The timing of the mechanism fits the timing of the clinical collapse. In the face of maximal exertion, the four sickling forces develop in 2 to 5 minutes. Sickle cells are seen in the blood in 2 to 5 minutes, and some football players with SCT have collapsed from exertional sickling after only 2 to 5 minutes of sustained sprinting. The explosive rhabdomyolysis from major exertional sickling can cause death in less than an hour from metabolic arrhythmia of a normal heart (e.g., pulseless electrical activity), or can cause death over the next several hours from metabolic complications of acute myoglobinuric renal failure (renal failure when myoglobin, which is released from muscle damage, saturates the kidneys).

Recognition of Exertional Sickling Collapse

Settings and Patterns of Collapse

It seems likely that the harder and faster SCT athletes go, the earlier and greater the sickling. That may be why sickling collapse occurs sooner, or at a shorter distance, in top college football players sprinting than in military recruits running. Many college football collapses have occurred after sustained or successive sprinting, totaling between 600 and 1200 meters, often on the first day of conditioning or early in the season (see Table 9.1). In contrast, most sickling collapses in military recruits have occurred while running 1 to 3 miles.[5]

The patterns of collapse teach other lessons. For example, sickling collapse in college football players is not typically triggered by an exertional heat illness (EHI). Army researchers concluded that EHI was a culprit in deaths in SCT recruits,[5] but most cases they gave as examples of EHI and sickling had no temperature recorded or the core temperature on collapse was 38.9°C (102°F) or lower. It seems that many of these recruits did not have an EHI but only the expected physiologic elevation of core temperature consistent with strenuous exercise.[14] The same applies to most of the football players who collapsed sickling. Some had been on the field only briefly, coming from an air-conditioned locker room and sprinting as briefly as 2 to 5 minutes before they collapsed. How could this be an EHI? Others collapsed on a cool day or had only mildly elevated core body temperature, or both.[14] And even one in whom the medical examiner diagnosed EHS as well as sickling had a core temperature of only 39°C (102.4°F) soon after collapse. It is likely that he had only the expected physiologic hyperthermia of the brief uphill successive sprinting he did before his exertional sickling collapse.

In other words, at least in college football, heat is no more a trigger for exertional sickling than is unaccustomed altitude, uncontrolled asthma, a heedless fervor on the part of the athlete, or a reckless intensity on the part of the coach. As one editorialist has said, problematic drills in football seem to have a common theme: too much, too fast, too soon, and too long.[20] The sickling trigger is maximal intensity, sustained for at least a few minutes, that pushes the athlete beyond his or her limits. Exertional sickling collapse is an *intensity* syndrome.

Diagnosis of Collapse

Bear in mind that when an athlete takes the field healthy—and barring trauma—most ominous collapses on the field are caused by one of four major problems: (1) heart conditions, (2) heat stroke, (3) severe asthma, or (4) exertional sickling. In general, the features of these four causes of sudden on-field collapse differ, and telltale clues can help observers differentiate among these medical emergencies.

Asthma tends to be unique and stark in its features. In general, asthma attacks severe enough to cause collapse occur in athletes with known asthma and prior problems with exercise-induced asthma, including frequent or urgent use of inhalers and a tendency for uneven control of their asthma. Thus, a grave asthma attack is usually easy to recognize.[21,22]

Heart conditions come in many forms, but there are common causes of sudden cardiac death in athletes.[23] It seems that, too often in the past two decades, sickling deaths have been misdiagnosed as cardiac deaths in athletes who had only athlete's heart.[24] Cardiac collapses typically differ from sickling collapses in that the former are not merely sudden but nearly instantaneous. The athlete hits the ground, does not speak, and is unresponsive and pulseless because of a grave abnormal heart rhythm. The only way to save the athlete is by immediate cardiopulmonary resuscitation (CPR) and the use of an automated external defibrillator (AED).

EHS is the condition that can most closely mimic exertional sickling collapse. Here too the setting and pattern of collapse can help. If it is the first hot day of summer training and a huge lineman collapses after 2 to 3 hours in the heat, it is likely EHS. However, if a small wide receiver fresh out of the locker room collapses after sprinting only 2 to 3 minutes, it is likely sickling. It also goes without saying that it pays to know your athletes—for example, who has asthma, who tends to struggle in the heat, and who has SCT.

The early symptoms indicating potential to collapse usually evolve more slowly in EHS than sickling, but the early features of pending EHS—confusion, bizarre behavior, and physical decline—may be subtle, especially in the heat of competition or hard training. Mental clouding prevents athletes from realizing they are overheating, so unless someone who knows them well is watching them closely, their EHS collapse may catch everyone unaware. A hallmark of EHS is a core temperature greater than 40.5 C (105°F) at the time of collapse. Usually, in EHS in football, core body temperature is higher than this—often 41°C to 43.3°C (106–110°F). An immediate, accurate, core body temperature taken rectally can help differentiate EHS from sickling (see **Table 9.2**), but when in doubt, treat for both.

Heat cramping is not life threatening, but sometimes, in the face of a sickling collapse, precious time is lost with sideline treatment for presumed heat cramping. Football players who have suffered both heat cramping and sickling can differentiate between the two:

prodrome An early indication or symptom of impending disease or illness.

- Heat cramping often has warning signs (or **prodrome**). Hours or minutes before the cramping, the athlete may see or feel twitches or twinges in tired muscles, those destined to cramp. Sickling has no prodrome.
- The pain is different. Heat-cramping pain is excruciating, from a sustained contraction of muscles, a "lock-up." Sickling pain tends to be milder; it is an ischemic (restricted blood flow) pain from muscles starved of blood supply.
- What stops the athlete is different. With heat cramping, athletes "hobble to a halt" or grab a cramping leg muscle and fall down. With sickling, athletes "slump to a stop," as their legs become weak and wobbly and no longer hold them up.
- The physical findings are different. In major heat cramping, one can see and feel large, rock-hard muscles in full tonic contraction, and the athlete often is writhing and yelling in pain.

TABLE 9.2	Differentiating Features Among Common Causes of On-Field Collapse			
Feature	Sickling	Heat Cramping	Cardiac	Heat Stroke
Cramping	Weakness > pain	Pain > weakness	No cramping	No cramping
Collapse	Slumps to ground	Hobbles to a halt	Falls like a rock	Staggers to ground
Mental Function	Can talk at first	Yelling from pain	Unconscious	Incoherent, bizarre behavior
Muscle Function	Muscles "normal" (may appear weak)	Muscles locked up	Limp or seizing	Muscles "normal" (may appear weak)
Body Temperature	< 104°F	< 104°F	< 104°F	> 104°F
Timing	Can occur early during exercise	Usually occurs late during exercise	No warning	Usually occurs late during exercise

With sickling, the exhausted athlete lies fairly still and complains little, except to say that he feels bad and his legs hurt and are weak. The muscles look and feel normal to the medical staff (Table 9.2).

Also vital to know is that exertional sickling collapse can occur during any season and in any setting. It can occur on a hot day or a cold day. It can occur on a misty day in the mountains, when the athlete is unaccustomed to a jump in altitude of as little as 2000 feet or so. It can occur early on the field, within the first few minutes of successive sprinting, as on the first day of summer camp, or at the end of an hour-long, fast-tempo, multistation, "agility-drill" workout. It can occur at the end of a mat drill that starts at dawn. It can occur when a high school player returns to football after a year off and joins the team in sprinting drills. It can occur when a college football player returns after an injury and joins the team for the first fast-tempo, multistation drill of winter conditioning, or when the football players are just back from a 1.5-week holiday. It can occur when a basketball player new to altitude sprints up and down the court only 10 times. It can occur when a coach (or drill instructor) joins the struggling athlete in running to urge him or her on to finish a planned series of uphill sprints or a timed 2-mile fitness run. It can occur when an athlete, a star sprinter in high school, walks on for college football and is told to sprint for 10 minutes: too much, too fast, too soon.

The common denominator is a perfect storm of irrational or undue intensity, sustained for at least a few minutes—an intensity beyond the fitness level or physical limits, or both, of that particular SCT athlete on that day in that setting. Sickling collapse is an intensity syndrome, and this fact shapes our precautions. In our experience in college football, it seems that some or many SCT players may occasionally have at least mild—and sometimes disabling—symptoms from what seems to be exertional sickling. Admittedly, no test exists to immediately prove on the field that a given event *is* exertional sickling. The risk may vary not only with the amount of hemoglobin S in each red cell, and with other inherited or acquired conditions, but also with the sport, setting, drill, or fitness of the athlete. We have seen an SCT player collapse writhing in severe back pain after a grueling conditioning drill that included pushing a weighted sled in a bear-crawl posture. He developed paraspinal **myonecrosis** (muscle death). We and others have reported other SCT football players with the same syndrome, some disabled for weeks or months. We do not argue that paraspinal myonecrosis is specific to SCT athletes, but rather that it seems more common in them.[25]

myonecrosis The death of muscle cell fibers.

Not all sickling collapses are the same, and not all football players describe them in the same way. However, they are unique enough that they can be differentiated from the other three common nontrauma causes of collapse on the field. Some SCT players say it begins with leg and/or low back pain or "cramps" that "spread up my body." Some complain of leg weakness more than pain, saying that their legs "got wobbly, like Jello." Some say even their chest muscles are "tight" and "I can't catch my breath," or "I just don't feel right." By this point, they can be on their hands and knees, very anxious, with rapid breathing (up to 50 to 60 times a minute). This rapid breathing is not asthma, but rather hyperventilation to blow off carbon dioxide to try to offset a rapidly progressing, profound lactic acidosis, which comes from running hard on muscles that are increasingly starved for blood. Some stoic players with exertional sickling will just stop, for example, after 700 yards of a planned 800-yard wind sprint, and sit or lie down, saying "I can't go on" or "my legs won't go." This self-limiting feature—the wisdom to read their body even in the heat of battle or with coaches yelling at them—has likely saved the lives of SCT athletes. They stop, refuse to go on, rest, "unsickle," walk home that day in good health, and return to their sport the next day.

Prevention

In our opinion, prevention hinges on knowing who has SCT so the SCT athletes and the staff can be educated on the early sickling symptoms and signs to heed, and so precautions can be taken. Some argue that these precautions could just be taken for the entire team, without knowledge of who has SCT. But in college football, at least, this seems unrealistic. Also, the medical staff and coaches are better able to respond quickly and properly if they know who has SCT. Athletes with SCT should never be disqualified, because education and simple precautions seem to work and enable SCT athletes to thrive in their sport.

TABLE 9.3	Sickle Cell Trait Training Precautions at University of Oklahoma

1. Stop at onset of symptoms (pain, cramping, weakness, breathlessness, fatigue).
2. Report any symptoms immediately to certified athletic trainer and coach.
3. Avoid "preseason conditioning tests."
4. Acclimate to onset of conditioning or lifting program.
5. Modify conditioning drills (no timed sprints, no sustained running without breaks).
6. Take part in a conditioning program each season before return to sport activity.
7. Hydrate before, during, and after all activity.
8. Decrease activity in hot and/or humid conditions.
9. Monitor if new to altitude, even a jump of 2000 feet. Cut effort; have an oxygen tank ready.
10. Decrease activity after any illness, especially with vomiting or diarrhea.
11. Control asthma to cut risk of exertional sickling.
12. Decrease activity after nights of poor sleep.

These precautions are outlined in the 2007 National Athletic Trainers' Association "Consensus Statement: Sickle Cell Trait and the Athlete"[26] and in the 2010 *NCAA Sports Medicine Handbook*.[27] All athletes with SCT should be familiar with these precautions, as well as the early signs and symptoms of exertional sickling, and institutions should establish an environment in which these precautions will be activated. These precautions include the following:

- SCT athletes should be allowed to set their own pace. This simple precaution is the heart of the matter. If followed, it is unlikely that any athlete would ever die from exertional sickling.
- SCT athletes should build up slowly in training, with paced progressions and longer periods of rest and recovery between repetitions, especially during "gassers" and intense station or "mat" drills.
- Extreme performance tests are especially risky and often unphysiologic for the sport. SCT athletes should not be urged to perform all-out exertion of any kind beyond 2 to 3 minutes without a breather. Serial sprinting, timed mile runs, and fast-tempo multistation drills with little or no rest between stations are especially risky for SCT athletes and are not advised.
- SCT athletes should stop activity immediately upon struggling, or upon any unusual muscle pain or weakness, "cramping," breathlessness, discomfort, or undue fatigue. They should seek and get immediate aid from medical staff.
- Predisposing factors include heat, altitude, dehydration, asthma, and other illness, because they make any workout harder. Adjust work/rest cycles for ambient heat stress and for a jump of even 2000 feet in altitude. Emphasize hydration. Control asthma. Have supplemental oxygen ready at altitude. An SCT athlete who feels ill should not begin a workout.

Table 9.3 provides a terse list of SCT precautions in football at the University of Oklahoma.

Management

An exertional sickling collapse is a medical emergency. The collapsed athlete can usually still talk or respond, but in some cases he or she can deteriorate rapidly and become unresponsive within minutes. Practice an emergency action plan. Check vital signs; watch especially for shock, decreased levels of arousal and responsiveness, or a rapid heart rate that may signal coming onset of a life-threatening abnormal heart rhythm. With the guidance of a medical professional, athletes with exertional sickling collapse should be treated with supplemental oxygen by face mask, even at sea level, to offset oxygen deficiency. The athlete should be cooled if necessary. Call 911, attach an AED, and be ready to start CPR if needed. Get the athlete to the hospital quickly. Tell the doctors to anticipate explosive rhabdomyolysis and its grave complications.

Return to Play

Return to play must be decided on an individual basis. First, it is key to know that the mortality rate is high for athletes who collapse from exertional sickling and deteriorate to shock and coma on site. They can die within an hour or so from cardiac arrhythmias caused by the complications of the explosive rhabdomyolysis. Their best chance of survival is a very rapid trip to the emergency department, where experienced physicians, including a cardiologist and a nephrologist, are ready to treat the dire metabolic emergencies.

Some athletes survive the sickling collapse but spend a long time in the hospital with major, debilitating rhabdomyolysis, compartment syndromes, kidney failure, and other complications. They may not return to play, either. One college football player in Texas survived the collapse but lost 55 pounds of muscle in the hospital, was too weak at first even to feed himself, spent 2 weeks on kidney dialysis and 2 months in hospitals, and then was not cleared to return to play because he had lost about half of his kidney function. He did, however, come back in all other ways and after college played some semiprofessional football. At the other extreme—the happy extreme—are the informed SCT athletes who stop at the first sign of sickling trouble and are attended to immediately with rest, supplemental oxygen, fluids, and, if needed, cooling. In our experience in football, these athletes can rebound quickly. Likely many or most of their sickle red cells revert to normal shape as they traverse the lungs and pick up oxygen, having done little damage to the tissues before the athlete stopped. These athletes can likely return to play the next day, with careful watching by trained medical staff.

Some SCT athletes fall between these two extremes. This has been the case for football players who develop moderate rhabdomyolysis, especially if associated with some lumbar paraspinal myonecrosis or a leg compartment syndrome. They present a clinical pattern of rhabdomyolysis but without kidney failure. We and others have seen occasional SCT football players who had two to four similar sickling bouts of disabling rhabdomyolysis, either because a new college coach intensified a conditioning drill or because the athlete had trouble elsewhere, such as in training for arena football or playing in an intense recreational basketball game. These athletes in the middle of the sickling spectrum tend to have limiting muscle pain and weakness for at least a week or two and need frequent assessment to ensure prudent, gradual return to play.

Summary

SCT, generally benign in everyday life, can pose a grave risk for some athletes. U.S. Army research first tied SCT to risk of sudden death in military recruits in basic training. The risk of fatal rhabdomyolysis in SCT recruits was increased 200-fold. Similar deaths have occurred for decades in young athletes, and in the past decade an alarming spate of exertional sickling death has occurred in NCAA Division I college football conditioning. SCT occurs in 3% to 4% of all these football players but is tied to 10 (63%) of 16 conditioning deaths, an excess of up to 21-fold.[24]

Exercise physiology research explains how and why sickle cells can accumulate during intense exercise bouts and "logjam" blood vessels, causing explosive rhabdomyolysis. Several lines of research suggest that sickling can begin after only 2 to 5 minutes of all-out exertion and can reach grave levels soon thereafter if the athlete struggles on or is urged on by coaches despite warning signs. The sickling collapse is an *intensity* syndrome that can be differentiated from the other three common causes of nontrauma collapse on the field. It is a medical emergency that calls for fast action to save lives. We believe that screening and tailored precautions[26,27] can prevent these tragic collapses and deaths and enable all SCT athletes to thrive in their sports.

Clinical Case Scenario

1. An 18-year-old African American football player in Florida collapsed during an outdoor conditioning session. He is a freshman on a Division I wrestling team. His medical history includes seasonal allergies and possible asthma when he was a young child. He has no history of EHIs and does not use tobacco, drugs, or alcohol. He does not know if he has SCT. When he collapsed, it was 75°F on a partly cloudy day with 80% humidity and partly overcast skies.

   a. What medical conditions would you suspect?

   b. Consider that the workout leading up to this athlete's collapse was at the end of a long training day and consisted of twelve 100-meter sprints with 1 minute of rest between each sprint and 2 minutes after the fourth and eighth sprints. The athlete seemed to be struggling but was capable of completing the sprints. What conditions would you suspect at this point?

   c. The athletic trainer examines the athlete. The athlete complains of shortness of breath and lower extremity discomfort. As he is being questioned, he becomes lethargic and his legs become too weak to support him. At this point the athletic trainer calls emergency medical services, suspecting exertional sickling. What are the primary objectives and what actions should be taken at this point?

   d. What are the main actions you can take to prevent an exertional sickling case from occurring?

   e. What are the factors that determine survival after an athlete with SCT begins an exertional sickling episode?

Key Terms

arrhythmia

exertional sickling

explosive rhabdomyolysis

fulminant ischemic rhabdomyolysis

myoglobinuric renal failure

myonecrosis

prodrome

sickle cell trait (SCT)

References

1. Eichner ER. Sickle cell trait and athletes: three clinical concerns. *Curr Sports Med Rep.* 2007;6:134–135.
2. Eichner ER. Exertional sickling. *Curr Sports Med Rep.* 2010;9:3–4.
3. Pretzlaff RK. Death of an adolescent athlete with sickle cell trait caused by exertional heat stroke. *Pediatr Crit Care Med.* 2002;3:308–310.
4. Bonham VL, Dover GJ, Brody LC. Screening student athletes for sickle cell trait—a social and clinical experiment. *N Engl J Med.* 2010;363:997–999.
5. Kark JA, Ward FT. Exercise and hemoglobin S. *Semin Hematol.* 1994;31:181–225.
6. Eichner ER. Sickle cell trait. *J Sport Rehabil.* 2007;16:197–203.
7. Kark JA, Posey DM, Schumacher HR, Reuhle CJ. Sickle-cell trait as a risk factor for sudden death in physical training. *N Engl J Med.* 1987;317:781–787.
8. Sanchez CE, Jordan KM. Exertional sickness. *Am J Med.* 2010;123:27–30.
9. Dincer HE, Raza T. Compartment syndrome and fatal rhabdomyolysis in sickle cell trait. *Wisc Med J.* 2005;104:67–71.
10. Makaryus JN, Catanzaro JN, Katona KC. Exertional rhabdomyolysis and renal failure in patients with sickle cell trait: is it time to change our approach? *Hematology.* 2007;12:349–352.
11. Helzlsouer KJ, Hayden FG, Rogol AD. Severe metabolic complications in a cross-country runner with sickle cell trait. *J Am Med Assoc.* 1983;249:777–779.
12. Eichner ER. Sickle cell trait, heroic exercise, and fatal collapse. *Physician Sportsmed.* 1993;21:51–64.

13. Rosenthal MA, Parker DJ. Collapse of a young athlete. *Ann Emerg Med.* 1992;21:1493–1498.
14. Anzalone ML, Green VS, Buja M, et al. Sickle cell trait and fatal rhabdomyolysis in football training: a case study. *Med Sci Sports Exerc.* 2010;42:3–7.
15. Hartley LH, Vogel JA, Landowne M. Central, femoral, and brachial circulation during exercise in hypoxia. *J Appl Physiol.* 1973;34:87–90.
16. Medbo JI, Sejersted OM. Acid-base and electrolyte balance after exhausting exercise in endurance-trained and sprint-trained subjects. *Acta Physiol Scand.* 1985;125:97–109.
17. Osnes J-B, Hermansen L. Acid-base balance after maximal exercise of short duration. *J Appl Physiol.* 1972;32:59–63.
18. Martin TW, Weisman IM, Zeballos J, Stephenson SR. Exercise and hypoxia increase sickling in venous blood from exercising limb in individuals with sickle cell trait. *Am J Med.* 1989;87:48–56.
19. Bergeron MF, Cannon JG, Hall EL, Kutlar A. Erythrocyte sickling during exercise and thermal stress. *Clin J Sport Med.* 2004;14:354–356.
20. McGrew CA. NCAA football and conditioning drills. *Curr Sports Med Rep.* 2010;9:185–186.
21. Becker JM, Rogers J, Rossini G, Mirchandani, D'Alonzo GE Jr. Asthma deaths during sports: report of a 7-year experience. *J Allergy Clin Immunol.* 2004;113:264–267.
22. Eichner ER. Asthma in athletes: scopes, risks, mimics, trends. *Curr Sports Med Rep.* 2008;7:118–119.
23. Maron BJ, Doerer JJ, Haas TS, Tierney DM, Mueller FO. Sudden deaths in young competitive athletes. Analysis of 1866 deaths in the United States, 1980–2006. *Circulation.* 2009;119:1085–1092.
24. Eichner ER. Sickle cell trait in sports. *Curr Sports Med Rep.* 2010;9:347–351.
25. Schnebel B, Eichner ER, Anderson S, Watson C. Sickle cell trait and lumbar myonecrosis as a cause of low back pain in athletes [abstract]. *Med Sci Sports Exerc.* 2008;40(suppl 5):537.
26. National Athletic Trainers' Association. *Consensus statement: sickle cell trait and the athlete.* Paper presented at: Annual Meeting of the National Athletic Trainers' Association; June 27, 2007; Anaheim, CA.
27. National Collegiate Athletic Association. Section 3c: the student-athlete with sickle cell trait. In: *2009–2010 NCAA Sports Medicine Handbook.* Indianapolis, IN: NCAA; 2009:86–88. http://www.nata.org/sites/default/files/SickleCellTraitAndTheAthlete.pdf. Accessed October 14, 2013.

Traumatic Injuries

Margot Putukian, MD, FACSM

Charlie Thompson, MS, ATC

From the Field Scenario

Bob has been the assistant football coach for Muskeegen Private Boarding School for 2 years. His team has just finished playing a game against a rival on an unusually hot and humid evening. One of the senior wide receivers, a starter and key player, came and sat down next to Bob and said "Coach, I just went to the bathroom and there was some blood when I peed. Am I dehydrated?" Bob asked him if he had any pain anywhere and if anything like this had happened before, and the player said that he had been fighting a sore throat for the past 2 weeks, had some left shoulder pain, and some pain in his back where he might have gotten hit in the first quarter. He also said he had never had anything like it before but thought "maybe I should just drink water and call my parents tomorrow morning if it happens again." Bob gave the player some water, and he felt a little better, but when the player stood up, he felt weak and the shoulder pain seemed to worsen. Bob told the player to sit back down and went to get the athletic trainer. When the athletic trainer evaluated the player, he found that the young man looked a little pale, had a significant drop in his blood pressure when he went from lying down to standing up, and that he had an increase in his heart rate. The team physician was asked to emergently evaluate the athlete, and emergency medical services (EMS) was called. The player's shoulder and abdominal pain increased, and he developed abdominal tenderness. The player was transported emergently to the hospital by EMS where he was found to have a renal contusion and a splenic rupture. Laboratory testing later confirmed that he also had infectious mononucleosis (Epstein-Barr virus infection). Given the immediate recognition that there might be something more serious going on, Bob was able to get a quick evaluation by the athletic trainer and team physician (who stabilized the patient while EMS arrived). The player had an emergency splenectomy and survived, going on to play in his spring lacrosse season.

Discussion Questions

1. What items were in place to allow Bob (the coach) to recognize the seriousness of this situation? (What knowledge do you expect he had? What policies were in place to help him appropriately handle this situation?)
2. What steps did the coach take that played an important role in the positive outcome for this athlete?
3. If you were the athletic director, what follow-up steps would you take after this incident to evaluate how it was handled and improve future cases?

Introduction

Catastrophic injury in sports is uncommon, and most commonly the injuries that do occur are to the head, spine, or heart. In children, trauma is a leading cause of injury and death, resulting in over 1.5 million injuries, 500,000 hospital admissions, and 20,000 deaths per year.[1] In 80% of these injuries, the mechanism of injury is blunt force trauma.[2] In children, the risk of catastrophic injury in sports has been reported to be 0.6 per 100,000 participants annually.[3] This compares favorably with the risk level of 10- to 15-year-olds in automobile accidents, where the risk of catastrophic injury is reported to be 5.0 per 1,000,000 participants annually.[4] Whereas most catastrophic injuries in sports are head and spinal cord injuries, as well as cardiac injuries, less common causes of sudden death also occur in sports and warrant consideration. These include injuries to joints and major vessels[5] as well as injuries to the chest and abdomen. This chapter will focus on these three areas (chest, abdomen, and vascular injuries), which house the organs and structures that are responsible for maintaining the body's day-to-day functions. See **Table 10.1** for a review of the basic organ functions.

TABLE 10.1   General Functions of the Abdominal and Chest Organs, Glands, and Muscles

Organ	Function
Liver	• Filters the blood for toxins • Serves as a storage site for glucose • Produces bile (which is stored in the gallbladder and is used to break down ingested fats)
Gallbladder	• Serves as a storage site for bile and releases bile when needed
Pancreas	• Produces the hormone insulin (to help control blood sugar levels) and pancreatic juice
Spleen	• Filters blood (destroys old blood cells) and helps control blood volume • Is part of the lymphatic system (which fights infection)
Kidneys (left & right)	• Filter blood to remove waste • Form urine to secrete waste
Stomach	• Initiates digestive process and secretes digestive juices
Intestines (large & small)	• Are responsible for metabolism of food and absorption of nutrients, eventually excreting any residual waste
Adrenal Glands (left & right)	• Produce hormones such as adrenaline, testosterone, and cortisol
Appendix	• Is vertigial organ (no known purpose) that branches off the large intestine
Diaphragm	• Contracts and relaxes to assist with lung expansion & contraction (breathing)
Heart	• Receives blood returning from the body & lungs (via veins) and pumps it to either the body or lungs (via arteries)
Lungs	• Are responsible for receiving oxygen from inhaled air and delivering it to the bloodstream • Exchange oxygen for carbon dioxide and remove carbon dioxide from the blood/body

Background

Injuries to the chest and abdomen are often associated with sudden deceleration impact injuries and are therefore more common in sports such as football, ice hockey, lacrosse, skiing, and snowboarding than in other sports. Injuries that occur in the chest and abdomen include injuries to the lung or heart or their linings, the space in between the heart and lungs in the middle of the chest, as well as injuries to the great vessel of the heart and other major blood vessels. Injuries that occur in the abdomen are often associated with high-velocity impact injuries that then cause injury to the organs within the abdominal cavity, most notably the spleen, kidney, and liver.[6] These types of injuries often occur if an individual is tackled and falls onto an object (e.g., a football), or falls and lands on a solid object (e.g., bicycle handlebars). Other mechanisms in sport include a solid structure penetrating or "almost penetrating" the body, which can occur when a hockey or lacrosse stick goes into the abdomen. The literature regarding traumatic injuries to the chest and abdomen is dominated by mechanisms outside of sports.[7–9] The most commonly reported injuries in sports that relate to chest wall trauma appear to be related to commotio cordis[10]; however, penetrating injuries from hockey sticks have been reported.[11]

Anatomically, the abdomen can be split into four regions, with the structures at risk grouped together on this basis (see **Table 10.2**). Injuries to the left and right chest region include lung contusions (bruises), a punctured lung, bleeding into the lung space, air in the middle of the chest (pneumomediastinum[PM]), and rib fractures, as well as abdominal injuries to the spleen, liver, kidneys, and adrenal glands. Rarely, rupture of the great vessel (aorta), the upper airways, or the diaphragm may occur. Understanding these anatomic regions is useful in considering injury to each location and the organs at risk.

TABLE 10.2 Abdominal Quadrants and Organs

Region	Organs
Left Upper Quadrant (LUQ)	1. Spleen 2. Left kidney 3. Left adrenal gland 4. Left hemidiaphragm 5. Left lobe of liver (small portion) 6. Pancreas 7. Stomach 8. Portions of intestines
Right Upper Quadrant (RUQ)	1. Liver 2. Right kidney 3. Right adrenal gland 4. Right hemidiaphragm 5. Gallbladder 6. Portions of intestines
Left Lower Quadrant (LLQ)	1. Appendix 2. Portions of intestines 3. Reproductive organs
Right Lower Quadrant (RLQ)	1. Intestines 2. Reproductive organs

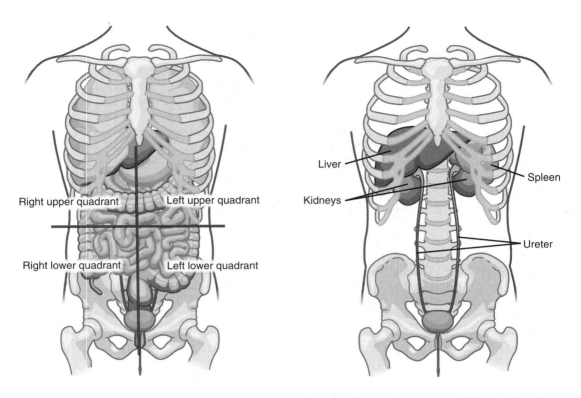

Right upper quadrant | Left upper quadrant

Right lower quadrant | Left lower quadrant

Liver

Spleen

Kidneys

Ureter

Children's abdominal organs sit lower in the body and are more exposed toward the front of the body. Their musculature is less developed, and where their ribs and cartilage meet, the costochondral junction, they are more pliable. These factors all increase the potential risk for chest and abdominal injury. In addition, because of the increased pliability, it takes more force for fractures to occur, and therefore the index of suspicion must be high in evaluating the youth athlete with traumatic injury.

This chapter focuses on injuries to the chest, including the space between the lungs and heart, the abdominal organs and great vessels. Injuries to the spinal cord, congenital issues, and cardiac injury are addressed in other chapters.

Specific Chest Injuries

Lung (Pulmonary) Contusion

There is a paucity of information regarding pulmonary contusion in sports, because most of the literature relates to high-speed motor vehicle accidents, falls, or suicide attempts, in which pulmonary contusion is often the most minor of multiple injuries that occur. Several case reports of pulmonary contusion in sports demonstrate that the most common mechanism is blunt trauma to the chest, most often during contact sports.[12–14] Pulmonary contusion often manifests as shortness of breath and decreased levels of oxygen in the blood, which can occur immediately or be delayed for several hours. Other common symptoms include coughing up blood, rapid respiratory rate, chest pain, and musical sounds while breathing or wheezing.[15] Coughing up blood can be an unsettling symptom that is infrequently present for more than a day or two. The majority of pulmonary contusions that occur in sports are mild, and these are rarely life threatening. When fatal, they are often seen in conjunction with other injuries that are more serious[16–20] and often unrelated to sports.

The initial management should include initiating the emergency action plan (EAP) and determining if emergency transportation is necessary. If the athlete is able to speak, has a normal respiratory rate, and is conscious without significant complaint, it may be possible to arrange for immediate assessment by a healthcare provider. If there is any question about the severity of the injury, emergent transportation should be arranged. If oxygen is available, it should be provided. Various imaging techniques may be used to rule out other possible conditions.[21-23] In more serious conditions a special procedure called a bronchoscopy may be necessary to evaluate the lungs.[24] The majority of pulmonary contusions are treated with relative rest, and return to play is often rapid—within 1 to 2 weeks based on the reported literature.[12-14]

Breastbone (Sternal) Fracture

Sternal fracture is uncommon in sports, although it can occur as a result of blunt trauma and, more important, is often associated with other injuries within the chest cavity. The chest wall in children is more compliant, and therefore these injuries within the chest may be more common in children and can be missed without a high index of suspicion. People often complain of chest pain, made worse with pushing directly onto the breastbone, along with shortness of breath and pain with breathing in and out. In addition, if the injury is at the joint between the collarbone and the breastbone (the sternoclavicular [SC] joint), an SC dislocation, particularly a dislocation where the bone pushes backward, must be considered. These dislocations should be referred emergently because there is a significant possibility of injury to the vessels that sit behind this joint. These dislocations are often relocated in the hospital where emergency surgical intervention is available if needed.

Punctured Lung and Air Within the Middle of the Chest (Pneumothorax and Pneumomediastinum)

Pneumothorax (PTX) and PM can both occur as a result of sports participation, although the literature reviewing their occurrence as well as management and return to play issues is sparse.[25-28] PTX is defined as air that has leaked into the space outside the lining of the lungs, either spontaneously or as a result of traumatic tears in the lining of the lung following chest injury, surgical procedures, or because of individual differences/lifestyle.[29-33] Treatment of PTX entails removing air from the pleural space, reexpanding the underlying lung, and preventing recurrence.[28]

pneumothorax (PTX) Air that has leaked into the pleural space, either spontaneously or as a result of traumatic tears in the pleura following chest injury or iatrogenic/surgical procedures.

There are approximately 20,000 cases of spontaneous PTX each year, but fewer than 10% of these are associated with exercise.[29,34] Spontaneous PTX can occur with Valsalva-type maneuvers (bearing down and holding one's breath) and has been reported with weightlifters[32,35] as well as divers holding their breath.[36] The incidence of spontaneous lung air leaks does not seem to be increased at high altitude, but may be during scuba or other compressed air diving activities, where the water pressure complications are felt to occur when the individual holds his or her breath during the ascent.[37,38] A PTX that occurs underwater during an ascent may rapidly progress to a tension PTX (described shortly), more so than one on land, and thus a history of spontaneous air leak is considered an absolute contraindication to scuba diving.[37,38]

Traumatic PTX can occur as a result of penetrating or nonpenetrating trauma. In sports, it is most common in contact or collision sports[26,39-41] and may be associated with fractures of the ribs, shoulder blade, or collarbone. Rib fractures are common, and certain rib segments are more likely to be associated with complications.[42] In children, given their more pliable chest wall and rib structures, more impact is necessary for fracture to occur, and thus a greater severity of injury and death rate is associated with these injuries.[43] Sixteen percent to 38% of shoulder blade fractures are associated with PTX, although one study reported a punctured lung in over 50%.[44-46] Therefore, in the case of shoulder blade fracture, a high index of suspicion is necessary for associated PTX.

Tension PTX is an uncommon, yet life-threatening, complication of pneumothorax and is defined as a progressive collection of air in the pleural space that produces a significant amount of pressure on the surrounding structures. It can cause death if untreated.[47] Tension PTX can develop slowly or quickly, depending on the degree of lung injury and the underlying health of the patient. A drop in blood pressure occurs late, just before heart–lung collapse. Additional symptoms include a progressive decrease in blood oxygen levels, increased heart rate, and respiratory distress. Tension PTX is a life-threatening emergency that must be considered in the athlete who presents with respiratory distress, and first responders should immediately initiate the EAP.

The presentation of PTX is classically shortness of breath and pain with inspiration, which is present in 80% to 90% of patients, although 10% will be asymptomatic.[30] The pain is generally on the same side where the injury is present and can travel to the shoulder, neck, and back. It worsens with inspiration and with exertion and, in addition to shortness of breath, it can also be associated with a dry cough.[26] Tension PTX should be considered if there is any deviation of the Adam's apple away from the side that the punctured lung is on, prominent neck veins, low blood pressure, respiratory distress, or a bluish discoloration of the face and skin. The presentation of air in the middle of the chest (PM) is slightly different in that the pain with inspiration is often accompanied by some "crunching" air just below the skin over the front of the neck and around the collarbones. In addition, complaints of pain with swallowing or talking or both are common.[26]

If an athlete is evaluated and PTX or PM is considered, then there should be an assessment of vital signs and breathing, and oxygen should be provided if it is available. Observation of breathing, looking for asymmetry or splinting, and confirming that the Adam's apple is midline is important. The EAP should be initiated and the athlete transported to an emergency facility where he or she can be evaluated and cared for by a healthcare professional. If the athlete is unstable, and these classic signs are evident, a trained healthcare provider, if on site, might proceed with immediate needle aspiration on the side of the tension (the side that the airway is deviating away from). Although this procedure is not without risk or complications, it can be life saving. Confirmation of PTX most often occurs with x-rays, which show the punctured lung (see **Figure 10.1**) and the absence of lung markings outside of it.

During the evaluation for PTX and PM, other injuries, such as disruption of the upper airway, injury to the great vessels, blood around the heart, bruising of the heart (cardiac contusion), or injuries to the diaphragm should also be considered. These injuries all present with chest symptoms, with a variable degree of hemodynamic compromise. If there is a significant drop in blood pressure, decreased mental status, or respiratory distress, then emergent stabilization and transportation to an emergency facility will be necessary. The evaluation in the emergency department will often include emergent x-rays and other tests such as ultrasound or computed tomography (CT) scanning.

For children with chest injuries, a clinical prediction protocol exists that helps to identify those with increased likelihood for injury.[48] The predictors of chest injury include low blood pressure, elevated

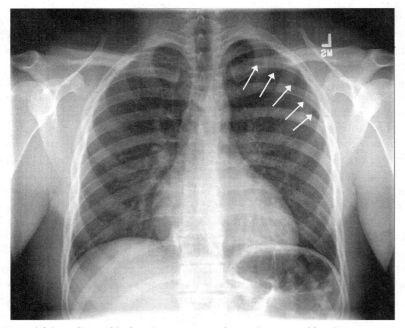

Figure 10.1   X-ray (plain radiograph) showing a pneumothorax (punctured lung).

age-adjusted respiratory rate, abnormal chest exam, abnormalities when the chest was listened to with a stethoscope, fracture of the thigh bone, and a decrease in mental status. In this series, 98% of patients with a chest injury had at least one of these predictive factors. It is important to recognize that this series was not specific to athletes, and that most injuries were not those seen in sports but rather were motor vehicle, auto–pedestrian, auto–bicycle, and bicycle accidents; assaults; crush injuries; and abuse injuries. However, these factors may be associated with significant injury and should be evaluated. The treatment of a punctured lung (PTX) depends on the clinical stability of the athlete as well as the size of the PTX.[49,50]

PM also presents as a result of trauma, although it has been reported in noncontact settings as well. Many of these cases are seen in conjunction with punctured lung (PTX) and are often not considered life threatening because they will resolve on their own without intervention. PM may be associated with significant compromise of swallowing or breathing, and therefore further evaluation with procedures to evaluate the upper airway or swallowing tube (esophagus) is essential to exclude any associated injuries. With blunt trauma, other associated injuries can include air around the heart lining.[51] Most cardiothoracic injuries can be treated successfully, and return to play is often uncomplicated. Tension PTX, bleeding into the chest, and diaphragmatic injury, as well as lung contusion with persistent bleeding, are issues that require emergent care because they are life threatening.[52]

Abdominal Injuries

Splenic Injury

Splenic injuries are the most common intra-abdominal organ injuries in sports; the spectrum of injury includes contusion, bleeding/hematoma within the spleen, laceration, and rupture.[53,54] Although splenic rupture can occur spontaneously, it often occurs as a result of direct or indirect trauma and usually occurs in conjunction with other abdominal organ injury.[54–56] Complicating factors include the addition of a rib fracture and an enlarged spleen, with the latter commonly caused by infectious mononucleosis. Splenic rupture in infectious mononucleosis is not common, although because of the risk of splenic rupture athletic participation is restricted for 3 to 4 weeks after the onset of symptoms.[57]

The symptoms and signs of splenic injury include a drop in blood pressure; abdominal pain with or without radiation to the left shoulder; abdominal bloating, tenderness, and significant pain and apprehension or guarding when the abdomen is pushed upon; and fainting or near fainting. If there is concern regarding possible intra-abdominal injury and the athlete has low blood pressure or significant abdominal findings, referral to an emergency facility should be arranged. Blood analysis, ultrasound, and specifically a focused assessment with ultrasound can be used to identify traumatic injury.[58–60] CT scanning remains the imaging of choice to best evaluate the severity of trauma as well as exclude other injuries, such as bony fracture of the ribs, pelvis, and spine or other abdominal organ injury.[2,61–65] CT can determine the extent of bleeding within the abdomen as well as detect and quantify the extent of injury to both solid and hollow organs.

Splenic injury is often graded from 0 to 5, with 0 being no injury and 5 being a "shattered spleen,"[66] which will also dictate time required for healing.[67] Treatment of splenic injury varies, although if the athlete is clinically stable, nonoperative treatment is preferred. With surgical removal of the spleen, case reports describe a return to play in 3 weeks in contact sports,[54] although the majority of reports describe a more lengthy return to play time, especially if nonoperative treatment is considered.[55,56,67–70]

Other intra-abdominal injuries that can occur are injuries to the liver, kidney, pancreas, or gastrointestinal (GI) tract. These are not common in sports, and most reports in the literature describe motor vehicle accidents or pedestrian–motor vehicle accidents. Both renal and liver laceration occur and evaluation and treatment of these injuries are important, although they are rarely life threatening. These injuries generally present similarly, with abdominal pain, low blood pressure, or both. Less commonly they may present with GI bleeding. The symptoms may be delayed, and a high index of suspicion should be present if there is a history of abdominal trauma. Blood in the urine is a common presentation,[71] although it is not always indicative of injury to the kidney.[72,73]

Evidence-based guidelines exist for children with isolated liver and spleen injury,[74] as well as for children with isolated spleen or liver injury.[62,74,75] The 2000 and 2005 guidelines from the American Pediatric Surgical Association provide some recommendations for the emergent treatment of these injuries.[62,74] These authors use CT grading to determine the appropriate utilization of resources. For grade I through III injuries, the guidelines do not recommend intensive care unit (ICU) stay. For grade IV injuries, they do recommend an ICU stay of 1 day. For grades I, II, III, and IV injuries, they recommend a hospital stay of 2, 3, 4, and 5 days, respectively, as well as activity restriction from "age-appropriate activities" of 3, 4, 5, and 6 weeks, respectively. The authors note that for return to full-contact competitive sports, the decision must be an individualized one made by the pediatric trauma surgeon.[62,74]

Prediction guidelines for the identification of both children and adults with intra-abdominal injuries after blunt trauma to the torso also exist that are useful in determining which athletes may need emergent treatment, but many of these items require medical or hospital equipment.[75–77] There are no clear guidelines for sideline assessment and what findings merit emergent transportation and evaluation. For adults with blunt torso trauma, a prediction rule using a Glasgow Coma Scale can be predictive of whether significant injury is present.[76] It is important to remember that in both of these studies, sports-related trauma was infrequent, and therefore the application of these rules to athletes may be limited.

Vascular Injuries and Conditions

Although sports-related orthopedic injuries are seldom considered "catastrophic" in the true definition of the word, they can often be season ending and even career ending, which in the eyes of athletes and possibly their family and coaches could be considered catastrophic. In the worst-case scenarios, these injuries are associated with injuries to the nerves and/or vessels (neurovascular injuries) secondary to the major injury that run the risk of being missed because of the severe nature of the original injury. It is imperative for those involved in the care of the athlete to be cognizant of the possibility of these neurovascular injuries.

Knee Dislocations

Knee dislocations, where the thigh bone dislocates from the lower leg bones, typically occur with high-velocity forces (car accidents) but also occur with low-velocity forces (sports). They were once thought to be relatively uncommon, and reports vary from relative low rates to higher incidence rates.[78–80] Many authors believe that knee dislocations are underdiagnosed because they most often spontaneously reduce.[81] There are four ligaments in the knee and when two or more ligaments are torn, significant instability can occur, including a transient dislocation. Patients with multiple-ligament knee injuries should be treated as having a reduced knee dislocation and must be monitored for nerve and/or vessel injury.[82] One study demonstrated vessel injuries in 38% of the patients presenting with multiple-ligament injuries of the knee.[83] It is imperative that close attention be paid for the potential of vascular and nerve damage when evaluating multiple-ligament injuries in the knee. All multiple-ligament injuries to the knee should be treated as a medical emergency, regardless of the findings during the on-field evaluation.[84]

Popliteal Artery Injuries

The popliteus is the space behind the knee, and the popliteal artery (PA) is the major artery in this location. PA injuries can result in amputation of the lower leg. In fact, amputation was at one time the treatment of choice for these injuries.[85] Because the PA is tethered up high at its origin as it emerges from the inner upper thigh, and also tethered down low in the lower leg, it is at risk for shear injuries. Ligamentous injury to the knee can also cause injury to the PA.[86] Johnson et al.[82] reported an 86% amputation rate if the integrity of the PA is not restored within 6 to 8 hours; they also reported an 89% salvage rate when the integrity is restored within 8 hours, making this issue critical.[82] If there is any question that a significant injury has occurred, the EAP should be initiated and the athlete transported for emergent evaluation by a healthcare provider.

Peroneal Nerve Injuries

Although not considered life or limb threatening, injury to the peroneal nerve, which runs on the outside of the knee, can be another significant cause of morbidity following knee dislocations.[82] The incidence of nerve damage following a knee dislocation varies from 25%[87] to 40%.[88] The peroneal nerve is considered to be superficial and relatively immobile, causing it to be susceptible to injury. The mechanism of injury is usually a stress that causes a traction-type injury[89] and fractures of the side of the knee (fibular head) where a small piece of bone is pulled off.[90] The degree of stretching will determine the extent of the injury, ranging from a mild stretch to a complete transection. Prognosis is usually poor, with a slow and often incomplete recovery. Foot drop (where the forefoot of the foot drops because of weakness) is considered a common manifestation of peroneal nerve damage.[82]

Examination of the Vessels

The incidence of PA injury associated with knee dislocation ranges from 23% to 32%.[83] It is important to note that vascular injury may not be readily apparent because vascular compromise may not be completely evident at the time of the dislocation.[84] For those dislocations that do not spontaneously reduce, it is important that the physician evaluates for pulses at the foot before and after reduction.[80] An athlete may not complain of numbness or decreased blood flow to the lower leg. All suspected knee dislocations or actual reduced dislocations should be transported and have serial evaluations performed every 4 to 6 hours for 48 hours, although recommendations vary.[82,91,92]

In addition to monitoring as mentioned previously, the use of the **arterial pressure index (API)** has been recommended by several authors.[82] The API is determined by dividing the systolic pressure of the lower extremity (cuff just above the ankle) by the systolic pressure of the upper extremity (brachial artery) (see **Table 10.3**). In one study, 11 of 38 patients had an API of less than 0.90, and all required vascular restoration. The remaining 27 had an API of more than 0.90 and did not require vascular restoration.[93] These data are often cited by authors advocating for noninvasive examination in these cases.[91]

Other studies used include duplex ultrasonography[94,95] and arteriography[82,91,96,97], which is considered the gold standard. Duplex ultrasonography is a noninvasive accurate and safe technique to evaluate vascular damage.[94] The downside is that it is reliant on the skill of the technician

arterial pressure index (API) A measure of arterial flow determined by dividing the systolic pressure of the lower extremity (cuff just above the ankle) by the systolic pressure of the upper extremity (brachial artery); acceptable level is greater than 0.90.

Table 10.3	**Arterial Pressure Index Information**	
Arterial Pressure Index Information		
Description	An effective diagnostic tool using the systolic pressure of the lower extremity (*dorsalis pedis* or posterior tibial artery, whichever is higher from both legs) divided by the highest systolic pressure of the upper extremity (brachial artery from both arms)	
Implications	API < 0.90 vascular restoration (arteriography) most likely needed	API > 0.90 vascular restoration unlikely needed
	Provides a noninvasive and safe method for diagnosing vascular injury from traumatic injuries (e.g., knee dislocations)	
Sensitivity (API < 0.90)	95%	
Specificity (API < 0.90)	97%	

Source: Adapted from Mills WJ, Barei DP, McNair P. The value of the ankle-brachial index for diagnosing arterial injury after knee dislocation: a prospective study. *J Trauma.* 2004;24:403–407; Bravman JT, Ipaktchi K, Biffl WL, Stahel PF. Vascular injuries after minor blunt upper extremity trauma: pitfalls in the recognition and diagnosis of potential "near miss" injuries. *Scand J Trauma, Resuscitation and Emerg Med.* 2008;16:16.

and radiologist.[95] Selective arteriography is recommended when noninvasive modalities such as pulse examination and API suggest the possibility of vascular compromise. The significant downside to arteriography is typically the delay of 2 to 3 hours to arrange the testing, which may not allow for vascular restoration in a timely manner.[96,97]

Neurologic Exam

A thorough neurologic evaluation should be performed, checking for sensation as well as motor functions of the superficial and deep branches of the peroneal nerve. An incomplete nerve injury could be indicated by loss of sensation with motor function intact or by a partial motor function loss. Further testing can help determine whether additional treatment is needed and to predict patient outcomes.[98]

Blood Clots in the Deep Veins of the Legs and Lungs (Deep Vein Thrombosis and Pulmonary Embolism)

deep vein thrombosis (DVT) A blood clot that forms in a vein deep in the body, most typically in the lower extremity but possibly in the upper extremity.

pulmonary embolism (PE) A complication of a venous thromboembolism; a clot (embolus) breaks off and travels through the blood to the lung, impeding blood flow.

The U.S. Department of Health and Human Services reported in a September 15, 2000, news release that between 350,000 to 600,000 people are affected by **deep vein thrombosis (DVT)** or **pulmonary embolism (PE)**, or both, each year, resulting in over 100,000 deaths per year.[99] Put simply, a DVT is a blood clot that forms in a vein deep in the body; most occur in the leg.[100] The three most common causes of clotting are local venous damage as the result of trauma or possibly surgery, venous stasis as the result of immobilization and pressure, and the effect of being in a hypercoagulable state.[101]

PE is not a disease in its own right, but rather it is a complication of venous thromboembolism.[102] Prandoni et al.[100] described a PE as a clot in a deep vein that breaks off (becoming an embolus) and travels through the bloodstream to the lungs, blocking blood flow to the lungs. The evidence that PE is predominantly a complication of venous thrombosis, typically occurring in the veins of the legs, is compelling.[102] It has been postulated that improved care of trauma patients has resulted in a decrease in morbidity from the actual trauma but may be the cause of an increase in the number of deaths related to PE in this same group of patients.[101] With trauma patients living longer after the trauma, the risk of DVT increases, and therefore the risk of PE increases.[103]

The majority of the research on DVT and PE has been done with major trauma patients, and much of the data includes elderly patients, who are frequently affected by either or both of the maladies. Although there is a lack of research regarding athletic injuries and DVT/PE, many athletes are faced with the prospect of suffering a significant injury and possibly major surgery, making them susceptible to these problems as a result of the actual trauma or the treatment that occurs subsequent to the trauma, thus forcing clinicians to be aware of the possibility of their occurrence.

Typical signs and symptoms of DVT include swelling, pain and tenderness, warmth, and red or discolored skin. However, it is thought that DVT can occur without any of the common symptoms being present, and that only objective testing can confirm its absence or presence.[103] Coaches need to be aware of this and medical professionals must monitor patients who have suffered significant injury, have had major surgery, or need to be immobilized for any length of time.

Treatment of lower extremity DVT includes the use of anticoagulant medicines as well as mechanical devices such as graded elastic compression stockings, intermittent compression, and electrical stimulation. The mechanical devices are considered effective in low- to medium-risk patients.[104] The discussion of specific pharmacologic treatment for DVT is beyond the scope of this chapter.

DVT is more common in the lower extremity, but it does occur in the upper extremity and is typically referred to as an "effort thrombosis," occurring in the dominant arm of overhead athletes. This is known

Paget-Schroetter syndrome (PSS) Axillosubclavian deep vein thrombosis without secondary cause (trauma).

as **Paget-Schroetter syndrome (PSS)** and generally refers to an upper extremity DVT without secondary cause (trauma, surgery etc.).[105] Although PSS normally occurs in the dominant arm, there is at least one report in the literature of a nondominant-arm PSS related to repetitive bilateral arm activity.[106] It has been reported that 80% of all PSS cases are associated with thoracic outlet syndrome, whereas only 1% to 12% of all thoracic outlet cases have complaints related to PSS.[107]

The signs and symptoms of PSS are typical of any DVT. They can improve with rest and can present with normal pulses.[105]

Thoracic outlet syndrome refers to a functional obstruction of the vessels and nerves going from the upper chest out to the upper extremity. This can occur either as a result of an extra rib or tight muscles, which can create pressure on the nerves and vessels. In the case of upper extremity clots, it is believed that the pressure on the veins can cause blood flow to be obstructed, and thus the likelihood of clot formation is increased. Venography, a study using dye injected into the vein followed by radiographs, is considered the gold standard for diagnosis, though it is an invasive procedure compared to ultrasound, which is noninvasive.

Treatment for upper extremity vein clots includes the use of medications to break up clots and blood thinner medications followed by surgical intervention to correct the underlying problem, often an extra rib resection.[108] Controversy remains regarding the indications for surgery, the timing of the surgery, and the technical approaches of surgery.[109]

Summary

The catastrophic nature of the conditions described in this section (see **Table 10.4**) do not have to cause devastating outcomes. The ability of the clinician to recognize secondary injuries in a timely manner when evaluating sports-related orthopedic injuries can be crucial to the outcome of the overall injury.

TABLE 10.4 Sampling of Traumatic Conditions, Standard Return to Play Implications Relative to Severity, and Common Signs and Symptoms

Injury	Severity	RTP Implications	Most Common Signs and Symptoms
Lung contusion	N/A	Rest, RTP within 1–2 weeks	Shortness of breath, diminished blood oxygen levels (possibly delayed for several hours), coughing up blood
Breastbone fracture	If occurring at the collarbone-breastbone joint, requires emergency response	Dependent upon severity, age (growth plate implications), and location of injury	Chest pain that worsens with pushing on the chest wall, shortness of breath
Punctured lung	N/A	Variable	Shortness of breath, sharp chest pain with breathing, decreased blood oxygen levels, increased heart rate and respiratory rate, respiratory distress, diminished breath sounds
Air in the middle of the chest (pneumomediastinum)	N/A	Variable	Sharp chest pain with breathing, air felt "crunching" under the skin, pain with swallowing, pain with speaking, "crunching" sound in sync with the heartbeat
Splenic rupture	Grade	Timeline (full-contact sports decision should be individualized)	Decreased blood pressure/dizziness, abdominal pain with or without pain radiating to the left shoulder, tenderness when the abdomen is pushed on or when taking the hand away from the abdomen
	1	3 weeks (hospital stay of 2 days)	

(continues)

TABLE 10.4 Sampling of Traumatic Conditions, Standard Return to Play Implications Relative to Severity, and Common Signs and Symptoms (*continued*)

Injury	Severity	RTP Implications	Most Common Signs and Symptoms
	2	4 weeks (hospital stay of 3 days)	
	3	5 weeks (hospital stay of 4 days)	
	4	6 weeks (ICU stay of 1 day, hospital stay of 5 days)	
	5	Probable splenectomy – variable	
Clot in the deep veins (DVT)	N/A	Dependent upon if surgical intervention is required	Pain and tenderness, swelling, warmth, red or discolored skin, highly susceptible athletes with a history of recent injury or immobilization

Abbreviations: DVT, deep vein thrombosis; ICU, intensive care unit; RTP, return to play.

Focusing only on the obvious and apparent damage can be devastating in some cases. Careful observation for signs of possible life- or limb-threatening conditions is critical in the overall care of the athlete.

Clinical Case Scenario

1. A 22-year-old male football player (offensive lineman, 288 pounds) suffered a right ankle sprain on October 19, 2009. He had no time loss because of this injury. He did, however, see the team physician and was prescribed diclofenac (Voltaren). On December 18, 2009, he went to a movie. After the movie, he felt like he had strained his calf. He tried stretching the calf, with no improvement. He was scheduled to fly home on December 20, but his flight was cancelled because of snow. He mentioned to his parents that his calf was sore and swollen, and they insisted he go to the local hospital emergency department. There, he had a Doppler ultrasound exam, which revealed a popliteal vein clot (DVT). He was administered a blood thinner by injection (enoxaparin [Lovenox]) and allowed to fly home the next day.

   Evaluation by a physician at home was arranged. Blood work was obtained that indicated he had a deficiency in one of the factors responsible for normal clotting, called factor V Leiden deficiency. On exam, he denied any chest pain, shortness of breath, cough, or coughing of blood, all of which might indicate that the clot had traveled to his lungs (PE). He only reported swelling in the calf and an occasional cramp. It was revealed that a family history of DVT existed.

   He was prescribed blood thinners (warfarin [Coumadin] and enoxaparin) for a period of 6 months. On January 18, 2010, he was allowed to commence biking and restricted weight lifting. He did not participate in winter or spring football drills or practice. After 6 months his blood thinners were discontinued. On August 24, he was cleared to play football during his senior season, which he did without incident. The following are questions that this athlete's healthcare providers would need to consider.
   a. What do you believe were the main factors contributing to this athlete's condition?
   b. What other conditions could present similarly? What signs would indicate that this was a DVT?
   c. Looking back, is there anything this athlete could have done to help prevent this incident?

Key Terms

arterial pressure index (API)

deep vein thrombosis (DVT)

Paget-Schroetter syndrome (PSS)

pneumothorax (PTX)

pulmonary embolism (PE)

References

1. Wegner S, Colletti JE, Van Wie D. Pediatric blunt abdominal trauma. *Pediatr Clin North Am.* 2006;53:243–256.
2. Sivit CJ. Abdominal trauma imaging: imaging choices and appropriateness. *Pediatr Radiol.* 2009;39(suppl 2):S158–S160.
3. Zemper ED. Catastrophic injuries among young athletes. *Br J Sports Med.* 2010;44:12–20.
4. The Disaster Center. Motor vehicle occupant fatality and injury rates per 100,000 population by age group, 1975–1997, per year. http://www.disastercenter.com/traffic/AgeGroup.html. Accessed March 2010.
5. Heller G, Immer FF, Savolainen H, et al. Aortic rupture in high-speed skiing crashes. *J Trauma.* 2006;61(4):979–980.
6. Ryan JM. Abdominal injuries and sport. *Br J Sports Med.* 1999;33:155–160.
7. Keel M, Meier C. Chest injuries—what is new? *Curr Opin Crit Care.* 2007;13(6):674–679.
8. McGillicuddy D, Rosen P. Diagnostic dilemmas and current controversies in blunt chest trauma. *Emerg Med Clin North Am.* 2007;25(3):695–711.
9. Galan G, Penalver JC, Paris F, et al. Blunt chest injuries in 1696 patients. *Eur J Cardiothorac Surg.* 1992;6:284–287.
10. Maron BJ, Pollac DC, Kaplan JA, Mueller FO. Blunt impact to the chest leading to sudden death from cardiac arrest during sports activities. *N Engl J Med.* 1995;333:337–342.
11. Kennedy J, Green RS, Henteleff H. Penetrating chest trauma secondary to a composite hockey stick injury. *Can J Emerg Med.* 2006;8(6):437–440.
12. Steinlight S, Putukian M. Hemoptysis in a varsity collegiate football athlete. *Med Sci Sports Exerc.* 2010;42(5):183.
13. Lively MW, Stone D. Pulmonary contusion in football players. *Clin J Sport Med.* 2006;16:177–178.
14. Meese MA, Sebastianelli WJ. Pulmonary contusion secondary to blunt trauma in a collegiate football player. *Clin J Sport Med.* 1997;7(4):309–310.
15. Cohn SM. Pulmonary contusion: review of the clinical entity. *J Trauma.* 1997;42:973–979.
16. Lotfipour S, Kaku SK, Vaca F, et al. Factors associated with complications in older adults with isolated blunt chest trauma. *West J Emerg Med.* 2009;10:79–84.
17. Balci AE, Kazez A, Eren S, et al. Blunt thoracic trauma in children: review of 137 cases. *Eur J Cardiothoracic Surg.* 2004;26:387–392.
18. Freixinet J, Beltran J, Rodriguez PM, et al. Indicators of severity in chest trauma [in Spanish]. *Arch Bronconeumol.* 2008;44(5):257–262.
19. Jones NS. An audit of the management of 250 patients with chest trauma in a regional thoracic surgical centre. *Arch Emerg Med.* 1989;6:97–106.
20. Perna V, Morera R. Prognostic factors in chest traumas: a prospective study of 500 patients [in Spanish]. *Cir Esp.* 2010;87(3):165–170.
21. Hayes D. Chest pain. *Clin Pediatr.* 2007;46(8):746–747.
22. Halil O, Gokhan G, Turkay K. A case of diaphragmatic rupture after strenuous exercise (swimming) and jump into the sea. *Turk J Trauma Emerg Surg.* 2009;15(2):188–190.
23. Trupka A, Waydas C, Hallfeldt KKJ, et al. Value of thoracic computed tomography in the first assessment of severely injured patients with blunt chest trauma: results of a prospective study. *J Trauma.* 1997;43:405–412.
24. Song JK, Beaty CD. Diagnosis of pulmonary contusions and a bronchial laceration after a fall. *AJR Am J Roentgenol.* 1996;167:1510.
25. Putukian M. Pneumothorax and pneumomediastinum. *Clin Sports Med.* 2004;23(3):443–454.
26. Curtin SM, Tucker AM, Gens DR. Pneumothorax in sports: issues in recognition and follow-up care. *Phys Sportsmed.* 2000;28(8):23–32.
27. Currie GP, Alluri R, Christie GL, Legge JS. Pneumothorax: an update. *Postgrad Med J.* 2007;83(981):461–465.
28. Jenkinson SG. Pneumothorax. *Clin Chest Med.* 1985;6(1):153–161.
29. Erickson SM, Rich BSE. Pulmonary chest wall emergencies: on-site treatment of potentially fatal conditions. *Phys Sportsmed.* 1995;23(11):95–104.
30. Volk CP, McFarland EG, Horsmon G. Pneumothorax: on field recognition. *Phys Sportsmed.* 1995;23(10):43–46.
31. Jantz MA, Pierson DJ. Pneumothorax and barotraumas. *Clin Chest Med.* 1994;15(1):75–91.
32. Marnejon T, Sarac S, Cropp AJ. Spontaneous pneumothorax in weightlifters. *J Sports Med Phys Fitness.* 1995;35(2):124–126.
33. Simons S. Pneumothorax and exercise. *Sports Med Consult.* 2000;1(6):1–6.
34. Voge VM, Anthracite R. Spontaneous pneumothorax in the USAF aircrew population: a retrospective study. *Aviat Space Environ Med.* 1986;57:939–949.

35. Simoneaux SF, Murphy BJ, Tehranzadeh J. Spontaneous pneumothorax in a weightlifter. *Am J Sports Med.* 1990;18:647–648.
36. Harker CP, Neuman TS, Olson LK, et al. The roentgenographic findings associated with air embolism in sport scuba divers. *J Emerg Med.* 1993;11:443–449.
37. Bove AA, Dabis JC. *Bove and Davis' Diving Medicine.* 3rd ed. Philadelphia, PA: WB Saunders; 1997:176–183, 270–277, 336–337.
38. Kizer KW. Dysbaric cerebral air embolism in Hawaii. *Ann Emerg Med.* 1987;16:535–541.
39. Partridge RA, Coley A, Bowie R, Woolard RH. Sports-related pneumothorax. *Ann Emerg Med.* 1997;30(4):539–541.
40. Fink DA, McGanity PL, Hagemeier KF 3rd, Schenck RC Jr. Pneumothorax in high school football. *Tex Med.* 1998;94(5):72–74.
41. Sadat-Ali M, Al-Arfaj AL, Mohanna J. Pneumothorax due to soccer injury. *Br J Sports Med.* 1986;20(2):91.
42. Miles JW, Barrett GR. Rib fractures in athletes. *Sports Med.* 1991;12(1):66–69.
43. Garcia VF, Gotschall CS, Eichelberger MR, et al. Rib fractures in children: a marker of severe trauma. *J Trauma.* 1990;30:695–700.
44. Armstrong CP, Vanderspuy J. The fractured scapula: importance in management based on series of 62 patients. *Injury.* 1984;15:324–329.
45. Ferro RT, McKeag DB. Neck pain and dyspnea in a swimmer: spontaneous pneumomediastinum presentation and return-to-play considerations. *Phys Sportsmed.* 1999;27(10):67–71.
46. Neer CS II. Fractures about the shoulder. In: Rockwood CA Jr, Green DP, eds. *Fractures.* Philadelphia, PA: JB Lippincott; 1984:713–721.
47. Barton ED. Tension pneumothorax. *Curr Opin Pulm Med.* 1999;5(4):259–274.
48. Holmes JF, Sokolove PE, Brant WE, Kuppermann N. A clinical decision rule for identifying children with thoracic injuries after blunt torso trauma. *Ann Emerg Med.* 2002;39(5):492–499.
49. Baumann MH, Strange C, Heffner JE, et al. Management of spontaneous pneumothorax. An American College of Chest Physicians Delphi Consensus Statement. *Chest.* 1999;112:789–804.
50. Kirby TJ, Ginsberg RJ. Management of the pneumothorax and barotraumas. *Clin Chest Med.* 1992;13(1):97–112.
51. Franklin WJ, Arora G, Ayres NA. Pneumopericardium and pneumomediastinum after blunt chest trauma. *Tex Heart Inst J.* 2003;30(4):338–339.
52. Shanmuganathan K, Killeen K, Mirvis SE, White CS. Imaging of diaphragmatic injuries. *J Thorac Imaging.* 2000;15(2):104–111.
53. Rifat SF, Gilvydis RP. Blunt abdominal trauma in sports. *Curr Sports Med Rep.* 2003;2:93–97.
54. Terrell T, Lundquist B. Management of splenic injury and return-to-play decisions in a college football player. *Clin J Sports Med.* 2002;12:400–402.
55. Flik K, Callahan LR. Delayed splenic rupture in an amateur hockey player. *Clin J Sport Med.* 1998;8:309–310.
56. Gangei JJ, Binns OA, Young JS. Splenic injury after athletic trauma: a case report of splenic rupture induced by a lacrosse ball. *J Trauma.* 1999;46:736–737.
57. Putukian M, O'Connor FG, Stricker PR, et al. Mononucleosis and athletic participation: an evidence based subject review. *Clin J Sports Med.* 2008;18:309–315.
58. Walter KD. Radiographic evaluation of the patient with sport-related abdominal trauma. *Curr Sports Med Rep.* 2007;6:115–119.
59. Lee BC, Ormsby EL, McGahan JP, et al. The utility of sonography for the triage of blunt abdominal trauma patients to exploratory laparotomy. *AJR Am J Roentgenol.* 2007;188:415–421.
60. Noble VE, Blaivas M, Benkenship R, et al. Decision rule for imaging utilization in blunt abdominal trauma—where is ultrasound? *Ann Emerg Med.* 2010;55(5):487–489.
61. Emery KH. Splenic emergencies. *Radiol Clin North Am.* 1997;35:831–843.
62. Stylianos S, APSA Trauma Committee. Evidence based guidelines for resource utilization in children with isolated spleen or liver injury. *J Pediatr Surg.* 2000;35:164–169.
63. Poletti PA, Mirvis SE, Shanmuganathan K. CT criteria for management of blunt liver trauma: correlation with angiographic and surgical findings. *Radiology.* 2000;216(2):418–427.
64. Poletti PA, Kinkel K, Vermeulen B, et al. Blunt abdominal trauma: should US be used to detect both free fluid and organ injuries? *Radiology.* 2003;227:97–103.
65. Richards JR, Knopf NA, Wong L, et al. Blunt abdominal trauma in children: evaluation at emergency US. *Radiology.* 2002;222:749–754.
66. Pranikoff T, Hirschl R, Schlesinger QE, et al. Resolution of splenic injury after nonoperative management. *J Pediatr Surg.* 1994;29:1366–1369.
67. Brown RL, Irish MS, McCabe AJ, et al. Observation of splenic trauma: when is a little too much? *J Pediatr Surg.* 1999;34:1124–1126.
68. Wasvary H, Howells G, Villala M, et al. Nonoperative management of adult blunt splenic trauma: a 15 year experience. *Am Surg.* 1997;63:73–76.
69. Pearl RH, Wesson DE, Spence LJ, et al. Splenic injury: a 5 year update with improved results and changing criteria for conservative management. *J Pediatr Surg.* 1989;24:428–431.
70. Croce MA, Fabian TC, Menke PG, et al. Nonoperative management of blunt hepatic trauma is the treatment of choice in hemodynamically stable patients; results of a prospective trial. *Ann Surg.* 1995;221:744–753.
71. Taylor GA, O'Donnell BA, Sivit CJ, et al. Abdominal injury score: a clinical score for the assignment of risk in children after blunt trauma. *Radiology.* 1994;190:689–694.

72. Taylor GA, Eichelberger MR, Potter BM. Hematuria: a marker of abdominal injury in children after blunt trauma. *Ann Surg.* 1988;208:688–693.

73. Stalker HP, Kaufman RA, Stedje K. The significance of hematuria in children after blunt abdominal trauma. *AJR Am J Roentgenol.* 1990;154:569–571.

74. Stylianos S. Outcomes from pediatric solid organ injury: role of standardized care guidelines. *Curr Opin Pediatr.* 2005;17:402–406.

75. McLeod RS, Webber E. Evidence-based guidelines for children with isolated spleen or liver injury. *Can J Surg.* 2004;44:458–460.

76. Holmes JF, Mao A, Awasthi S, et al. Validation of a prediction rule for the identification of children with intra-abdominal injuries after blunt torso trauma. *Ann Emerg Med.* 2009;54:528–533.

77. Holmes JF, Wisner DH, McGahan JP, Mower WR, Kuppermann N. Clinical prediction rules for identifying adults at very low risk for intra-abdominal injuries after blunt trauma. *Ann Emerg Med.* 2009;54:575–584.

78. Hegyes MS, Richardson MW, Miller MD. Knee dislocation: complications of non-operative and operative management. *Clin Sports Med.* 2000;19(3):519–543.

79. Shields L, Mital M, Cave EF. Complete dislocation of the knee: experience at the Massachusetts General Hospital. *J Trauma.* 1969;9(3):192–215.

80. Twaddle BC, Bidwell TA, Chapman JR, Simonia PT, Escobedo EM. MRI in complete knee dislocation: a prospective study of clinical, MRI, and surgical findings. *J Bone Joint Surgery Br.* 1996;18(4):573–579.

81. Schenck RC, Stannard JP, Wascher DC. Dislocations and fracture: dislocations of the knee. In: Bucholz RW et al., eds. *Rockwood and Green's Fractures in Adults.* 6th ed. Philadelphia, PA: Lippincott Williams & Wilkins; 2006:2031.

82. Johnson ME, Foster L, DeLee J. Neurologic and vascular injuries associated with knee ligament injuries. *Am J Sports Med.* 2008;36:2448–2462.

83. Green NE, Allen BL. Vascular injuries associated with dislocation of the knee. *J Bone Joint Surgery Am.* 1977;59(2):236–239.

84. Nicandri G, Chamberlain A, Wahl C. Practical management of knee dislocations. *Clin J Sports Med.* 2009;19:125–129.

85. DeBakey ME, Simeone FA. Battle injuries in the arteries in World War II; an analysis of 2471 cases. *Ann Surg.* 1946;123(4):534–579.

86. Kennedy JC. Complete dislocation of the knee joint. *J Bone Joint Surg Am.* 1963;45:889–904.

87. Niall DM, Nutton RW, Keating JF. Palsy of the common peroneal nerve after traumatic dislocation of the knee. *J Bone Joint Surg Br.* 2005;87:664–667.

88. Sisto DJ, Warren RF. Complete knee dislocation: a follow-up study of operative treatment. *Clin Orthop Relat Res.* 1985;198:94–101.

89. LaPrade RF, Terry GC. Injuries to the posterolateral aspect of the knee: association of anatomic injury patterns with clinical instability. *Am J Sports Med.* 1997;25(4):433–438.

90. Bottomley N, Williams A, Birch R, et al. Displacement of the common peroneal nerve in posterolateral corner injuries of the knee. *J Bone Joint Surg Br.* 2005;87(9):1225–1226.

91. McDonough B, Wojyts E. Multiligamentous injuries of the knee and associated vascular injuries. *Am J Sports Med.* 2009;37(1):156–159.

92. Barnes CJ, Pietrobon R, Higgins LD. Does the pulse examination in patients with traumatic knee dislocation predict a surgical arterial injury? *J Trauma.* 2002;53(6):1109–1114.

93. Mills WJ, Barei DP, McNair P. The value of the ankle-brachial index for diagnosing arterial injury after knee dislocation: a prospective study. *J Trauma.* 2004;24:403–407.

94. Byone RP, Miles WS, Bell RM, et al. Noninvasive diagnosis of vascular trauma by duplex ultrasonography. *J Vasc Surg.* 1991;14:346–352.

95. Levy BA, Zlowodzki MP, Graves M, Cole PA. Screening for extremity arterial injury with arterial pressure index. *Am J Emerg Med.* 2005;23:689–695.

96. Johansen K, Lynch K, Paun M, Copass M. Noninvasive vascular tests reliably exclude occult arterial trauma in injured extremities. *J Trauma.* 1991;31(4):515–519.

97. Treiman GS, Yellin AE, Weaver FA, et al. Examination of the patient with knee dislocation: the case for selective arteriography. *Arch Surg.* 1992;127:1056–1063.

98. Frykman GK, Wolf A, Coyle T. An algorithm for management of peripheral nerve injuries. *Orthop Clin North Am.* 1981;12(2):239–244.

99. U.S. Department of Health and Human Services, National Heart Lung and Blood Institute. Deep vein thrombosis. http://www.nhlbi.nih.gov/health/dci/Diseases/Dvt/DVT_WhatIs.html. Accessed October 16, 2013.

100. Prandoni P, Polistena P, Bernardi E, et al. Upper-extremity deep vein thrombosis: risk factors, diagnosis, and complications. *Arch Intern Med.* 1997;157(1):57–62.

101. Verstraete M. Prevention and treatment of venous thromboembolism after major surgery. *Trauma.* 1991;1:39–51.

102. Seed WA. Pulmonary embolism: part 1. *Vasc Med.* 1991;2:71–83.

103. Shackford S, Moser K. Deep vein thrombosis and pulmonary embolism in trauma patients. *J Intensive Care Med.* 1988;3:87–98.

104. Knudson MT, Dawson R. Prevention of venous thromboembolism in trauma patients. *J Trauma.* 1994;37:480–487.

105. Treat SD, Smith PA, Wen DY, Kinderknecht JJ. Deep vein thrombosis of the subclavian vein in a college volleyball player. *Am J Sports Med.* 2004;32:529–532.

106. Snead D, Marberry KM, Rowdon G. Unique treatment regimen for effort thrombosis in the non-dominant extremity of an overhead athlete: a case report. *J Athl Train.* 2009;44(1):94–97.

107. Adelman MA, Stone DH, Riles TS, et al. Multidisciplinary approach to the treatment of Paget-Schroetter syndrome. *Ann Vasc Surg.* 1997;11:149–154.

108. Rutherford RB, Hurlbert SN. Primary subclavian-axillary vein thrombosis: consensus and commentary. *Cardiovasc Surg.* 1996;4:420–423.

109. Nemmers DW, Thorpe PE, Knibbe MA, Beard DW. Upper extremity venous thrombosis: case report and literature review. *Orthop Rev.* 1990;19:164–172.

Lightning

Katie Walsh Flanagan, EdD, ATC

From the Field Scenario

It is late August and Tameka was just hired as the girls' lacrosse coach for Flantech High School. She was excited to teach the girls about the sport she loved so much. Tameka had recently moved to this North Carolina town from California, and she was still adjusting to the heat and humidity of the southern summers. For that reason, she held practices in the late afternoon—early evenings from 5:00–7:30 PM. Today, she was quite happy when the clouds rolled in and the wind picked up, because the forecasted rain would cool the sticky, humid weather. When the clouds rumbled and the rain began, Tameka was surprised that the girls wanted to stop the drills. In California, lacrosse practice was never suspended for rain, so she blew the whistle louder over the noise of the storm and yelled for the girls to continue the skills. When lightning flashed between the clouds, some of the girls screamed and ran toward the bleachers for shelter. Tameka was confused about why they would be so afraid of a silly storm, but when lightning flashed nearby, she told the girls to run from the bleachers to the trees along the side of the field. "Don't they know," she thought, "that lightning is attracted to metal?" Some of the girls ran to the picnic shelter that was on the opposite side of the field. "Well," Tameka thought, "At least they are smarter than I was—they will be dry." The rain arrived in sheets and the thunderstorm raged on for 15 minutes. As soon as the rain let up, she blew the whistle for the girls to return to the field and continue drills. Some of the girls whined about the lightning still flashing between the clouds, but Tameka explained that everyone knows that that type of lightning never hurts anyone and will not come to the ground. The next day, Tameka was very surprised to be called into a meeting with both the principal and athletic director, where she was reprimanded for violating student safety.

Discussion Questions

1. What misconceptions did Tameka have about lightning?
2. What should the athletic director have done to prevent this from occurring?
3. If you were the principal or athletic director, what would you have said in the meeting and what would the outcome have been?

Introduction

Lightning intrigued people long before Ben Franklin first flew a kite in a thunderstorm. The phenomenon has been viewed with both awe and fear throughout history. Death by lightning is the second-highest storm-related fatality; only flooding kills more people annually.[1,2] Lightning kills approximately 50 people and injures hundreds more each year[3-7] and causes millions of dollars in property damage.[8] Of the fatalities, the overwhelming majority are attributed to being outdoors during a thunderstorm. There are about 25 million cloud-to-ground lightning strikes annually in the United States.[9] Although more and more people know how to prevent lightning injury, there are always some who refuse to acknowledge lightning's danger. This chapter addresses the properties of lightning, the medical consequences of being injured by lightning, prevention strategies to lower the risk of being injured or killed by lightning, and treatment strategies.

Background and Causes

Although there have been reports of lightning striking "out of the blue,"[10] the typical approach of a thunderstorm is quite noticeable. Lightning is an extremely high current (tens of kiloamperes) electrical discharge most often resulting from interaction within or between clouds, and between clouds and the ground.[11] Most lightning is cloud to cloud and does not cause harm on the earth. This chapter focuses on cloud-to-ground lightning, which does cause harm.

As clouds form over the earth, an electric charge is generated between the cloud (typically negative) and the earth (positive) as the thunderstorm passes over. Leader strokes leave the cloud, while each subsequent stroke (stepped leader) follows the established path downward in an intermittent progression (hence the term *stepped* leader). A leader stroke channels through virgin air, whereas the stepped leader follows the channel created by the leader stroke.[11] This intermittent drive toward the earth occurs in milliseconds, giving lightning a flickering appearance. In reality, each leader stroke is moving closer to completing the channel with the earth. When lightning gets within a few tens of meters of the ground, upward streamers are induced in any objects that project above ground level. Attachment occurs when one or more downward leader joins with one or more upward streamer. Upward return strokes fill the channel[11,12] and create a wave that rapidly heats the lightning channel to temperatures of up to 50°K (five times hotter than the surface of the sun) and generates a channel pressure upward of 10 atm (the earth is 1 atm).[11-13] The pressure wave created expands the channel and creates an outward-propagating shock wave that produces the associated thunder.[11]

The shock wave produced by lightning can cause property damage in addition to casualties. Thunder can cause glass windows to be broken, which is why it is wise to stay away from windows in a thunderstorm.[8,13] Thunder noise is expressed in decibels (dB) and registers about 120 dB close to the ground stroke.[13] That noise level is comparable to sitting in front of the speakers at a rock concert. One of the more common consequences of lightning injury is a ruptured eardrum. Given the noise level and concussive pressure of lightning, this is understandable.

The lightning channel reportedly traveled up to 10 miles away from the main thunderstorm body.[14] People have been killed from a distant storm, while the sky overhead is relatively clear of clouds.[10] Lightning does occur in the winter during snowstorms.[15] In recent years, there have been reports of snow-related lightning deaths.[13] Lightning can also form in other scenarios such as volcanic eruptions, as a result of the dust created in forest fires, near fireballs created by nuclear explosions, and it is also very common with tornadoes.[11,13]

Signs of impending thunderstorms are very noticeable. Clouds thicken and darken, the wind shifts or becomes faster, and the humidity changes. Paying attention to the weather in the local and surrounding vicinity can make the difference between life and death, particularly with fast-moving violent weather. The National Weather Service (NWS) broadcasts severe storm warnings to the public. A *watch* indicates that conditions are favorable for severe weather, whereas a *warning* indicates that severe weather has been detected in the area. Neither a watch nor a warning is definitive to a particular storm cell, nor to lightning in general.

The warning sign of thunder must not be ignored, because lightning causes thunder. As the NWS advises, "When thunder roars, go indoors." On occasion, thunder may be muffled by snow, mountainous terrain, or local noise. As loud as thunder is near the ground strike, it is rarely heard over a distance of 10 miles.[16] It is important to observe weather patterns and forecasts prior to participating in outdoor events in the summer.

Mechanisms and Causes of Electrical Injury

Lightning and generated electricity are the same physical phenomenon. However, that is about where any similarity, including in the immediate injuries they cause, ends (see **Table 11.1**). The physics (and the mathematics to describe them) of these two common types of electrical phenomena are as dissimilar as the physics of Newton and Einstein. The rise and fall of lightning energy levels is quite different from the more familiar household AC or DC current. Extrapolation of knowledge of electrical injuries to the effects of lightning will almost always be wrong, because lightning injury is not "scalable" to electrical injury. It is far better to learn what lightning does than to try to predict its effects using "common sense."

For instance, most people assume that given the incredibly high amperage and voltage of lightning, the primary cause of death from lightning must be burns. In reality, burns occur in fewer than one third of lightning survivors and, in the vast majority of cases, are quite superficial when they do occur.[17] Lightning is not in contact with skin long enough to cause significant burns. In addition, most lightning injuries are indirect, so that not all of the energy is delivered to the victim.[18,19] It is unlikely that burns from lightning will require even basic treatment and even more rare for them to require grafting, in contrast to high-energy electrical injuries, which often result in deep muscle damage, extensive time in the intensive care and burn care units, and major amputations. The vast majority of lightning survivors, on the other hand, can be safely discharged from the emergency department. In fact, a significant number of lightning survivors do not present to an emergency department or seek medical care for several days after the injury.

Technically, produced electricity is a voltage phenomenon. Lightning, on the other hand, is a current phenomenon, and when attachment of lightning from a cloud to an object on the ground occurs, all voltage disappears. The classic six Kouwenhoven factors often discussed in electrical injury have little application to lightning injury. To be fair, there are two similarities: (1) in some circumstances, both types of injury may have significant barotrauma (trauma caused by changes in air pressure, usually affecting the eardrum) with blunt injuries in addition to any burn or electrical injury; and (2) both may cause significant neurologic damage that may display after the initial phase as chronic pain, brain injury, cognitive deficits, and other neurologically based disability. The critical difference is the amount of time that a victim receives the electrical charge.

TABLE 11.1   A Comparison of the Properties of Lightning and Electricity

	Lightning	Power Line/Electricity
Voltage	10 million to 2 billion V	110 to 70,000 V
Amperage	20,000 to 200,000 A	< 1000 A
Duration	1/1000 to 1/10 second	Seconds
Pathway	Flashover	Internal
Burns	Uncommon and superficial	Deep

Source: Reprinted from *Burns.* 2001;27, Muehlberger T, Vogt PM, Munster AM. The long-term consequences of lightning injuries, Pages 829–833, Copyright © 2001 with permission from Elsevier.

In electrical injuries, a victim remains in contact with current (although a lower voltage and amperage than lightning) until the power source is terminated. This could take several seconds. Providing care to a victim of an electrical shock injury is not safe until the current is turned off. If the current is on, the first responder would join the connection between the victim and the circuit and receive the same charge as the victim. In lightning injuries, contact with current lasts only milliseconds. Lightning current tends to "flash over" a person. Because lightning victims are not connected to a power source, they are safe to touch and treat as long as the rescuer does not endanger himself or herself by entering the storm before the lightning danger has passed. Both injuries require prompt, aggressive resuscitative efforts.[20,21]

More than 99% of the body's resistance to electric current is at the skin.[22] Once a current has breached the skin, it can cause great damage internally, largely because of the watery nature of the internal tissues. Because lightning flashes over the skin, the deep internal injuries typical of electrical shock victims are not common in the lightning victim. The rapid heating of the lightning channel has been demonstrated to cause sweat to evaporate with such force and speed that victims' clothing and shoes are literally blown off.[16,23] In flashover injuries, this energy rarely exceeds the normal resistance of the skin.[24] In both electrical shock and lightning injuries, cardiovascular consequences are likely.

Casualty Demographics

The National Oceanic and Atmospheric Administration (NOAA) maintains casualty demographics on lightning through its publication *Storm Data*. Consistently, lightning has been confirmed to occur most frequently in the summer months (May through September) and between the hours of 10:00 AM and 7:00 PM.[9] This time frame coincides with athletic and outdoor activity, which makes awareness even more critical. As with most weather-related casualties, July is the month with the most fatalities. The southeastern and midwestern United States have the greatest number of casualties. Florida has led national lightning fatality statistics for decades.[9,25] It also leads the country in the number of lightning flashes, with nearly 1.5 million cloud-to-ground flashes annually.[26] Between 2000–2009, the top 10 states with the highest fatalities caused by lightning were (in descending order) Florida, Colorado, Texas, Georgia, North Carolina, Alabama, South Carolina, Ohio, Pennsylvania, and Louisiana.[25] The data for 2007 to 2009 also demonstrate that 95% of lightning fatalities involved people who were outdoors when they were injured.[27]

Military and occupational data are consistent with NOAA records. Lightning strikes injured 350 military personnel in the 3-year period between 1998 and 2001.[28] In a 10-year period, lightning was identified as being among the top 10 mechanisms of injury from external causes in relation to years of life lost.[29] The occupations with the greatest tendency for fatal lightning injury were agriculture, forestry, fishing, construction, and manufacturing.[30,31] All of the occupations had a common denominator: they were outdoor professions. The military report also demonstrated the danger of multiple people being affected at once, because 87% of the strikes involved more than one person. One strike injured 44 persons.[28] Other reports have also documented multiple casualties from lightning, which underlines the importance of vacating to a safe place prior to lightning danger becoming imminent.[32–35]

The activities in which people were engaged at the time of being injured by lightning also show a trend. Eighteen percent of recent deaths involved people in or around the water.[27] They were swimming, fishing, boating, jet skiing, or scuba diving. Swimming pools, regardless of whether they are indoors or outdoors, are not safe from the effects of lightning.[36,37] Eight percent of victims were headed to a safe place to wait out the storm when they were fatally injured. These data do not include lightning strike survivors, who tend to constitute 10 times the number of fatalities.[38]

Being indoors does not completely eliminate the risk posed by lightning. Lightning can enter a building via the plumbing or electrical system. Therefore, using water (e.g., washing dishes, showering) or electrical devices or appliances (e.g., computers) is not safe during a thunderstorm. Neither is using a landline telephone. The electrical charge from the strike can travel through telephone lines into buildings and injure people.[39] Other unsafe areas in buildings are open doors and windows. Because current has an affinity for the path of least resistance, it tends to follow electrical, telephone, and plumbing lines. Staying indoors and away from these channels increases protection from lightning.

Places That Are Not Safe for Waiting Out a Lightning Storm

Tent

Screened-in porch

Picnic shelter

Rain shelter

Beach pavilion

Bus stop shelter

Dugout

Convertible car

Golf cart

In garage with open garage door

Storage shed (garden/tools/athletic equipment)

Under a tree

Under an awning

Under bleachers

Some places that people sought refuge from a storm have contributed to their demise. Nearly all fatalities occurred while the victim was outdoors,[27] with the majority of victims being sheltered under trees. Many fatalities also occurred when people erroneously sought protection from a storm under "shelters" that provided no safety from lightning. **Box 11.1** lists places that do not provide adequate protection from lightning.

Mechanisms of Injury

To fully appreciate the type of damage people suffer as a consequence of lightning, one must understand the basic mechanisms of how lightning can create injury. There are six mechanisms by which lightning strikes can injure people:

1. A **direct injury** occurs when lightning hits the person with no intermediary object taking the impact. These are typically strikes to the head, because that is often the highest point between the ground and the cloud. This type of injury is thought to be the most common mechanism of lightning injury but in fact is very rare.[18]
2. A **contact injury** is sustained when a person is in contact with an object struck by lightning. Examples include leaning against a tree or tent pole, holding an umbrella, sitting on bleachers, holding hardwired telephones, and being in contact with plumbing or another object that transmits the charge to the person.
3. A **side flash** is the mechanism that causes injury to those seeking shelter under trees, in a dugout or picnic shelter, and so on (see Box 11.1). People mistakenly believe that if they are out of the rain, they are safe from lightning. In a side flash, lightning strikes an object (a tree, for example) and a portion side steps to a nearby person. Thirty to 35% of lightning fatalities are caused by a side flash mechanism.[18]
4. The mechanism most disconcerting for participants in athletics and outdoor recreation is when a single bolt hits the ground and creates a **step voltage** (also known as a **ground current**). In this situation, there is danger of suffering the effects of lightning energy for a considerable distance from where the lightning hit the ground. The step voltage can radiate outward from the strike and cause multiple casualties. This is by far the most common mechanism of lightning fatalities.[18]

direct injury A mechanism of lightning injury by which the lightning strikes the person or object directly.

contact injury A mechanism of lightning injury by which the lightning strikes an object to which the victim is connected.

side flash A mechanism of lightning injury by which the lightning strikes a nearby object, then a portion of the strike side steps to a nearby person.

step voltage A mechanism of lightning injury by which the lightning strikes the ground and radiates outward from the strike to affect those within the radiating current. Also known as *ground current*.

ground current See *step voltage*.

upward leader A mechanism of lightning injury by which the victim becomes a weak, incomplete part of an electrical channel attempting to complete the lightning channel to earth.

blunt injury A mechanism of lightning injury by which the lightning strike causes a concussive force creating blunt injuries such as ruptured tympanic membranes or violent muscular contractions that cause dislocations or fractures.

5. An **upward leader** is an incomplete lightning channel arising from the ground through a person.[40] It does not complete the lightning channel, but nevertheless the person suffers the effects of the energy generated by the upward leader.

6. In a **blunt injury**, the energy created by the lightning channel acts similarly to an explosion, creating a shock wave. A person can sustain violent muscular contractions, be thrown a distance, or suffer internal damage because of the concussive nature of the strike. Injuries sustained via blunt injury include ruptured eardrums, fractures, dislocations, and contusions.

Prevention

The most critical aspect of lightning safety is to have a clear, written emergency action plan (EAP) specific to not only lightning, but to each venue. Identifying a reliable means of monitoring the local weather is a major component of the EAP. Because thunderstorms can arise and dissipate quickly, the NWS will never be able to warn of each dangerous lightning situation as it does for weather hazards such as tornadoes, hurricanes, and floods. Avoiding becoming a casualty of lightning thus requires personal responsibility for safety. Being aware of the weather conditions, especially in the summer months, is very important. **Table 11.2** includes federal weather-monitoring websites (NOAA and NWS) that can assist with the gross estimation of current weather. There is often a significant time lag between detection and broadcast of the data, so caution should be used in relying on these sites for real-time warning. No place outside is safe when thunderstorms are in the area. Modifying, postponing, or canceling outdoor activities and events may prevent injury and loss of life. The vast majority of deaths since 2005 have been people who were within a few feet of safety but chose to continue their outdoor activity or left a good shelter prior to the storm passing.

Prevention begins with education and appreciation of the danger of lightning. It is absolutely critical that adults who supervise or are responsible for children (e.g., teachers, lifeguards, coaches, scout leaders, camp directors) know and execute lightning safety guidelines.[41–44] Further, teaching children simple lightning safety guidelines is strongly recommended. The NOAA's Lightning Safety website (see Table 11.2) has outstanding educational materials suitable for youth, as well as catchy phrases to teach children to remember what to do in the event of a storm **(Box 11.2)**. In other situations, adults may be under the direction of others, such as in collegiate athletics, where young adults are led by coaches. The National Collegiate Athletic Association (NCAA) declares that an identified individual must have "unchallengeable authority" to modify or cancel workout sessions or events if lightning is a threat.[43]

Strategies to employ for prevention include adhering to published lightning safety guidelines. The NCAA, the National Athletic Trainers' Association, and the American Meteorological Society have all published documents addressing lightning safety. All of these guidelines stress the importance of knowledge

---

TABLE 11.2 Related Websites

Lightning Safety	http://www.lightningsafety.noaa.gov/
Lightning Strike and Electric Shock Survivors, International (LSESSI)	http://www.lightning-strike.org
National Athletic Trainers' Association	http://www.nata.org
National Collegiate Athletic Association	http://www.ncaa.org
National Lightning Safety Institute	http://www.lightningsafety.com
National Oceanic and Atmospheric Administration (NOAA)	http://www.noaa.gov
National Weather Service (NWS)	http://www.nws.noaa.gov

Lightning Safety Catch Phrases and Educational Tools

No Place Outside Is Safe When Thunderstorms Are in the Area!

When Lightning Roars, Go Indoors!

When You Hear It [thunder], Clear It; When You See It [lightning], Flee It

Half an Hour Since Thunder Roars, Now It's Safe to Go Outdoors!

Source: Modified from National Weather Service. Lightning Safety. Available at: http://www.lightningsafety.noaa.gov/. Accessed April 15, 2011.

of weather in the region, clear directions regarding when to vacate and return to the outdoors, and knowledge and use of buildings or areas deemed safer from lightning.[41–44]

Keeping on top of developing weather can include using the NWS website and weather radios. Subscribing to a professional lightning detection service that has been externally verified may be worth the cost when working with large groups of people. It requires considerably more time to evacuate masses at large events to safe buildings than it does to clear a swimming pool. Hand-held personal lightning detectors have not been sufficiently reviewed to determine their effectiveness.[44,45]

Identifying and knowing the properties of a safe place to go to prevent a lightning injury is also a part of lightning safety strategy and the lightning EAP. Substantial buildings where people live and work are a good place to wait out storms.[4] Too often, people resort to a *shelter* instead of a building. A shelter typically will not prevent lightning from striking the person via a side flash.[46,47] Most people identify shelters with a place of refuge from the rain. Current lightning protection codes establish that a building is safe from total destruction by lightning, but these codes do not address the safety of the occupants within these dwellings. Whereas structures and safe buildings all have a roof, certain structures often do not have the other properties required for safety from lightning hazard—namely, four solid walls, a roof, plumbing, and wiring, all of which are common to places people live or work. Lightning protection and grounding of a building is different from what is needed to protect individuals in a shelter. Certain structures are safer than others. Substantial buildings that have wiring, plumbing, and telephone service have consistently been determined to be safe places, as long as individuals avoid the indoor hazards discussed previously (e.g., landline telephones and game boxes, water use, computer use, etc.).[3,11–13,44,48–50] Another safe place is a fully enclosed metal car, bus, or van with all the windows fully rolled up.[2,6,13,44,48–50]

When a large group of children were injured by lightning while sleeping in a tent, a contributory factor may have been their body positions on the ground.[33] Because they were unprotected by not being in a substantial building, and lightning travels along the ground, lying flat afforded more opportunity for the lightning strike to traverse through the children. This mass casualty situation might not have occurred had the children been in a building deemed safe from lightning.

In addition to the unsafe shelters listed in Box 11.1, people often have mistakenly sought protection from lightning hazard in other places. Flagpoles; open fields; near or on elevated coaching stands, deer stands, or bleachers; metal fences; and beaches, swimming pools, lakes, and the ocean are not safe. Golf carts, bicycles, motorcycles, and open farm equipment offer no protection from lightning injury.[51,52] When outdoors in an unfamiliar area, be certain to inquire about the nature of weather systems indigenous to the regions. For example, in some mountainous areas, lightning occurs much earlier in the day than in the Southeast. Tracking storms that suddenly appear through valleys is challenging, so a clear appreciation of the characteristics of thunderstorms specific to the locale is paramount.[53]

It is important to note that nothing "attracts" lightning, including metal. Holding mobile phones and iPods does not cause a person to be injured. Instead, it is likely that victims using such devices were distracted by them and not paying attention to the weather surrounding them.[54–58] Another aspect of the EAP is to clearly establish criteria for suspending and resuming activity if lightning is in the area. Time must be allowed for all participants and spectators to get completely within a safe location, car, bus, or van long before the threat of lightning is in the area. If thunder is heard, or lightning is seen, the EAP must be put into effect. At minimum, everyone must be completely within the identified safe location when the leading edge of the storm reaches 6 miles from the venue. Everyone must stay within the safe location until there is a full 30 minutes without either thunder or lightning. Every time thunder is heard or lightning seen, the 30-minute clock is re-started. All participants and spectators should be made aware of this 30-minute clock prior to vacating the outdoor venue.[59]

Recognition

Sometimes it is difficult to unravel the cause of injury when a lightning incident is not witnessed or when an entire group is affected and members remember only that they encountered inclement weather at the time of their disaster. In contrast, team sporting and mass participation events disrupted by lightning often have many witnesses, although they may have differing accounts. Immediate response to injured individuals by athletic trainers, coaches, and emergency personnel shifts the focus to a multicasualty incident response. Because it is unlikely that the lightning is an isolated event, the main concern becomes to secure the scene and move everyone to safety until all lightning danger has passed.

Management of a Lightning Victim

Death by lightning is a result of a heart attack at the time of the injury.[59,60] A lightning strike can cause the heart muscle to quiver or stop beating. Cardiac physiology allows the heart to spontaneously restart itself, but if the person is not breathing, the heart will stop beating a second time, and without intervention, that person will die.

Victims often present pulseless, and with fixed and dilated pupils. It is absolutely essential for rescuers to violate the basic principle of triage (that is, "treat the living first") and provide cardiopulmonary resuscitation to those who appear to be dead. People injured by lightning and found with no pulse and fixed and dilated pupils have survived following aggressive resuscitation.[61-64] Those who receive delayed care often suffer brain damage because of lack of oxygen and do not usually fully recover. [65,66]

keraunoparalysis A transient paralysis, extreme vasoconstriction, and sensory disturbance caused by a lightning strike.

Survivors of lightning strikes suffer a number of physical and psychological symptoms. Nerve and brain symptoms are the most common, but damage to the eyes, ears, and skin often occurs as well. There are a few unique physical manifestations of lightning injury. **Keraunoparalysis** designates a transient paralysis, extreme vasoconstriction, and sensory disturbance caused by a lightning strike.[67]

Cherington noticed that the majority of damage involved the brain and spinal cord[68] and established four levels of neurologic complications subsequent to lightning strikes.[69] Category I includes transient symptoms of numbness, weakness, loss of consciousness, and headaches. Patients in this category rarely require long-term intervention or rehabilitation.[59-60] Category II involves protracted or permanent symptoms. Most serious is swelling of the brain due to lack of oxygen resulting from delayed resuscitation. This condition, if not fatal, can be extremely debilitating and is irreversible.[68] Bleeding within the brain and persistent and progressive neuropsychological dysfunction are also in category II.

Category III patients have delayed neurologic syndromes, often displaying new neurologic signs or symptoms long after the initial damage has occurred. The link between the lightning strike and the subsequent damage is not always established. Syndromes in this category include movement disorders, seizures, and amyotrophic lateral sclerosis. All have been rarely reported in lightning strike survivors, and a definite relationship has not been established.[68,70]

The final category of neurologic complications of lightning strikes is category IV: lightning-linked complications resulting from the barotrauma from lightning. Blunt trauma injuries, including intracranial bleeding caused by trauma and spinal injuries, fall into this category. Eye and ear injuries are common in lightning strike survivors. The intense optical radiation can create a number of eye injuries. Cataracts have been reported to occur fairly early, within the first few weeks to months of the injury.[71] Unequal pupil size, pooling of blood in the eye, retinal detachment, sensitivity to light, and transient blindness have also been reported.[16,46,72] Ruptured tympanic membranes (eardrums) are reported in 30% to 50% of survivors,[16,39] and a few suffer fractured ear bones. Follow-up studies indicate that the majority of

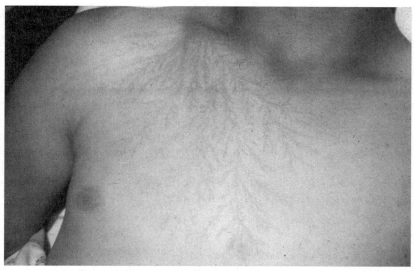

Figure 11.1 Keraunographic markings on a lightning strike patient.

hearing deficits have been restored to pre-injury levels.[47] Conductive hearing loss has been infrequently documented in association with eardrum rupture.[57] Injuries to the eighth cranial nerve cause dizziness, persistent ringing in the ears, and uncoordinated muscle movements. Facial paralysis may also occur.[16,39]

Fewer than one third of survivors have burns or skin markings. This is most likely because of the frequently indirect nature of lightning injury and the very short time of exposure. Lightning flashes over the superficial layer of the skin, preventing the deep penetrating burns that are common to electric shock injuries. Burns are found, however, along the sweat patterns in the skin. They tend to congregate below the armpit, below the breasts, and down the midchest and are first- or second-degree burns. Other burns are caused by contact with metal (e.g., jewelry, belt buckles, underwire in bras, body piercings, cleats on shoes). Specific skin markings, also referred to as Lichtenberg figures, are a sign unique to strike but rarely occur. These markings are passing and may be attributed to blood vessel and skin reactions to lightning; they are not true burns (see **Figure 11.1**).[16,73]

Recovery from Lightning Strikes

The majority of lightning strike victims survive, but many have significant disability. Their symptoms may be debilitating, persistent, and have little chance of improving over time. Complications of the nervous system are found in 70% of lightning survivors.[24,74] **Box 11.3** summarizes the common chronic symptoms reported by lightning strike survivors. The symptoms are similar to those of a traumatic brain injury and are difficult to quantify via traditional medical testing.[69] Electroencephalograms, computed tomography, radiography, and magnetic resonance imaging typically yield results within normal ranges.[23,69]

Box 11.3

Long-Term Complications of Lightning Survivors

Headache	Depression	Behavioral changes
Dizziness	Self-isolation	Absence-type seizure activity
Personality changes	Chronic pain	Palpitations
Concentration issues	Sleep disturbances	

Source: Adapted from Cooper MA. Disability, not death, is the main problem with lightning injury. *Natl Weather Digest.* 2001;25(1,2):43–47; and Muehlberger T, Vogt PM, Munster AM. The long-term consequences of lightning injuries. *Burns.* 2001;27:829–833.

Life skills may be altered in the lightning survivor. Despite the fact that nearly one third of lightning injuries are work related and survivors may qualify for disability benefits, it is often difficult for them to be awarded these benefits.[2] Frequently, short-term memory is impaired, and survivors returning to work may be unable to learn new skills, organize thoughts, or multitask, resulting in unemployment.[23] Survivors may also suffer unrelenting headaches that do not respond to traditional relief medications. Personality changes, depression, loss of cognitive reasoning, and self-isolation are common as well.[23]

Neuropsychological tests, similar to those used to determine return to play following concussions, have recently been strongly suggested for those affected by lightning.[39,69] Cognitive therapy and counseling have also been shown to be beneficial.[39] An international support group for survivors and loved ones has been successful in addressing issues and concerns germane to survivors.[75] Within the group organization, support can be found for both survivors and family members who seek to better understand the effects of lightning injury. There is solidarity and comfort in knowing that others (both survivors and family) are experiencing and coping with the life changes associated with the trauma.

Return to Play

Most of the time, it is not a question of whether an individual can return to the same game, because it is likely that the entire event has been disrupted. Whether someone was injured by direct strike, contact, ground current, or upward streamer makes little difference. The individual injuries are what will direct the individual's care.

The vast majority of victims will not need hospitalization, although some may be too confused or shaken up to resume play. It is safe for an individual to return to play in a later game if he or she is clear minded enough to follow commands, is physically coordinated, has good balance, has overcome most of the musculoskeletal pain, and can pass on-field concussion assessments. For the individual who only experienced tingling, hair standing on end, or similar static electrical feeling with no other symptoms, there is no danger in immediately returning to play.

Summary

Death from lightning is a largely preventable occurrence. There is no place outdoors that is safe from lightning, and most so-called shelters under which people seek refuge from the rain are not proper protection from this phenomenon either. The best practice is to identify a substantial building in which to wait out a storm. Everyone should be inside the building by the time the leading edge of the thunderstorm comes within 6 miles of the activity site. Waiting a full 30 minutes after the last lightning or thunder is critical before resuming outdoor activity.

Those injured by lightning are safe to touch and treat, as long as the rescuer is not also in danger of being struck. Lightning victims may appear to be dead (pulseless, with fixed and dilated pupils), but it is critical to begin aggressive cardiopulmonary resuscitation immediately on any victims who appear lifeless.

With education, most lightning injuries and deaths can be averted. It is imperative that the message gets out that there is no place outdoors that is safe during a thunderstorm. It is critical that everyone be responsible for his or her own safety and also act as a vocal spokesperson promoting lightning safety.

Clinical Case Scenarios

1. An adult male was working on his lawn mower in his open garage during a lightning storm. He was using an electric drill to repair his lawn mower when lightning struck the power transformer on the power line outside of his home. The resulting surge traveled through the electrical wires to the drill and threw him across the garage floor. He suffered no reported permanent damage.
   a. How could he have prevented this injury?
   b. How did this injury occur?

2. An 18-year-old woman and her grandmother were in a park in Omaha, Nebraska, on a July afternoon waiting for fireworks. They decided to pass the time during a storm by sitting on the lawn under a tarp. The grandmother reported that the victim screamed and was lifted off the ground 6 inches when she was struck by lightning. She remained conscious but was confused and disoriented. She was combative in the ambulance but discharged from the hospital 3.5 hours after she arrived. Her resulting injuries included temporary right-sided paralysis/weakness, chronic fatigue syndrome, migraines, and lethargy.

   a. How could the women have prevented this injury?

   b. How many different things can you identify that these two women did wrong in terms of their personal safety?

   c. What other long-term effects could lightning cause?

3. A North Carolina mother was home with her teenage daughter during a thunderstorm when she decided to call her husband, who was working at an outdoor construction site, and warn him of the impending storm. The mother was using the landline telephone when lightning struck and thunder resounded over the house. Because she was conscious and functional, she did not seek medical attention. A few weeks after the incident, she began to suffer seizures because of the traumatic brain injury caused by the lightning strike.

   a. How did this injury occur?

   b. How could it have been prevented?

   c. If lightning hit the house, why wasn't the daughter affected?

Key Terms

blunt injury

contact injury

direct injury

ground current

keraunoparalysis

side flash

step voltage

upward leader

References

1. Curran EB, Holle RL, López RE. *Lightning Fatalities, Injuries, and Damage Reports in the United States: 1959–1994*. Washington, DC: National Oceanic and Atmospheric Administration; 1997. Technical Memorandum NWS SR-193.
2. López RE, Holle RL, Heitkamp TA, et al. The underreporting of lightning injuries and deaths in Colorado. *Bull Am Meteorol Soc*. 1993;74:2171–2178.
3. Duclos PJ, Sanderson LM. An epidemiological description of lightning-related deaths in the United States. *Int J Epidemiol*. 1990;19:673–679.
4. Craig SR. When lightning strikes: pathophysiology and treatment of lightning injuries. *Postgrad Med*. 1986;79:109–112, 121–123.
5. Zegel FH. Lightning deaths in the United States: a seven-year survey from 1959 to 1965. *Weatherwise*. 1967;20:169.
6. López RE, Holle RL. Demographics of lightning casualties. *Semin Neurol*. 1995;15:286–295.
7. National Weather Service. Lightning safety. http://www.lightningsafety.noaa.gov. Accessed June 2010.
8. National Lightning Safety Institute. Lightning costs and losses from attributed sources. http://www.lightningsafety.com/nlsi_lls /nlsi_annual_usa_losses.htm. Accessed June 2010.
9. National Weather Service. Lightning science. http://www.lightningsafety.noaa.gov/science.htm. Accessed June 2010.
10. Dwyer JR. A bolt out of the blue. *Sci Am*. 2005;292(5):64–71.
11. Rakov VA, Uman MA. *Lightning: Physics and Effects*. Cambridge, England: Cambridge University Press; 2003.
12. Uman MA. *All About Lightning*. New York, NY: Dover Publications; 1986.

13. Vavrek JR, Holle RL, López RE. Updated lightning safety recommendations. In: *Preprints of the American Meteorological Society 8th Symposium on Education; January 10–15, 1999; Dallas, TX*. 1993;22(pt 2):378–387.

14. Holle RL, López RE, Howard KW, Vavrek J, Allsopp J. Safety in the presence of lightning. *Semin Neurol*. 1995;15:375–380.

15. Cherington M, Breed DW, Yarnell PR, Smith WE. Lightning injuries during snowy conditions. *Br J Sports Med*. 1998;32(4):333–335.

16. Gatewood MO, Zane RD. Lightning injuries. *Emerg Med Clin North Am*. 2003;22(2):369–403.

17. Cooper MA, Andrews CJ, Holle RL. Lightning injuries. In: Auerbach PS, ed. *Wilderness Medicine*. 5th ed. St. Louis, MO: Mosby/Elsevier; 2007.

18. Cooper MA, Holle RL, Andrews C. *Distribution of lightning injury mechanism*. Presented at 20th International Lightning Detection Conference, Tucson, AZ. http://www.vaisala.co.jp/files/Short_notice_outdoor_lightning_risk_reduction_-_evaluating_its_performance_and_discussion_on_why_it_should_not_be_taught.pdf. Accessed January 19, 2011.

19. Cooper MA, Holle RL. How to use public education to change lightning safety standards (and save lives and injuries). Paper presented at: American Meteorological Society 14th Symposium on Education; January 2005; San Diego, CA.

20. Fontanarosa PB. Electrical shock and lightning strike. *Ann Emerg Med*. 1993;22(pt 2):378–387.

21. Adukauskiene D, Vizgirdaite V, Mazeikiene S. Electrical injuries [in Lithuanian]. *Medicina (Kaunas)*. 2007;43(3):259–266.

22. Fish RM, Geddes LA. Conduction of electrical current to and through the human body: a review. *Eplasty*. 2009;9:e44.

23. Cooper MA. Disability, not death, is the main problem with lightning injury. *Natl Weather Digest*. 2001;25(1,2):43–47.

24. Muehlberger T, Vogt PM, Munster AM. The long-term consequences of lightning injuries. *Burns*. 2001;27:829–833.

25. Holle RL. Number of lightning deaths by state from 2000–2009. http://www.nws.noaa.gov/om/hazstats.shtml. Accessed May 2010.

26. Holle RL. Number of cloud-to-ground flashes by state from 1996–2008. National Lightning Detection Network. May 2009.

27. Holle RL. Summary of 2007–2009 US lightning fatalities. National Lightning Detection Network. November 2009.

28. Lightning-associated injuries and deaths among military personnel—United States, 1998–2001. *MMWR*. 2002;51(38):859–862.

29. Bailer AJ, Bena JF, Stayner LT, Halperin WE, Parks RM. External cause-specific summaries of occupational fatal injuries. Part II: an analysis of years of potential life lost. *Am J Ind Med*. 2003;43:251–261.

30. Robinson CF, Halperin WE, Alterman T, et al. Mortality patterns among construction workers in the United States. *Occup Med*. 1995;10(2):269–283.

31. Adekoya N, Nolte KB. Struck-by-lightning deaths in the United States. *J Environ Health*. 2005;67(9):45–50, 58.

32. Cherington M, Martorano FJ, Siebuhr LV, Stieg RL, Yarnell PR. Childhood lightning injuries on the playing field. *J Emerg Med*. 1994;12(1):39–41.

33. Carte AE, Anderson RB, Cooper MA. A large group of children struck by lightning. *Ann Emerg Med*. 2002;39(6):665–670.

34. Duppel H, Lobermann M, Reisinger EC. Hit by lightning out of the blue. *Dtsch Med Wochenschr*. 2009;134(23):1214–1217.

35. Delaney JS, Drummond R. Mass casualties and triage at a sporting event—review. *Br J Sport Med*. 2002;36:85–88.

36. Wiley S. Shocking news about lightning and pools. *USA Swimming Safety Q*. 1998;4:1–2.

37. Cherington M. Lightning injuries in sports—situations to avoid. *Sports Med*. 2001;31(4):301–308.

38. Cherington M, Walker M, Boyson R, et al. *Closing the gap on actual numbers of lightning casualties and deaths*. Paper presented at: American Meteorological Society's 11th Conference on Applied Climatology; January 10–15, 1999; Dallas, TX.

39. Gluncic I, Roje Z, Gluncic V, Poljak K. Ear injuries caused by lightning: report of 18 cases. *J Laryngol Otol*. 2001;115:4–8.

40. Cooper MA. A fifth mechanism of lightning injury. *Acad Emerg Med*. 2002;9(2):172–174.

41. Walsh KM, Bennett B, Cooper MA, et al. National Athletic Trainers' Association Position Statement: lightning safety for athletics and recreation. *J Athl Train*. 2000;35(4):471–477.

42. Zimmermann C, Cooper MA, Holle RL. Lightning safety guidelines. *Ann Emerg Med*. 2002;39(6):660–665.

43. Bennett BL, Holle RL, López RE. Lightning safety guideline 1D. In: Klossner D, ed. *2009–2010 National Collegiate Athletic Association Sports Medicine Handbook*. Overland Park, KS: National Collegiate Athletic Association; 2009.

44. Roeder WP, Vavrek RJ. Lightning safety for schools—an update. http://www.weather.gov/os/lightning/resources/ASSE-Schools.pdf. Accessed May 2010.

45. Roeder WP. *Last minute outdoor lightning risk reduction—a method to estimate its effectiveness and comments on its utility in public education*. Paper presented at: The American Meteorological Society's Fourth Conference on the Meteorological Applications of Lightning Data; January 11–15, 2009; Phoenix, AZ.

46. Cooper MA. Emergent care of lightning and electrical injuries. *Semin Neurol*. 1995;15(3):268–278.

47. Soni UK, Mistry B, Mallya SV, Grewal DS, Varadkar S. Acoustic effects of lightning. *Auris Nausus Larynx*. 1993;20(4):285–289.

48. Holle RL, Lopez RE, Vavrek J, Howard KW. *Educating individuals about lightning*. Paper presented at: American Meteorological Society 7th Symposium on Education; January 11–16, 1998; Phoenix, AZ.

49. Holle RL, López RE. Lightning: impacts and safety. *World Meterol Bull*. 1998;47:148–155.

50. Holle R. Lightning-caused deaths and injuries in and near dwellings and other buildings. www.lightningsafety.com/nlsi_lls/lightning-caused-deaths.pdf. Accessed June 2010.

51. American Meteorological Society. Lightning safety awareness statement. *Bull Am Met Soc*. 2002;83. http://www.ametsoc.org/policy/lightningpolicy_2002.html. Accessed June 2010.

52. Cherington M. Hazards of bicycling: from handlebars to lightning. *Semin Neurol*. 2000;20(2):247–254.

53. Zafren K, Durrer B, Herry JP, Brugger H. Lightning injuries: prevention and on-site treatment in mountains and remote areas. Official guidelines of the International Commission for Mountain Emergency Medicine and the Medical Commission of the International Mountaineering and Climbing Federation (ICAR and UIAA MEDCOM). *Resuscitation*. 2005;65:369–372.

54. Faragher RM. Injury from lightning strike while using mobile phone. Statistics and physics do not suggest a link. *BMJ*. 2006;333(7558):96.

55. Esprit S, Kothari P, Dhillon R. Injury from lightning strike while using a mobile phone. *BMJ*. 2006;332(7556):1513.

56. Althaus CW. Injury from lightning strike while using mobile phone—mobile phones are not lightning strike risk. *BMJ*. 2006;333(7558):96.

57. Cooper MA. More on thunderstorms and iPods. *NEJM*. 2007;357(14):1447–1448.

58. Andrews CJ, Darveniza M. Telephone-mediated lightning injury: an Australian survey. *J Trauma*. 1989;29:665–671.

59. Walsh KM, Cooper MA, Holle R, Rakov VA, Roeder WP, Ryan M. National Athletic Trainers' Association Position Statement: Lightning Safety for Athletics and Recreation. 2013;48(2):258–270.

60. Cooper MA. Lightning: prognostic signs for death. *Ann Emerg Med*. 1980;9:134–138.

61. Steinbaum S, Harviel JD, Haffin JH, Jordan MH. Lightning strike to the head: case report. *J Trauma*. 1994;36(1):113–115.

62. Slesinger TL, Bank M, Drumheller BC, et al. Immediate cardiac arrest and subsequent development of cardiogenic shock caused by lightning strike. *J Trauma*. 2010;68(1):E5–E7.

63. Dronacharya L, Poudel R. Lightning induced atrial fibrillation. *Kathmandu Univ Med J*. 2008;6(24):514–515.

64. Dhawan S, Sultan-Ali IA. Lightning-induced ECG changes and hydrostatic pulmonary edema. *Clin Cardiol*. 2009;32(8):E71.

65. Rash W. Cardiac injury and death by lightning strike. *J Emerg Nurs*. 2008;34(5):470–471.

66. Saglam H, Yavuz Y, Yurumez Y, Ozkececi G, Kilit C. Lightning strike at St. Albans game kills Bethesda student, injures 10. *Washington Post*. May 18, 1991:A1.

67. Ten Duis HJ, Klasen HJ, Reenalda PE. Keraunoparalysis, a 'specific' lightning injury. *Burns Incl Therm Inj*. 1985;12(1):54–57.

68. Cherington M. Central nervous system complications of lightning and electrical injuries. *Semin Neurol*. 1995;15:233–239.

69. Cherington M. Neurologic manifestations of lightning strikes. *Neurology*. 2003;60(2):182–185.

70. Jafari H, Courztier P, Camu W. Motor neuron disease after electric injury. *J Neurol Neurosurg Psychiatry*. 2001;71:265–267.

71. Cooray V, Cooray C, Andrews CJ. Lightning caused injuries in humans. *J Electrostatics*. 2007;65:386–394.

72. Zane RD. Lightning injuries. *Emerg Med Clin North Am*. 2004;22:369–403.

73. Andrews CJ, Cooper MA, Darveniza M. *Lightning Injuries: Electrical, Medical, and Legal Aspects*. Boca Raton, FL: CRC Press; 1992.

74. Lewis AM. Understanding the principles of lightning injuries. *J Emerg Nurs*. 1997;23:535–541.

75. Cooper MA, Marshburn S. Lightning Strike and Electrical Shock Survivors, International. *Neuro Rehabil*. 2005;20:43–47.

Asthma

Michael G. Miller, PhD, EdD, ATC, CSCS, FNATA

Robert J. Baker, MD, PhD, ATC, FACSM, FAAFP

From the Field Scenario

Adalyn, a sophomore high school athlete, has been running for approximately 2 years, both on her own and as part of a team. During this time, she has had episodes of breathlessness that resulted in cessation of her running activity. She sought medical attention about her breathing difficulties and was diagnosed by her primary care physician as having asthma. She was prescribed both controller and relief medications to treat her condition. During a cloudy day in the early fall, outside Chicago, she was participating in a cross-country meet. At mile 2, Adalyn started to experience breathing exacerbations. She proceeded to stop running to catch her breath; however, cessation of activity did not produce significant improvements in her breathing patterns. An assistant coach noticed Adalyn on the side of the course and decided to summon the athletic trainer, who determined that Adalyn was having an asthma attack and sought a relief inhaler to treat the condition. The assistant coach stood by to aid the athletic trainer if necessary. After several minutes, Adalyn began to breathe easier and feel better. While she did not resume her running activities that day, she was fully recovered by the end of the meet.

Discussion Questions

1. A relief inhaler can effectively treat an acute bout of asthma, but it must be administered correctly. What are the steps necessary to deliver the medication to the athlete?
2. If the asthma attack progressed in intensity, emergency medical services activation would be necessary. For a cross-country meet, what should be included in an emergency action plan for that facility/site?
3. What methods could Adalyn, the coach, or the athletic trainer have performed earlier in the day or before the meet, to reduce the risk of an asthma attack?

Introduction

Asthma is a chronic inflammatory disease of the lungs that affects millions of individuals throughout the world. Asthma is triggered by various agents such as allergens, exercise, and the environment but can be controlled and treated successfully. When an asthma attack does occur, proper identification and immediate management is paramount to prevent death or severe complications. Athletes, regardless of their participation level, should follow management guidelines. Coaches working with athletes diagnosed with asthma must know how to activate an asthma management plan when medical professionals are absent. Therefore, it is apparent that all nonmedical personnel associated with coaching or supervising athletes should be aware of how to recognize, treat, and manage an asthma attack. This chapter will discuss asthma and asthma management plans for nonmedical personnel and provide strategies for successful asthma treatment when the situation arises.

Definition

Asthma occurs when the airways become inflamed and airflow is restricted.[1,2] Airway inflammation limits airflow in response to an asthma trigger. This can produce symptoms of chest tightness, shortness of breath, and coughing or wheezing. Airway inflammation will also reduce the available lung surface for oxygen exchange during respiration. Asthma episodes can be variable and symptoms may resolve spontaneously; however, early identification and management of signs and symptoms are paramount to preventing severe complications or loss of life. Sudden death from asthma, although rare, may be associated with risk factors such as a previous severe or life-threatening attack, previous hospital admission for asthma, and/or failure to control asthma.[3,4] However, the benefits of athletic participation and exercise far exceed the potential of death from asthma.[5]

Background and Occurrence of Asthma

In 2009, asthma was thought to affect approximately 22 million people in the United States alone, with nearly 6 million of all affected persons being children.[1] Worldwide, asthma prevalence ranges from 1% to 18% of the population in different countries.[2,6] Individuals who have allergies, eczema (severe dry skin), or a genetic predisposition appear to be at higher risk for developing the disease.[2] Boys tend to have higher incidences than girls; however, in the adult population, women appear to have a higher rate of asthma than do males.[2] The annual death toll from asthma worldwide has been hypothesized to be 250,000, although the specific link to death is not known.[6]

Sudden death from asthma varies by geographic location and population characteristics. Trends for asthma death appear to be decreasing in the United States and other countries. In the United States, the mortality rate from 1994 to 1996 was 2.1 per 100,000; during the years from 1997 to 1998, the rate dropped to 2.0 per 100,000.[7] In 2002, the rate declined to 1.4 per 100,000, suggesting the existence of either better asthma control or better intervention methods when life-threatening exacerbations occurred.[7] The number of sudden deaths from asthma in children and adolescents is lower than other age populations. This is likely because of the lower frequency of children participating in organized sports.[8]

Asthma is one of the leading causes of nontraumatic sudden death in athletes, after all other cardiac causes of sudden death.[9] Although the mortality rate for individuals participating in athletics is low, deaths do occur. A study examining asthma mortality rates from 1993 to 2000 before and after athletic competition showed 61 deaths met the criteria for death from asthma-related complications. Eighteen athletes died during competition and 14 during a practice event. Of these, 57% were competitive athletes and 43% were recreational athletes. For sporting activities, basketball and track appeared to have the highest rate of asthma deaths.[10] Early fall, followed by the summer and spring, appeared to be the seasons in which the most asthma deaths occurred.[10] In a review of asthma deaths in U.S. schools from 1990 to 2003, 42% of asthma deaths were attributed to children participating in some form of physical activity prior to death.[11]

Mechanisms and Causes of Asthma

Asthma is associated with both chronic and acute effects. Exposure to the appropriate stimuli will result in inflammation and airway constriction. Acutely, this can lead to respiratory distress, decreased oxygen absorption, decreased oxygen in the blood, and, in the extreme case, asphyxia (extreme lack of oxygen, which usually results in unconsciousness). Long-term effects of persistent airway inflammation can also lead to airway remodeling, which in turn leads to a decline in lung function.

Airway inflammation is almost always persistent in patients with asthma, regardless of whether an asthmatic is having symptoms.[2] The airway inflammation results from an increase in mast cell production.[12-19] Mast cells release inflammatory substances that lead to mucous secretion and inflammation. These events cause inflammation, leading to structural changes that result in narrowing of the airways. Remodeling of the airways is also a result of altered extracellular matrix (the substance surrounding cells) changes, with depositions of various proteins.[20-23] These changes cause thickening of the walls (large and small airways), representing the chronic inflammation associated with asthma, and appear to be pronounced in the small airways and small air sacs.[24,25] Individuals with fatal asthma also showed signs of increased protein content in the inner and outer sections of the small airways in the lungs.[26]

Airway restriction is also linked to fatal asthma attacks. In postmortem studies, damage has been found within the tissue lining the bronchial tubes, along with blockage of the **airway lumen** with mucus, and an increased airway size, suggesting that death was a result of chronic and persistent airway inflammation.[27-30]

airway lumen The inner lining of the bronchial airways.

Asthma in Athletes

Asthmatic symptoms can occur in athletes participating in any event throughout the year. Studies have shown that cross-country skiers and track and field athletes have a higher risk for asthma than control subjects.[31,32] Factors such as training periods and prolonged hyperventilation associated with these respective sports and exposure to environmental conditions and pollens or allergens may explain the increased incidence.[33] Environmental factors, such as allergens, smoke, and pollution may cause an asthma exacerbation, or even death.[34] Allergens to dust mites, dander, and mold are inherent risk factors shown to cause asthma exacerbations.[35-37] Pollution (indoor and outdoor) has been shown to decrease lung function in people exposed to the polluted areas and may cause breathing problems in athletes with asthma.[38,39]

Asthma severity is variable, depending on the cause or risk factors of the breathing difficulty. When asthma deaths do occur, the symptoms can progress rapidly, irrespective of triggers.[40-42] In one study, 10 asthma deaths were attributed to severe exacerbations that required hospitalization within 1.3 hours of the onset of symptoms. Another report showed that 50% of asthma deaths were attributed to individuals with a history of "severe" asthma.[31,43] Other studies have indicated that a family link may be involved in asthmatic death.[44,45] An examination of the Utah Population Database for genealogy from 1904 to 2006 found a significantly higher risk of death when first-degree relatives rather than second- or third-degree relatives were affected.[46] Racial or ethnic differences may also contribute to a higher risk for asthma and asthma exacerbations. This increased risk may be correlated with socioeconomic factors,[2] but a correlation with sudden asthma death remains unproven. Studies show the ratio of African American athletes with asthma to be higher than the rate for white athletes.[47]

Asthma and Medications

Over-the-counter and prescription asthma medications may affect athletes with asthma. Nonsteroidal anti-inflammatory drugs (NSAIDs), such as ibuprofen, were found to be associated with a rapid onset of asthma exacerbation in a review of cases of asthma fatality.[48] Although the death rate is relatively low, athletes with asthma need to be monitored closely when taking NSAIDs. Beta-blockers may predispose an individual to severe asthma exacerbations because they cause bronchoconstriction. This may either block the effects of β-agonist medications used to treat asthma or directly cause airway constriction.

Recognition and Management of Asthma

Acute respiratory distress in the athlete must be treated emergently whether the athlete has known asthma or not. In their review of asthma death in children, Rainbow and Browne[49] suggest that asthma exacerbations be monitored closely to ensure that the athlete is suffering from asthma symptoms, not anaphylaxis (a life-threatening allergic reaction). Symptoms of anaphylaxis mimic asthma exacerbations, and differentiating between the two conditions is necessary for proper treatment. A slow or absent response to asthma medications given to alleviate respiratory distress may help differentiate the asthma attack from anaphylaxis.[49] Vocal cord dysfunction and hyperventilation syndrome are other conditions that can often be confused with an asthmatic episode. Although these conditions are not very harmful, they can occur alone or along with asthma, in which case they may further complicate the asthma.

The major symptoms of an athlete suffering from asthma are:

- Breathing difficulties
- Breathlessness (rapid and shallow breathing)
- Wheezing (whistling or rattling when breathing out)
- Difficulty speaking in complete sentences
- Confusion
- Drowsiness
- Sweating
- Increased pulse rate
- Chest tightness
- Chest pain
- Bluish skin
- Coughing or any combination of the symptoms listed here[50–52]

These symptoms may be brought on or made worse by exercise. Athletes with exercise-induced bronchospasm may experience these same symptoms after several minutes of exercise. Symptoms of exercise-induced bronchospasm can be as subtle as coughing or wheezing after exercise.

At the time of a severe asthma attack, pending respiratory failure, the athlete may present with mental status changes because of low blood oxygen. The skin, especially of the mouth, fingers, and feet, may appear blue or cyanotic. As respiratory distress progresses, the work of breathing will lead to poor air movement and fatigue, and the use of accessory muscles (usually neck and chest muscles) for breathing will be required. As respiratory complications worsen, the athlete may become drowsy or experience mental status changes such as agitation or loss of consciousness. All of these findings are ominous and should be identified to initiate the potential need for cardiopulmonary resuscitation, recovery breathing, and/or notification of emergency medical services.

When an athlete presents with the aforementioned physical findings, proper and immediate treatment is crucial to alleviate the breathing difficulty.

- First, have the athlete use an inhaled short-acting beta$_2$ agonist (often referred to as a rescue or relief medication). Have the athlete exhale, place the inhaler into the mouth, release the medication, and breathe in the medication over a 10-second period and hold. This may be repeated if necessary (in 10- to 15-second intervals). Relief should occur over several minutes.
- Multiple treatments over 4 hours may be necessary, but they should be spaced apart by 20 minutes, and airflow changes should be monitored with a peak flow meter (PFM), if available.[53,54] Medication can be repeated as often as every 1 to 2 hours if needed.[55]
- Most times, a spacer (a tubular device connected to the inhaler that allows the medication to gather within and then be breathed into the lungs through the mouth) should be used.
- Athletes who require β_2-agonist therapy more often than every 2 to 3 hours or who require supplemental oxygen need to be admitted to the hospital.
- Other factors that may necessitate hospitalization include a history of rapid progression of severity in past exacerbations, poor adherence to an outpatient medication regimen, or inadequate access to medical care.
- If respiratory failure occurs, ventilatory support can be provided via an artificial airway by trained medical personnel.

Any athlete presenting with respiratory difficulty or respiratory arrest should immediately be removed from practice or competition. The medical professional must differentiate causes of respiratory difficulty

Box 12.1

Asthma Emergency Action Plan

1. If an athlete is suspected of having an asthma attack, cease exercise.
2. If feasible, move the athlete into a well-ventilated environment.
3. Measure peak expiratory flow (PEF) if applicable.
    a. If PEF is below 15% of normal baseline measurements:
        i. Have the athlete use his or her prescribed inhaler (2 to 3 times)
4. Monitor airway and breathing for several minutes.
5. Re-measure PEF and administer additional inhaler medication.
6. If symptoms worsen or do not subside, refer immediately to a medical facility.

and treat accordingly. If an athlete is suspected of having an asthma attack but has an unconfirmed diagnosis, follow the guidelines for respiratory support. Management of respiratory difficulty or arrest includes the following interventions: Call emergency services, give oxygen, open the airway if needed, have medical providers provide basic ventilation when needed, provide respiratory support with the use of artificial airways, and suction to maintain a clear airway where indicated. Maintain airway with advanced airway device/technique if the airway is obstructed and the athlete has become unconscious. Severe cases of respiratory difficulty (or if respiratory difficulty quickly worsens) should have medical referral. If the athlete recovers with oxygen and rest, proper medical diagnosis is required to determine the causative factors and the likelihood of having asthma.

Another important aspect of asthma management is developing an asthma emergency action plan.[1] The asthma emergency action plan should be part of each athletic venue's or facility's emergency action plan and address how to treat an asthma emergency (see **Box 12.1**). The specific instructions about how to recognize an asthma attack, the medications required, techniques to administer the medications, lung function zones, and values must be addressed (see **Table 12.1**). Additionally, the asthma action plan should identify who will respond at each venue to asthma emergencies, their roles and functions, and how to contact emergency services when needed. In one study, 31% of cases resulting in asthma deaths in school-aged children had delays of treatment medication, with 17% of all treating respondents stating they had no knowledge that the asthmatic child had asthma or that quick relief medications were

TABLE 12.1   Equipment List for Management of Acute Exacerbation of Asthma

Available to Athlete

1. Short-acting β-agonist inhaler with spacer
2. Spacer: may be improvised with a tape roll
3. Peak flow meter: to monitor lung function
4. Nebulizer
5. Epinephrine (EpiPen)

Available to Coach

1. Spacer: may be improvised with a tape roll
2. Communication device: cell phone to call 911 if indicated
3. First-generation antihistamine (diphenhydramine): for allergen-triggered attacks or anaphylaxis

---

TABLE 12.2   Peak Flow Meter Directions

1. Have the athlete either stand or sit in the upright position.
2. Place the peak flow meter (PFM) value indicator in the zero position.
3. Have the athlete take a deep breath.
4. Place the athlete's mouth over the mouthpiece of the PFM, making sure to close lips around mouthpiece.
5. Have the athlete blow out as fast as possible.
6. Record the number represented by the indicator.
7. Repeat this process two more times.
8. Use the best value as the indicator of lung function.

---

available.[11] One of the most common causes of treatment failure is poor inhaler technique with inhaled metered-dose medications. Therefore, the coach or other first responder should be able to help properly administer asthma medications in the event of an emergency.

Prevention

One of the best preventive steps for asthma exacerbations is requiring a preparticipation physical examination with a good review of the medical history, combined with pulmonary tests and exercise challenge tests, as necessary for athletes with possible asthma. Athletes who are identified as at risk should have a pulmonary function test to assess control and rule out other diagnoses. One of the most cost-effective and convenient tests for athletes is measure of peak expiratory flow using a peak flow meter (PFM). The peak flow can be measured daily, preferably in the morning to determine lung function (see **Table 12.2** and **Table 12.3**). Based on the peak flow and baseline percentage, an individual asthma action plan can be determined for the athlete. The color zones on the individual asthma action plan help the athlete determine management steps based on the percentage of his or her personal bests: green (breathing is good), yellow (hard to breathe, coughing or wheezing), and red (very difficult to breathe, accessory muscle activation, hypoxia). The plan can also be used on the sidelines to assess asthma exacerbations. The values

---

TABLE 12.3   Severity of Asthma Based on Peak Flow Meter Values[1,53]

Severity Classification	Signs/Symptoms	PFM Values
Mild	Difficulty breathing with exercise	PEF ≥ 70% of personal best
Moderate	Hard to breathe with exercise or normal activities	PEF is between 40% to 70% of personal best
Severe	Difficulty breathing at rest, difficulty speaking in normal conversations	PEF is below 40% of personal best
Life threatening	Cannot speak, sweating, gasping for air	PEF < 25% of personal best

Abbreviations: PEF, peak expiratory flow; PFM, peak flow meter.

---

measured during an asthma attack or when the athlete experiences breathing difficulty are compared to personal bests and are usually classified and correlated to the percentage of lung volume flow found in Table 12.3. Predicted peak flow rate can be determined based on age, sex, and size.

Another method for assessing lung function is office **spirometry**. This procedure should be conducted in a medical office by trained personnel using appropriate equipment. Athletes with an asthma history or who are suspected of having asthma should be referred for an office lung assessment prior to practices and competitions. Office spirometry assesses lung function via forced expiratory volume in the first second of expiration (FEV1). Airflow obstruction based on spirometry is graded as mild, moderate, severe, and very severe according to the FEV1 and is similar to PFM classifications found in Table 12.3. If obstruction is found, reversibility of the obstructive abnormality can be assessed after administration of a bronchodilator. An increase in FEV1 of 12% or greater following bronchodilator administration indicates asthma.

> **spirometry** A pulmonary function test that measures the volume of air as a function of time.

Blood oxygen concentration can be measured using a hand-held pulse oximeter, and blood concentrations below 90% typically reflect hypoxemia (low blood oxygen concentration). These measurements can be taken in the field and on the sidelines. The pulse oximeter should not be used to diagnosis asthma or monitor long-term asthma control but may help in determining breathing difficulties.

Other Tests

A majority of athletes with asthma can be diagnosed based on history, physical examination, and pulmonary testing. In rare cases, the diagnosis may not be clear and further testing will be required. Methacholine is known to evoke a bronchoconstriction response. Individuals with asthma tend to respond to lower concentrations of this drug. Methacholine testing is generally considered the gold standard in diagnosing asthma. The eucapnic hyperventilation test is an alternative test for exercise-related bronchospasm. This test requires the individual to hyperventilate while breathing in controlled concentrations of carbon dioxide. This allows the tested individual to safely and voluntarily increase ventilatory rate as might be expected in response to exercise. The increase in ventilation will lead to **bronchoconstriction** in individuals with exercise-induced asthma. This technique is accepted by the International Olympic Committee as diagnostic of exercise-induced asthma.

> **bronchoconstriction** Constriction of the airways.

Medications

Short-Acting β-Agonists

Short-acting β-agonists are the first-line treatment for an acute asthma **exacerbation**. They are often referred to as rescue inhalers. They are effective during an asthma attack. Athletes with known asthma should have a short-acting β-agonist readily available. Onset of action is 5 to 15 minutes. Inhaled β-agonists can be repeated as often as every 1 to 2 hours if need.[55] Nebulized β_2-agonists are often used for severe asthma exacerbations, although a **metered dose inhaler** with a spacer is as effective as a **nebulized** β_2.[55-59] Continuous nebulization of short-acting β-agonist medication may improve lung function over the course of intermittent treatment during acute exacerbations.

> **exacerbation** Worsening of a disease or condition.
>
> **metered dose inhaler** A pressurized hand-held device that uses propellants to deliver medication to the lungs.
>
> **nebulizer** A device used for delivering medication into the lungs during inhalation.

Inhaled Atropine or Ipratropium Bromide

Inhaled ipratropium bromide may be used as a second-line drug. Ipratropium bromide is used to inhibit receptors in airway smooth muscle to reduce airway constriction and appears to be effective when added to β_2-agonist administration, with little or limited adverse effects.[50,60,61] Ipratropium bromide showed promising results when administered early and frequently to treat acute asthma exacerbations.[62,63]

Magnesium Sulfate

Magnesium sulfate has been postulated to be an effective medical therapy for acute asthma exacerbations because of its inhibition of airway smooth muscle constriction.[50] Magnesium sulfate inhibits acetylcholine and histamine release; it also inhibits calcium ion intake in the airway bronchial smooth muscle in acute asthma exacerbations.[64] When used in combination with other asthma therapies, magnesium sulfate has been effective in improving lung function in patients who have severe asthma.[65,66] The side effects of magnesium sulfate are relatively minimal, but toxicity can occur with high doses and thus intake should be monitored.[50]

Management of Chronic Asthma

Long-Acting Inhaled β-Agonists

The long-acting inhaled β-agonist medications are best used as controller medications, often in conjunction with an inhaled steroid. These medications are used for long-term control of asthma and therefore are often referred to as controller medications. These are not effective in treating an acute asthma attack and should not be used for this. Long-acting β-agonist medications may accumulate in the body and result in tachycardia (usually fast heartbeat). Decreased effectiveness of this type of medication can occur. The Food and Drug Administration warns that these medications should be used only in conjunction with steroids and for the shortest amount of time necessary.[67,68] Other studies show that long-acting β_2-agonists, particularly salmeterol, may increase the risk of severe adverse effects and death.[69] The exact mechanism is unknown. Some suggest that inappropriate use of this type of medication as a rescue medication is to blame. Although the use of long-acting β_2-agonists has increased since the early 1990s, asthma death rates, particularly in European and South American countries, actually decreased, suggesting that other factors may influence asthma mortality.[70,71]

Mast Cell Stabilizers

Inhaled mast cell stabilizers remain an option for exercise-induced asthma, but they should never be used for rescue. These medications will only prevent the release of inflammatory mediators in the airway in response to stimuli. They do not directly treat inflammation or lead to bronchodilation. This type of medication needs to be used regularly prior to exposure or exercise.

Steroids

Long-term relief may require either oral or inhaled steroids. These medications also are used for long-term control of asthma and therefore are referred to as controller medications. The national guidelines for the treatment and prevention of asthma recommend a stepwise treatment plan for asthma based on the severity of the asthma. For mild to moderate asthma, the addition of inhaled steroids is recommended.

For severe exacerbations of asthma, systemic steroids are recommended. Oral steroids are as effective as intravenous steroids and may be used for control of asthma symptoms to prevent worsening of exacerbations as part of a stepwise treatment plan based on symptoms and **peak flow meter** monitoring.[50,64]

Other Medications

Leukotriene inhibitors may be beneficial as third-line medications to block the products of inflammation. Theophylline is a third-line medication, the exact effect and benefit of which for asthmatics is unknown. This medication seems to increase respiratory drive and may have some bronchodilating effect.[72]

Education

Education plays a vital role in controlling and recognizing an asthma attack. Athletes who have asthma must understand their condition, how to effectively manage and control asthma, and how to treat breathing exacerbations when they occur. When an athlete is diagnosed with asthma, educational information must be presented, and it is the duty not only of the physician or asthma specialists but also of parents, coaches, and others who will be involved in the athlete's daily life to educate the athlete. Allied healthcare providers should use a pharmacologic and psychological approach to educate athletes on common procedures along with avoidance of triggers that may predispose an athlete to asthma exacerbations.[73] Education should include the rationale and the need for asthma medications, address the individual's concerns over the adverse effects of prescribed medications, and address any barriers that preclude them from using their medications. Reasons for medication noncompliance are speculated to include forgetfulness, lack of understanding about how to use the asthma medication as prescribed by physicians, intentional factors of taking the medication differently than prescribed (e.g., decreased dosage or frequency), or even lack of understanding of the need to take medication.[73-75] In addition, athletes need to know the best management strategies to control their asthma, which also includes assessing environmental conditions, learning about potential allergens that may predispose them to attacks, and informing others about their condition and how to treat breathing emergencies in emergency situations. In fact, a written asthma action plan, has been shown to increase medication compliance and improve management of their asthma.[76,77]

Return to Play

There are no specific guidelines regarding return to play following an asthma attack in the *NCAA Sports Medicine Handbook* or other published literature. Initial treatment with inhaled β-agonist medication should relieve symptoms as well as return lung function to baseline. If asthma exacerbation symptoms are not resolved after three repeated uses of a short-acting β-agonist inhaler (preferably with a spacer), the athlete should be referred to an appropriate healthcare facility.[78] Lung function may be monitored on the sidelines with a PFM. It is important that the asthmatic athlete be familiar with this type of device in order to perform this monitoring appropriately and obtain reliable information. It is best to have a baseline reading and a stepwise treatment plan based on peak flow readings for the specific athlete; however, predicted norms are available based on height, gender, and age. It is important to consider that ethnicity may also affect lung function.[78] These general management strategies can be found in the National Athletic Trainers' Association asthma position statement for control of asthma exacerbations and can be used by clinicians to determine if and when an athlete could return to play.[79]

Once the athlete's symptoms have resolved and lung function has returned to baseline, the athlete can potentially return to play. However, thought should be given to the circumstances that led to the exacerbation. These may include external stimuli that can be avoided, a change in environmental conditions, or infections.[80] In the latter case, further evaluation of the athlete may be necessary prior to return.

There are likewise no specific guidelines for return to play after hospitalization for asthma. An appropriate workup looking for common inciting factors should be performed. Should pneumonia be the underlying cause, 2 to 6 weeks of convalescence may be necessary. Activity should begin on a low aerobic level and be increased slowly, while monitoring the athlete for recurrent symptoms. The athlete's lung function should be at baseline prior to any activity. The athlete may need to repeat the use of a rescue inhaler during or following activity if symptoms return. If this occurs on a regular basis, the athlete should decrease or stop the inciting activities altogether until a physician fully evaluates the athlete. The physician may consider referring difficult-to-control asthma patients to a pulmonologist.

Summary

Asthma that is controlled properly should not limit athletes' participation in sports or other recreational activities. Research has shown the best way to manage asthma is to have an individualized asthma action plan to improve medication compliance and identify asthma triggers. In the athletic venue, a written emergency action plan, including how to treat asthma exacerbations with medications, should be posted and rehearsed by all medical and nonmedical personnel on a regular basis. The guidelines and information presented in this chapter should act as a resource for coaches and other individuals who work in an athletic environment to implement for all levels and types of athletes to properly control, understand, and manage asthma.

Clinical Case Scenarios

1. Justin, an athlete on the men's cross-country team, finished his practice, which consisted of an 8-mile run. Approximately 10 minutes after he finished, he began to experience wheezing and chest tightness. Jessica, the cross-country coach, is the only staff present. Justin's symptoms begin

to worsen and it is obvious, based upon his past medical history of asthma, that Justin needs medical assistance.

   a. What are the steps that can be taken to help alleviate Justin's breathing difficulties?

   b. What environmental conditions or factors could be contributing to his breathing difficulties?

   c. What measures could have been implemented earlier to prevent Justin's asthma attack?

2. Michelle is a high school hockey player who complains of new onset tiredness, shortness of breath, and fatigue after playing hockey. For 3 weeks, she has had a nonproductive cough that is worse after she plays hockey. She thought she had a fever the day before. As a young child she was diagnosed with asthma and treated with a mouth inhaler. She felt she outgrew asthma and does not take the medication anymore.

   a. What immediate steps may be taken to help relieve her breathing problems and cough?

   b. What factors may have contributed to her new onset symptoms?

   c. When might she return to play?

Key Terms

airway lumen

bronchoconstriction

exacerbation

metered dose inhaler

nebulizer

peak flow meter

spirometry

References

1. National Asthma Education and Prevention Program . *Expert Panel Report 3: Guidelines for the Diagnosis and Management of Asthma*. National Heart, Lung and Blood Institute. http://www.nhlbi.nih.gov/guidelines/asthma. Accessed November 29, 2012.
2. Global Initiative for Asthma (GINA). From the Global Strategy for Asthma Management and Prevention, Global Initiative for Asthma (GINA) 2011. http://www.ginasthma.org/. Accessed November 26, 2012.
3. Rea HH, Scragg R, Jackson R, et al. A case-control study of deaths from asthma. *Thorax*. 1986;41(11):833–839.
4. Sears MR, Rea HH. Patients at risk for dying of asthma: New Zealand experience. *J Allergy Clin Immunol*. 1987;80:477–481.
5. Martinez FD. Sudden death from respiratory disease in sports [in Spanish]. *Arch Bronconeumol*. 2008;44(7):343–345.
6. Masoli M, Fabian D, Holt S, Beasley R. The global burden of asthma: executive summary of the GINA Dissemination Committee report. *Allergy*. 2004;59(5):469–478.
7. Sly RM. Decreases in asthma mortality in the United States. *Ann Allergy Asthma Immunol*. 2000;85(2):121–127.
8. Byard RW, James RA, Gilbert JD. Childhood sporting deaths. *Am J Forensic Med Pathol*. 2002;23:364–367.
9. Maron BJ. Sudden death in young athletes. *N Engl J Med*. 2003;349:1064–1075.
10. Becker JM, Rogers J, Rossini G, Mirchandani H, D'Alonzo GE. Asthma deaths during sports: report of a 7-year experience. *J Allergy Clin Immunol*. 2004;113:264–267.
11. Greiling AK, Boss LP, Wheeler LS. A preliminary investigation of asthma mortality in schools. *J School Health*. 2005;75(8):286–290.
12. Akbari O, Faul JL, Hoyte EG, et al. CD4+ invariant T-cell–receptor+ natural killer T cells in bronchial asthma. *N Engl J Med*. 2006;354(11):1117–1129.
13. Galli SJ, Kalesnikoff J, Grimbaldeston MA, et al. Mast cells as "tunable" effector and immunoregulatory cells: recent advances. *Annu Rev Immunol*. 2005;23:749–786.
14. Kay AB, Phipps S, Robinson DS. A role for eosinophils in airway remodeling in asthma. *Trends Immunol*. 2004;25(9):477–482.
15. Peters-Golden M. The alveolar macrophage: the forgotten cell in asthma. *Am J Respir Cell Mol Biol*. 2004;31(1):3–7.
16. Wenzel S. Mechanisms of severe asthma. *Clin Exp Allergy*. 2003;33(12):1622–1628.
17. Barnes PJ. Cytokine modulators as novel therapies for asthma. *Annu Rev Pharmacol Toxicol*. 2002;42:81–98.
18. Miller AL, Lukacs NW. Chemokine receptors: understanding their role in asthmatic disease. *Immunol Allergy Clin North Am*. 2004;24(4):667–683.
19. Ricciardolo FL, Sterk PJ, Gaston B, Folkerts G. Nitric oxide in health and disease of the respiratory system. *Physiol Rev*. 2004;84(3):731–765.

20. Chakir J, Shannon J, Molet S, et al. Airway remodeling-associated mediators in moderate to severe asthma: effect of steroids on TGF-beta, IL-11, IL-17, and type I and type III collagen expression. *J Allergy Clin Immunol.* 2003;111:1293–1298.

21. de Medeiros Matsushita M, da Silva LF, dos Santos MA, et al. Airway proteoglycans are differentially altered in fatal asthma. *J Pathol.* 2005;207:102–110.

22. Laitinen A, Altraja A, Kampe M, et al. Tenascin is increased in airway basement membrane of asthmatics and decreased by an inhaled steroid. *Am J Respir Crit Care Med.* 1997;156:951–958.

23. Roche WR, Williams JH, Beasley R, Holgate ST. Subepithelial fibrosis in bronchi of asthmatics. *Lancet.* 1989;1:520–524.

24. de Magalhaes Simoes S, dos Santos MA, da Silva Oliveria M, et al. Inflammatory cell mapping of the respiratory tract in fatal asthma. *Clin Exp Allergy.* 2005;35:602–611.

25. Hamid Q, Song Y, Kotsimbos TC, et al. Inflammation of small airways in asthma. *J Allergy Clin Immunol.* 1997;100:44–51.

26. Dolhnikoff M, da Silva LFF, de Araujo BB, et al. The outer wall of small airways is a major site of remodeling in fatal asthma. *J Allergy Clin Immunol.* 2009;123:1090–1097.

27. Carroll N, Carello S, Cooke C, James A. Airway structure and inflammatory cells in fatal attacks of asthma. *Eur Respir J.* 1996;9:709–715.

28. Dunnill MS. The pathology of asthma with special reference to changes in the bronchial mucosa. *J Clin Pathol.* 1960;13:27–33.

29. Heard BE, Hossain S. Hyperplasia of bronchial muscle in asthma. *J Pathol.* 1971;110:319–331.

30. Saetta M, Di Stefano AD, Rosina C, Thiene G, Fabbri LM. Quantitative structural analysis of peripheral airways and arteries in sudden fatal asthma. *Am Rev Respir Dis.* 1991;143:138–143.

31. Hessel PA, Mitchell I, Tough S, et al. Risk factors for death from asthma. *Ann Allergy Asthma Immunol.* 1999;83:362–368.

32. Larsson K, Ohlsen P, Larrson L, et al. High prevalence of asthma in cross-country skiers. *Br Med J.* 1993;307:1326–1329.

33. Helenius IJ, Tikkanen HO, Sarna S, Haahtela T. Respiratory pathophysiologic responses. *J Allergy Clin Immunol.* 1998;101:646–652.

34. Busse WW, Lemanske RF Jr. Asthma. *N Engl J Med.* 2001;344(5):350–362.

35. Hogaboam CM, Carpenter KJ, Schuh JM, Buckland KF. Aspergillus and asthma—any link? *Med Mycol.* 2005;43(suppl 1): S197–S202.

36. Sporik R, Holgate ST, Platts-Mills TA, Cogswell JJ. Exposure to house dust mite allergen (Der p l) and the development of asthma in childhood. A prospective study. *N Engl J Med.* 1990;323(8):502–507.

37. Wahn U, Lau S, Bergmann R, et al. Indoor allergen exposure is a risk factor for sensitization during the first three years of life. *J Allergy Clin Immunol.* 1997;99(6):763–769.

38. American Thoracic Society. What constitutes an adverse health effect of air pollution? Official statement of the American Thoracic Society. *Am J Respir Crit Care Med.* 2000;161(2 pt 1):665–673.

39. Gauderman WJ, Avol E, Gilliland F, et al. The effect of air pollution on lung development from 10 to 18 years of age. *N Engl J Med.* 2004;351(11):1057–1067.

40. Sur S, Crotty TB, Kephart GM, et al. Sudden-onset fatal asthma. A distinct entity with few eosinophils and relatively more neutrophils in the airway submucosa? *Am Rev Resp Dis.* 1993;148:713–719.

41. Campbell S, Hood I, Ryan D, Biedrzycki L, Mirchandani H. Death as a result of asthma in Wayne County Medical Examiner cases, 1975–1987. *J Forensic Sci.* 1990;35(2):356–364.

42. Robertson CF, Rubinfeld AR, Bowes G. Deaths from asthma in Victoria: a 12-month survey. *Med J Aust.* 1990;152(10):511–517.

43. Wasserfallen JB, Schaller MD, Feihl F, Perret CH. Sudden asphyxic asthma: a distinct entity? *Am Rev Respir Dis.* 1990;142:108–111.

44. Burke W, Fesinmeyer M, Reed K, Hampson L. Family history as a predictor of asthma risk. *Am J Prev Med.* 2003;24:160–169.

45. Hao K, Chen C, Wang B, et al. Familial aggregation of airway responsiveness: a community-based study. *Ann Epidemiol.* 2005;15:737–743.

46. Teerlink CC, Hegewald MJ, Cannon-Albright LA. A genealogical assessment of heritable predisposition to asthma mortality. *Am J Respir Crit Care Med.* 2007;176:865–870.

47. Kukufka DS, Lang DM, Porter S, et al. Exercise-induced bronchospasm in high school athletes via a free running test: incidence and epidemiology. *Chest.* 1998;116:1613–1622.

48. Plaza V, Serrano J, Picado C, Sanchis J. Frequency and clinical characteristics of rapid-onset fatal and near-fatal asthma. *Eur Respir J.* 2002;19:846–852.

49. Rainbow J, Browne GJ. Fatal asthma or anaphylaxis. *Emerg Med J.* 2002;19:415–417.

50. Holley AD, Boots RJ. Review article: management of acute severe and near-fatal asthma. *Emerg Med Aus.* 2009;21:259–268.

51. Rodrigo GJ, Rodriquez Verde M, Peregalli V, Rodrigo C. Effects of short-term 28% and 100% oxygen on PaCO2 and peak expiratory flow rate in acute asthma: a randomized trial. *Chest.* 2003;124:1312–1317.

52. Papiris SA, Manali ED, Kolilekas L, Triantafillidou C, Tsangaris I. Acute severe asthma. New approaches to assessment and treatment. *Drugs.* 2009;69(12):2363–2391.

53. Pollart SM, Compton RM, Elward KS. Management of acute asthma exacerbations. *Am Fam Physician.* 2011;84(1):40–47.

54. Murta A, Ling PM. Asthma diagnosis and management. *Emerg Med Clin N Am.* 2012;30:203–222.

55. Dennis RJ, Solarte I, FitzGerald M. Asthma in adults. In: Young C, et al., eds. *BMJ Clinical Evidence Handbook.* London: BMJ Publishing Group; 2008:502–503.

56. Rodrigo GJ, Rodrigo C. Continuous vs. intermittent β agonists in the treatment of acute adult asthma. A systematic review with meta-analysis. *Chest.* 2002;122:160–165.

57. Lin RY, Sauter D, Newman T, et al. Continuous versus intermittent albuterol nebulization in the treatment of acute asthma. *Ann Emerg Med.* 1993;22:1847–1853.

58. Papo MC, Frank J, Thompson AE. A prospective, randomized study of continuous versus intermittent nebulized albuterol for severe status asthmaticus in children. *Crit Care Med.* 1993;21:1479–1486.

59. Woolcock AJ. Inhaler technology: new concepts for the millennium. A special report. *Postgrad Med.* 1999;106(suppl 7):18–21.

60. Silverman R. Treatment of acute asthma. A new look at the old and at the new. *Clin Chest Med.* 2000;21:361–379.

61. Stoodley RG, Aaron SD, Dales RE. The role of ipratropium bromide in the emergency management of acute asthma exacerbation: a metaanalysis of randomized clinical trials. *Ann Emerg Med.* 1999;34:8–18.

62. Plotnick LH, Ducharme FM. Acute asthma in children and adolescents: should inhaled anticholinergics be added to beta(2)-agonists? *Am J Respir Med.* 2003;2:109–115.

63. Rodrigo GJ, Castro-Rodriguez JA. Anticholinergics in the treatment of children and adults with acute asthma: a systematic review with meta-analysis. *Thorax.* 2005;60:740–746.

64. Dominguez LJ, Barbagallo M, Di Lorenzo G, et al. Bronchial reactivity and intracellular magnesium: a possible mechanism for the bronchodilating effects of magnesium in asthma. *Clin Sci (London).* 1998;95:137–142.

65. Rowe BH, Bretzlaff JA, Bourdon C, Bota GW, Camargo CA Jr. Intravenous magnesium sulfate treatment for acute asthma in the emergency department: a systematic review of the literature. *Ann Emerg Med.* 2000;36:181–190.

66. Silverman RA, Osborn H, Runge J, et al. IV magnesium sulfate in the treatment of acute severe asthma: a multicenter randomized controlled trial. *Chest.* 2002;122:489–497.

67. Butland BK, Anderson HR, Cates CJ. The association between recent asthma medication and asthma death in a British case-control study. *Thorax.* 2009;64(suppl IV):A28.

68. Suissa S, Ernst P. Current reviews of allergy and clinical immunology. *J Allergy Clin Immunol.* 2001;107:937–944.

69. Castle W, Fuller R, Hall J, Palmer J. Serevent nationwide surveillance study: comparison of salmeterol with salbutamol in asthmatic patients who require regular bronchodilator treatment. *BMJ.* 1993;306:1034–1037.

70. Chatenoud L, Malvezzi M, Pitrelli A, La Vecchia C, Bamfi F. Asthma mortality and long-acting beta2-agonists in five major European countries, 1994–2004. *J Asthma.* 2009;46:546–551.

71. Neffen H, Baena-Cagnani C, Passalacqua G, Canonica GW, Rocco D. Asthma mortality, inhaled steroids, and changing asthma therapy in Argentina (1990–1999). *Resp Med.* 2006;100:1431–1435.

72. Finnish Medical Society Duodecim. Treatment of acute exacerbation of asthma. In: *EBM Guidelines. Evidence-Based Medicine* [Online]. Helsinki, Finland: John Wiley & Sons; 2007. Accessed June 2010.

73. Horne R. Compliance, adherence, and concordance: implications for asthma treatment. *Chest.* 2006;130:65S-72S.

74. Cochrane GM, Horne R, Chanez P. Compliance in asthma. *Respir Med.* 1999;93:763–769.

75. Horne R, Weinman J. Self-regulation and self-management in asthma: exploring the role of illness perceptions and treatment beliefs in explaining non-adherence to preventer medication. *Psychol Health.* 2002;17:17–32.

76. Patel MR, Valerio MA, Sanders G, Thomas LJ, Clark NM. Asthma action plans and patient satisfaction among women with asthma. *Chest.* 2012;142(5):1143–1149.

77. Wilson SR, Strub P, Buist AS, et al. Better Outcomes of Asthma Treatment (BOAT) Study Group. Shared treatment decision making improves adherence and outcomes in poorly controlled asthma. *Am J Respir Crit Care Med.* 2010;181(6):566–577.

78. Allen TW. Sideline management of asthma. *Curr Sports Med Rep.* 2005;4:301–304.

79. Miller MG, Weiler JM, Baker R, Collins J, D'Alonzo G. National Athletic Trainers' Association position statement: management of asthma in athletes. *J Athl Train.* 2005; 40(3):224–245.

80. Weiler JM, Layon T, Hunt M. Asthma in United States Olympic athletes who participated in the 1996 Summer Games. *J Allergy Clin Immunol.* 1998;102:722–726.

Exertional Hyponatremia

Lawrence E. Armstrong, PhD, FACSM
Brendon P. McDermott, PhD, ATC

© Giorgio Michieletti/ShutterStock, Inc.

From the Field Scenario

On a warm day (82°F) in the first few weeks of the regular season, Alice, a high school cross-country coach at Forest High, was faced with a difficult situation involving one of her runners. The team had just finished their long distance run for the week (8 miles) and one of the female runners, Elizabeth, seemed dizzy and staggered when finishing the run. Alice went to check on her as she lay on the ground. Elizabeth said that she felt nauseous and bloated and was dizzy. She said that she would be fine and just needed to lie there for a little bit. After a few minutes, Alice checked on Elizabeth, but she was not responding and seemed to be sleeping or unconscious. The other girls started to worry. Alice was able to get Elizabeth awake and talking, but her speech was slurred and she seemed confused. One girl ran to get one of the athletic trainers on the nearby football field. Because this situation seemed serious, Alice had another girl use a mobile phone to summon emergency medical services (EMS). When the athletic trainer arrived, he asked Elizabeth questions about her fluid and food intake during the day. Her friends began answering questions for Elizabeth and told the athletic trainer that she drank "a ton" of water during the school day in preparation for the run. Then, she drank another 32 ounces of water just prior to running. EMS arrived a short time after and assessed blood glucose, electrolyte levels, and rectal temperature. Her blood sodium level was 128 mmol/L, indicative of exertional hyponatremia. Quickly, a hypertonic saline intravenous (IV) line was attached and administered while she was transported to the emergency department for monitoring and follow-up.

Discussion Questions

1. How was the initial management for this case handled by the coach (Alice)? What steps seemed to be in place as part of the emergency action plan that was followed in this case?
2. What steps did the coach take that played an important role in the positive outcome for this athlete?
3. What, if anything, could have improved the outcome in this case?

Introduction

Symptomatic exertional hyponatremia (EH$_s$) is among the few noncongenital, nontraumatic conditions that can result in sudden death, pulmonary or cerebral edema, and coma. Among athletes, EH$_s$ typically results from consumption of a large volume of **hypotonic** fluid (i.e., having a concentration lower than blood) at a rate that greatly exceeds the capacity of the kidneys to excrete water. Thus, the excess water is retained inside and outside the cells of virtually all organs. It is important to recognize the distinct signs and symptoms (see **Table 13.1**), which herald a potentially life-threatening illness. This chapter addresses the causes, symptoms, treatment, and prevention strategies for EH$_s$.

Mechanisms and Causes of Exertional Hyponatremia

Blood sodium levels are vital for healthy cell functioning and body fluid balance; they normally range from 135 to 145 milliequivalents per liter of blood (mEq·L^{-1}). In sport, industrial, and military settings, EH$_s$ involves a blood sodium concentration of less than 130 mEq·L^{-1}. This is the approximate threshold for the appearance of the signs and symptoms of this illness (see Table 13.1). Sodium concentrations below 125 mEq·L^{-1} almost always result in symptoms and require immediate medical treatment. The approximate threshold for coma is 120 mEq·L^{-1}. In sedentary adults who consume a high volume of water chronically, these thresholds may be lower.[1]

Although few authors doubt that **fluid overload** is involved in EH$_s$,[2–4] published evidence demonstrates that retention of excess water is not always present. Some athletes experience hyponatremia when dehydrated. In a study examining blood sodium concentration and percent body mass change after an Ironman triathlon, blood was sampled from 330 competitors at the finish line; 11 were hyponatremic with weight gain, 47 were hyponatremic with weight loss, and the vast majority of triathletes (272 or 82%) were not hyponatremic.[5] See **Table 13.2**.

Generally, finishers with the lowest blood sodium concentrations (and therefore the greatest risk of serious medical complications) either gained weight or had the smallest weight losses. Such a weight gain (interpreted as fluid retention) supports excessive water consumption as a primary component of the cause of EH$_s$. Further, a weight gain during an Ironman triathlon is noteworthy considering that

TABLE 13.1 Signs and Symptoms of EH$_s$	
Change of mental status	Brain dysfunction
Nausea	Disorientation, confusion
Vomiting	Incoordination
Headache	Combative behavior
Dizziness	Physical exhaustion
Muscular twitching	Muscular weakness
Grand mal seizure	Cardiac arrest
Coma	Respiratory arrest
Strong desire for sleep	Pulmonary fluid accumulation
Tingling in extremities	Cerebral fluid accumulation

TABLE 13.2 Post-Ironman Blood Sodium Concentration with Associated Weight Changes in Hyponatremic Participants

Total Hyponatremic Subjects	Hyponatremic Subjects with Weight Loss, (%)	Hyponatremic Subjects with Weight Gain, (%)
58/330 (18%)	47/58 (81%)	11/58 (19%)

Source: Data from Speedy DB. Hyponatremia in ultradistance triathletes. *Medicine & Science in Sports & Exercise.* 31(6):809–815, 1999.[5]

these endurance athletes likely lost 0.8 to 1.0 liter of sweat per hour, or about 9 to 12 liters total (average duration of 12.4 hours).[3] See **Figure 13.1** to highlight how weight losses and weight gain can both result in hyponatremia.

Retention of Excess Fluid

As shown in **Table 13.3**, Montain and colleagues[6] calculated the volume of *excess fluid* (specifically, excess fluid refers to fluid intake that exceeds sweat loss volume + urine loss volume) required to dilute blood sodium to 120 mEq·L^{-1} in three hypothetical ultramarathon runners with body masses of 50, 70, and 90 kilograms (110, 154, and 198 pounds, respectively). All began with the same initial blood sodium concentration (140 mEq·L^{-1}) and ran at a pace of 10 km·h^{-1} for 9 hours. The volume of fluid that would induce serious EH$_s$ (at 120 mEq·L^{-1}) was different, primarily because of differences of total body water and sweat sodium concentration. The reader should note that this critical volume (refer to the bottom row of Table 13.3) is only 2.2 liters for the 50-kilogram athlete who has "salty sweat" (60 mEq·L^{-1}). This volume is relatively small; it represents only 200 milliliters (7 ounces) of excess fluid per hour when consumed during a 9-hour event.

In a unique case report, a healthy 21-year-old man consumed a total of 10.3 liters during intermittent treadmill walking, but his fluid loss (urine plus sweat) of 7.5 liters was greater than nine other participants who served as a comparison group.[7] His total urine volume of 2.3 liters demonstrated that kidney function was not impaired, once he stopped exercising and drinking. Thus, he retained 2.8 liters in 7 hours; this represented the excess fluid consumed (i.e., intake minus fluid lost in urine and sweat) and demonstrates

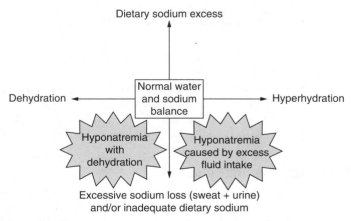

Figure 13.1 Interactions of sodium and water turnover (i.e., gain versus loss).

TABLE 13.3 Calculated Water Excess Required to Dilute Blood Sodium to 120 mEq·L⁻¹, in Ultramarathon Runners with Different Body Masses and Sweat Sodium Levels

		Light-Weight Runner			Middle-Weight Runner			Heavy-Weight Runner		
Body mass (kg)		50			70			90		
(lb)		110			154			198		
Total body water (L)		31.5			44.0			56.6		
(qt)		33.3			46.5			59.8		
Initial blood sodium concentration (mEq·L⁻¹)		140.0			140.0			140.0		
Volume of pure water consumed (L·9h⁻¹)		6.1			8.6			11.1		
(qt·9h⁻¹)		6.4			9.1			11.7		
Sweat loss (L·9h⁻¹) ^{a}		6.1			8.6			11.1		
(qt·9h⁻¹)		6.4			9.1			11.7		
Three sweat sodium levels ^{b}		L	M	H	L	M	H	L	M	H
Resultant blood sodium concentration (mEq·L⁻¹)		136	132	128	136	132	128	136	132	128
Fluid excess that dilutes blood sodium to 120 mEq·L⁻¹ ^{c,d}	(L)	4.2	3.2	2.2	5.9	4.5	3.0	7.6	5.8	3.9
	(qt)	4.4	3.4	2.3	6.2	4.8	3.2	8.0	6.1	4.1
	(L·h⁻¹)	0.5	0.4	0.2	0.7	0.5	0.3	0.8	0.6	0.4
	(qt·h⁻¹)	0.5	0.4	0.2	0.7	0.5	0.3	0.8	0.6	0.4

Pure water intake equals sweat loss, in all columns in the table.
^{a} Running at 10 km·h⁻¹ for 9 hours.
^{b} Sweat sodium concentration decreases with physical training, heat acclimatization, and low-sodium diets.
^{c} (Initial TBW volume) x [(Sodium concentration after exercise)/(120 mEq·L⁻¹)] = Final TBW volume.
^{d} Fluid excess = (Final TBW volume) – (Initial TBW volume).
Abbreviations: L, liters; L·h⁻¹, liters per hour; mEq, milliequivalents; TBW, total body water; L, low (20 mEq·L⁻¹); M, moderate (40 mEq·L⁻¹); H, high (60 mEq·L⁻¹)

Source: Data from Montain SJ, Cheuvront SN, Sawka MN. Exercise associated hyponatremia: quantitative analysis to understand the aetiology. *Br J Sports Med.* 2006;40:98–106.

total body water The water content of the human body, in both intracellular and extracellular fluid compartments.

a key causative factor. The 2.8 liters was a small part (5%) of his **total body water** (estimated as 64% of body mass or 52.1 liters), but retaining this much excess fluid was enough to alter the concentration of extracellular (the fluid surrounding cells) sodium to the point that his hyponatremia became symptomatic. Further, his sweat rate (range, 0.54–0.84 L·h⁻¹) and his urinary excretion rate (range, 0.28–0.63 L·h⁻¹) were normal during 7 hours in the heat. This demonstrates that little excess fluid (2.8 liters in 7 hours = 400 mL·h⁻¹) can induce symptoms.

Occurrence of Exertional Hyponatremia

The incidence of EH$_s$ in competitive athletics is not well documented, with the exception of mass-participation distance events. However, there has been a widespread increase in public awareness regarding EH$_s$ in recent years. Siegel et al.[2] assessed blood sodium levels in collapsed runners following the Boston marathon and found that 4.8% had experienced EH$_s$. Interestingly, this represents fewer than 1% of participants at this race between 2001 and 2008 and only includes collapsed runners. In other observational studies, the incidence of EH_s ranged from 0%[8] to 29%[9] of participants.

Thus far, incidence rates of EH_s are unreported in many sports, including American football. This condition is typically an afterthought for the medical staff covering the sidelines of such sports, but EH_s may occur more often than reported. Presumably, an athlete may overestimate the need to hydrate prior to and during activity, leading to EH_s. Any symptoms athletes exhibit are assumed to be a result of exertion and heat exposure, and they typically resolve with the consumption of meals following workouts. It is important to note, however, that this assumption has not been proven. Further, EH_s is most commonly reported in events or contests lasting longer than 4 hours.[9,10] A much more common condition resulting from team sports activities lasting 2 to 3 hours is exercise dehydration,[11] the signs and symptoms of which often mimic those of mild EH_s (light-headedness, fatigue, dizziness). It is difficult to pinpoint the prevalence of either condition in team sports because both are rapidly corrected when athletes consume meals (including sodium) and fluids following exercise (provided fluids are not consumed in excess). Given the overwhelming percentage of athletes who lose weight during activity,[11] the incidence of exercise dehydration clearly exceeds that of EH_s. Future research should identify the prevalence of both conditions following team sports activities.

What Happens in Organs and Systems of the Body?

The regulation of sodium and potassium concentration, both within and surrounding a cell, is critical for proper nerve conduction, muscle contraction, movement of fluids and solutes throughout the body, and optimal health. This explains the skeletal muscular twitching and cramps, muscular weakness, and physical exhaustion that are part of the clinical picture of advanced EH_s.[12,13] A delayed onset of symptoms, sometimes reported long after exercise ends,[7] likely occurs because fluid equilibration between the brain and blood may require more than 2 hours to achieve.[14]

When a large volume of dilute fluid (e.g., water or commercial sports drink) is consumed, the extracellular fluid in turn becomes dilute because water moves from the intestine directly into the blood. As extracellular concentration falls, water flows into cells and they swell.[15] This explains the pulmonary edema (fluid accumulation within the lungs) that occurs in severe cases of EH_s, as well as the neurologic symptoms of nausea, vomiting, grand mal seizure, and coma.[12,16] If the hyponatremia is not corrected, edema often leads to pulmonary arrest.

Brain edema usually accompanies severe EH_s. If the brain does not compensate for this accumulation of fluid, the pressure of the swollen brain on the skull can lead to reduced blood flow, poor oxygen delivery, and tissue death.[17] Autopsies have revealed obliteration, flattening, and herniation (protrusion) of brain structures.[16,18,19] Autopsies also have identified fluid accumulation and congestion of the heart, liver, kidneys, and intestine as well as pink, frothy fluid in the trachea (windpipe) and bronchi (lungs).[16]

Prevention

After reviewing the clinical and scientific literature, we have identified nine factors that predispose athletes to EH_s. The following list summarizes the factors and provides targeted strategies to prevent or counteract each threat to health.

1. A large volume of hypotonic fluid (e.g., water or commercial sports drink) is consumed within a few hours.[7] When compared to the volume of fluid lost during exercise (e.g., in sweat or urine), the excess fluid is small (see previous discussion and Table 13.3).

   Prevention: Consume fluids during exercise to prevent exceeding a weight loss of 2% of body mass, because this compromises performance. On the other hand, weight gain should not occur during activity. Simple body weight measurements can be used to determine individual body mass loss or sweat rate.[20]

2. Exercise duration is a primary predisposing factor. Reports of EH_s occur most often in distance running events that are 42.2 kilometers (a marathon) or longer,[3-5,9,10,21,22] triathlons that last 7 to 17 hours,[23] repeated days of military training,[24] and long hikes.[25] Slower runners may be at greater

risk of EH$_s$ because they linger at aid stations or do not pass aid stations without drinking. Further, Davis and colleagues[21] observed a significant inverse relationship between postrace blood sodium level in marathoners and the time elapsed before presentation at a hospital emergency department. None of the marathon runners who experienced EH$_s$ completed the race in less than 4 hours.

> *Prevention:* Avoid overconsumption of fluid by using a personalized hydration plan that is based on sweat rate. Sports drinks contain low levels of sodium and thus do little to maintain normal whole-body sodium balance. Instead, during postexercise meals, consume foods that are high in sodium (e.g., canned soups, pretzels). Consuming salty foods or salt capsules with water during ultraendurance events may or may not be useful depending on the whole body balance of sodium.

3. A genetic tendency for high sweat sodium concentration (e.g., 80–100 mEq·L^{-1}) increases the risk of a whole-body sodium deficit, as found in individuals who carry the trait (those who have one of potentially two genes) for cystic fibrosis but do not have all of the symptoms associated with the condition.[26] For example, Vrijens and Rehrer[27] reported one case of EH$_s$ that occurred after 2.5 hours of cycling. Their calculations indicated that the cyclist's sweat contained a sodium concentration of at least 100 mEq·L^{-1}. An athlete should check for white salt deposits on a uniform, jersey, or shorts after a strenuous bout of exercise in a hot environment. This indicates that he or she has a high sweat sodium concentration.

> *Prevention:* At meals, consume foods that are high in sodium (e.g., canned soup).

4. Sodium or sodium chloride (table salt) losses in sweat and urine may not be replaced adequately by dietary food or fluids. This is especially true for athletes who have a high sweat rate and salty sweat.

> *Prevention:* Consume ample dietary sodium when training in a hot environment and during daily meals. Easy ways to ensure an adequate intake are to use the salt shaker more liberally with meals, or to eat processed foods such as canned soups, potato chips, or pretzels on a daily basis. *Note:* Sports drinks are relatively dilute and vary in sodium concentration; they do little to retard the development of EH$_s$.[28]

5. The absence of heat acclimatization predisposes active individuals to EH$_s$ because of relatively large sodium losses in sweat and urine. A decreased sweat sodium concentration is one of several physiologic adaptations that occur during heat acclimatization.[29] Opposing this, sweat rate increases during a 2-week heat acclimatization period, increasing the likelihood that a sodium deficit will occur.

> *Prevention:* Undertake 8 to 14 days of training in the heat, gradually increasing the exercise duration and intensity.

6. Published evidence suggests that environmental heat stress (see later discussion) interacts with the mindsets or personality characteristics of some individuals to increase the desire to consume a large amount of hypotonic fluid. Considerable evidence indicates that EH$_s$ often occurs in those who premeditate drinking a large volume of water[7,30,31] or believe that consuming excess water will prevent heat illness (see From The Field Scenario).[32]

> *Prevention:* Educate athletes about the risk of EH$_s$ because of fluid overload; train them to drink adequately but not excessively, according to individual needs. Athletes will be less likely to overconsume fluids if they understand their personal body water losses through exercise.

7. Although no systematic study has verified this hypothesis, some authorities[31] believe that the instructions of race organizers and medical directors to "drink as much water as possible" resulted in overdrinking and EH$_s$ at numerous road races during the 1980s and 1990s. As a result of educational efforts and recent position statements of professional sports medicine organizations,[33,34] this disturbing trend has changed considerably. Simple body weight measurements can be used to determine individual body mass loss or sweat rate.[20]

> *Prevention:* Explain the risk of EH$_s$ because of fluid overload; encourage competitors to drink adequately but not excessively, according to individual needs.[8]

8. At least four previous studies have indicated that female hikers and marathon runners were more likely than males (19 women versus 4 men) to develop serious symptomatic EH$_s$ (see Armstrong et al.[7] for a summary of these cases). This may occur because the average woman has less total body water than the average man and therefore requires a smaller volume of water to dilute blood sodium (see Table 13.3).

Prevention: Drink no more fluid than the volume lost in sweat and urine; do not *gain* weight during a workout or race, because this represents fluid excess. Additionally, we have observed that women are generally more ardent about following advice and instructions about drinking and thus may err on the side of excess with respect to hydration, or at least fail to adjust volume for their size. Thus, the notion of hydration recommendations for the masses has less value and perhaps some danger. Rather, individuals should ascertain their own needs.[35]

9. Annual seasons influence development of EH$_s$. Because exercise in a hot environment and the resulting rise of internal body temperature stimulate considerably greater water turnover (i.e., sweat loss with hypotonic fluid intake) than comparable exercise in a cool environment, most cases of EH$_s$ occur during summer months.

    Prevention: During summer months, heed the recommendations in items 1 through 9 of this list.

Two potential predisposing factors require further research before their validity can be established. The first involves abnormal secretion of the hormone **arginine vasopressin (AVP)**, which regulates water excretion by the kidneys. One case report[7] involved an abnormal AVP (i.e., antidiuretic hormone) response (+460% despite a fluid intake of 10.3 liters) in a young, healthy male. In contrast, another publication reported that 14 runners with symptomatic EH$_s$ all had normal blood AVP concentrations.[36] The second potential predisposing factor involves the use of nonsteroidal anti-inflammatory drugs (NSAIDs). These medications are known to exaggerate the effect of AVP on the renal collecting ducts, with the result of impaired diuresis (excretion of urine). Therefore, an abnormal AVP response, as well as NSAID use, may contribute to an episode of EH$_s$. Specific recommendations are not warranted at this time, but athletes should know that interactions may exist.

> **arginine vasopressin (AVP)** Pituitary hormone that limits production of urine by stimulating water reabsorption in the kidneys (also known as antidiuretic hormone or ADH).

Recognition

We believe that there are two periods in which EH$_s$ can be recognized. First, an athlete may sense symptoms during or shortly after exercise. Second, EH$_s$ symptoms may occur hours after an event, when the athlete is likely to perceive initial symptoms to be a result of exercise and may not be aware of EH$_s$. (See the Clinical Case Scenario later in the chapter.)

Early Recognition

Early recognition involves the prompt identification of signs and symptoms related to EH$_s$ during, or even before, exercise. Prior to exercise, an athlete may overhydrate with the goal of avoiding dehydration-related decrements in exercise performance. Although slight hyperhydration prior to an event may be recommended,[33,34] extreme overhydration should be discouraged. Signs and symptoms of overhydration include dizziness, light-headedness, and puffiness.[3] A preparticipation body weight can help identify pre-exercise hyponatremia, if body weight is greater than a predetermined baseline measure. Athletes exhibiting signs or symptoms prior to exercise should not participate until a normal blood sodium state is verified. As a general rule, it is wise to assess body weight just prior to competition so that a postexercise weight can be used to quantify weight gain or loss.

Athletes may recognize symptoms during exercise, including headache, dizziness, muscular twitching, extremity tingling or swelling, and physical exhaustion (see Table 13.1). The most common symptoms reported by patients include (in order of occurrence) nausea, vomiting, dizziness, light-headedness, headache, and puffiness.[37] Because many of these symptoms are also symptoms of intense exercise, low blood glucose level, dehydration, head injury, or heat illness, these disorders are difficult to distinguish from EH$_s$. Athletes experiencing these symptoms during exercise should pay close attention to their fluid consumption and take steps to correct what may be the cause. During workouts or competition, athletes should not gain weight.

Management of Exertional Hyponatremia

After an exercise bout or competition, symptoms of EH$_s$ may appear acutely or as a gradual progression over several hours.[7] Because vital treatment for these conditions varies widely (from on-site whole-body cooling for exertional heat stroke to prompt IV hypertonic saline for EH$_s$, whether on site or during transport), an efficient assessment by a trained medical professional is necessary.[38–43] The key differential for correct diagnosis of EH_s is blood sodium assessment, which should be measured in collapsed athletes suspected of having EHs. If the medical staff does not have access to a portable sodium analyzer, the medical staff must rule out other conditions (e.g., exertional heat stroke, ruled out with a rectal temperature < 40°C [104°F]) prior to emergency transport. Clinical symptoms matched with a blood sodium concentration below 125 mEq·L^{-1} warrant a diagnosis of EH_s and initiation of treatment. This is a medical emergency.

When athletes complain of mild symptoms following an exercise bout, a complete history should be taken that includes questions regarding fluid volume consumed, use of NSAIDs, and food consumption. If the history suggests EH_s, blood sodium levels should be measured by the medical staff. Some athletes in this state may worsen over time. Athletes should be educated to recognize the symptoms of EH_s that may occur immediately after an event. The medical staff should determine an appropriate action plan based on clinical assessment and patient history.

Athletes also may experience symptoms of EH_s hours after the event. Emergency department personnel should include EH_s in differential diagnoses, and blood sodium concentration should be assessed prior to treatment. Any question regarding the signs and/or symptoms of EH_s warrant transport to and evaluation by emergency medical professionals.

The medical staff should determine an appropriate course of treatment and/or referral based on their assessment of EH_s. Treatment goals hinge upon normalizing physiology and blood sodium levels while avoiding complications. The most common treatment for EH_s includes hypertonic saline (3% to 5% NaCl) to increase whole body sodium levels. Because signs and symptoms of EH_s can mimic other conditions, trained medical staff should be involved rather than nonmedical personnel who cannot diagnose or treat.

Recovery

When treated appropriately with IV hypertonic saline, EH_s spontaneously resolves without complications. Chronic complications are rare.[38,40] Although the expected time course of recovery following EH_s is not well documented, it appears to be largely dependent on the severity and duration of the condition.[3] Rapid recognition and appropriate treatment reduce the risk of brain or central nerve damage.[3,38–40]

We recommend that EH_s patients follow up with a primary care physician within 3 to 7 days of their episode, to ensure that no physical or mental complications exist. The physician will ensure normal fluid turnover, kidney function, diet, neuropsychological processing, and daily function. A plan for future prevention should be developed with a knowledgeable athletic trainer, exercise physiologist, or sports medicine–trained physician. An appropriate course of return to activity should be discussed when the patient is discharged.

Return to Play

To our knowledge, few complications exist following mild or moderate EH_s when treatment is prompt and appropriate. In such cases, return to activity should be guided by a plan to avoid future episodes of EH_s, specifically, an individualized hydration plan.[33] This plan should incorporate individual exercise intensity and duration, environmental conditions, sweat rate, and sweat sodium concentration.[44] This plan also should be influenced by specific history and factors that contributed to the initial EH_s episode.

It is true that most EH_s can be avoided if athletes do not consume fluids during exercise. However, severe dehydration (i.e., > 7% body mass loss) compromises health. Further, exercise performance and cardiovascular, thermoregulatory, and cognitive function are all compromised by dehydration of more than 2% of body mass and should be avoided.[33,34] Therefore, athletes should strive to maintain hydration within a relatively narrow range by considering both dehydration and EH_s when developing a personalized hydration plan.

Current Return to Play Recommendations

Specific civilian and military recommendations do not exist for return to activity following EH_s. The National Athletic Trainers' Association position statement regarding exertional heat illnesses recommends a gradual increase in activity following physician clearance, but this recommendation lacks scientific or case report confirmation.[45] Recent expert panels have avoided this aspect of EH_s management and have instead focused on acute treatment.[38] If prompt recognition and treatment occur, the athlete should be encouraged to return to activity. Competitor education should be designed to prevent a subsequent episode. With a hydration and nutrition plan in place, most athletes should be able to return within 48 to 72 hours.

In our opinion, the following actions will raise athlete awareness about EH_s:

- Distribute electronic/paper based information sheets to describe EH_s and strategies to avoid it.
- Provide accurate digital floor scales to allow body weight to be compared, before and after prolonged endurance exercise. During workouts or competition, athletes should not gain weight (provided they do not go to the bathroom or eat food during this time).
- Teach athletes how to measure sweat rate, with a goal of replacing lost fluid (i.e., in sweat or urine) so that body weight loss does not exceed 2%.
- Encourage athletes to heed thirst sensations during training and competition. Athletes should drink when thirsty and stop drinking when they feel full.
- Teach athletes what 4-, 6-, and 8-ounce containers look like, so they know how much fluid to replace.

For large athletic events, event directors should seek consults with athletic trainers and sports dietitians so that EH_s educational information can be disseminated in race packets, at race trade shows and expositions, at exhibits, and to medical staffs.

Summary

EH_s is one of a few illnesses that are potentially fatal to otherwise healthy athletes, laborers, and military personnel. This illness involves a blood sodium concentration below 130 mEq·L^{-1}. The signs and symptoms of severe EH_s include disorientation, depression, nausea, vomiting, muscular twitching, and grand mal seizure. Severe cases (blood sodium level < 125 mEq·L^{-1}) may involve coma, fluid retention in the lungs and brain, and respiratory arrest. Despite these facts, few athletes realize that excessive fluid consumption may cause illness, hospitalization, or occupational disability.

Reports of EH_s most often arise from military training, long hikes, distance running events ($\geq$ 42.2 kilometers), and triathlons (7–17 hours). Many individuals who experience EH_s are self-motivated to drink "as much fluid as possible" during or after exercise. Body size, total body water, beverage composition, sweat rate, and sweat sodium concentration are important etiologic factors. The simplest way to reduce the risk of EH_s is to ensure that fluid is consumed at a rate that equals, or is slightly less than, the sweat rate. After exercise, consumption of sodium-rich beverages and foods (e.g., low-fat soup, dissolved bouillon, or stew with crackers) also reduces long-term complications caused by EH_s.

Clinical Case Scenario

1. To our knowledge, there is only one case report[7] with published data that continuously tracked EH_s as it developed. A 21-year-old, healthy man (K.G.) was participating in a research investigation in which dietary sodium was controlled for 7 days prior to the onset of symptoms. In a hot environment (41°C [106°F]), hyponatremia was verified as a blood sodium concentration of 126 mEq·L^{-1} after only 4 hours of exercise. Prior to the blood sample, this man had consumed breakfast and a snack containing 17 and 6 mEq·L^{-1} sodium, respectively.

   Four etiologic factors caused his blood sodium to fall to 122 mEq·L^{-1} by hour 7: (1) K.G. entered the day with a "low normal" blood sodium (134 mEq·L^{-1}) because he had hyperhydrated the previous night; (2) K.G. consumed 10.3 liters of fluid in 7 hours; (3) his blood sample indicated an inappropriately large release of AVP (i.e., antidiuretic hormone), which coincided with a decrease of urine volume to 0 mL·h^{-1}; and (4) his personal goal was to consume as much water as possible during exercise, because he believed that this would help him avoid heat illness. This constellation of four factors resulted in fatigue and nausea (hour 4).

Later that evening, despite no eating or drinking, he complained of increasing nausea and malaise, which prompted the attending physician to transfer him to a nearby hospital. At time of admission, his blood sodium level was still 122 mEq·L^{-1}. Treatment consisted of administration of hypertonic IV saline solution (5% NaCl) and overnight fluid restriction. The patient was released at 11:00 AM the next morning in an asymptomatic state.

a. What are the main factors that contributed to this case of hyponatremia?

b. What could this athlete have done to help prevent this incident from occurring?

c. What take-home instructions would you give this man, upon his release from the hospital?

Key Terms

arginine vasopressin (AVP)

blood sodium

fluid overload

hypotonic

symptomatic exertional hyponatremia (EH$_s$)

total body water

References

1. Farrell DJ, Bower L. Fatal water intoxication. *J Clin Pathol.* 2003;56:803–804.
2. Siegel AJ, d'Hemecourt P, Adner MM, et al. Exertional dysnatremia in collapsed marathon runners. *Am J Clin Pathol.* 2009;132:336–340.
3. Armstrong LE. Exertional hyponatremia. In: *Exertional Heat Illnesses.* Champaign, IL: Human Kinetics; 2003:103–135.
4. Noakes TD, Norman RJ, Buck RH, et al. The incidence of hyponatremia during prolonged ultradistance exercise. *Med Sci Sports Exerc.* 1990;22:165–170.
5. Speedy DB, Noakes TD, Rogers IR, et al. Hyponatremia in ultradistance events. *Med Sci Sports Exerc.* 1999;31:809–815.
6. Montain SJ, Cheuvront SN, Sawka MN. Exercise associated hyponatremia: quantitative analysis to understand the aetiology. *Br J Sports Med.* 2006;40:98–106.
7. Armstrong LE, Curtis WC, Hubbard RW, et al. Symptomatic hyponatremia during prolonged exercise in heat. *Med Sci Sports Exerc.* 1993;25(5):543–549.
8. Schenk K, Gatterer H, Ferrari M, et al. Bike Transalp 2008: liquid intake and its effect on the body's fluid homeostasis in the course of a multistage, cross-country, MTB marathon race in the central Alps. *Clin J Sport Med.* 2010;20:147–152.
9. Hiller WDB, O'Toole ML, Massimino F, Hiller RE, Laird RH. Plasma electrolyte and glucose changes during the Hawaiian Ironman Triathlon. *Med Sci Sports Exerc.* 1985;17:S219.
10. Almond CSD, Shin AY, Fortescue EB, et al. Hyponatremia among runners in the Boston Marathon. *NEJM.* 2005;352:1550–1556.
11. Mueller F, Colgate B. *Annual Survey of Football Injury Research, 1931–2009.* Chapel Hill, NC: National Center for Catastrophic Injury Research; 2009. http://www.unc.edu/depts/nccsi/. Accessed July 2, 2010.
12. Arieff A. Central nervous system manifestations of disordered sodium metabolism. *Clin Endocrin Metab.* 1984;13:269–294.
13. Ayus JC, Achinger SG, Arieff A. Brain cell volume regulation in hyponatremia: role of sex, age, vasopressin, and, hypoxia. *Am J Physiol Renal Physiol.* 2008;295:F619–F624.
14. Pollock AS, Arieff AI. Abnormalities of cell volume regulation and their functional consequences. *Am J Physiol.* 1980;239:F195–F205.
15. Goldberger E. *A Primer of Water, Electrolyte, and Acid-Base Syndromes.* 6th ed. Philadelphia, PA: Lea and Febiger; 1980:58–120.
16. Chen X, Huang G. Autopsy case report of a rare acute iatrogenic water intoxication with a review of the literature. *Forensic Sci Int.* 1995;76:27–34.
17. Arieff AI. Management of hyponatremia. *BMJ.* 1993;307:305–308.
18. Helwig FC, Schultz CB, Curry DE. Water intoxication: report of a fatal case with clinical, pathological, and experimental studies. *JAMA.* 1935;104:1569–1574.
19. Rashkind M. Psychosis, polydipsia, and water intoxication: report of a fatal case. *Arch Gen Psych.* 1974;30:112–116.
20. Casa DJ. For distance running—identifying individual fluid needs. *Track Coach.* 2004;167:5321–5328.

21. Davis D, Marino A, Vilke G, Dunford J, Videen J. Hyponatremia in marathon runners: experience with the inaugural Rock'n'Roll Marathon. *Ann Emerg Med.* 1999;34:540–541.
22. Speedy DB, Noakes TD, Rogers IR, et al. Hyponatremia in ultradistance triathletes. *Med Sci Sports Exerc.* 1999;22:165–170.
23. Noakes TD, Norman RJ, Buck RH, et al. The incidence of hyponatremia during prolonged ultradistance exercise. *Med Sci Sports Exerc.* 1990;22:165–170.
24. U.S. Army Center for Health Promotion and Preventive Medicine. Hyponatremia hospitalizations, U.S. Army 1989–1996. *Med Surv Monthly Rep.* 2000;6:9–11.
25. Garigan T, Ristedt DE. Death from hyponatremia as a result of acute water intoxication in the Army basic trainee. *Mil Med.* 1999;3:234–238.
26. Smith HR, Dhatt GS, Melia WMA, Dickinson JG. Cystic fibrosis presenting as hyponatraemic heat exhaustion. *BMJ.* 1995;310:579–580.
27. Vrijens DM, Rehrer NJ. Sodium-free fluid ingestion decreases plasma sodium during exercise in the heat. *J Appl Physiol.* 1999;86(6):1847–1851.
28. Weschler LB. Exercise-associated hyponatremia. A mathematical review. *Sports Med.* 2005;35(10):899–922.
29. Armstrong LE, Maresh CM. The induction and decay of heat acclimatization in trained athletes. *Sports Med (New Zealand).* 1991;12(5):302–312.
30. Romero JC, Stameloni RJ, Dafu ML, et al. Changes in fluid compartments, renal hemodynamics, plasma renin, and aldosterone secretion induced by low sodium intake. *Metabolism.* 1968;37:10–19.
31. Speedy DB, Noakes TD, Boswell T, et al. Response to a fluid load in athletes with a history of exercise induced hyponatremia. *Med Sci Sports Exerc.* 2001;33:1434–1442.
32. Noakes TD, Goodwin N, Rayner BL, Branken T, Taylor RKN. Water intoxication: a possible complication during endurance exercise. *Med Sci Sports Exer.* 1985;17:370–375.
33. Sawka MN, Burke LM, Eichner ER, et al. American College of Sports Medicine position stand. Exercise and fluid replacement. *Med Sci Sports Exerc.* 2007;39:377–390.
34. Casa DJ, Armstrong LE, Hillman SK, et al. National Athletic Trainers' Association position statement: fluid replacement for athletes. *J Athl Train.* 2000;35:212–224.
35. Chorley J, Cianca J, Divine J. Risk factors for exercise-associated hyponatremia in non-elite marathon runners. *Clin J Sport Med.* 2007;17(6):471–477.
36. Speedy DB, Rogers IR, Noakes TD, et al. Exercise-induced hyponatremia in ultradistance triathletes is caused by inappropriate fluid retention. *Clin J Sport Med.* 2000;10:272–278.
37. Hew TD, Chorley JN, Cianca JC, Divine JG. The incidence, risk factors, and clinical manifestations of hyponatremia in marathon runners. *Clin J Sport Med.* 2003;13:41–47.
38. Hew-Butler T, Ayus JC, Kipps C, et al. Statement of the Second International Exercise-Associated Hyponatremia Consensus Development Conference, New Zealand, 2007. *Clin J Sport Med.* 2008;18:111–121.
39. Hew-Butler T, Anley C, Schwartz P, Noakes T. The treatment of symptomatic hyponatremia with hypertonic saline in an Ironman triathlete. *Clin J Sport Med.* 2007;17:68–69.
40. Speedy DB, Noakes TD, Schneider C. Exercise-associated hyponatremia: a review. *Emerg Med.* 2001;13:17–27.
41. Lien YH, Shapiro JI. Hyponatremia: clinical diagnosis and management. *Am J Med.* 2007;120:653–658.
42. Hiller WD, O'Toole ML, Fortess EE, et al. Medical and physiological considerations in triathlons. *Am J Sports Med.* 1987;15:164–167.
43. Casa DJ, Armstrong LE, Ganio MS, Yeargin SW. Exertional heat stroke in competitive athletes. *Curr Sports Med Rep.* 2005;4:309–317.
44. Armstrong LE, Casa DJ. Methods to evaluate electrolyte and water turnover of athletes. *Athl Train Sport Health Care* 2009;1:169–179.
45. Binkley HM, Beckett J, Casa DJ, Kleiner DM, Plummer PE. National Athletic Trainers' Association position statement: exertional heat illnesses. *J Athl Train.* 2002;37:329–343.

Anaphylaxis, Hypothermia, Diabetes, and Altitude Illnesses

Susan W. Yeargin, PhD, ATC

© Giorgio Micheletti/ShutterStock, Inc.

From the Field Scenario

Payton had been the women's cross-country coach at First District High School for 1 year. She brought the team 40 minutes away to a new running venue, a state park. The team warmed up and she dispersed the running groups among the four trail runs she had created. Thirty minutes later a teammate returned, explaining that another teammate, Jessica, had been stung by a bee on the trail and was not feeling well. Payton started to follow the teammate down the trail toward Jessica. Jessica came jogging down the trail about 5 minutes later. She had labored breathing, was warm and flushed from running, and was complaining of not feeling well. Once Payton had Jessica stop moving, she noticed hives on all the body parts she could see. Upon lifting Jessica's shirt part way, Payton noticed that her entire body was covered by hives as well. Jessica said she had no history of asthma or allergic reaction to bee stings. Jessica started to complain of an itchy throat and feelings of nausea as they walked back. By the time they reached the parking lot, Jessica was unable to walk by herself and the hives had progressed in number, prominence, and redness. Payton pulled a camp chair out of her trunk for Jessica to sit on. She then called 911. The operator asked for the address of the state park.

Discussion Questions

1. What are the key symptoms that indicate to Payton that emergency medical services (EMS) should be called and that Jessica is most likely having an anaphylactic reaction?
   a. What other key symptoms might exist but were not mentioned in the story?
   b. Why might Jessica's symptoms be progressing faster than normal?
2. What preliminary steps is the coach taking to help treat the situation?
3. What should be Payton's next steps in treating Jessica while waiting for EMS to arrive?
4. What are some preventive measures Payton should have had in place prior to taking the team to the state park to prepare for such a situation?

Anaphylaxis

Anaphylaxis, also known as an anaphylactic reaction, is a potentially life-threatening allergic reaction that impacts the entire body.[1] It can happen to anyone, anywhere, and at any time. Athletic populations are continuously exposed to allergens that may induce anaphylaxis. Because of the rapid onset of symptoms, early recognition and appropriate treatment are imperative to lower the potential for death.

Anaphylactic reactions progress as part of a continuum. An allergen exposure may initially cause relatively minor symptoms but can rapidly progress to life-threatening heart and lung compromise. One research study indicated the time interval from allergen exposure to death for food-induced anaphylaxis was between 25 and 35 minutes.[2] The interval found for an insect sting was 10 to 15 minutes, whereas fatal drug-induced anaphylaxis occurred at 10 to 20 minutes. Therefore, any delay in recognition and appropriate treatment can increase the incidence of death.[2]

Background and Occurrence of Anaphylaxis

Anaphylaxis is a relatively common problem, affecting up to 2% of the population.[3] Recent studies have shown an increase in the number of anaphylaxis cases presenting in the emergency department (ED).[4] It has been reported that up to 1500 deaths per year result from anaphylaxis in the United States.[5] Individuals working with athletic populations must be able to recognize signs and symptoms, as well as be able to provide appropriate initial care.

Mechanisms and Causes of Anaphylaxis

An allergic reaction begins only when a **trigger** introduces an allergen and it crosses into the bloodstream. Organs with the greatest response include the skin (90% of cases), respiratory tract (70%), gastrointestinal tract (30% to 45%), cardiovascular system (10% to 45%), and the central nervous system (10% to 15%).[6]

Response chemicals sent to attack the allergen include histamines. Histamine release is directly responsible for increased blood flow, increased permeability, and over secretion of mucus. The histamine levels present in the blood of anaphylaxis victims are directly related to the severity of their anaphylactic reactions.[7]

Triggers

The potential triggers that can cause an anaphylactic reaction are infinite.[8] Anaphylactic reactions can be associated with foods, medications, latex products, and insect stings. There are other triggers as well, for example, exercise and cold. Foods, medications, and insect stings are among the most common provoking factors for anaphylaxis.[7]

Food-associated anaphylaxis is the most common cause treated in EDs across the United States in younger populations.[9] Most food cases are not fatal and have a gradual onset of signs and symptoms. The most common food culprits are tree nuts, peanuts, cow's milk, eggs, soy, wheat, shellfish, and fish. However, any food may be implicated.[9]

Exercise-induced anaphylaxis (EIA) is most commonly associated with food ingestion. Food-dependent EIA tends to occur when food ingestion is followed by exercise within 2 to 4 hours; athletes may not experience a reaction from ingestion of the food or exercise alone, but in conjunction they pose a risk.[9] EIA, on the other hand, may be triggered by other cofactors or can occur with exercise alone. Additional cofactors include alcohol, temperature, drugs, humidity, seasonal changes, and hormonal changes.

The onset of anaphylaxis following an insect sting is generally rapid. Fatal reactions begin within 30 minutes of the sting, emphasizing the importance of prompt recognition and appropriate treatment. Most fatal reactions are not preventable because the reaction commonly occurs on the first sting or subsequent stings with no prior history of anaphylactic shock.[1]

Anaphylaxis does not discriminate on the basis of age, race, sex, or socioeconomic status. Some populations with diseases that impede prompt recognition of a known trigger or the presentation of signs and symptoms are at greater risk of a life-threatening, or even fatal, reaction. Such diseases include vision or auditory impairment, and neurologic and psychiatric disorders.[10]

Factors that increase the risk of a fatal episode include exercise, exposure to extreme temperature or humidity, general illness, use of certain medications (e.g., nonsteroidal anti-inflammatory drugs), acute infection, increased emotional stress, and menses. Additionally, individuals with respiratory or cardiovascular diseases such as asthma are at greater risk.[8] Minimizing those factors that are modifiable may lower the risk for an anaphylactic event.

Recognition

Anaphylaxis cases are commonly under-recognized by individuals, including healthcare professionals, and therefore are undertreated.[3,8,11,12] Several national anaphylaxis organizations came together to develop criteria for recognition of anaphylaxis.[13] These criteria are reported to capture 95% of anaphylaxis cases.[1] If a victim presents with one of the three criteria, he or she is likely to have anaphylaxis (see **Figure 14.1**). These criteria can be invaluable to healthcare professionals, as well as support staff acting as first responders, for the initial recognition and early appropriate treatment of anaphylaxis.

Anaphylaxis cases have an initial acute onset (<60 minutes) of signs and symptoms that may be followed by a secondary reaction,[14–16] which occurs 1 to 24 hours after the initial reaction. The secondary reaction usually affects the same organ systems as the original reaction and presents in up to 20% of anaphylaxis cases.[17] There is no clear consensus regarding factors that predispose a victim to a secondary reaction. It has been speculated that the predisposing factors include reaction severity, time to onset of symptoms after allergen introduction, and history of a secondary reaction. Additionally, secondary reactions tend to be associated with a delay in epinephrine administration, as well as inadequate dosage.[18]

Table 14.1 lists signs and symptoms associated with anaphylaxis. The most common manifestations of an anaphylactic reaction are hives and welts.[8] Signs that show up on the skin may not always be present

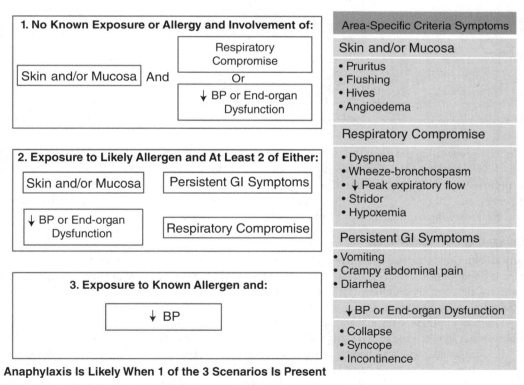

Anaphylaxis Is Likely When 1 of the 3 Scenarios Is Present

Figure 14.1 Visual representation of the anaphylaxis criteria of the National Institute of Allergy and Infectious Diseases and the Food Allergy and Anaphylaxis Network.

Source: Data from Manivannan V, Decker WW, Stead LG, Li JT, Campbell RL. Visual representation of National Institute of Allergy and Infectious Disease and Food Allergy and Anaphylaxis Network criteria for anaphylaxis. *Int J Emerg Med*. 2009;2(1):3–5.

TABLE 14.1 Signs and Symptoms of Anaphylaxis

Skin and Mucosal Tissues

General: flushing, itching, hives, rash, arm and leg hair standing up

Eyes: itching, redness, and swelling

Lips, tongue, and mouth: itching and swelling

Ears, genitalia, palms, and soles of feet: itching

Respiratory

Nasal: itching, congestion, runny nose, sneezing

Throat: itching and tightness in throat, trouble talking and hoarseness, dry cough, wheezing, difficulty swallowing

Lungs: temporary lack of breathing, chest tightness, deep cough, wheezing

Lips, fingertips, and toes: blue coloring

Gastrointestinal

Nausea, cramping, abdominal pain, vomiting, diarrhea

Cardiovascular

Chest pain, palpitations, fast pulse, slow pulse, or other dysrhythmia

Altered mental status, low blood pressure, shock, cardiac arrest

Central Nervous System

Aura of impending doom, anxiety, irritability, throbbing headache, disorientation

Other

Metallic taste in mouth

Uterine contractions in postpubertal females

---

in rapidly progressing reactions, however; first responders should not rule out anaphylaxis because of a lack of skin involvement. Exacerbation of allergy-type symptoms will present, followed by complaints of "tightness" in the throat and chest. As anaphylaxis progresses, the victim will experience coughing, wheezing, and shortness of breath. A fast pulse is an early reliable sign of cardiovascular involvement. Most fatal cases of anaphylaxis result from respiratory compromise and cardiovascular collapse.[19]

Management of Anaphylaxis

Early recognition is the first life-saving measure in the acute treatment of anaphylaxis. Emergency treatment is dependent on the training of available personnel on the scene and available equipment. All victims of anaphylaxis should be transported to the hospital for advanced medical care and observation of potential secondary reactions.

The most important drug in the treatment of anaphylaxis is epinephrine (adrenaline).[19] The drug should be administered when the initial signs and symptoms present, regardless of their severity. Epinephrine injected into a large muscle group eases respiratory distress and restores adequate cardiac function. Anaphylaxis-related fatalities usually result from delayed administration of epinephrine.[19] There is no absolute reason not to use epinephrine in a patient with anaphylaxis (i.e., there are no contraindications to using epinepherine even if the person was actually not having an anaphylactic reaction).[8] Athletes with a history of reactions should be prescribed and carry an **epinephrine autoinjector** ("Epi Pen"). Healthcare professionals or parents trained to administer

epinephrine autoinjector An intramuscular drug delivery system preloaded with a specific dosage of epinephrine for use during an emergency anaphylactic reaction.

an autoinjector should immediately utilize the drug at the first sign of anaphylaxis. If healthcare professionals or parents are normally not available, then coaches or support staff should be trained to use the prescribed injector.[20,21] However, those authorized to administer a prescribed injector should be determined by medical care.

Once anaphylaxis is recognized in an individual, EMS should be immediately activated. Airway, breathing, and circulation should be continuously monitored and epinephrine administered. The athlete should be placed in a comfortable position until advanced medical personnel arrive. An automated external defibrillator should be brought to the scene as a precautionary measure. Victims should be encouraged to remain still, minimizing movement, until advanced medical personnel arrive on scene.

It may be difficult to determine the trigger causing a reaction. If a stinger from a bee is present, the first responder should remove it as quickly as possible. The method of removal is not as important as early removal.[22] Vomiting should not be induced in victims of food or drug allergies. Airway, breathing, and circulation should be continuously monitored and cardiopulmonary resuscitation (CPR) begun if necessary. **Figure 14.2** lists key steps in the treatment of acute anaphylaxis.

Return to Play

An athlete who experiences an anaphylactic reaction must follow up with his or her primary care physician (PCP) prior to returning to activity. If warranted, the PCP may refer the patient to an allergist/immunologist. In most cases of anaphylaxis, the trigger can be determined and avoidance measures developed. The athlete should be educated on avoidance measures, signs and symptoms of recurrence, and appropriate use of a prescribed epinephrine autoinjector.[19] A detailed anaphylaxis emergency action plan can be developed with the athlete, athletic trainer, coaches, and additional support staff. These strategies will help reduce the risk of recurrence and provide life-saving skills for the athlete if the condition returns. Return to participation is individualized and gradual, with close monitoring of the athlete.

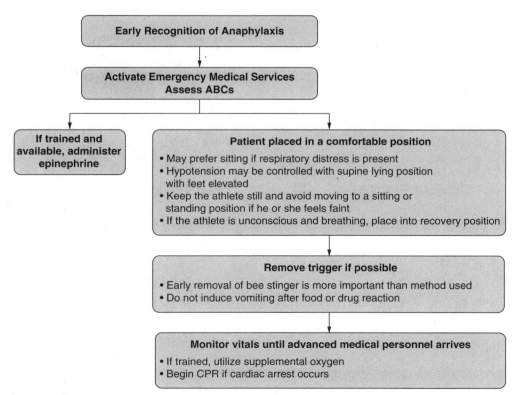

Figure 14.2 Emergency treatment of acute anaphylaxis.

Prevention

Implementation of prevention strategies is imperative for athletes with a history of anaphylaxis. Avoidance of known triggers is the basis of all long-term risk reduction for recurrence of anaphylaxis. Additional strategies include development of an anaphylaxis emergency action plan; wearing a medical identification tag; and education of patients, first responders, and healthcare professionals concerning the recognition and acute treatment of anaphylaxis.[8] Individuals with a history of anaphylactic reactions should never exercise alone.

Despite aggressive avoidance measures, research[23] indicates that 1 in 12 anaphylaxis victims will have a recurrence that will require emergency administration of epinephrine or hospitalization in any given year. When this situation occurs, emergency preparedness is essential. Those at risk for recurrence of anaphylaxis should carry one or more epinephrine autoinjectors and have an anaphylaxis emergency action plan.[8]

hypothermia Defined as being when core body temperature drops below 95°F as a result of the human body losing more heat than it can produce. Mental confusion is also present in this condition. This occurs in an outdoor setting in which hypothermia happened unintentionally.

accidental hypothermia Hypothermia that occurs in natural settings.

Hypothermia

Another condition that is of concern with participation in sports because of the possibility of death is **hypothermia**. Hypothermia is defined as a core body temperature below 95°F. Even though hypothermia is usually associated with cold-weather conditions, it has been recorded in situations as warm as 50–60°F.[24] A total of 4607 hypothermia deaths occurred from 1999 to 2002.[25] Common situations include a winter sport athlete who is working out alone, an organized sport event in which check-in stations are far apart, accidental water immersion while exercising, or a sudden unexpected change in environmental conditions (see **Table 14.2**). Death from hypothermia can be prevented through prompt diagnosis in combination with fast treatment and immediate transport.

Hypothermia is classified into different degrees of severity (see **Table 14.3**).[26–29] It can be progressive if the person is left untreated. When hypothermia occurs in a natural setting, it is termed **accidental hypothermia**. This is important to note because there are cases in which hypothermia is purposefully induced in a controlled hospital setting for surgical procedures.

TABLE 14.2   Examples of Sports and Physical Activity in Which Hypothermia Is Possible

Sport or Activity	Example
Snow sports	Cross-country skiing
	Snowshoeing
	Biathlon
	Outdoor hockey
	Skating
	Snowboarding
	Snowmobiling
Physical activity commonly done in wet and/or cold conditions	Jogging
	Marathons, ultramarathons, triathlons
Adventure	Adventure racing
	Open-water swimming
	Mountaineering
	Rock or ice climbing
	Exploring

TABLE 14.3   Classification of Hypothermia

Classification	Core Body Temperature
Mild hypothermia	32–35°C (89.6–95.6°F)
Moderate hypothermia	28–32°C (82.4–89.6°F)
Severe hypothermia	<28°C (<82.4°F)

For the purposes of this chapter, the term *hypothermia* will refer to accidental hypothermia. This occurs in an outdoor setting in which hypothermia happened unintentionally.

Hypothermia seen in organized sport involves victims exposed to cold conditions or cold water for a short period of time. An example is falling through the ice while cross-country skiing. However, hypothermia can also occur when an individual is slowly cooled over time because of exposure. An example is an individual who is not dressed appropriately for the cold weather while competing in a long-term outdoor event.[29]

Background and Occurrence of Hypothermia

Reported death rates caused by hypothermia vary greatly. One survey reported an overall rate of 17%, but these were primarily moderate to severe hypothermia cases.[30] Older individuals (60 years of age and older) may have physiologic differences that predispose them to hypothermia. Individuals with chronic medical conditions such as cardiac conditions and diabetes are also more susceptible to hypothermia. Individuals without significant family or friends are at risk because of lack of accountability. Examples are unmarried individuals, the homeless, and the elderly. Without the accountability of social ties, individuals may go missing without others realizing that they need to look for them.[26,29]

Mechanisms and Causes of Hypothermia

Several **cold stressors** can encourage heat losses to be greater than heat gain opportunities. Ambient conditions that are colder than the skin create a primary pathway for heat loss. With the temperature gradient in favor of the environment, the only source of heat gain is through metabolic (muscle contraction) production. Wind conditions also increase heat loss. If clothing is wetted through rain, snow, or water immersion, heat is lost at a faster pace. Athletes exercising in the cold may have an additional cold stress in the form of dry air. The lack of humidity causes irritation of the lungs.[28,29,31]

cold stressor Any intrinsic or extrinsic factor that encourages heat loss from the body.

The creation of heat through **shivering** depends on the contraction of muscle. This is an involuntary process initiated by the nervous system. Shivering starts in the trunk musculature and progresses to the extremities as hypothermia progresses.[26,28,32] The intensity of shivering increases as the cold stress or length of exposure increases. As more muscles are used for shivering, the need for oxygen increases.

shivering A response initiated by the brain in order to produce heat to combat cold stressors.

The release of hormones activates the mobilization of metabolic fuels into the blood. Fats, lipids, and carbohydrates can be used for energy in voluntary and involuntary muscle contractions.[26,28] The generation of heat through voluntary muscle contraction can easily be accomplished through physical activity if the victim still has coordination. Moving in place, walking, and jogging are all good examples.

As core body temperature decreases, the body redirects blood to keep it warmed centrally in the body and to protect vital organs. This will limit the amount of heat being transferred from the skin to the environment.[27-29] As a result, though, skin and extremity temperatures decrease, placing them at risk for frostbite. At first, the heart rate increases to compensate for the shift in blood flow.[33] As hypothermia progresses, however, the heart rate slows. This can potentially lead to the medical emergency, ventricular fibrillation (uncoordinated heart contractions).[28]

The lungs initially respond to hypothermia with an increased respiration rate (hyperventilation) to meet the demands of oxygen for heat production. Similar to the reaction of the heart, respiration slows as hypothermia progresses. Sporadic breathing patterns and cessation of breathing are possible at very low body temperatures.[26,28]

The redirection in blood flow also causes an increased urine output by the kidneys. This "cold diuresis" leads to an initial loss of body fluids through urine.[28] If the athlete begins competition in a hydrated state, this urine loss may not be significant. However, because most athletes begin exercising in a dehydrated state, this urine loss often has practical implications for performance and physiologic responses.[28]

Prevention

Extrinsic Predisposing Factors

- *Environmental:* Ambient temperatures below skin and core temperatures encourage heat loss over heat gain. Air movement and wind accelerate heat loss. Wind chill (a combination of low temperature and wind) also hastens heat loss.
- *Cold water:* Water causes heat loss at a rate that is 70 times greater than air. Therefore, individuals in conditions of rain, melting snow, or cold water immersion are at risk for hypothermia regardless of whether they are in mild or extreme cold conditions. The water temperature, amount of immersed body surface, and number of body parts involved with exercise can all encourage heat loss, leading to the development of hypothermia.[27,28] Whole or partial water immersion is a common factor in death from hypothermia.[25] An example of an athlete at risk is an open water swimmer because this sport involves cold water continuously flowing by the skin while both arms and legs exercise, resulting in significant heat loss.[34]
- *Wet clothing:* Unexpected wetting of clothing can double heat loss in cold-weather conditions as compared with dry clothing[27] and is a common factor found in hypothermia death cases.[30] This particular predisposing factor is significantly relevant not only in cold conditions but also in mild conditions.
- *Body type:* Individuals who have less body fat are susceptible to greater amounts of heat loss.[27] During hypothermia skin and fat are responsible for insulating the body to retain heat. There is an inverse relationship between heat loss and fat. Therefore, the less fat a person contains, the more heat loss is possible.[28] Individuals with less body fat have demonstrated less tolerance for cold water and begin shivering earlier.[35,36] Another body type at a disadvantage in combating cold conditions includes those individuals who do not have significant muscle mass to generate sufficient heat.[28] Examples include children, the elderly, and women.
- *Age and gender:* Individuals who are older than 60 years may be predisposed to hypothermia. A reduced heat retention,[37,38] decreased metabolic rate,[39] and decreased sensitivity to cold sensation are key factors.[27] Children may be predisposed to hypothermia because of their body type and lower amounts of fat. However, their physiologic responses are still appropriate and they can adjust to handle cold as well as adults, possibly just differently.

There is no overwhelming evidence that there are gender differences in terms of hypothermia risk.[27] However, with a higher incidence of hypothermic males found outdoors and already injured, it may be safe to assume that males engage in riskier behavior that possibly can predispose them to the condition.[30,40]

Intrinsic Predisposing Factors

- *Substance abuse:* Alcohol increases heat loss, inhibits shivering, and decreases heat production. Alcohol also increases urine production, resulting in mild dehydration. An intoxicated individual's sensations are decreased; therefore, cold and pain are not fully felt or comprehended by the individual, which may affect appropriate self-preserving behaviors. Additionally, alcohol increases risky behavior, often resulting in an immobilizing injury while in cold conditions and increased length of outdoor exposure.[28,41] The rate of oxygen released decreases during hypothermia. In smokers this rate declines even further; thus smokers develop hypothermia faster.[29]
- *Exercise intensity:* When an individual is exercising in cold or wet conditions but at moderate to high intensities, core body temperature can be maintained. However, if the exercise intensity is

low (such as walking or slow jogging), body temperature can actually decrease. Exercise in rainy conditions or exercising prior to getting wet in cold conditions leads to a greater decline in core body temperature as compared to not exercising.[27,28,42]

- *Physical fitness:* A physically fit person may be able to exercise and shiver for longer during hypothermic risk situations, allowing heat generation to maintain core body temperature.[28,43,44] Individuals with low physical fitness will fatigue earlier, leading to an earlier decrease in body temperature.[45]
- *Hypoglycemia:* Because shivering is dependent on energy sources within the body, an individual who has not been eating appropriately to prepare for the needs of exercising in the cold may be predisposed to hypothermia.[27] Shivering may actually be impaired in this situation. If an individual does not have significant carbohydrate stores or has low caloric intake as a result of underfeeding, this becomes a significant predisposing factor.[46–48] Dehydration does not affect shivering; therefore it may not play a role in predisposing someone to hypothermia.[26,49]
- *Time and place:* The majority of accidental hypothermia cases within Northern America occur between October and March, the coldest and wettest months of the year, respectively. Weekends have the highest incidence, probably because of alcohol consumption and lack of accountability for longer time periods. There is no specific geographic demographic in hypothermia; cases have been documented in all 50 U.S. states.

Recognition of Hypothermia

The key diagnostic criterion for hypothermia is a temperature of less than 95°F.[27–29] Only a temperature assessed rectally can be trusted to obtain an accurate measurement in an emergency situation in the field.[50]

Signs and symptoms can differ among individuals, the earliest being sensation of coldness, shivering, apathy, and personality changes. As hypothermia progresses, other signs and symptoms usually include uncontrollable shivering, grayish pale skin color, palpable cold skin, immobile extremities progressing from fingers and toes to elbows and knees, inability to move after rest, decreased pulse, decreased blood pressure, delayed pupil responses, decreased respiration rate, and mental orientation/awareness issues.

Nervous system dysfunction can manifest in many ways (see **Table 14.4**). An easy way to remember important key signs is "the umbles" (see **Table 14.5**).[27–29] It may be relevant to briefly assess a suspected victim using standard concussion assessments. These tools cover orientation questions, word recall, and saying numbers and months backward. They also assess balance function. All are relevant if one is trying to confirm a case of mild hypothermia but probably are not needed to recognize moderate to severe hypothermia.

Hypothermic individuals can lack "behavioral thermoregulation" because of the condition's effect on the brain. Examples include not adding clothing for warmth, not looking for shelter, and not drinking or eating. As the condition worsens, hypothermic individuals have actually been found to start taking off all their clothing.[28]

Management

The first responder and the transitional responder are mainly limited to external treatments. It should be noted that because of the significant decrease and possible absence of vital signs (e.g., pulse, breathing) as hypothermia progresses, actions and treatments should always be initiated even if no vital signs are found.[27] Great care should be taken not to jostle or move the victim a great deal while providing initial care and transport. Increased movement or jostling may cause ventricular fibrillation.[26,33,51] Keeping the victim as horizontal as possible is recommended.

No matter the circumstances, actions and treatment should include the following:[28–30]

- Place the individual in a warm, dry, environmentally protected, safe shelter while waiting for transitional care to arrive.
- Place the individual in a comfortable position while minimally jostling him or her.
- Those trained to do so should obtain and monitor vital signs such as pulse, respiration rate, blood pressure, pupil response, and consciousness level.
- If possible, attempt to gain a history of the length and circumstances of exposure.

TABLE 14.4   Manifestations of Central Nervous System Dysfunction by Categories

Category	Progressive Signs or Symptoms
Personality	Apathetic Withdrawn Belligerent Combative behavior Irritability Any exaggerated emotional responses
Behavior	Lethargy Drowsiness Removing clothing Lack of behavioral thermoregulation Vague communication Marked memory disturbances and lapses
Coordination	Slow and slurred speech Lack of dexterity Staggering Collapse Decreased to absent reflexes
Consciousness	Complete exhaustion Responds verbally but not oriented Responds to only painful stimuli Coma

- If the victim is shivering, allow shivering to continue and do not limit or discourage it. Spontaneous rewarming can occur with successful productive shivering.
- Remove wet clothing (preferably by cutting, in order to minimize movement).
- Administer CPR if indicated.

Rewarming falls into the following categories: passive and active. Passive rewarming aims to remove sources of heat loss and use the body's own shivering or physical activity to rewarm the individual.[52] Active rewarming uses forced air and other warming products. Forced air rewarming has been supported as more effective compared with passive rewarming in a few foundational studies.[53–55] It has been suggested that the trunk should be targeted in rewarming efforts.[23,33,56]

The external treatment options that are possible in the field are as follows:

- Warm forced-air circulation around the body (commercial products)
- Layering traditional or heating blankets

TABLE 14.5   Common Signs Associated with Hypothermia: The "Umbles"

"Umbles"	Sign or Symptom
Grumbles	Irritability, personality change
Mumbles	Slurring of speech, difficulty articulating speech
Stumbles	Coordination issues, trouble walking/moving
Fumbles	Issues with small tasks

- Hot water bottles placed on major arteries
- Another person's body heat
- Warm drinks that contain carbohydrates if the victim is conscious and can tolerate them
- Natural inhalation of warm air (not forced)

The goal of the first responder should be to initiate the actions and treatments just discussed as soon as possible in all hypothermia cases. An individual with hypothermia should be warmed slowly. However, this is a controversial subject in the research and may be dependent on the severity of the hypothermia being treated.[33]

Recovery and Return to Play

Only a sparse amount of research on the recovery of hypothermic individuals has been done, and none on athletes who have experienced hypothermia. One study followed up with survivors of severe hypothermia and found no difference in quality of life after the incident.[57] After being released from the hospital, subjects indicated an ability to return to normal lifestyles. The subjects in this study were young and healthy. Return to participation is individualized and gradual, with close monitoring of the athlete. Published guidelines should be sought to help with decisions.[58]

Prevention

Table 14.6 addresses each predisposing factor listed earlier with simple preventive measures. Additional discussion follows.

TABLE 14.6 Prevention of Hypothermia

Predisposing Factor	Preventive Measure
Environmental conditions	Layer warm clothing Wear appropriate underwear Wear mittens and a hat to cover fingers, head, and ears Limit length of time outside
Breathing dry air	Lightly cover the mouth and nose with outerwear
Extended length of exposure outside alone	Tell one to two people your estimated start and end time and the exact place you are exercising, and agree upon a plan should you not contact them at the estimated end time
Thin or unseen ice	Ensure that the path that is taken is either free of water or that all ice is safe to cross before moving forward
Wet clothing	Bring additional clothing to change into if the current weather becomes wet Wear shoes that will keep snow and water out Wear wicking and breathable material
Body type	Be aware and increase vigilance during events or situations with athletes of low body fat and/or low muscle mass
Age	Be aware and increase vigilance during events or situations with athletes older than 60
Substance abuse	Avoid drinking any type of alcohol within 24 hours of exercising or traveling in the cold Stop smoking
Exercise intensity	Keep a moderate to high intensity of exercise when risks of hypothermia are greater Avoid getting wet while exercising at low intensities

(continues)

TABLE 14.6   Prevention of Hypothermia (*continued*)

Predisposing Factor	Preventive Measure
Physical fitness	Be aware and increase vigilance during events or situations in which normally sedentary people are participating
Hypoglycemia	Ensure appropriate carbohydrate feeding prior to exercising in the cold
Time and place	Be aware and increase vigilance during events or situations that occur between October and March Ensure accountability
Illness and injury	Consider participation or length constraints on individuals who are injured All athletes with a chronic medical condition should be cleared by a physician prior to participation

Organized Sport and Event Planning

For cold-weather sporting events, have medical personnel and check-in stations in place in order to appropriately monitor participants (see **Box 14.1**). Evaluating the environmental conditions and then comparing them to predeveloped tables and charts are suggested. (The National Athletic Trainers' Association [NATA] position statement on cold-weather injuries contains such charts.[26]) Following wind chill risk charts is recommended to assess risk, develop plausible time frames in which to exercise if it is necessary, or make participation or event decisions. Limiting the duration of cold exposure during a practice or an event is an easily implemented preventive measure.[26–28]

Clothing

Appropriate clothing is the best preventive measure against hypothermia. An inner, middle, and outer layer should be used. The inner layer lies against the skin and wicks away sweat and moisture. The purpose of the middle layer is to provide warmth and insulation. The outer layer should allow moisture to evaporate and defend against air, wind, and rain.[26,27] It should be noted that individuals have different clothing needs and that a strict standard may not be useful in events in which multiple people are exercising. Research varies, and there is no "perfect" choice of clothing fabric materials. However, clothing that will not hold moisture, that dries easily, is breathable, and is loose fitting is best.[26–28,59] Additional tips include wearing outerwear on the head to prevent significant heat loss through this area of the body and wearing appropriately fitted socks, shoes, and gloves to allow adequate blood flow.

Box 14.1

List of Recommended Prevention Measures for Cold-Weather Events

1. Send educational materials to athletes, coaches, and/or parents prior to the event regarding the recognition and prevention of cold-weather injuries and illnesses.

2. Have an appropriate number of medical personnel for the number of participants and length of event.

3. Provide fluids at the start and finish of the race as well as at numerous stations along the event. Fluids at the start and finish can be a mix of cool and warm. Fluids should contain carbohydrates and electrolytes.

4. Set up numerous medical stations throughout the event. If stations are far apart, have personnel responsible for sweeping the course in between. Communication should be coordinated so that all stations are involved.

5. The main medical station and key course stations should be equipped with warming products and additional medical equipment.

6. Ensure that local hospitals are aware of the event in order to be prepared.

Nutrition

Good diet and hydration habits may help prevent hypothermia. Exercising in the cold requires more energy, dictating higher caloric needs to meet the metabolic demand. Good hydration is a basic habit of good health.

Cold Acclimatization

Cold acclimatization can be defined as a set of beneficial adaptations by the body to handle repetitive cold exposure. Some examples of adaptations include enhanced shivering, a lower shivering threshold, and improved muscle blood flow. This response by the body is a beneficial and important preventive measure.[28,60]

Diabetes

Diabetes is not a common cause of sudden death in young athletes. However, in addition to the long-term risks of the disease, diabetes and its treatment can be a source of short-term risk. It is **hypoglycemia** that carries the greatest degree of risk to the young athlete.

In discussing diabetes, it is important to understand the difference between type 1 and type 2 diabetes. **Type 1 diabetes** is an autoimmune illness involving the destruction of the cells that produce **insulin**. Insulin is a hormone that helps to regulate sugar (glucose) in the blood. Individuals with type 1 diabetes do not produce adequate amounts of their own insulin and require the administration of insulin to survive. **Type 2 diabetes** is a disease of insulin resistance. Individuals with type 2 diabetes produce copious amounts of their own insulin, but over time they become less sensitive to it. It is largely a disease of lifestyle, particularly obesity. The type 2 diabetic patient is managed via promotion of physical activity and dietary interventions, rather than with insulin. Type 2 diabetes remains very uncommon in young athletes, largely because of their active lifestyle. Therefore, for the remainder of this section the focus is on the young athlete with type 1 diabetes.

Mechanisms and Causes

The primary risks faced by the diabetic athlete are hypoglycemia and hyperglycemia.[61] Signs and symptoms associated with hypoglycemia include fast pulse, sweating, palpitations, hunger, anxiety, and tremor. These symptoms are triggered by the release of the hormone epinephrine. Additional symptoms of hypoglycemia are triggered by the direct effect of diminished glucose supply to the brain. Glucose is the primary fuel for the brain, so glucose depletion has dramatic effects on the brain's function. These symptoms include drowsiness, confusion, stupor, weakness, slurred speech, and dizziness. Severe symptoms include seizures and loss of consciousness.[61] It is important to note that the diabetic athlete who is sleeping or has a blunted response to hypoglycemia is at particular risk because of his or her inability to detect the warning symptoms.

A related and somewhat poorly understood phenomenon is the "dead in bed" syndrome. This syndrome involves a young diabetic person who retires to bed at night in otherwise excellent health, only to be found dead the next morning.[62] The lack of disruption of the bedding of these individuals indicates a rather sudden event leading to their demise.[63] The exact nature of this event remains unknown, but overnight hypoglycemia is suspected.[64,65]

On the other end of the spectrum lies the risk associated with hyperglycemia. With hyperglycemia, the elevated glucose levels result in spillage of glucose into the urine. This effect increases urine output, which can lead to progressive dehydration and further hyperglycemia.

Despite the high glucose levels, the lack of insulin diminishes the capability to utilize glucose as an energy source. An internal cascade causes marked dehydration, dramatic hyperglycemia, and electrolyte imbalances. This is the process known as diabetic ketoacidosis (DKA). DKA accounts for 8% to 29% of all hospital admissions for patients with diabetes.[66,67]

Glycemic Control with Exercise

Glycemic control during exercise in the normal individual is intricately controlled by a variety of interactions. The precise hormonal responses to exercise vary with the type of exercise (moderate vs. intense,

cold acclimatization A series of beneficial adaptations made over 14 days that enhances heat production and minimizes heat loss while exposed to cold conditions.

hypoglycemia A low blood glucose level that affects physiologic function.

type 1 diabetes An autoimmune illness that causes the pancreas to not produce adequate amounts of insulin.

insulin A hormone produced by the pancreas that helps glucose move into cells for use.

type 2 diabetes A disease in which the pancreas produces large amounts of insulin but cells become less sensitive and more resistant to it.

aerobic vs. resistance), the duration of exercise (short, intermediate, or long), and environmental conditions. The most commonly discussed mode of exercise is intermediate to prolonged moderate activity, such as with distance running. In this scenario, the body functions in the optimal manner to provide an adequate supply of glucose to exercising muscle and subsequently adapts to diminishing glycogen stores.[68] In fact, it has been previously established that muscle can take up glucose in the absence of insulin.[69] This fine control is lost in athletes with type 1 diabetes because their insulin level is determined not by the body's innate response, but by their insulin dosing.

Intense exercise elicits a somewhat different response. The tremendous need for glucose in the setting of intense exercise necessitates a dramatic rise in blood catecholamines (epinephrine and norepinephrine).[70] This surge helps provide the necessary glucose, but when the intense exercise ceases, it takes time for catecholamine levels to decline, creating a state of temporary hyperglycemia.[71] It is even possible for people with well-controlled type 1 diabetes to experience significant hyperglycemia secondary to intense exercise.[72,73]

To complicate matters further, many sports are not purely moderate or purely high intensity. Rather, they involve a baseline of moderate activity with overlying bouts of intense energy demand. Sports such as soccer, basketball, field hockey, and football are typical of this scenario. In this setting, the normal hormonal response of the athlete is constantly adjusting to maintain glucose normalcy. This is a substantial challenge to the diabetic athlete.

Finally, the body's response to falling glucose levels can also be altered by previous episodes of hypoglycemia. The athlete with type 1 diabetes must practice added caution with exercise that occurs 12 to 24 hours after a hypoglycemic episode.

Insulin Delivery

Intensive treatment of diabetes is the current standard of care, with evidence that tight control of blood glucose values alters the risk of long-term complications.[74,75] However, with this intensive control, the risk of hypoglycemia increases twofold to threefold, especially during exercise.[75,76] Intensive treatment of diabetes requires insulin infusion either via multiple daily injections or, optimally, the use of an insulin pump.

Injections given once or twice a day can provide a baseline level of insulin for the athlete with type 1 diabetes. Then, prior to meals, the athlete uses an injection of insulin.[76] The drawbacks to multiple daily injections are the number of daily injections the athlete must perform (three to four) and, more important, the lack of flexibility this offers in insulin dosing. When a fixed dose of insulin has been injected, there is little room for flexibility if exercise plans change, which is common in team sports.

The insulin pump has greatly assisted athletes in the control of their glucose levels. It works by providing a steady infusion of insulin that can be adjusted by the athlete depending on the demands of a particular time of day. In addition to this infusion, the athlete can also trigger additional injections of insulin to cover carbohydrate intake. The insulin pump is connected via tubing that is inserted subcutaneously. It can typically stay in place for 2 to 3 days but then needs to be moved to prevent infection. Between the tubing and the pump there is an interlocking connector that allows the pump to be disconnected for short periods of time. The pump can be removed, if needed, during athletic participation as long as the athlete monitors his or her blood glucose level.

It is difficult to make concrete insulin dosing recommendations that apply to all situations. Several variables need to be taken into account. Insulin absorption will vary with the site of injection or infusion.[77,78] Additionally, ambient conditions will have an effect, with hot and humid conditions potentially enhancing absorption.[79] Working with the athlete and the PCP is the best way to become knowledgeable about the best delivery route for the individual and the sport-specific demands.

The optimal prevention of diabetic complications comes from education of the athlete. Athletes need to be educated regarding the proper nutritional intake for exercise, the basics of insulin dosing and administration during exercise, the importance of testing blood glucose, the guidelines for proper blood glucose levels for exercise, and the proper response to abnormal glucose levels.

Prevention

In athletic participation, the type 1 diabetic must be very vigilant of blood glucose levels in order to control them. Although the benefits of exercise are as substantial for the diabetic athlete as they are for the nondiabetic athlete, the type 1 diabetic faces the risk of hypoglycemia, which can occur during exercise and up to 12 to 24 hours afterward.[80,81] The type 1 diabetic also faces the risks of hyperglycemia, as noted previously.[82,83] Managing the dosing of insulin is imperative to diminish this risk.

Maintenance of Normal Glucose Levels

Athletes who use multiple daily injections of insulin for control will need to alter both their insulin doses and nutritional intake depending on their status, exercise demand, and timing of their exercise sessions.[80,81] It is recommended that athletes who plan on exercising after eating alter their injection amount to account for both the duration and type of exercise planned. Some athletes train prior to eating in the morning, which makes alteration of their insulin dosing more difficult as well as important. Exact alterations should be planned with the athlete, his or her physician, and athletic trainer.

It is difficult to determine exactly how to alter doses. Athletes with type 1 diabetes need to check their blood glucose level regularly and note how they respond to different alterations.[82] Because of the somewhat unpredictable response of blood glucose levels to these alterations, it is essential that the athlete always have a source of carbohydrate available to him or her.

The use of the insulin pump gives an athlete greater control and flexibility regarding insulin dosing.[83–85] As mentioned earlier, the insulin pump may need to be removed for certain types of exercise such as collision or water sports. It is recommended that the pump be removed approximately 30 minutes prior to exercise because insulin can remain active for approximately 30 minutes. For prolonged exercise of an hour or more, additional doses of insulin should be administered for that hour in order to prevent a hypoinsulinemic state.[83] The exact dosage should be determined by the athlete with his or her physician and the support of healthcare providers.

Dosage decisions should be made based on other variables as well. As noted earlier, a previous episode of hypoglycemia can increase the risk of hypoglycemia with subsequent exercise in the next 12 to 24 hours.[74] Also, fluctuations in ambient temperature can affect insulin sensitivity. Insulin sensitivity is also increased as an athlete becomes more fit. Therefore, the insulin plan may need to change as an athlete becomes better conditioned. If an athlete is sick, this will raise blood glucose levels. The same effect can be seen with injury.[76] Regardless of the alterations made to insulin dosing, athletes must pay close attention to the responses of their blood glucose level to various situations. They face numerous alterations to their training and practice schedules, as well as to their eating schedules. Athletes should always be equipped with an ingestible source of carbohydrate should their blood glucose level dip too low. Support staff and healthcare providers should also be prepared to help with a quick source of appropriate carbohydrate if this situation occurs.

Recognition

Athletes with type 1 diabetes should know their blood glucose level going into exercise. Beginning exercise with a blood glucose level that is either too low or too high will predispose to hypoglycemia or hyperglycemia, so alterations need to be made to address these issues before exercise is started.[86]

NATA recommends measuring blood glucose levels two to three times at 30-minute intervals prior to exercise to determine the trend of the glucose levels that day. During exercise, its recommendation is to measure blood glucose every 30 minutes if possible. After exercise, NATA recommends that athletes who experience delayed postexercise hypoglycemia check their blood glucose every 2 hours for up to 4 hours.[76] Coaches, support staff, and healthcare providers should aid the diabetic athlete by making accommodations before, during, and after practices/games to allow these measurements to occur.

Once an athlete with type 1 diabetes develops a stable schedule of insulin, diet, and exercise, it may not be necessary to check his or her blood glucose level as regularly during exercise. However, if there is change to an athlete's food intake, exercise schedule and intensity, insulin dosing, or internal situation (as a result of illness, injury, or environment), the athlete should be diligent about checking his or her blood glucose level periodically during exercise. Exhaustive exercise and hypoglycemia share many common symptoms, so it is important to check blood glucose levels in these situations to ensure that hypoglycemia is addressed early, if it develops. Also, if the athlete has experienced a recent episode of hypoglycemia, added attentiveness is necessary because of the increased risk of recurrent hypoglycemia. The athlete also needs to know not to use insulin to treat temporary hyperglycemia during intense exercise.[71] The hormonal response of intense exercise will elevate blood glucose levels, so if athletes chase these levels with additional insulin, they place themselves at greater risk of postexercise hypoglycemia.

Late Hypoglycemia

After exercise, muscle and liver stores are replenished and muscle sensitivity to insulin increases. These combined factors can lead to a delayed hypoglycemic response to exercise, which can occur 6 to 24 hours after exercise.[87] It most commonly occurs at times when activity levels change, such as progression to a new level of competition or with two-a-day practices in the preseason. Late hypoglycemia often occurs overnight. In addition to the significant risks of hypoglycemia, it can disturb sleep patterns, impair recovery, and contribute to subjective feelings of fatigue and shrinking of a sense of well-being.[79]

Prevention of late hypoglycemia may require as little intervention as the addition of a late-night snack before bed. Also, insulin doses can be reduced, either as part of a multiple daily injection or an insulin pump regimen. Exercise interventions have been studied in research,[88,89] but it is unknown whether these interventions have any effect on hypoglycemia occurring after exercise.

Management of Hypoglycemia and Return to Play

Hypoglycemia is generally defined as a blood glucose level less than 70 mg/dL. If the athlete is conscious, coherent, and able to follow directions, the hypoglycemia is considered mild. If the athlete is unconscious, combative, disoriented, or unable to follow directions, the hypoglycemia is considered severe. Obviously, management of mild and severe hypoglycemic episodes differs.

Mild Hypoglycemia

The management of mild hypoglycemia centers on oral carbohydrate replacement. In this setting, the athlete should be removed from exercise and given 15 to 20 grams of fast-acting carbohydrate. This can be attained with 4 to 6 glucose tablets, 2 tablespoons of honey, 4 to 6 ounces of fruit juice or sweetened carbonated beverage, or 8 ounces of low-fat milk.[61,71,76] Higher-fat foods such as candy bars should be avoided because they delay the absorption of carbohydrate. Also, sports beverages contain lower amounts of carbohydrate, so larger volumes are required to achieve 15 to 20 grams of carbohydrate. For instance, an equal volume of Gatorade has just less than one half of the carbohydrate of apple or grape juice.[61] This makes sports drinks suboptimal sources of carbohydrate to treat hypoglycemia, and the other alternatives noted previously should be made available. After the athlete ingests the carbohydrate, the blood glucose level should be reassessed every 15 minutes. If there is no response in symptoms or blood glucose level after 15 minutes, the initial carbohydrate dose can be repeated. If there is still no response after a second dose, NATA recommends activating EMS.[76] It is important to keep in mind that proper dosing of the carbohydrate is important. Blindly giving an amount of carbohydrate that is too large is likely to stimulate a hyperglycemic rebound.

If the athlete responds properly to the oral carbohydrate dose, he or she may be returned to exercise once symptoms resolve and the blood glucose level is above 80 mg/dL. In returning an athlete to exercise, it is prudent to have him or her also ingest some low-glycemic-index carbohydrate, such as a bagel or bread, to prevent a recurrence of the hypoglycemia.

Severe Hypoglycemia

Severe hypoglycemia obviously requires more emergent intervention. The emergency medical system should be activated, and measures should immediately be taken on site to raise blood glucose levels. If the athlete has an injectable **glucagon** kit, a healthcare provider or parent can inject into the deltoid, quadriceps, or gluteal muscle groups. In a situation in which an athlete is traveling without an athletic trainer or parent, the coach should be trained to be able to administer the glucagon.

It should be obvious that there is no role for the use of oral carbohydrate in the unresponsive athlete. Attempts to force oral consumption of carbohydrate can lead to choking and aspiration.

glucagon A hormone produced by the pancreas that helps blood glucose by stimulating glycogen release.

Altitude Illnesses

There are several towns and cities in the United States that are 9800 feet or more above sea level (e.g., Cheyenne, Wyoming; Denver, Colorado; and Santa Fe, New Mexico). There are many more regions that fit this classification internationally. Athletes who travel to these towns to compete from lower elevations are susceptible to several illnesses associated with altitude: Acute Mountain Sickness (AMS), **high-altitude pulmonary edema (HAPE)**, and **high-altitude cerebral edema (HACE)**.

high-altitude pulmonary edema (HAPE) A condition that only manifests in high-altitude outdoor settings in which low oxygen levels trigger swelling of lung tissue, filling them with fluid.

Mechanisms and Causes of Altitude Illness

HAPE and HACE are both life threatening and caused by a reduction in blood oxygen levels. The organs most sensitive to a decrease in oxygen are the lungs and brain. HACE is caused by an increase in blood flow to the brain. HAPE is caused by pulmonary hypertension. In both cases, there is significant swelling of the organ tissues. HACE tends to develop over 24 hours, whereas HAPE tends to develop over several days. Predisposing factors for both conditions include a past history of altitude illness and rapid ascent (e.g., airplane transportation into an area or hiking numerous miles in one day to a higher elevation). Additionally, being a "low-lander" (a person who lives below 3200 feet elevation), exercise, and cold air are also predisposing factors. Prevention of HACE and HAPE includes a gradual ascent, frequent rests, frequent descents intermixed with ascents, avoidance of depressants, and staying well hydrated and fed.[90–94]

high-altitude cerebral edema (HACE) A condition that only manifests in high-altitude outdoor settings in which low oxygen levels cause trigger swelling of brain tissue.

Recognition and Management of Altitude Illness

These illnesses are possible in sports situations, particularly AMS, but are more commonly encountered in outdoor activities (hiking, climbing, camping, etc.). AMS is a non–life threatening illness, but symptoms can be incapacitating. AMS usually develops within 6 to 12 hours and reaches greatest strength in 24 to 48 hours. Common signs and symptoms are similar to the flu with headache, vomiting, dizziness, nausea, and general sensations of not feeling well. Other symptoms that have been reported with AMS include a feeling of "overwhelming oppression," significant intensity of headaches, and irritability. Treatment includes nonemergent transportation to advanced medical care (i.e., the hospital) and/or descent. Some measures athletes can take to prevent AMS include a good diet and hydration habits, avoiding significant exertion upon arrival, and acclimatization to the higher altitude.

HACE's early signs and symptoms include headache, loss of appetite, and nausea. As swelling increases skull pressure, these symptoms progress in severity. Mental confusion arises and is similar to the signs and symptoms of concussion. Mental status, consciousness, orientation, and coordination are all affected. Vomiting might also be present and persistent at a progressed stage. Treatment is simply to get the athlete to advanced medical care and/or descend as fast as possible to transitional care.[90–94]

HAPE's early signs and symptoms include shortness of breath and a dry cough. A low-grade fever may be present. Individuals with an existing or recent respiratory illness are at greater risk. As HAPE progresses, "crackly" breathing can be heard in the chest with or without a stethoscope. Difficulty in breathing and cough worsen. Descent should be immediate, as well as transportation to advanced care. If descent means strenuous exercise, it is possible that staying at the location and resting might be the better treatment because exertion will worsen the lung swelling. Without treatment, however, respiratory failure and death are possible.[90–93]

Clinical Case Scenarios

1. John is a 22-year-old white NCAA Division I cross-country athlete. His teammates reported to athletic training personnel that he had been stung by a hornet and was not feeling well. The incident occurred at the beginning of a workout in August running trails a half mile away from campus (starting point). Environmental conditions that day included a dry bulb temperature of 26.7°C (80.1°F) and a relative humidity of 76%. The athlete continued to run after the sting for approximately 1 mile (approximately 7 minutes) in order to arrive at the water break point, where athletic training personnel were stationed. He initially complained of itching on his palms and feet, his face was red and hot, and he was sweating profusely. Hives were slightly recognizable on his body at this time. During the conversation, hives started to progressively form on his body. No previous history of an anaphylactic reaction existed prior to this incident. EMS was activated when the athlete's throat started swelling and he began having difficulty breathing. The athlete was kept in a supine position and made as comfortable as possible. His vital signs were monitored. The athlete was turned to a recovery position as he started to vomit. An ambulance arrived at the site approximately 17 minutes after the sting. John received an epinephrine shot, a Benadryl shot, and intravenous (IV) fluids on the ambulance. At the hospital, he received an additional liter of IV fluids. A second shot of epinephrine and Benadryl was administered approximately 45 minutes after the first injections.

   a. What triggers played a role in this reaction?

   b. What factors mediated the severity of the response?

   c. What precautions will the medical staff need to have in place before John practices again?

2. Hailey is a 5-foot, 4-inch, 110-pound cross-country skier in Vermont. She is a freshman on the college's intercollegiate team. She was "initiated" onto the team Friday night. It was late October but early in the training season. The team was hosting its first meet the following week. Hailey and her roommate went for an additional workout on the cross-country trails Saturday morning in order to better prepare for the meet. Hailey's ski caught on a rock, making her fall onto a thin sheet of ice on the small creek they were skiing next to. As she scrambled to get up, she fell through the ice and ended up sitting in waist-high cold water. Her friend helped her out of the creek, and they continued their workout for another hour. The environmental conditions were a temperature of 1.6°C (35°F) with 10% humidity. By the time they returned to the ski shack, Hailey was complaining, grumpy, and cold. As soon as they stopped to remove their skis and outwear, Hailey began to shiver violently. The athletic trainer took her pulse and blood pressure, which were 160 and 150/90, respectively. The athletic trainer had Hailey remove all her wet clothing, put dry clothing on from her team locker with the help of her friend, and wrap herself in blankets. Hailey was placed in front of a heat blower and was asked to sip hot chocolate and eat granola bars. Within 30 minutes, Hailey felt better and her vital signs had returned to normal.

   a. What were the major predisposing factors to Hailey developing hypothermia? Which factors were within Hailey's control? Which ones were not?

   b. Why did the athletic trainer choose these particular treatments? What precautions should be taken with these treatments?

3. Brayden had been training for his first triathlon all summer. Race day came on September 30th in Colorado, with beautiful fall conditions: 15.6°C (60°F) and 20% humidity. As he dove into the mountain lake, it felt shockingly cold compared to the pool in which he had been training. He completed the half-mile swim, dried off, and changed into his new biking and running clothes. As he neared the finish of the bike portion, the sky turned cloudy, the air cooled, and it started to drizzle. Brayden was already shivering when he began running the 10 miles. His clothes and socks were wet after 2 miles of running. Brayden became increasingly frustrated as he kept tripping on rocks and cracks in the road. At the finish line Brayden refused to wave at his parents as they cheered for him. He was unable

to remove the time chip from his shoe and became upset with the volunteer helping him. Brayden ignored the offers of mylar blankets, food, and hot fluids from the volunteers.

    a. What predisposing factors of hypothermia are at play in this scenario that are not discussed in the text?

    b. What signs, symptoms, and behavior is Brayden exhibiting at the end of the scenario?

    c. How might this situation progress further?

    d. What should medical volunteers do to help Brayden?

4. Dan and Jen were hiking in the Sierra Nevada with four other friends. They hiked 10 miles on the first day, set up camp, ate a full dinner, and got 7 hours of sleep. On the beginning of the second day of hiking, Jen became hungry and tried a handful of berries she found next to the trail. As the group continued to hike, Jen told Dan that she was not feeling well and needed to stop. Dan turned to Jen and noticed hives on her arms, neck, and chest. Dan stopped the rest of the group. A trained provider in the group found Jen's pulse to be 130, and her respiratory rate was increased. As the group member began to take a history, Jen started to have significant difficulty with breathing. The group member gave Jen 0.3 milligram of epinephrine through intramuscular injection, made her comfortable, and monitored her vital signs while calming her.

    a. What will need to be done once Jen starts to recover?

    b. What will need to be done if Jen's signs and symptoms continue or get worse?

    c. How would this situation differ if it were to occur at a soccer field?

Key Terms

accidental hypothermia

anaphylaxis

cold acclimatization

cold stressor

epinephrine autoinjector

glucagon

high-altitude cerebral edema (HACE)

high-altitude pulmonary edema (HAPE)

hypoglycemia

hypothermia

insulin

shivering

trigger

type 1 diabetes

type 2 diabetes

References

1. Sampson HA, Munoz-Furlong A, Bock SA, et al. Symposium on the definition and management of anaphylaxis: summary report. *J Allergy Clin Immunol*. 2005;115(3):584–591.
2. Pumphrey R. Anaphylaxis: can we tell who is at risk of a fatal reaction? *Curr Opin Allergy Clin Immunol*. 2004;4(4):285–290.
3. Lieberman P, Camargo CA Jr, Bohlke K, et al. Epidemiology of anaphylaxis: findings of the American College of Allergy, Asthma and Immunology Epidemiology of Anaphylaxis Working Group. *Ann Allergy Asthma Immunol*. 2006;97(5):596–602.
4. Poulos LM, Waters AM, Correll PK, Loblay RH, Marks GB. Trends in hospitalizations for anaphylaxis, angioedema, and urticaria in Australia, 1993-1994 to 2004-2005. *J Allergy Clin Immunol*. 2007;120(4):878–884.

5. Neugut AI, Ghatak AT, Miller RL. Anaphylaxis in the United States: an investigation into its epidemiology. *Arch Intern Med.* 2001;161(1):15–21.
6. Simons FE. Anaphylaxis. *J Allergy Clin Immunol.* 2010;125(suppl 2):S161–S181.
7. Kemp SF, Lockey RF. Anaphylaxis: a review of causes and mechanisms. *J Allergy Clin Immunol.* 2002;110(3):341–348.
8. Simons FE. Anaphylaxis: recent advances in assessment and treatment. *J Allergy Clin Immunol.* 2009;124(4):625–636; quiz 637–638.
9. Sampson HA. Anaphylaxis and emergency treatment. *Pediatrics.* 2003;111(6 pt 3):1601–1608.
10. Lieberman P. Anaphylaxis. *Med Clin North Am.* 2006;90(1):77–95.
11. Campbell RL, Luke A, Weaver AL, et al. Prescriptions for self-injectable epinephrine and follow-up referral in emergency department patients presenting with anaphylaxis. *Ann Allergy Asthma Immunol.* 2008;101(6):631–636.
12. Klein JS, Yocum MW. Underreporting of anaphylaxis in a community emergency room. *J Allergy Clin Immunol.* 1995;95(2): 637–638.
13. Sampson HA, Muñoz-Furlong A, Campbell RL, et al. Second symposium on the definition and management of anaphylaxis: summary report—Second National Institute of Allergy and Infectious Disease/Food Allergy and Anaphylaxis Network symposium. *J Allergy Clin Immunol.* 2006;117(2):391–397.
14. Brazil E, MacNamara AF. "Not so immediate" hypersensitivity—the danger of biphasic anaphylactic reactions. *J Accid Emerg Med.* 1998;15(4):252–253.
15. Douglas DM, Sukenick E, Andrade WP, Brown JS. Biphasic systemic anaphylaxis: an inpatient and outpatient study. *J Allergy Clin Immunol.* 1994;93(6):977–985.
16. Stark BJ, Sullivan TJ. Biphasic and protracted anaphylaxis. *J Allergy Clin Immunol.* 1986;78(1 pt 1):76–83.
17. Lee JM, Greenes DS. Biphasic anaphylactic reactions in pediatrics. *Pediatrics.* 2000;106(4):762–766.
18. Lieberman P. Biphasic anaphylactic reactions. *Ann Allergy Asthma Immunol.* 2005;95(3):217–226.
19. Kemp SF, Lockey RF, Simons FE. Epinephrine: the drug of choice for anaphylaxis. A statement of the World Allergy Organization. *Allergy.* 2008;63(8):1061–1070.
20. Korenblat P, Lundie MJ, Dankner RE, Day JH. A retrospective study of epinephrine administration for anaphylaxis: how many doses are needed? *Allergy Asthma Proc.* 1999;20(6):383–386.
21. Uguz A, Lack G, Pumphrey R, et al. Allergic reactions in the community: a questionnaire survey of members of the anaphylaxis campaign. *Clin Exp Allergy.* 2005;35(6):746–750.
22. Visscher PK, Vetter RS, Camazine S. Removing bee stings. *Lancet.* 1996;348(9023):301–302.
23. Mullins RJ. Anaphylaxis: risk factors for recurrence. *Clin Exp Allergy.* 2003;33(8):1033–1040.
24. Reynolds K, Williams J, Miller C, Mathis A, Dettori J. Injuries and risk factors in an 18-day Marine winter mountain training exercise. *Mil Med.* 2000;165(12):905–910.
25. Murphy T, Zumwalt R, Fallico F, et al. Hypothermia-related deaths—United States, 1999–2002 and 2005. *MMWR.* 2006;55(10):282–284.
26. Cappaert TA, Stone JA, Castellani JW, et al. National Athletic Trainers' Association position statement: environmental cold injuries. *J Athl Train.* 2008;43(6):640–658.
27. Castellani JW, Young AJ, Ducharme MB, et al. American College of Sports Medicine position stand: prevention of cold injuries during exercise. *Med Sci Sports Exerc.* 2006;38(11):2012–2029.
28. Armstrong LE. *Performing in Extreme Environments.* Champaign, IL: Human Kinetics; 2000.
29. Martyn JW. Diagnosing and treating hypothermia. *Can Med Assoc J.* 1981;125(10):1089–1096.
30. Danzl DF, Pozos RS, Auerbach PS, et al. Multicenter hypothermia survey. *Ann Emerg Med.* 1987;16(9):1042–1055.
31. Regnard J. Cold and the airways. *Int J Sports Med.* 1992;13(suppl 1):S182–S184.
32. Tikuisis P, Bell DG, Jacobs I. Shivering onset, metabolic response, and convective heat transfer during cold air exposure. *J Appl Physiol.* 1991;70(5):1996–2002.
33. Giesbrecht GG. Emergency treatment of hypothermia. *Emerg Med (Fremantle).* 2001;13(1):9–16.
34. Castro RR, Mendes FS, Nobrega AC. Risk of hypothermia in a new Olympic event: the 10-km marathon swim. *Clinics (Sao Paulo).* 2009;64(4):351–356.
35. Smith RM, Hanna JM. Skinfolds and resting heat loss in cold air and water: temperature equivalence. *J Appl Physiol.* 1975;39(1):93–102.
36. Glickman-Weiss EL, Nelson AG, Hearon CM, et al. Effects of body morphology and mass on thermal responses to cold water: revisited. *Eur J Appl Physiol Occup Physiol.* 1993;66(4):299–303.
37. Budd GM, Brotherhood JR, Hendrie AL, Jeffery SE. Effects of fitness, fatness, and age on men's responses to whole body cooling in air. *J Appl Physiol.* 1991;71(6):2387–2393.
38. Falk B, Bar-Or O, Smolander J, Frost G. Response to rest and exercise in the cold: effects of age and aerobic fitness. *J Appl Physiol.* 1994;76(1):72–78.
39. Wagner JA, Robinson S, Marino RP. Age and temperature regulation of humans in neutral and cold environments. *J Appl Physiol.* 1974;37(4):562–565.
40. Graham TE. Thermal, metabolic, and cardiovascular changes in men and women during cold stress. *Med Sci Sports Exerc.* 1988;20(suppl 5):S185–S192.
41. Fox GR, Hayward JS, Hobson GN. Effect of alcohol on thermal balance of man in cold water. *Can J Physiol Pharmacol.* 1979;57(8):860–865.

42. Patton JF, Vogel JA. Effects of acute cold exposure on submaximal endurance performance. *Med Sci Sports Exerc*. 1984;16(5): 494–497.

43. Bittel JH, Nonotte-Varly C, Livecchi-Gonnot GH, Savourey GL, Hanniquet AM. Physical fitness and thermoregulatory reactions in a cold environment in men. *J Appl Physiol*. 1988;65(5):1984–1989.

44. Sugahara M, Taimura A. Relationship between thermoregulation and cold induced vasodilation during cold exposure with regard to maximal oxygen uptake. *Jpn J Physiol Fitness Sports Med*. 1996;46(1):101–110.

45. Young AJ, Castellani JW, O'Brien C, et al. Exertional fatigue, sleep loss, and negative energy balance increase susceptibility to hypothermia. *J Appl Physiol*. 1998;85(4):1210–1217.

46. Vallerand AL, Jacobs I. Energy metabolism during cold exposure. *Int J Sports Med*. 1992;13(suppl 1):S191–S193.

47. Giesbrecht GG, Goheen MS, Johnston CE, et al. Inhibition of shivering increases core temperature afterdrop and attenuates rewarming in hypothermic humans. *J Appl Physiol*. 1997;83(5):1630–1634.

48. Askew EW. Environmental and physical stress and nutrient requirements. *Am J Clin Nutr*. 1995;61(suppl 3):631S–637S.

49. O'Brien C, Young AJ, Sawka MN. Hypohydration and thermoregulation in cold air. *J Appl Physiol*. 1998;84(1):185–189.

50. Bagley JR, Judelson DA, Spiering BA, et al. *Validity of Field Expedient Measurement Devices to Assess Core Body Temperature During Rest and Exercise in the Cold*. Fullerton, CA: California State University, Fullerton; 2010.

51. Rogers I. Which rewarming therapy in hypothermia? A review of the randomized trials. *Emerg Med*. 1997;9:213–220.

52. Kempainen RR, Brunette DD. The evaluation and management of accidental hypothermia. *Respir Care*. 2004;49(2):192–205.

53. Goheen MS, Ducharme MB, Kenny GP, et al. Efficacy of forced-air and inhalation rewarming by using a human model for severe hypothermia. *J Appl Physiol*. 1997;83(5):1635–1640.

54. Steele MT, Nelson MJ, Sessler DI, et al. Forced air speeds rewarming in accidental hypothermia. *Ann Emerg Med*. 1996;27(4): 479–484.

55. Ittner KP, Bachfischer M, Zimmermann M, Taeger K. Convective air warming is more effective than resistive heating in an experimental model with a water dummy. *Eur J Emerg Med*. 2004;11(3):151–153.

56. Zachary L, Kucan JO, Robson MC, Frank DH. Accidental hypothermia treated with rapid rewarming by immersion. *Ann Plast Surg*. 1982;9(3):238–241.

57. Walpoth BH, Walpoth-Aslan BN, Mattle HP, et al. Outcome of survivors of accidental deep hypothermia and circulatory arrest treated with extracorporeal blood warming. *N Engl J Med*. 1997;337(21):1500–1505.

58. McDermott BP, Casa DJ, Yeargin SW, et al. Recovery and return to activity following exertional heat stroke: considerations for the sports medicine staff. *J Sport Rehabil*. 2007;16(3):163–181.

59. Rissanen S, Rintamaki H. Thermal responses and physiological strain in men wearing impermeable and semipermeable protective clothing in the cold. *Ergonomics*. 1997;40(2):141–150.

60. Young AJ. *Homeostatic Responses to Prolonged Cold Exposure: Human Cold Acclimatization*. New York, NY: Oxford University Press; 1996.

61. Kirk SE. Hypoglycemia in athletes with diabetes. *Clin Sports Med*. 2009;28(3):455–468.

62. Tattersall RB, Gill GV. Unexplained deaths of type 1 diabetic patients. *Diabet Med*. 1991;8(1):49–58.

63. O'Reilly M, O'Sullivan EP, Davenport C, Smith D. "Dead in bed": a tragic complication of type 1 diabetes mellitus. *Ir J Med Sci*. 2010;179(4):585–587.

64. Tu E, Twigg SM, Semsarian C. Sudden death in type 1 diabetes: the mystery of the 'dead in bed' syndrome. *Int J Cardiol*. 2010;138(1):91–93.

65. Tanenberg RJ, Newton CA, Drake AJ. Confirmation of hypoglycemia in the "dead-in-bed" syndrome, as captured by a retrospective continuous glucose monitoring system. *Endocr Pract*. 2010;16(2):244–248.

66. Kitabchi AE, Nyenwe EA. Hyperglycemic crises in diabetes mellitus: diabetic ketoacidosis and hyperglycemic hyperosmolar state. *Endocrinol Metab Clin North Am*. 2006;35(4):725–751.

67. Henriksen OM, Roder ME, Prahl JB, Svendsen OL. Diabetic ketoacidosis in Denmark: incidence and mortality estimated from public health registries. *Diabetes Res Clin Pract*. 2007;76(1):51–56.

68. Thorell A, Hirshman MF, Nygren J, et al. Exercise and insulin cause GLUT-4 translocation in human skeletal muscle. *Am J Physiol*. 1999;277(4 pt 1):E733-E741.

69. Richter EA, Ploug T, Galbo H. Increased muscle glucose uptake after exercise. No need for insulin during exercise. *Diabetes*. 1985;34(10):1041–1048.

70. Sigal RJ, Fisher S, Halter JB, Vranic M, Marliss EB. The roles of catecholamines in glucoregulation in intense exercise as defined by the islet cell clamp technique. *Diabetes*. 1996;45(2):148–156.

71. MacKnight JM, Mistry DJ, Pastors JG, Holmes V, Rynders CA. The daily management of athletes with diabetes. *Clin Sports Med*. 2009;28(3):479–495.

72. Berger M, Berchtold P, Cuppers HJ, et al. Metabolic and hormonal effects of muscular exercise in juvenile type diabetics. *Diabetologia*. 1977;13(4):355–365.

73. Mitchell TH, Abraham G, Schiffrin A, Leiter LA, Marliss EB. Hyperglycemia after intense exercise in IDDM subjects during continuous subcutaneous insulin infusion. *Diabetes Care*. 1988;11(4):311–317.

74. Davis SN, Galassetti P, Wasserman DH, Tate D. Effects of antecedent hypoglycemia on subsequent counterregulatory responses to exercise. *Diabetes*. 2000;49(1):73–81.

75. The effect of intensive treatment of diabetes on the development and progression of long-term complications in insulin-dependent diabetes mellitus. The Diabetes Control and Complications Trial Research Group. *N Engl J Med*. 1993;329(14):977–986.

76. Jimenez CC, Corcoran MH, Crawley JT, et al. National Athletic Trainers' Association position statement: management of the athlete with type 1 diabetes mellitus. *J Athl Train*. 2007;42(4):536–545.
77. Koivisto VA, Felig P. Effects of leg exercise on insulin absorption in diabetic patients. *N Engl J Med*. 1978;298(2):79–83.
78. Frid A, Ostman J, Linde B. Hypoglycemia risk during exercise after intramuscular injection of insulin in thigh in IDDM. *Diabetes Care*. 1990;13(5):473–477.
79. Peirce NS. Diabetes and exercise. *Br J Sports Med*. 1999;33(3):161–172; quiz 172–173, 222.
80. Tuominen JA, Karonen SL, Melamies L, Bolli G, Koivisto VA. Exercise-induced hypoglycaemia in IDDM patients treated with a short-acting insulin analogue. *Diabetologia*. 1995;38(1):106–111.
81. Rabasa-Lhoret R, Bourque J, Ducros F, Chiasson JL. Guidelines for premeal insulin dose reduction for postprandial exercise of different intensities and durations in type 1 diabetic subjects treated intensively with a basal-bolus insulin regimen (ultralente-lispro). *Diabetes Care*. 2001;24(4):625–630.
82. Ruegemer JJ, Squires RW, Marsh HM, et al. Differences between prebreakfast and late afternoon glycemic responses to exercise in IDDM patients. *Diabetes Care*. 1990;13(2):104–110.
83. Schiffrin A, Parikh S. Accommodating planned exercise in type I diabetic patients on intensive treatment. *Diabetes Care*. 1985;8(4):337–342.
84. Edelmann E, Staudner V, Bachmann W, et al. Exercise-induced hypoglycaemia and subcutaneous insulin infusion. *Diabet Med*. 1986;3(6):526–531.
85. Sonnenberg GE, Kemmer FW, Berger M. Exercise in type 1 (insulin-dependent) diabetic patients treated with continuous subcutaneous insulin infusion. Prevention of exercise induced hypoglycaemia. *Diabetologia*. 1990;33(11):696–703.
86. Zinman B, Ruderman N, Campaigne BN, Devlin JT, Schneider SH. Physical activity/exercise and diabetes mellitus. *Diabetes Care*. 2003;26(suppl 1):S73–S77.
87. Lisle DK, Trojian TH. Managing the athlete with type 1 diabetes. *Curr Sports Med Rep*. 2006;5(2):93–98.
88. Bussau VA, Ferreira LD, Jones TW, Fournier PA. A 10-s sprint performed prior to moderate-intensity exercise prevents early post-exercise fall in glycaemia in individuals with type 1 diabetes. *Diabetologia*. 2007;50(9):1815–1818.
89. Bussau VA, Ferreira LD, Jones TW, Fournier PA. The 10-s maximal sprint: a novel approach to counter an exercise-mediated fall in glycemia in individuals with type 1 diabetes. *Diabetes Care*. 2006;29(3):601–606.
90. Isaac JE, Johnson DE. *Wilderness and Rescue Medicine: A Practical Guide for the Basic and Advanced Practitioner*. 3rd ed. Portland, ME: Wilderness Medical Associates; 2007.
91. Stream JO, Grissom CK. Update on high-altitude pulmonary edema: pathogenesis, prevention, and treatment. *Wilderness Environ Med*. 2008;19(4):293–303.
92. Bartsch P, Mairbaurl H, Maggiorini M, Swenson ER. Physiological aspects of high-altitude pulmonary edema. *J Appl Physiol*. 2005;98(3):1101–1110.
93. Hackett PH, Roach RC. High-altitude illness. *N Engl J Med*. 2001;345(2):107–114.
94. Hackett PH. The cerebral etiology of high-altitude cerebral edema and acute mountain sickness. *Wilderness Environ Med*. 1999;10(2):97–109.

CHAPTER

Emergency Action Plans

15

Ron Courson, ATC, PT, NREMT-I, CSCS

© Giorgio Micheletti/ShutterStock, Inc.

Introduction

Although most injuries in athletics are relatively minor, life-threatening injuries are unpredictable and can occur without warning. Because of the relatively low incidence of catastrophic injuries, coaches may develop a false sense of security. However, **catastrophic injuries or illnesses** can occur during any physical activity and at any level of participation. The most common causes of sudden death in athletics are cardiac events, head and spinal cord injuries, exertional heat illness, asthma, and sickle cell crisis (exertional sickling). There is often a heightened public awareness associated with the nature and management of these events. Legal issues that are related to these medical issues may lead to questions regarding the qualifications of the personnel involved, the preparedness of the organization, and the actions taken.

> **catastrophic injury or illness** A sudden death or disability in which there is life-altering physical or mental impairment, or both.

Proper management of emergencies in athletics is critical (see **Figure 15.1**). Emergencies should be handled by trained personnel. Preparation should include education and training, maintenance of emergency equipment and supplies, appropriate use of personnel, and formation and implementation of an **emergency action plan (EAP)**.[1–6]

> **emergency action plan (EAP)** A written document that defines the standard of care for the management of emergencies in athletics.

The Need for an Emergency Action Plan

Emergencies are rarely predictable, and they call for a rapid, controlled response. An EAP should include all necessary contingencies, even the worst-case scenario. First responders should take lessons from past emergencies: Experience is a great teacher. The National Athletic Trainers' Association (NATA) position statement *Emergency Planning in Athletics* provides guidelines for the development and implementation of an EAP.[2]

All personnel involved with the organization or sponsorship of athletic activities share a professional and legal responsibility to provide for the emergency care of an injured person and a legal duty to develop, implement, and evaluate an emergency plan for all sponsored athletic activities. A written EAP document defines the **standard of care**. The absence of an EAP frequently is a basis for claims and lawsuits based on negligence. Thus, each institution or organization that sponsors athletic activities should have a written emergency plan. The EAP should be comprehensive, practical, and flexible enough to adapt to any emergency situation. The EAP should be developed in consultation with local emergency medical services (EMS) personnel, and the written

> **standard of care** The manner in which an individual must act based on his or her training and education.

203

Figure 15.1 A copy of the emergency action plan should be posted by the telephone.

document should be approved and signed by the medical director for the athletic organization. The EAP should be distributed to all involved with the sports program, from attending physicians to athletic trainers and athletic training students, to institutional and organizational safety personnel to administrators, coaches, and strength and conditioning staff.

The Legal Basis for an Emergency Plan

The existence of an emergency plan for athletics is an accepted standard of care. Sports programs have a duty to provide reasonable and prudent care in a timely manner. Sports programs additionally have a duty to foresee the possibility of emergency situations in athletics and to develop a plan to address such situations. Court cases in recent years have addressed or alluded to emergency care and the emergency plan. In a landmark legal case in 1993 regarding emergency action planning, *Kleinknecht v. Gettysburg College*, the parents of a college lacrosse player who suffered sudden cardiac arrest during lacrosse practice brought a negligence action against the college. The Court of Appeals held that the college owed the player a duty of care as well as a duty to take reasonable precautions against the risk of reasonably foreseeable life-threatening injuries during participation in athletic events.[7] Adequate planning includes expediting emergency vehicles to the site of an accident and ensuring the availability of medical personnel qualified to care for the injured athlete.

The Team Concept

The goal in emergency care is the delivery of the highest possible quality health care to the athlete. An athletic emergency situation may involve certified and student athletic trainers, emergency medical technicians, physicians, and coaches working together. Just as with an athletic team, the sports medicine team must work together as an efficient unit in order to accomplish its goals. In an emergency situation, the team concept becomes even more critical, because seconds may mean the difference between life and death or permanent disability. The sharing of information, training, and skills among the various emergency medical providers helps to reach the goal of the delivery of the highest-quality emergency health care to the athlete.

Components of the Emergency Plan

The EAP should be specific to each individual athletic venue and cover the following:

- Emergency personnel
- Emergency communication
- Emergency equipment
- Medical emergency transportation
- Venue directions with map

Box 15.1 provides a sample venue-specific EAP for football practice.

Box 15.1

Example Venue-Specific Emergency Action Plan

FOOTBALL PRACTICE EAP: Butts-Mehre Hall: Woodruff Practice Fields
July 2010

Address: 1 Selig Circle

Venue Directions:

Butts-Mehre Hall is located on Pinecrest Street (cross street Lumpkin). Two entrances provide access to building:

1. Main Entrance: front of building on Pinecrest Street (directly across from Barrow Elementary School)

2. Locker Room Entrance: rear of building, access from driveway off of Smith Street

Football Practice Fields are located with two fields adjacent to Smith Street. Two gates located on Smith Street provide access to artificial turf practice fields and access road. Be aware that construction may modify EAP: plan accordingly each day prior to practice!

GPS Coordinates (in event of the need for a medical helicopter transport): 33 56.54 / 83 22.83 (practice field 2)

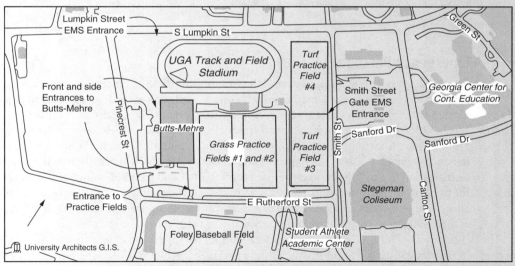

Football: Butts-Mehre Hall, Woodruff Practice Field

Emergency Personnel:

Butts-Mehre Hall: certified athletic trainers, student athletic trainers, and physician (limited basis) on site in athletic training trailer, located on grass practice field 2 during construction

Football Practice Fields: certified athletic trainers and student athletic trainers on site for practice & workouts

(continues)

Example Venue-Specific Emergency Action Plan (*continued*)

Emergency Communication:
    Butts-Mehre Hall: fixed telephone lines in athletic training trailer adjacent to practice fields:
                     (706-542-9060) or (706-542-7900)

    Football Practice Fields: certified athletic trainers carry cellular telephones
         Ron Courson 000-000-0000; Emily Miller 000-000-0000; Philip Young 000-000-0000;
         Anish Patel 000-000-0000; Ryan McGovern 000-000-0000
         Fixed telephone line under practice shed 000-000-0000

Emergency Equipment:
    Butts-Mehre Hall: emergency equipment (AED, trauma kit, splint kit, spine board, Welch Allen vital signs
    monitor, Philips MRx 12 Lead EKG/defibrillator) located within athletic training trailer
    Football Practice Fields: emergency equipment (AED, trauma kit, splint kit, spine board) maintained on
    motorized medical cart parked adjacent to practice shed during practice; additional supplies maintained under
    practice shed; additional emergency equipment accessible from athletic training trailer adjacent to practice fields

Roles of First Responders
    1. immediate care of the injured or ill student-athlete

    2. activate emergency medical system (EMS)

        a. 9-911 call (provide name, address, telephone number, number of individuals injured, condition of
            injured, first aid treatment, specific directions, other information as requested)
        b. Notify campus police at 542-2200
    3. emergency equipment retrieval

    4. direct EMS to scene

        a. open appropriate gates (Smith Street gate has keycard entry; other gates secured with padlocks
            for M60 key)
        b. designate individual to "flag down" EMS and direct to scene
        c. scene control: limit scene to first aid providers and move bystanders away from area

Courtesy of the University of Georgia Sports Medicine.

---

first responder The first person present at the scene of a sudden illness or injury.

Emergency Personnel

For athletic practices and competitions, the **first responder** to an emergency situation is typically a member of the sports medicine staff—most commonly a certified athletic trainer—or EMS personnel. A team physician is not always present at every organized practice or competition. The type and degree of sports medicine coverage for an athletic event may vary widely, based on such factors as the sport or activity, the setting, and the type of training or competition. The first responder in some instances may be a coach, strength and conditioning staff, or other institutional personnel.

first aid Emergency treatment administered to an injured or sick person before professional medical care is available.

Certification in cardiopulmonary resuscitation (CPR)[8] and **first aid**, knowledge concerning the prevention of disease transmission, and review of the existing EAP should be required for all athletic personnel associated with practices, competitions, skills instruction, and strength and conditioning; copies of training certificates or cards should be maintained.

The development of an EAP cannot be complete without the formation of an emergency team. The emergency team may consist of a number of healthcare providers, including physicians, emergency medical technicians, certified athletic trainers, athletic training students, coaches, equipment managers, and, possibly, bystanders. For example, game officials may play a critical role in the emergency plan by keeping the field clear of others when an emergency arises, allowing the healthcare providers room to work. The roles of these individuals within the emergency team may vary depending on various factors such as the number of members of the team, the athletic venue itself, or the preference of the head athletic trainer.

There are four basic functions of the emergency team. The first and most important is establishing the safety of the scene and providing immediate care to the athlete. Acute care in an emergency situation should be provided by the most qualified individual on the scene. Individuals with lesser qualifications should yield to those with more appropriate training. The second role, EMS activation, may be necessary in situations in which emergency transportation is not already present at the sporting event. This should be done as soon as the situation is deemed an emergency or a life-threatening event. Time is the most critical factor under emergency conditions. Activating the EMS system may be done by anyone on the team. However, the person chosen for this duty should be someone who is calm under pressure and who communicates well over the telephone. This person should also be familiar with the specific location and address of the sporting event.

The third function, equipment retrieval, may be carried out by anyone on the emergency team who is familiar with the types and location of the specific equipment needed. Athletic training students, equipment managers, and coaches are good choices for this role. The fourth role of the emergency team is that of directing EMS personnel to the scene. One member of the team should be responsible for meeting emergency medical personnel as they arrive at the site of the emergency. Depending on ease of access, this person should have keys to any locked gates or doors that may slow the arrival of medical personnel. An athletic training student, equipment manager, or coach may be appropriate for this role.

When forming the emergency team, it is important to adapt the team to each situation or sport. It may also be advantageous to have more than one individual assigned to each role. This allows the emergency team to function even though certain members may not always be present. Preparation is the key to emergency response. The healthcare team should regularly review the EAP (annually or when alterations to the EAP occur) and rehearse emergency simulations (with all individuals involved) to work effectively as a team. These rehearsals should be realistically staged and performed completely to ensure thorough proficiency and understanding by the emergency healthcare team. In conjunction with reviewing the EAP, an inventory check should be performed and a log of regular equipment checks/maintenance recorded by a qualified and designated member of the healthcare team.

Emergency Communication

Communication is the key to quick emergency response. First responders and emergency medical personnel must work together to provide the best emergency response capability and should have contact information, such as a telephone tree, established as a part of preplanning for emergency situations. Communication prior to events is a good way to establish boundaries and to build rapport between both groups of professionals. If emergency medical transportation is not available on site during a particular sporting event, then direct communication with the emergency medical system at the time of injury or illness is necessary.

Access to a working telephone or other telecommunications device, whether fixed or mobile, should be ensured. The communication system should be checked prior to each practice or competition to verify that it is in proper working order. A back-up communication plan should be in effect in case a failure of the primary communication system occurs. At any athletic venue, whether home or away, it is important to know the location of a functioning telephone. Prearranged access to the phone should be established if it is not easily accessible.

Other considerations include:

- What number do you call?
- Is 911 universal?
- Do you have to dial a prefix number (such as "9") to get off campus?
- Are 911 calls screened by the campus or venue operator before they go out?
- Do security personnel/police/sheriff have radio contact with "public service access points" or dispatch centers to get EMS activated?

A copy of the EAP should be posted by the telephone (see Figure 15.1). When activating EMS, the following information should be provided:
- Name and telephone number of the caller and the address to which to respond
- Number of athletes affected

- Condition of athlete(s)
- First aid treatment initiated
- Specific directions
- Other information as requested by the dispatcher

Emergency Equipment

All necessary emergency equipment should be at the site and easily accessible. Personnel should be familiar with the function and operation of each type of emergency equipment. Equipment should be in good operating condition, and personnel must be trained in advance to use it properly. Emergency equipment should be checked on a regular basis and its use rehearsed by emergency personnel. The emergency equipment available should be appropriate for the level of training of the emergency medical providers. **Table 15.1** is an example of the items that would be found in a trauma bag.

TABLE 15.1   University of Georgia Trauma Bag Checklist

AIRWAY	GENERAL SUPPLIES
• Emergency airway kit OPA—6 sizes NPA—6 sizes *King LT—sizes 4 and 5 and/or* *Combitube and syringe*	• Adult BP cuff
	• Large adult BP cuff
	• Stethoscope
	• *EpiPen (youth)*
• Bite blocker	• *EpiPen (adult)*
• V-Vac suction with extra canister	• *Aspirin*
BREATHING	• *Glucagon kit **
• Pocket mask	• *Insta-Glucose tube **
• Bag-valve-mask	• *Blood glucose kit **
• Nonrebreather mask	• *Penlight*
• *Oxygen tank with regulator*	• Paramedic shears
• Oxygen tubing	• Scissors
• *Pulse oximeter*	• Gloves
• *Albuterol inhaler/spacer*	• PPE kit
CIRCULATION	• Protective glasses
• *AED with extra pads*	• Thermal blanket
• Wound dressing kit	• Cervical collar
• Tourniquet	• Sterile saline
	• Betadine solution
	• Emergency management guidelines
	• Notepad
	• Pen

* As needed
Check regularly for proper functioning and/or expiration date (if applicable)

Abbreviations: AED, automated external defibrillator; BP, blood pressure; NPA, nasopharyngeal airway; OPA, oropharyngeal airway; PPE, personal protective equipment.

TABLE 15.2   Recommended Emergency Equipment for Athletic Venues

Automated external defibrillator (AED)

Airway management supplies (oropharyngeal and nasopharyngeal airways)

Oxygen delivery system and pulse oximeter

Suction device (manual, battery, or oxygen powered)

Body substance isolation equipment (per OSHA guidelines)

Wound care supplies

Vital signs assessment: blood pressure cuff, stethoscope, penlight

Emergency shears

CPR pocket mask

Bag-valve-mask

Rigid cervical collar

Long spine board, strapping system, cervical/head immobilization device

Extremity splints

Face mask removal tools if the sport involves use of a helmet with face mask

Abbreviations: CPR, cardiopulmonary resuscitation; OSHA, Occupational Safety and Health Administration.

* Note: The emergency equipment available should be appropriate for the level of training of the emergency medical providers.

The creation of an equipment inspection log book for continued inspection is strongly recommended. A few members of the emergency team should be trained and responsible for the care of the equipment. It is also important to know the proper way to care for and store the equipment. Equipment should be stored in a clean and environmentally controlled area. It should be readily available when emergency situations arise.

The equipment available should be based on the type of event being covered and the possible emergency scenarios anticipated. For example, when covering an outdoor event with the possibility of exertional heat illness, such as a distance road race, first responders should have ready in advance an ice-water immersion tub and other necessary equipment. **Table 15.2** lists recommended emergency equipment for athletic venues.

Medical Emergency Transportation

Emphasis should be placed on having an ambulance on site at high-risk sporting events. EMS response time should be factored in when determining whether on-site ambulance coverage is warranted (see **Box 15.2**). In the event that an ambulance is on site, it should be in a designated location with rapid access to the site and a cleared route for entering and exiting the venue.

In the medical emergency evaluation, the primary survey assists the emergency care provider in identifying emergencies requiring critical intervention and in determining transport decisions. In an emergency situation, the athlete should be transported by ambulance to a hospital, where the necessary staff and equipment are available to deliver appropriate care. First responders should refrain from transporting unstable athletes in inappropriate vehicles. Care must be taken to ensure that the activity areas are supervised should the emergency care provider leave the site to transport the athlete. Any emergency situations in which there is impairment in level of consciousness or in airway, breathing, or circulation or there is neurovascular compromise should be considered a "load and go" situation, and emphasis should be placed on rapid evaluation, treatment, and transportation.

Box 15.2

Emergency Action Plan Tip: EMS Response Time

It is beneficial to know the average EMS response time for your region. This information is available through your local EMS agency. The length of your region's EMS response time may factor into your emergency plan. For example, a metropolitan high school with a local fire/rescue station two blocks away will generally have a quicker response time than a rural high school with the closest station 15 miles away. If a longer response time is anticipated, it may be prudent for care providers to have the necessary equipment to provide extended emergency care until EMS arrives. When reviewing the EMS response, factor in both horizontal and vertical response times. *Horizontal response time* is measured from the time the EMS call goes out until the dispatched unit arrives on scene. Once the unit arrives, time is required to remove emergency equipment from the unit and travel to the site of the patient. *Vertical response time* is measured from the time the dispatched unit arrives on the scene until patient treatment begins.

Venue Directions with Map

The EAP should include specific directions to the venue, including the exact street address, cross streets, and any landmarks that may make the site easier for EMS to locate. Ideally, prior to the start of the athletic season, a meeting should be held at the athletic venue site with sports program staff members and EMS personnel to familiarize everyone with the exact location and discuss emergency management issues. Plans should be made for ambulance ingress and egress to the site in terms of gates, stadium portals, and so forth. Host providers should orient visiting athletic staffs to the venue and discuss emergency procedures prior to competitions.

Emergency Care Facilities

In designing the EAP, incorporate the emergency care facilities to which injured individuals will be taken. It is helpful, if possible, to notify emergency receiving facilities in advance of scheduled events and contests. Factors to consider in the selection of the appropriate emergency care facilities include location with respect to venue and level of capabilities. Reviewing the plan with facility staff is helpful. Additionally, in-service training of emergency department physicians and nurses may be beneficial. For example, reviewing emergency football equipment removal on an annual basis prior to the start of football season may help to facilitate proper removal of helmet and shoulder pads in the management of a head or cervical spine injury in the emergency department.

EAP Pocket Emergency Card

Coaches should consider preparing pocket emergency cards. This index card–sized item can be laminated and carried on their person in the event of an emergency. The EAP cards should include the EAP with written directions and a highlighted map on one side and the pertinent medical information of participating athletes, such as medical conditions, allergies, and medications, on the other side. **Table 15.3** provides an example of pertinent medical information that can be printed on a pocket emergency card.

Emergency Documentation

A written emergency plan should be reviewed and approved by the team members and institutions involved. If multiple facilities or sites are used, each will require a separate plan. Documentation should encompass the following:

- Who is responsible for documenting the events of the emergency situation
- Follow-up documentation to evaluate the response to the emergency situation, such as time of injury, treatment start, EMS call, arrival, treatment provided, and departure
- Documentation of periodic rehearsal of the emergency plan
- Documentation of institutional personnel training

TABLE 15.3	Sports Medicine–Pertinent Medical Conditions
Athlete A	hx concussion
Athlete B	sickle cell trait
Athlete C	allergic to Septra (sulfa drugs), yellow jackets
Athlete D	hx asthma, hx concussion
Athlete E	hx concussion with LOC, amnesia
Athlete F	hx concussion, catheter ablation, PSVT
Athlete G	heart murmur, concussion
Athlete H	hx concussion, hx heat cramps
Athlete I	hx heat cramps, exertional headaches
Athlete J	hx concussion, EIB, endocarditis prophylaxis, hx stingers
Athlete K	hx asthma
Athlete L	hx concussion x 2
Athlete M	hx asthma
Athlete N	hx concussion
Athlete O	hx heat cramps
Athlete P	allergic to penicillin
Athlete Q	family hx cardiomyopathy
Athlete R	exercise-induced headaches, hx heat illness
Athlete S	allergic to sulfa and Ceclor, hx concussion
Athlete T	hx heat syncope, hx concussion, exertional headaches
Athlete U	hx hypertension, allergic to Penicillin, hx concussion, Norvasc

Abbreviations: EIB, exercise-induced bronchoconstriction; hx, history; LOC, loss of consciousness; PSVT, paroxysmal supraventricular tachycardia.

When an athletic emergency occurs, postepisode documentation is an important component and should not be neglected. Reasons for documentation include the medicolegal record, continuity of care, quality assurance, organization of thought processes, and research and statistical review. Written documentation of all actions taken during treatment and transport can be very useful in situations in which liability is an issue. It should also be noted that consent is implied during most athletic emergencies.

Catastrophic Incident Guidelines

Catastrophic incident guidelines should be developed in the event of a sudden death or of an injury that results in disability or an alteration of the quality of life of a student-athlete, coach, or staff member. A catastrophic incident management team should be put together, along with a checklist of chain of command responsibilities. Although there are many types of catastrophic incidents, not all will require activation of the emergency plan. However, a catastrophic injury/incident plan can be considered a companion document to the emergency plan. This written plan should include both direct and indirect catastrophic athletic injuries and incidents.

Either direct or indirect catastrophic incidents can affect a sports program. Direct or sport-related fatalities include heat stroke, brain injury, and commotio cordis; indirect fatalities can be from natural causes (e.g., heart attack, stroke), crime related (e.g., homicide or assault), or accidental (e.g., fall, car crash). Disabling or life-altering catastrophic incidents can also be divided into direct or indirect causes. Direct incidents include catastrophic events occurring during organization-sponsored sport participation or travel, including spinal cord injury, coma, loss of paired organs or use of an extremity or extremities, and severe brain injury. Indirect incidents could include any of these injuries to a member of the sports organization that occur outside of a sport-related activity.

Depending on the sport sponsor, sport venue, and nature of the emergency, certain notifications may need to be made; these should be described in the emergency plan. Obviously, in the high school setting, a minor athlete's parents will need to be notified. Depending on the school or system size, the athletic coordinator, principal, and possibly the district superintendent may also need to be notified of the incident.

Notifications at the collegiate level might include the athletic director, one or more deans or vice-presidents, and, in the event of a catastrophic event, possibly the president or chief executive officer of the college or university. The parents, spouse, or other family members of the injured student-athlete may also need to be notified. Travel plans for the parents or spouse of the injured athlete should be considered if distance is a factor. Counseling may need to be made available for students, team members, and the sports medicine team. When there is considerable media interest, the sports information director or other institutional media relations personnel should be included to handle media inquiries. The institutional insurance carrier, risk management office, legal counsel, or a combination of these should also be notified.

As mentioned, the catastrophic injury plan should include the formation of a catastrophic injury team. Obvious members of this team include the organization's athletic director or coordinator, the head athletic trainer, sports information or media relations personnel, senior administrators, the team physician, and the organization's legal counsel. This team will direct all aspects of crisis management, including providing appropriate counseling (for the athlete, family, and team), releasing information to the media, and documenting the incident. **Figure 15.2** provides an example of a catastrophic incident guideline card and emergency contact information card.

Emergency Contact Information Card

Emer. Contact	Department/Area	Office	Home	Cell/Pager
Michael Adams	University President			
Steve Bryant	Assoc. Athletic Trainer			
Eric Baumgartner	NCAA Compliance			
Ron Courson	Assoc. Athletic Director			
Frank Crumley	Interim Dir. of Athletics			
Claude Felton	Assoc. AD/SID			
Greg McGarity	Director of Athletics			
Kevin Hynes	Chaplain			
Tom Jackson	University Spokesperson			
Arthur Johnson	Assoc. Athletic Director			
Barbara Boyd	UGAA Travel Coordinator			
Robert Miles	Asst. Ath. Dir.: Life Skills			
Fred Reifsteck	Head Team Physician			
Joe Scalise	Counselor			
Tricia Searels	Counselor			
Steve Shewmaker	University Legal Affairs			
Ed Tolley	UGAA Legal Counsel			
Jeanne Vaughn	UGAA Insurance Coord.			
Craig White	Assoc. Athletic Director			
Peggy Whitfield	Human Resources			
Carla Williams	Assoc. Athletic Director			
Jimmy Williamson	Chief of Police			

A

CRISIS MANAGEMENT GUIDELINES

Contact Ron Courson/Steve Bryant; Fred Reifsteck, MD
  • work with medical specialists assisting athlete
Contact UGAA/UGA administration
  • Greg McGarity notifies Michael Adams, notifies legal counsel
  • Claude Felton notifies Tom Jackson
  • Contact Frank Crumley/Carla Williams
Designate athletic administrator point person
Contact/update sport staff if not yet familiar with situation
Contact family by appropriate individual (assist as needed):
  • Eric Baumgartner: compliance
  • Barbara Boyd: travel
  • Air Med International   000-000-0000
Assign athletic staff member to be with family at all times upon
  arrival; assist family as needed; protect from outside persons
Involve appropriate counseling/ministerial support
Coordinated media plan
  • No contact with media/comments from athletic training
    staff, hospital staff or med. personnel except through SID
Meeting with athletes to discuss situation
  • No outside discussion of meeting with media
Contact catastrophic/malpractice insurance providers
  • Borden Perlman: 000-000-0000
  • NCAA: American Specialty: 000-000-0000
  • Seabury & Smith (malpractice): 000-000-0000
  • HPSO (malpractice):   000-000-0000
Complete documentation of events from everyone involved in
  incident
Collect and secure all equipment/materials involved
Construct detailed time line of events related to the incident
Catastrophic incident stress management as necessary for
  individuals involved in incident

B

Figure 15.2   Emergency contact information card (A) and crisis management guidelines (B).

Summary

It is critically important to properly prepare for athletic emergencies. An athlete's survival may hinge on how well trained and prepared athletic healthcare providers are. Organizations sponsoring athletic activities invest "ownership" in an EAP by involving athletic administration personnel, sports coaches, and sports medicine personnel. It is important to review the EAP yearly with all athletic personnel, including CPR and first aid refresher training. Through development and implementation of an EAP, healthcare providers help to ensure that athletes have the best care provided when an emergency situation does arise.

Clinical Case Scenario

1. A 13-year-old white male baseball player was struck in the chest by a baseball while attempting to bunt. He stumbled a couple of steps and then collapsed face down at home plate. He had no previous symptoms of palpitations, dizziness, or syncope and no family history of sudden death or cardiac abnormalities. He was evaluated by the baseball coach and found to have no signs of life. The coach had heard of commotio cordis, where a healthy athlete receives a hard blow to the chest over the heart and goes into sudden cardiac arrest. He suspected this condition based upon the mechanism of injury and the athlete's condition and immediately started CPR. The coach directed bystanders to call 911 and retrieve the automated external defibrillator (AED) from the park office. The AED was applied in less than 3 minutes from the time of collapse. One shock was delivered and the athlete regained consciousness, and normal circulation and breathing resumed. Paramedics arrived and the coach turned over care, providing details of what had happened. The athlete was transported to a nearby hospital by ambulance for further evaluation. He was examined by cardiologists. The physical examination, which included an electrocardiogram and an echocardiogram, was normal. The athlete was ultimately cleared for return to full athletic activity and remains in good health.

    a. What were critical components that saved the athlete's life in this scenario?

    b. Knowledge of the steps required for this EAP was critical to saving this athlete's life. Who should be instructed and knowledgeable of the school's EAP?

    c. What other monthly or yearly maintenance or planning had to occur to ensure that all of the steps within this EAP worked as planned?

Key Terms

catastrophic injury or illness

emergency action plan (EAP)

first aid

first responder

standard of care

References

1. Courson RW. Preventing sudden death on the athletic field: the emergency action plan. *Curr Sports Med Rep*. 2007;6:93–100.
2. Andersen J, Courson RW, Kleiner DM, McLoda TA. National Athletic Trainers' Association position statement: emergency planning in athletics. *J Athl Train*. 2002;37(1):99–104.
3. Guideline 1c: emergency care and coverage. In: Klossner D, ed. *2010–11 NCAA Sports Medicine Handbook*. Indianapolis, IN: National Collegiate Athletic Association; 2010. http://www.ncaapublications.com/productdownloads/MD11.pdf. Accessed November 8, 2010.
4. Sideline preparedness for the team physician: consensus statement. *Med Sci Sports Exerc*. 2001;33(5):846–849.
5. Drezner JA, Courson RW, Roberts WO, et al. Inter-Association Task Force recommendations on emergency preparedness and management of sudden cardiac arrest in high school and college athletic programs: a consensus statement. *J Athl Train*. 2007;42(1):143–158.

6. Hazinski MF, Markenson D, Neish S, et al. Response to cardiac arrest and selected life-threatening medical emergencies: the medical emergency response plan for schools. A statement for healthcare providers, policymakers, school administrators, and community leaders. *Circulation*. 2004;109(2):278–291.

7. *Kleinknecht v. Gettysburg College*, 989 F2d 1360 (3rd Cir 1993).

8. 2005 American Heart Association guidelines for cardiopulmonary resuscitation and emergency cardiovascular care. *Circulation*. 2005;112(suppl 24):IV1–IV203. Part 4: adult basic life support. *Circulation*. 2005;112(suppl 24):IV19–IV34. Part 5: electrical therapies: automated external defibrillators, defibrillation, cardioversion, and pacing. *Circulation*. 2005;112(suppl 24): IV35–IV46.

Sport Law and Sudden Death

Gil Fried, JD

Lesley W. Vandermark, MS, ATC, PES

Douglas J. Casa, PhD, ATC, FACSM, FNATA

Introduction

We are often challenged with new ideas or concepts that impact how we do our job. New technologies have the potential to revolutionize what we do. Imagine someone from the 1960s who has been in a coma for 50 years and then wakes up to see modern society. He or she would obviously be taken aback by all the changes that have occurred in the world. Then imagine how this person would feel when he or she saw all the changes that have occurred in the sport industry. From high definition TVs, to online tracking of fantasy football teams, to the current debates going on about concussions in sports—it would seem like a brand new world. But it is also a brand new world for many of us who have been here all along when we start examining how sport law has changed and evolved.

Numerous legal issues arise in sport on a daily basis. For the average layperson it is very hard to keep track of such changes. It is that much more difficult for those who have never been exposed to studying legal theories or issues. This chapter is written assuming that you do not know a thing about sport law. We will walk you through the critical areas with which you should at least be familiar to avoid potential liability. We will make a special effort to get you to understand the legal implications of sudden death in sport.

The chapter will get you up to speed on sport law by providing a brief description of various critical legal concepts, presenting several scenarios of different concerns, reviewing some of the issues an athletic administration might face, and, finally, offering several real-world case examples that emphasize the gravity and seriousness of sport law.

Legal Concepts

How the Law Is Developed

Laws can be developed by legislative bodies (e.g., Congress or city councils) or by courts. A large swatch of the world (primarily English-based systems/countries) uses common law to help determine or clarify laws developed by others, such as legislative bodies. Take, for example, the evolution of comparative and contributory negligence standards. The rule of contributory negligence was developed as a defensive theory against negligence claims (see later discussion) made in the court system. The basis of the contributory negligence standard is that if an injured party is responsible in any way for his or her own injury, that person should be barred from recovering an award. Contributory negligence evolved over a number of centuries and is still the law of the land in a number of states. Some courts, however, felt this standard was too harsh because under it an injured party who is only 1% responsible for his or her own injury can be penalized. Thus, some courts developed a so-called "50% rule," meaning that if an injured party was less than 50% at fault, he or she could recover.

Other courts were not willing to change their rule, so it was up to legislative bodies to develop the concept of comparative negligence. Under this theory the injured party's own negligence does not preclude him or her from recovery, but instead reduces the amount the injured person can receive based on what percentage he or she is at fault. With such a statute in place, courts can then try to apply these laws to cases they face and develop variations that are both consistent with the statute and help clarify any confusion. This example helps show that the two law-making bodies, courts and legislatures, can work together (although they sometimes work against each other!) to help create a stronger legal system.

This backdrop is important, because the primary legal challenges in the sport industry relate to the ways that courts interpret laws and apply them to the facts. However, laws are ever evolving and can be changed by courts or legislative bodies. A law might be valid one day, and the next day a court or legislative body can change it.

The following sections provide brief descriptions of two of the biggest legal challenges or theories—contract law and tort law.

Contract Law

While it might seem that contracts only relate to professional athletes, there are numerous other contracts that arise in the sport world, such as waivers, releases, consent to treat forms, do not resuscitate orders (DNRs), orders for athletic training equipment, employment contracts, student-athletes' letters of intent, insurance policies, and a host of others. For a contract to pass muster with the courts it needs to contain four elements:

agreement This is the meeting of the minds where there is an offer and acceptance. The terms need to be specific and understood by both parties.

consideration This is an exchange of value where both parties need to give something such as a waiver where one party gives another the right to participate in exchange for agreeing not to sue if injured through normal negligence.

capacity This means that the contracting parties need to meet certain criteria. They need to be the right age (those under 18 can void many contracts), they cannot be drunk/under the influence of drugs, and they cannot be certified insane by the courts.

legality This means that the subject matter of the contract has to be for a legal purpose.

1. *Agreement*: This is the meeting of the minds where there is an offer and acceptance. The terms need to be specific and understood by both parties.
2. *Consideration*: This is an exchange of value where both parties need to give something such as a waiver stating that one party gives the other the right to participate in exchange for agreeing not to sue if injured through normal negligence.
3. *Capacity*: This means that the contracting parties need to meet certain criteria. They need to be the right age (those under 18 can void many contracts), they cannot be drunk/under the influence of drugs, and they cannot be certified insane by the courts.
4. *Legality*: This means that the subject matter of the contract has a legal purpose.

Athletic administrators need to make sure that all the contracts they enter into are clear. Specific clauses should be added to provide the athletic program with additional protection. These clauses can include the following:

- *Mediation/arbitration clause*: Such a clause requires parties to go to arbitration or mediation before a neutral third party to attempt to resolve a dispute before heading to court.
- *Venue clause*: This clause requires all disputes under a contract to be brought in a specific jurisdiction. The contract author can require, for example, that any dispute be brought in New York to prevent having to defend cases all over the United States and thus save money.
- *Noncompete clause (trade secrets)*: Such a clause prohibits an employee from leaving his or her current employer and starting a competing business in a specific area for a specific time period. Any such limitations need to be reasonable. For example, the courts would support a clause that would limit an athletic trainer from working in the field for 2 years within 40 miles of where the trainer was employed when he or she entered their contract.

- *Damages clause*: This clause establishes what damages might be incurred by a party that breaches a contract. These damages can include compensating someone for actual harm done or punishing a party for breaching a contract.
- *Indemnity/hold harmless clause*: This is one of the most commonly seen clauses in contracts, including waivers and rental agreements. Under this term a contracting party agrees to defend another party if anyone is injured and brings suit. For example, a gym might let a group rent the gym after they have agreed to such a clause. If, when the renter is running an event, a party is injured and then sues, the renter would normally have to pay defense costs, defend the gym, and pay any settlement or judgment (often covered by insurance that the renter is required to purchase under a different contract clause requiring the gym to be named as an additional insured and requiring the renter to provide proof of insurance before being able to rent the gym).

Tort Law

The two types of **torts** are *intentional* torts (such as assault, defamation, and intentional infliction of emotional distress) and *unintentional* torts (negligence). **Negligence** is the primary concern faced by those in the sport industry. Negligence is the failure to act in a reasonable manner, in such a way that the action causes harm to another. **Table 16.1** shows the way the authors teach negligence to our students, dividing it into three categories.

Elements of Negligence

This section will review each of the elements of negligence. In order for an injured party to bring a negligence claim, he or she needs to prove all four negligence elements. Plaintiffs need to show (1) that the defendant (person or entity being sued) owed them a duty, (2) that the duty was breached, (3) that the breach of duty caused an injury, and (4) that the **plaintiff** (person suing) is injured. Each element is critical; if even one element is missing, the plaintiff cannot recover.

A duty is an obligation one person owes to another person based on a statute, common law, or industry practice. There are numerous duties that arise in the sport context. These duties include providing the following:

- Proper instruction
- Proper supervision
- Proper first aid assistance
- Proper matching of opponents
- Safe facilities
- Safe equipment
- Safe transportation options

tort A civil wrong or wrongful act that may be intentional or accidental from which injury occurs to another.

negligence Conduct that falls below the standards of behavior currently established by law for the purpose of protecting others against unreasonable risk or harm.

plaintiff The party who initiates a lawsuit by filing a complaint with the clerk of the court against the defendant in a civil action.

TABLE 16.1   Elements of Negligence

Elements	Status	Defenses
Duty	Youth	Assumption of risk
Breach of duty	Seniors	Contributory/comparative negligence
Proximate cause	Government	Act of God
Injury	Nonprofit	Missing an element
		Waiver
		Immunity
		Insurance

For example, if you operated a swimming pool, you would have a number of duties. By statute, most pools open to the public need to meet minimum cleanliness standards. They also have duties regarding the proper number of lifeguards. The number of lifeguards might be dictated by statute, but it might also be established through industry standards such as what other local pools of the same size and participation numbers do. People can also have specific duties. A swimming coach, for example, has a duty to provide proper instruction to his or her charges. This could entail making sure the athletes know basic skills and have access to water, not playing hurt athletes without clearance, and a number of other duties. These duties or obligations are often referred to as a *reasonable person standard* because the focus is on what a reasonable person would do under the same or similar circumstances.

The label is a bit misleading, however, because the standard does not refer to just any regular person. In this case, it would refer to a coach with comparable skills, training, and experience as the coach being sued. If the coach does not allow athletes to drink water on a hot day and someone suffers from a heat stroke, the coach will not be compared to any other mother or person walking down the street, but rather to other local coaches who have the same number of years of experience and work with the same type of athletes. The coach's behavior will also be compared to what any local coaching organizations might mandate. This represents the "industry standard." The coach will not be compared to just one person, but several people. We like to use the "7 out of 10 rule," which in this example means that if 7 out of 10 coaches in a given area would have acted a given way, then that represents the standard and other coaches should likewise have acted in that way to avoid violating a duty.

After it is established that a duty exists, the plaintiff needs to show that the duty was breached. Did the coach (continuing with the same example) violate his or her duty? If there is a duty to allow athletes to have water breaks, then did the coach allow for such a break? If not, then the coach breached that duty.

The next question is whether the breached duty actually caused the plaintiff's injury. This might seem like an obvious issue, but it actually can be complicated. The proximate cause element is often called the "but for" test. This test requires the court to determine whether the plaintiff would not have been injured, but for what the defendant did. For example, if a car is rear-ended by another car, it is pretty easy to show that the rear driver hit the driver in front of him or her. However, what if the cars collided because the road was defective or the rear car malfunctioned in some way (often referred to as an *intervening cause*)? If the reason the cars collided had nothing to do with the rear driver, then why should the driver be held responsible? The driver might not have breached any duty.

The last element is that the plaintiff needs to suffer an injury. The court cannot speculate, so it has to be a demonstrable injury. Injuries can include actual medical costs, pain and suffering, lost wages, the potential for lost future wages, the potential for future medical expenses, and even punitive damages to punish a defendant for egregious conduct.

Status of the Involved Parties

Once all four elements of negligence are established, it is important to look at the status of all parties, because that can impact the duty and possible defenses to a claim. The first status component is whether the plaintiff is a minor. A minor is anyone under the age of 18. This is important because the duty of care normally increases for a minor. A coach working with adults needs to be careful, but the coach working with youths has a higher duty of protection. This is because adults presumably have a better understanding of the risks and issues that can impact them and are better able to protect themselves. In contrast, children, especially if they are under age 14, do not have the same knowledge base and cannot appreciate all the risks they face. This is akin to a parent having a duty to protect his or her child from running into the street. This duty is much greater when the child is young, but by the time the child is a teen he or she does not need to be warned as much, and when the child becomes an adult, it is assumed the person wholly knows about the risks of crossing a street.

Youths are thus owed a higher duty of care, and a defendant's ability to claim that a child assumed the risk of injury from participating in a sport is reduced—children cannot assume all risks. Seniors are also owed a heightened duty of care, as well as those with disabilities. The key is to determine what a person would normally do to protect others. A senior who does not have the same amount of physical strength as a younger adult should be closely supervised by a personal trainer. Similarly, coaches for the Special Olympics have a higher duty to protect their athletes compared to other coaches.

The next status area deals with the defendant(s) and whether they are private, government, or nonprofit entities. Government entities sometimes benefit from statutory protection of *immunity*. The concept of government immunity dates back to the historical idea that the king (government) could do no wrong. Total immunity means that if the government messes up, the injured party is barred from recovery. In some states the law is that severe. For example, Alabama has immunity protection included in its state constitution. In most states, however, the immunity protection applies only to discretionary acts. *Discretionary acts* involve planning and developing programs. In contrast, *ministerial acts*, which involve just execution, do not have such protection. For example, a public high school coach who decides to put on an event will have immunity protection. If the same coach is required to have an athletic trainer at all practices and fails to have one, however, the coach (and the high school) can lose the immunity protection.

Nonprofit immunity provides the same basic protection as government immunity, but it applies only to nonprofit organizations. Such legislative protection exists in only a few states, for example, Texas and New Jersey. The law is very strict and serves as a bar for an injured party's claim of simple negligence. These laws, as well as government immunity, do not protect entities or persons engaged in intentional tort or willful, wanton, or reckless misconduct.

Defenses

The last category is *defenses*. Defenses do not prevent a negligence claim but can be used by the defendant to minimize damages or dismiss a claim. The most commonly used defense (other than one of the four elements being missing) is *assumption of risk*. If a plaintiff voluntarily undertook an activity knowing the possible risk of injury, then he or she should not be able to recover. The key is that the injured party needs to know the risk and then voluntarily pursue an activity knowing that risk exists. Because children often do not appreciate all risks, it is harder to raise this defense in cases involving children. However, if adults engage in sky diving, for example, they know it is dangerous, and if they jump from an airplane and get injured, they should not be allowed to recover money from others.

There are two different types of assumption of risk, primary versus secondary. **Primary assumption of risk** usually involves a situation in which two participants play together in a sport and one gets injured by the other. Such an injury is not intentional, but rather a part of the game. For example, during a one-on-one basketball game, one player is injured when hit in the face while trying to gather a rebound. The other player was not trying to cause an injury, but both players were going for the ball. This type of accident occurs on a regular basis and can include injuries that resulted from fouls or just accidents. In such a scenario the court will rule that those who engage in playing sports face normal risks of the games and as such if they are injured they should be barred from recovery under the theory that they assumed the risk by participating in the sport. This defense can come into play even without coparticipants. If someone gets injured landing poorly after a long jump, the primary assumption of risk defense would apply and possibly bar a negligence claim.

> **primary assumption of risk** Involves two participants engaged in sport where one participant's injuries have resulted from an accident because of the inherent nature of participation.

The **secondary assumption risk** is not between coparticipants, but rather between a player and another party such as a coach, athletic trainer, or event manager. The duty owed by a coach or event administrator is higher than the duty owed by coparticipants. Coaches or event administrators need to make sure they are putting on as safe an event as possible. If they have put on a safe event and someone is injured, then the person cannot recover because he or she assumed the risk. However, if the event was unsafe, then the injured party can recover. In the skydiving example, the injured party would not be able to recover if injured on a jump. However, if the sky diver were injured because a parachute was not packed correctly by the skydiving company, then he or she would not be barred from recovery by assumption of risk. In the basketball example, if the injured party was injured because the other player slipped on a wet floor, he or she likewise would not be barred from the traditional assumption of risk defense. The key in these cases is the person putting on an event cannot assume that an injured party will automatically be barred from recovery. If the event is safe and someone is injured,

> **secondary assumption of risk** The duty owed by a coach or event administrator to participants.

the event planner can use the assumption of risk defense (it is raised anyway as a defense in almost every case). However, if the event was not safe, then the injured party will not be barred from recovering. Thus, event administrators, coaches, and others in charge need to make sure they put on an event that is as safe as possible.

Other key defense claims are contributory and comparative negligence, mentioned briefly at the beginning of the chapter. Under these theories, an injured party should not be able to recover if he or she contributed to the injury. Under *contributory negligence* (established by court precedents), if injured parties contributed in any way to their injuries, then they are prohibited from ever recovering for their injuries. State legislatures felt that this rule was too harsh and in response they created the *comparative negligence* rule. Under this rule, the injured party can contribute to the injury and still recover. Liability is allocated based on a percentage basis; for example, if the injured party was 40% at fault and was awarded $1 million by a jury, he or she would receive only $600,000.

Waivers represent the blend of a defense and a preemptive strategy using contract law. Through a waiver a party can agree not to sue another party. The terms *waiver* and *release* are sometimes used interchangeably, but they are very different. A waiver says that an injured party will not sue in the future for the negligent acts of another party. A release says that an already injured party will not bring a claim or will cancel a claim in exchange for something, often money. The injured party might have already filed a claim; as a condition of settlement, the defendant will ask the plaintiff to sign a release to receive the settlement funds.

This chapter's focus is on waivers, because they represent the opportunity for a party to agree (in a written contract) that he or she will not sue for a given injury. Some states do not allow such a contract because they feel it is a violation of public policy. Other states allow it, but they specifically allow a party to waive a claim only for simple negligence. Thus, if an event has an unsafe slippery surface and the person is injured, he or she would not be able to recover. However, if the event engages in some horrible conduct that is considered reckless or willful, then the waiver would not provide any protection to the venue. That is why the waiver applies only to negligence, and the waiver language has to specifically use the term negligence so there is no confusion.

Even in states that do not allow waivers, they are still very important tools. Someone who signs a waiver might feel he or she has given up some valuable rights and might not think about suing.

Insurance is not really a defense, but it is a protective device used throughout the sport industry. It will not limit or prevent a suit; however, if an event or entity purchases insurance, it can obtain very valuable protection similar to a hold harmless clause. Insurance is another type of contract where a party agrees to pay a premium based on the perceived risks of an event and the insurance company agrees to provide attorney fee/expense coverage and/or pay any resulting damage claims. There are numerous insurance policies covering every facet of an event or organization. Some examples include comprehensive general liability (the broadest coverage), automobile, workers' compensation, business interruption, key person, and prize insurance.

Other Considerations

While we have made every effort to make the discussion of contract and tort law as simple as possible, there are numerous minor issues that can change the outcome of a lawsuit. That is why it is so essential to have an attorney available who can help interpret and apply legal principles. In addition, everyone working in the sport industry can be proactively involved in risk management. Waivers and other contracts can help deflect liability from the very beginning. Whenever someone sees something dangerous or operates with safety as the number-one concern, these actions help prevent lawsuits. More importantly, they help prevent injuries.

What Would You Do?

One of the best ways to address all the legal concerns associated with sport medicine is to assume the role of an athletic trainer to see what areas can raise legal concerns. Imagine that you are an athletic trainer working with a women's high school volleyball team. You see a play where an athlete gets hit in the head with a smash. What would you do?

You would probably evaluate the athlete for any signs of concussion or other injuries. Remember that your actions would be compared to a similar athletic trainer who has the same number of years of experience and similar knowledge. Thus, if the coach says the athlete is fine and you are scared to challenge him or her, you could be held accountable if a similarly situated athletic trainer would not have allowed the athlete to return to play.

The key to preventing these types of situations is to have a preseason meeting with all managers, coaches, and athletic training personnel highlighting what can be done and who is in charge. State statutes, medical industry standards, and athletic training standards can serve as a guide to determine what can be done and by whom. All personnel need to be on the same page, and athletes also need to know that the decision to play or not to play rests with the athletic trainer. The stakes are higher when the high school does not employ an athletic trainer or the athletic trainer is not present during a workout. In these circumstances, the coach must make all the appropriate decisions regarding the prevention, recognition, and treatment of conditions to avoid a catastrophic outcome. This may not be possible because the coach typically is not an expert on medical conditions that can cause sudden death in sport. The following quote from an important case offers a realistic precedent for the level of care a high school or college is expected to deliver:

> When medical treatment is undertaken by a school or its agent, public policy considerations dictate an obligation to ensure that it is competently rendered. To hold school districts to an ordinary care standard in this area does not appear unduly burdensome.
>
> —*O'Brien v. Township High School*, No. 77-1673, Appellate Court of Illinois,
> First District, Fourth Division 73 Ill. App. 3d 618; 392 N.E.2d 615;
> 1979 Ill. App. LEXIS 2957; 29 Ill. Dec. 918 June 28, 1979, Filed

Many civil cases involving sudden death result in successful jury verdicts or satisfactory settlements. The reason for this is usually the relative ease with which the plaintiff is able to show that the level of care delivered by the entity sponsoring the athletic activity fell below a "competently rendered" standard. This is especially true in cases related to exertional heat stroke. Given the excellent research that has been generated in the past 10 years, the availability of best practices documents, and the proactive efforts of professional/ governing organizations such as the National Athletic Trainers' Association (NATA), the American College of Sports Medicine (ACSM), the American Medical Society for Sports Medicine (AMSSM), the National Collegiate Athletic Association (NCAA), the National Federation of State High School Associations (NFHS), and others, the sponsoring entity has access to extremely useful information. Failure on the part of the sponsoring entity to heed these recommendations places the burden of responsibility squarely on the entity's shoulders. With regard to exertional heat stroke, the evidence has shown that if rectal temperature is obtained and whole-body rapid cooling via cold water immersion is implemented within 10 minutes of collapse, then survival will consistently be the outcome. When a principal, superintendent, or athletics director at a high school chooses to not employ an athletic trainer or limits the scope of practice of the athletic trainer (e.g., not allowing rectal temperatures or not following the strategy of cool first, transport second), the school district will have a harder time defending itself. The authors of this chapter are not aware of any circumstance in which a school successfully litigated a civil case involving a heat stroke death of a high school athlete. Insurance carriers should take note and give discounts to those schools that offer the services of an athletic trainer and follow best practices, because these schools are much lower risk to insure. The process of incentivizing the insurance structure can motivate high schools and colleges to optimize care.

Real Cases

The following cases offer vivid and heartbreaking accounts of what can happen when appropriate prevention, recognition, and treatment strategies are not implemented. These cases provide examples from high schools and colleges from a variety of sports such as football, baseball, and basketball. Because these cases really occurred, and most traversed the legal system, they provide great insight. The authors do not intend to place blame, but instead hope the extremely valuable learning experiences from these cases can help to dictate future policies. Our goal is to prevent future tragedies. The interpretations of the cases are the opinion of the authors of this chapter. For educational purposes, we specifically chose a majority of cases in which the school or university settled or lost in litigation. It is important to note that many cases are successfully resolved on behalf of the defense. In some cases, sensitive information was altered to respect the families or patients discussed, but all information pertaining to the case remains true.

Case 1: Henry White

Case Overview[1]

- On August 14, 2009, Henry White, a 21-year-old male basketball player at Grambling State University, died from an exertional heat stroke suffered after a punishment running session before preseason workouts.
- White and other teammates did a weight lifting session, then a 4.5-mile timed punishment run outside.
- White collapsed at the same time as another player with a heat illness, who survived after spending the night in the hospital. White spent 12 days in the hospital; his organs lost function, and he died on August 26, 2009.

Case Analysis

Prevention	What They Did	What They Could Have Done
Appropriate medical care	The athletic trainer was not aware of the workout session and was not on site. None of the athletes had been cleared to participate. This workout session happened before any allowable NCAA-sanctioned practices could occur. One coach followed the team in a golf cart.[1]	Appropriate medical care (the athletic trainer) should be on site at all athletic events. The athletic trainer at the school should have at least been notified of the workout session. The workout session should not have happened, as per NCAA guidelines.[2,3]
Acclimatization	White and other athletes were forced to run a 4.5-mile timed punishment run outside after not having done any other activity at the university in previous days. The athletes, including White, were likely not acclimatized.[1]	The athletes should have performed an acclimatization protocol, which includes a gradual return to exercise that allows the body to adapt to the exercise and environmental conditions. Exercise in any form should not be used as punishment or discipline. The additional risk of injury or death should not be considered an appropriate consequence for any unsatisfactory behavior.[4]
Hydration and rest	No water was allowed during the disciplinary run session.	Water should not be restricted during exercise. The goal of drinking during exercise should be to maintain less than a 2% body weight loss.[5]
Environmental conditions	Clear, temperature 91–95° F, 30–50% relative humidity; black top, 135° F. No activity modifications based on environmental conditions occurred.[1]	Exercise should be modified based on environmental conditions. In this case, environmental conditions were so stressful that the athletes should have been restricted from participating at all.[6–8]

Recognition	What They Did	What They Could Have Done
Sign and symptom recognition	Signs and symptoms were neither recognized nor assessed until after the athlete had collapsed. Another athlete also collapsed with a heat illness at the same time. Other players were the first on the scene.[1]	Central nervous system (CNS) dysfunction and the possible presence of other signs and symptoms may have been recognized if appropriate medical staff had been in attendance at the practice.[6-8]
Rectal temperature	No rectal temperature was performed at the scene to determine the presence of a high body temperature.	Had appropriate medical staff been at the scene, the best course of action would have been to determine the presence of a body temperature > 104°F. This, along with CNS dysfunction, would have indicated exertional heat stroke.[6-8]

Treatment	What They Did	What They Could Have Done
Rapid cooling	Fellow players took water in their hands from the water fountain to dump it on the head of the unconscious White.[1]	Cold water immersion, the gold standard for heat stroke treatment, should have been used to treat both White and the other player.[6-9]
Cool first, transport second	White was transported to the hospital without effective cooling. Players reported that it took 20 minutes for emergency medical services (EMS) to be called and arrive.[1]	Rapid cooling should have occurred while waiting for EMS to arrive and should have continued until rectal temperature reached < 102°F.[6-8]

Lessons Learned

- Appropriate medical staff should be on site at all athletic events to initiate appropriate preventive strategies, early recognition, and appropriate treatment for injured athletes.
- Appropriate recognition and treatment strategies should be implemented as quickly as possible to increase chances of survival from an exertional heat stroke.
- Rapid cooling via cold water immersion is an easy and accessible modality for the treatment of exertional heat stroke.

Legal Outcome

- Civil suit for wrongful death, *Family of Henry White v. Grambling State University*. The jury awarded $3 million to the family for negligence on the part of the university.

Case 2: John Gaston

Case Overview[10]

- On September 12, 2010, John Gaston, a 19-year-old freshman baseball player at LaGrange College, collapsed as a result of heat stroke during his first baseball practice at the college.
- The team was doing sprints, jump rope, tire drills, base running, batting, fielding, and other conditioning activities. The practice lasted over 4 hours and there were no scheduled water or rest breaks.
- Gaston had to have emergency surgery to relieve the pressure buildup in his head as a result of the heat stroke and spent several months in rehabilitation before he could resume daily activities.

Case Analysis

Prevention	What They Did	What They Could Have Done
Appropriate medical staff	There was no certified athletic trainer on site during the practice, which was held from 1 to 4:30 PM. Coaches were certified in cardiopulmonary resuscitation (CPR), first aid, and the use of automated external defibrillators (AED). They were also educated somewhat about heat illness, but not comprehensively.	An athletic trainer should have been on site for the practice.[2-3]
Environmental guidelines	The weather was moderately hot (the highest temperature was 91°F, humidity was 40%, and the heat index was 90).[10]	Wet bulb globe temperature and the heat index should have been monitored by the head athletic trainer or coach prior to the practice in order to determine the safety of environmental conditions.[6-8]
Nutritional plan	There was speculation that Gaston may have been at a party drinking alcohol the night before the practice and he may have been taking a supplement (Jack3d), but this was not proven. Players were educated about hydration, heat illness, and supplement use in the preseason meeting.	Gaston should not have consumed alcohol the night before the practice.[6-8] The preseason meeting about hydration, heat illness, and supplement use was a good way to educate the players.
Acclimatization period	The team held practice for over 4 hours outside on the first day.[10]	An acclimatization period should have taken place starting on the first official practice day. It should have included a gradual return to participation and careful monitoring of environmental conditions.[4,11]
Hydration and rest	Water breaks were not scheduled into practice. If players wanted water, they could get it quickly between drills.[10]	Water should never be limited or restricted during exercise. Water breaks should have been spaced out so that dehydration was limited to 2% of body weight loss. The breaks should have increased in frequency and length when the environmental conditions became more stressful. Work-to-rest ratios should always be modified in stressful environmental conditions.[5]
Emergency action plan (EAP)	The facility did not have a comprehensive EAP.	All athletic facilities should have an EAP to expedite emergency care and ensure athletes have the best care possible.[2]

Recognition	What They Did	What They Could Have Done
Sign and symptom recognition	Gaston showed unusually poor throwing skills along with difficulty during fielding drills and collapsed toward the end of practice during a bunting drill. Coaches recognized that Gaston was suffering from a heat illness immediately after he collapsed. When he regained consciousness, he displayed erratic behavior toward EMS, which indicates CNS dysfunction.[10]	Coaches should have taken action as soon as they observed erratic behavior. Recognition of possible CNS dysfunction prior to collapse leads to earlier treatment.[6-8]

Recognition	What They Did	What They Could Have Done
Rectal temperature	No rectal temperature was taken until the athlete was in the emergency department (ED).[10]	Rectal temperature should have been taken on site by appropriate medical personnel to determine if the athlete had a high body temperature. Rectal temperature should be taken any time an athlete displays signs and symptoms of exertional heat stroke and CNS dysfunction.[6–8]

Treatment	What They Did	What They Could Have Done
Rapid cooling	The coach immediately called 911 and started cooling with ice bags.[10]	Activation of EMS immediately is crucial without proper medical staff. While any cooling is helpful, rapid cooling is necessary for improving survival rate. Gaston should have been cooled via cold water immersion, which is the gold standard treatment for exertional heat stroke.[6–9]
Cool first, transport second	Coaches began cooling with ice bags but stopped upon EMS arrival.[10] There was an 18-minute transportation delay by EMS because Gaston was combative. EMS waited for the police to arrive to restrain the athlete, thinking he was having a drug overdose.	The athlete should have been cooled until his rectal temperature was below 102°F. Ideally, monitoring the rectal temperature continuously during the cooling process ensures the cooling and cessation of cooling are implemented appropriately. The cooling should not have been interrupted by transportation.[6–9]

Lessons Learned

- Appropriate medical coverage at an athletic event may help prevent sudden death by providing preventive strategies, early recognition, and appropriate treatment.
- Adhere to proper NCAA, NATA, and ACSM guidelines for care and prevention of heat illness and have proper policies and procedures for such guidelines documented in an EAP.
- Athletes and coaches should be educated on basic prevention, recognition, and treatment of heat illness.

Legal Outcome

- Civil suit for negligence, *Gaston family v. LaGrange College and Kevin Howard*. Howard was the head baseball coach. The family settled for an undisclosed amount.

Case 3: Max Gilpin

Case Overview[12]

- Max Gilpin, a 15-year-old high school football offensive lineman at Pleasure Ridge Park (PRP) High School in Louisville, KY, died after suffering exertional heat stroke at a football practice on August 20, 2008.
- During the last part of football practice, athletes performed 12 to 15 gassers. Gilpin collapsed at the end of the conditioning. He was taken to a water fountain and to have water run over

his back. EMS was called. Gilpin was taken to the hospital, where he died a few days later. Witnesses from a nearby soccer game attested that even they were concerned about what was happening at the football practice, that it was too intense for such a hot day.

- The event occurred about a month after practices began, in the afternoon, with a hygrometer reading of 94°F.

Case Analysis

Prevention	What They Did	What They Could Have Done
Activity modification	The coaching staff did not enact any activity modifications based on environmental conditions.[12]	Although the Kentucky High School Athletic Association (KHSAA) guidelines did not require activity modification, it may have been prudent to modify the practice, given the environmental conditions.[6-8]
Hydration	No mandated hydration, 2 to 3 possible breaks for < 5 minutes during a 1.5-hour practice.	KHSAA guidelines have no mandate for water breaks for < 95°F heat index, which is still imperative.[5]
Appropriate medical care	PRP High School did not have an athletic trainer or any other form of appropriate medical care.	An athletic trainer should have been present on site to implement preventive strategies as well as provide appropriate care.[2-3]
Appropriate supervision	Only the head coach attended the safety training related to heat illnesses.	All coaches should have basic education on recognition and treatment of causes of sudden death in sport.[2-3]

Recognition	What They Did	What They Could Have Done
CNS dysfunction and core body temperature > 104°F	Witnesses noticed Gilpin struggling while running gassers during practice. The coaches at PRP High School did not come to Gilpin's aid until he became unconscious.[12]	As soon as any altered mental status or other unusual behavior was recognized, coaches should have gone to Gilpin's aid. If appropriate medical care was on site, a rectal temperature should have been attained.[6-8]
Activation of EMS	It was not until after Gilpin was brought over to the water station that EMS was called by coaches, who thought he was just "overheating." In the 911 call, Gilpin can be heard in the background moaning incoherently.[12]	As soon as Gilpin was recognized as having a medical problem, EMS should have been activated via an EAP.[2]
Appropriate medical coverage	There was no medical coverage present to get an accurate body temperature to determine if Gilpin was suffering from an exertional heat stroke; and the only coach who had any training (Stinson) never assessed or treated Gilpin for exertional heat stroke in any way.	An athletic trainer on site should have been utilized to recognize Gilpin's signs and symptoms, perform a proper assessment, and activate EMS in a timely manner.[3]

Treatment	What They Did	What They Could Have Done
Rapid cooling	Gilpin was cooled initially by running a hose over his back and placing two ice bags over peripheral arteries.[12]	Better methods of on-site cooling, such as the gold standard cold water immersion, should have been used; aggressive on-site cooling, such as cold water immersion, has been shown to guarantee survival.[6-9]

Treatment	What They Did	What They Could Have Done
Ice towels	Coaches did not have ice towels at practice and claimed they knew nothing about ice towels.[12]	As per KHSAA guidelines, coaches should have had ice towels at practice in the event of a heat illness.
Cold water immersion	PRP High School had a whirlpool tub located inside the school, but it was not used to treat Gilpin.	As part of the EAP, coaches should have transported Gilpin the short distance to the school to immerse him in cold water while waiting for EMS.[2,9]

Lessons Learned

- Appropriate medical coverage, that is, an athletic trainer, on site can decrease the risk of death from exertional heat stroke; athletic trainers can implement appropriate recognition and treatment in a reasonable amount of time.
- All states should mandate appropriate guidelines when it comes to athletic participation in the heat. States need to have appropriate heat acclimatization guidelines as well as appropriate guidelines for work-to-rest ratios and hydration breaks in extreme environmental conditions specific to their normal climate.
- All coaches should undergo basic education related to all causes of sudden death in sport so they are aware of potential signs/symptoms and any treatment modalities that can be used prior to the arrival of EMS.
- All schools should have an appropriate EAP that is rehearsed annually.

Legal Outcomes

- Civil case for wrongful death, *Parents of Max Gilpin v. Jefferson County Public Schools*. The case was settled out of court for approximately $2 million.
- Criminal case for reckless endangerment and wanton endangerment, *David Jason Stinson v. Commonwealth*. The coach was acquitted of both charges.

Case 4: Ja'Quayvin Smalls

Case Overview[13]

- On July 8, 2009, Ja'Quayvin Smalls, a 20-year-old male football player at Western Carolina University (WCU), died of exertional sickling during his first preseason conditioning session at the school.
- Ja'Quayvin was aware of his sickle cell trait status, as indicated in his medical history forms; however, the medical care on site this day was not aware of this.
- Environmental conditions were mild: early evening, cool, ~60°F, light rain, altitude 2400 feet.

Case Analysis

Prevention	What They Did	What They Could Have Done
Informed medical staff	An athletic trainer was on site during the practice but had no knowledge of Smalls's sickle cell trait (SCT) status. The school did not test for SCT in athletes, but Smalls had written on a medical questionnaire that he had SCT prior to the practice on July 8.[13]	As per NCAA standards, all members of the medical staff and necessary members of the coaching staff should have been informed and educated about all their SCT athletes. This means testing for the trait and educating athletes and coaches.[4,8]

(continues)

Prevention	What They Did	What They Could Have Done
Acclimatization	The practice was Smalls's first practice at WCU and his first ever at altitude (2400 feet, about 2000 feet higher than Smalls was accustomed to).[13]	Smalls could have been provided a more gradual introduction to exercise at this altitude. High altitude environments are more stressful for athletes because of the limited availability of oxygen. This is especially important for SCT athletes, because they require more oxygen during exercise than non-SCT athletes.[4,8]
Activity modification	Athletes ran roughly 700 yards during conditioning within 1 hour of a 1-hour maximum repetition weight lifting session.	High-intensity anaerobic exercise may need to be moderated for SCT positive athletes. This may include planning and testing sessions to determine which exercises the athlete should and should not perform. This should always be done in the presence of appropriate medical staff.[4,8]

Recognition	What They Did	What They Could Have Done
Sign and symptom recognition	Smalls complained of a cramping sensation without palpable muscle cramps, extreme fatigue, and the inability to physically complete activity. He was taken out of activity to stretch, then lost consciousness and went into cardiac arrest.[13]	Medical staff should have been able to recognize signs and symptoms of exertional sickling at onset with knowledge of his SCT status.[8]

Treatment	What They Did	What They Could Have Done
Activity modification	No activity modification or early recognition was implemented for Smalls. When he was finally removed from exercise, it was to stretch and he was offered water.	Smalls should have been monitored and immediately removed from exercise when signs and symptoms presented.[8]
CPR and AED	When Smalls stopped breathing, the athletic trainer began to perform CPR. No AED was used because of the rain.[13]	Smalls would have benefitted greatly by having CPR with an AED. He should have been moved to an area that was covered and then received defibrillation from an AED. The school was only 2 minutes from the team, which is a viable distance to move to in order to administer the AED.[14]
EAP activation	It is not clear whether or not an EAP was in place or enacted.	An EAP, which leads to earlier activation of EMS as well as higher treatment standards, should have been used to give Smalls the best treatment possible.[2]

Lessons Learned

- Athletes should be aware of their SCT status and educated about it. They should understand the signs and symptoms associated with exertional sickling and exercise modifications to decrease the likelihood of a sickling event.
- All athletic staff, including coaches, strength coaches, and medical staff, should be aware of each athlete's SCT status and techniques for recognition, exercise modification, and treatment.
- Activity modifications should include workout progressions and awareness of altitude and environmental conditions, which may increase exercise intensity in an SCT-positive athlete.

Legal Outcome

- Civil suit for wrongful death, *Smalls v. Western Carolina University athletic personnel*. The family settled out of court for $600,000.

Case 5: Ereck Plancher

Case Overview[15]

- Ereck Plancher, 19 years old, died from exertional sickling during a University of Central Florida (UCF) football practice session.
- Practice took place on March 18, 2008. It was the first practice after returning from spring break.
- Practice began with a morning weight lifting session, followed by three 5-minute agility sessions. All players had to perform a 200-yard high-intensity obstacle course two times. However, during the second repetition Plancher had to be assisted by his teammates. Immediately following, players performed a single gasser. Plancher, a wide receiver, struggled through the gasser, falling at the beginning and finishing in last place behind the linemen. After two team huddles and a cool-down, Plancher collapsed on the indoor practice field.

Case Analysis

Prevention	What They Did	What They Could Have Done
SCT testing	UCF tested for SCT. However, only the head athletic trainer, head football coach, and head strength and conditioning coach were aware that Plancher had SCT.[15]	UCF was right in testing for SCT; however, this information could have been utilized more extensively, including informing the medical staff of this condition.[8]
SCT protocol	UCF had a protocol in place to follow if an athlete tested positive for SCT. However, no documentation was produced showing they did the testing and followed the protocol.	UCF should have followed the protocol they had put in place for cases of a positive SCT test. This protocol detailed who is to be notified, education on SCT and exertional sickling, and education on activity modifications to avoid a medical emergency.[2,4,8]
EAP	UCF had an EAP in place for the training facilities that football was using that day.	In this case, the EAP was appropriate and was followed.

Recognition	What They Did	What They Could Have Done
Sign and symptom recognition	Plancher presented with cramping, muscle weakness, rapid breathing, and slumped to the ground (not a sudden collapse). The athletic trainer did not intervene until Plancher was unconscious.[15]	His signs and symptoms should have been recognized earlier. Early recognition is easier when coaching and medical staff are aware of a preexisting condition.[2,4,8]

Treatment	What They Did	What They Could Have Done
CPR and AED	After Plancher collapsed he was carried outside the practice facility and became unconscious. 911 was called and they began administering CPR while an assistant athletic trainer went to get an AED. Unfortunately the first AED obtained was dropped and broke, but another AED was obtained very quickly. It was applied to the athlete, but no shock was advised.[15]	At the first onset of symptoms, the player should have been removed from the activity and monitored to determine if return to play was possible. A medical professional should always check a player's vital signs and call 911 if necessary. Administering oxygen may also be helpful in preventing sickling. EMS and the hospital staff should have been warned to expect explosive rhabdomyolysis.[8]

Lessons Learned

- Athletes should be tested for SCT before participating in sports. When an athlete tests positive for SCT, the player, all coaches, and all athletic trainers working with the athlete should be informed of the player's test results and educated regarding prevention, recognition, and treatment of exertional sickling.
- Positive SCT athletes should be given appropriate work-to-rest ratios during intense training to minimize the risk of an exertional sickling event.
- Proper acclimatization to environmental conditions, session intensity, and duration must be accomplished, especially during the first 1 to 3 days of training or return to training.
- All interactions, forms, and educational sessions with the athlete, coach, and medical staff must be documented extensively.

Legal Outcome

- Civil suit for wrongful death, *Plancher v. University of Central Florida Athletic Association*. Ten million dollars was awarded to the Plancher family on the charge of negligence.
- In August of 2013 an appellate court overturned the amount awarded in this settlement because of a disagreement regarding whether the University of Central Florida Athletic Association is categorized as a private corporation or if it falls under the University as a state agency (under which the athletic association would have a sovereign immunity cap that limits civil liability for public agencies at $200,000). Under this decision the family would be awarded $200,000, the maximum amount that could be awarded to the family as a state agency. As of October 2013, the Florida Supreme Court had decided to hear an appeal of this decision, but a date to hear the case has not been set.

Case 6: Preston Plevretes

Case Overview[16]

- On November 5, 2005, Preston Plevretes, a 19-year-old sophomore football player at La Salle University, sustained a catastrophic blow to the head, which resulted in second impact syndrome.
- Plevretes had sustained a blow to the head during a previous football practice, went through student health services for clearance, and returned after a total of 12 days while still symptomatic. Plevretes continued to participate with symptoms until the game on November 5 against Duquesne University.
- The hit on November 5 came from a block on a punt return, which knocked Plevretes unconscious. He briefly regained consciousness for a few minutes, was combative, and then lapsed into a coma. Plevretes underwent brain surgery to release the pressure in his skull caused by brain swelling caused by second impact syndrome. Extensive therapy has aided his recovery, but he still has significant difficulty speaking.

Case Analysis

Prevention	What They Did	What They Could Have Done
Hitting technique	Plevretes reported sustaining head-to-head contact during a practice. He also sustained head-to-head contact during his final football game.[16]	Athletes should be coached and practice safe hitting techniques. Head-to-head contact should be protected against and corrected if it occurs.[17]

Prevention	What They Did	What They Could Have Done
Appropriate concussion management	After Plevretes reported a headache (symptom) and head-to-head contact (a mechanism of injury) to the athletic trainer, he was removed from the game and referred to student health services. Two days later, he saw a nurse practitioner, a day later he went to the ED for an eye exam, and the following day he went back to student health services. He was cleared to participate 4 days later.[16]	As soon as the athlete reported signs and symptoms, he should have been referred to appropriate medical care. Also, medical staff should have had Plevretes go through a gradual exercise-based return to play program prior to returning to full activity.[18,19]

Recognition	What They Did	What They Could Have Done
Sign and symptom recognition	When Plevretes initially reported symptoms, he was referred to student health services. He complained of eye problems, went to the ED, and was referred back to student health services. He was cleared, but he told his friends that he still had symptoms.[16]	Players and coaches should be educated on sign and symptom recognition. They should be encouraged to watch for signs and symptoms within themselves and teammates and report them to appropriate medical personnel if a problem arises.[18,19]

Treatment	What They Did	What They Could Have Done
Removal from play	When the athletic trainer heard about Plevretes's initial symptoms, he removed him from participating.[16]	Initially removing Plevretes was correct. Upon any indication of signs or symptoms of a concussion, the athlete should be immediately evaluated and removed from participation until further evaluation by an appropriate medical care provider.[18,19]
Concussion management	Management of the athlete was coordinated primarily through nurses at student health services.[16]	Concussions should be managed by appropriate medical care providers who are trained in concussion management. This includes athletic trainers, sports physicians, and neurologists.[18,19]
Return to participation	Return to participation clearance was given by a nurse practitioner at student health services.[16]	Only appropriate medical care providers with training in concussion management should be allowed to clear an athlete to return to participation following a traumatic brain injury. Also, a gradual return to exercise protocol should be followed to determine the effects of exercise on an athlete prior to full participation.[18,19]

Lessons Learned

- Appropriate medical care should be on site to recognize and manage traumatic brain injury. Clearance from traumatic brain injury should be managed by appropriate medical personnel.
- Instruction of proper hitting techniques should include heads-up contact as well as avoidance of head-to-head contact with other players.

Legal Outcome

- Civil Suit for negligence, *La Salle University v. Plevretes family*. La Salle settled out of court for $7.5 million to the Plevretes family.

Case 7: Team Examples

Case Overviews[20,21]

- After a strenuous workout on January 20, 2011, 13 members of the University of Iowa (UI) football team were hospitalized for exertional rhabdomyolysis (rhabdo). A school issued a report in March of 2011 and a follow-up report providing details of this event.[20]
  - The workout included new, high-intensity, high-repetition drills as part of the team's first lift after returning from winter break.
  - Several players noted extreme pain and muscle fatigue, along with discolored urine and the inability to perform daily tasks such as walking or putting on their shoes. However, no one disclosed their symptoms to UI athletic trainers or physicians. Players were admitted to the UI Health Center between January 24 and 25; the last athlete was released from the hospital on January 31, 2011.
- Following a workout on March 9, 2012, Ohio State University (OSU) Women's Lacrosse players were hospitalized for exertional rhabdo.
  - The team performed a workout that included pull-ups, chin-ups, and tricep dips without rest for 20 minutes. The athletes complained of extreme upper body weakness, pain, loss of motion, shaking, and tingling.

Case Analysis

Prevention	What They Did	What They Could Have Done
Acclimate to exercise	At UI, the athletes were given a winter workout to perform unsupervised for 3 weeks. The damaging workout was their first workout back as a team.[21]	After so long on their own, the strength and conditioning coaches should have acclimated the athletes to intense exercise again by progressively increasing their training volume over time.[4]
Education	At both schools, the coaches and athletes were not educated on what rhabdo is or how it might be recognized.[21,22]	Strength coaches, athletic trainers, and sport coaches should be educated on ways to implement exercises appropriately, how to determine an appropriate amount of exercise, and how to recognize signs and symptoms should they arise.[4]
Inclusion of new exercises	At OSU, the athletes performed a series of intense upper body workouts unlike anything they had done in the past.[22] At UI, the athletes performed a higher training volume than they ever had in the past.[21]	Rhabdo is commonly caused by performing too large a volume of a new exercise in too short a period of time.

Recognition	What They Did	What They Could Have Done
Symptoms	At OSU, one athlete reported severe muscle soreness to the athletic trainer and was referred to the team physician, who sent her to the ED. There she was diagnosed with rhabdo. The rest of the team was evaluated and five more athletes were found to have similar symptoms.[22] At UI, the strength coaches thought the complaints of soreness from the athletes were just general soreness.[21]	Early recognition is the key to treatment. The athlete who let the appropriate people know about the soreness at OSU was instrumental in recognizing the other athletes. At UI, the coaches did not recognize the soreness as anything serious. Athletes and strength coaches should be educated to recognize the signs and symptoms in themselves and others. The athletic trainers should have the knowledge to recognize symptoms of rhabdo and refer to the ED.[4,8]

Recognition	What They Did	What They Could Have Done
Urine color	At OSU, one athlete described cola-colored urine 2 days after the conditioning session but did not tell anyone.[22]	The athletes should have been educated about urine color and what it can mean in terms of hydration and rhabdo.

Treatment	What They Did	What They Could Have Done
Referral to the ED	At OSU, the athlete who came forward was sent to the physician before being referred to the ED.[22]	Severe rhabdo requires hospitalization, intravenous fluids, and pain management. Rhabdo has the potential to cause compartment syndrome and kidney damage. These conditions may require surgery or dialysis. Prompt treatment, without delay, may reduce some of the potential damage caused by rhabdo.

Lessons Learned

- Athletes should be educated and informed about rhabdo recognition and what to do if they have symptoms.
- Medical and coaching staff should be educated on ways to prevent rhabdo from occurring, how to recognize rhabdo, and what to do about it. Medical and coaching staff should also have open communication about practice activities, and concerns should be raised to prevent harm to the athletes.
- New exercises should be introduced progressively into strength and conditioning programs. Exercise should be phased in after any time away from exercise, including school breaks, season breaks, and injury. Athletes should be allowed to acclimate to exercise gradually and new exercises should be implemented with caution.

Legal Outcome

- Currently, no lawsuit has been brought against the UI athletic staff for the incident. No lawsuit has been brought against OSU athletic staff for the incident there either. Parents in both cases are calling for changes in current practices in athletics.

Model Case Examples

The following cases are provided to demonstrate positive outcomes from events that posed the potential for a fatal outcome, but because of proper planning and swift actions, these lives were saved.

Case 1: Davis Nwankwo[23]

Case Overview

- Davis Nwankwo, a 19-year-old African American male basketball player at Vanderbilt University, went into cardiac arrest during a basketball practice.
- Nwankwo had no previous or family history of cardiac problems. He displayed no signs or symptoms prior to collapse. When he collapsed on March 6, 2006, the athletic trainer determined Nwankwo was in cardiac arrest, began CPR, applied an AED, and activated EMS. After a shock and two rescue breaths, Nwankwo started breathing on his own. He was given oxygen and transported to the hospital for further evaluation.

- Nwankwo was disqualified from future athletics with a diagnosis of hypertrophic cardiomyopathy.

Case Analysis

Prevention	What They Did
Preparticipation physical exam	The school had screened the athlete for previous family history of cardiac issues and current problems that would indicate the presence of a cardiac abnormality.
Appropriate medical staff	All athletic activities, including practices, should be covered by an appropriate medical care provider, as was provided in this case by the athletic trainer.
AED access	Every athletic venue should have an AED that can be accessed within 3 minutes in case of emergency. This case had a successful outcome in part because of the speed at which the AED was applied.
EAP	The athletic trainer on site initiated the EAP upon the athlete's collapse. This allowed quick access to the AED and contact with other emergency personnel.

Recognition	What They Did
Loss of consciousness and the ABCs (airway, breathing, circulation)	When Nwankwo collapsed, the athletic trainer recognized the athlete was in cardiac arrest by assessing pulse and breathing.
Previous/family history	Nwankwo had no family history or previous history of cardiac problems.

Treatment	What They Did
CPR and AED	Upon collapse, the athletic trainer began performing CPR. The AED was applied within 2 minutes of collapse.
Oxygen therapy	Oxygen was applied after the athlete began breathing on his own. Oxygen therapy was maintained during transport to the hospital.

Lessons Learned

- Every athletic venue should have a comprehensive EAP that details the procedures to follow in case of an emergency.
- Having appropriate medical personnel on site at athletic events allows for quick and necessary action during emergency medical situations.
- Quick access, under 3 minutes, to an AED may be the key to saving an athlete's life who is suffering from cardiac arrest.

Legal Outcome

- No legal action was necessary in this case.

Case 2: Jane Doe

Case Overview

- A 25-year-old female endurance runner, Jane Doe, had an exertional heat stroke while running a 7-mile road race in New England. The weather conditions were sunny, 71°F, and 65% humidity. Just after crossing the finish line, Doe collapsed and lost consciousness.

- Doe had no previous history of illness or significant medical conditions. She did not stop at any aid stations along the course. Upon collapse, she was transported to the finish line medical tent, where her temperature was assessed and she was cooled via cold water immersion. After 16 minutes, Doe was removed from the tub and evaluated for any additional injuries.
- Doe went home with her family the afternoon of the race and had no future complications. Doe returned to running approximately 1 month after the race.

Case Analysis

Prevention	What They Did
Participant education	Race officials sent out educational materials to the runners prior to the event. The materials gave recommendations for hydration and race strategy.
Aid stations	On the course, water and aid stations were staffed with athletic trainers, nurses, and EMS personnel to assist runners in need of care.
Medical tent preparation	Historically, this event has had several exertional heat stroke incidents each year. Race organizers recognized this and prepared by having at least 12 immersion tubs prepared with ice and water prior to the first runners crossing the finish line. They also had several rectal thermometers on hand to accurately assess body temperature.
Medical staff education	After setting up the finish line medical tent, medical staff were briefed about the possibility of exertional heat stroke, appropriate diagnosis and treatment, and how the medical teams should operate.

Recognition	What They Did
CNS dysfunction/collapse	When the athlete collapsed, Doe was immediately taken to the medical tent by the medical staff manning the finish line. After about 2 minutes, Doe regained consciousness but was disoriented and combative. Doe had to be restrained by medical staff during assessment and the beginning portion of the treatment.
Rectal temperature	As soon as Doe was brought into the medical tent, rectal temperature was assessed via a flexible rectal thermistor, which remained in place for the entire treatment. Doe's temperature approximately 2 minutes after collapse was 108.7°F, well above the normally accepted temperature that indicates exertional heat stroke.

Treatment	What They Did
Rapid cooling	Once a high rectal temperature was found, Doe was immediately lifted into an immersion tub filled with ice and water. A towel was placed around her chest and under her armpits to help support her in the tub. The water was moved continuously by medical staff to enhance cooling. After approximately 7 minutes of cooling, Doe was no longer combative, but she remained in the tub for another 13 minutes.
Temperature monitoring	Rectal temperature was monitored continuously during the treatment to ensure that Doe's temperature was decreasing and to determine when she should be removed from the tub. Treatment took approximately 20 minutes.
After-care	Once her temperature was down to 102.1°F, Doe was removed from the tub. Doe had become verbally coherent and responsive to medical staff. She was able to stand up and walk to a cot at the back of the medical tent with some support from medical staff. After approximately 2 hours of temperature monitoring, fluid and food consumption, and tending to an unrelated foot injury, Doe was released from the medical tent with her family.

Lessons Learned

- Preparation for exertional heat stroke prior to an event where exertional heat stroke is common can help expedite the care and treatment of injured athletes.
- Appropriate recognition via rectal temperature, in addition to CNS dysfunction, is a key criterion for identifying exertional heat stroke. CNS dysfunction may include loss of consciousness or other mental impairments, including combativeness.
- Rapid cooling via cold water immersion with circulating water yields cooling rates that are acceptable for reducing body temperature within 30 minutes of collapse.

Legal Outcome

- No legal actions were necessary in this instance. Doe returned to running approximately 1 month after the exertional heat stroke incident with no sequelae.

Summary

While the law might seem foreign to many in the sport medicine area, it really is simple at a basic level. The simplicity lies in doing what is right. Many resources are available to help guide medical and administrative practice to appropriately prepare and manage emergency medical scenarios.[2–8,14,18,19,20,24] One test of reasonable conduct is to think about what your mother would say if she saw that you could have prevented an injury. We also call this the "front headline test." This test examines how it would look on the front page of the local newspaper if you did something that injured or killed someone. The key to preventing such issues is effective risk management, whether through contracts or avoiding negligence claims.

Key Terms

agreement

capacity

consideration

legality

negligence

plaintiff

primary assumption of risk

secondary assumption of risk

tort

References

1. Fainaru-Wada, Mark. Questions linger for Grambling State. http://sports.espn.go.com/espn/otl/news/story?id=4693697. Published November 30, 2009. Accessed November 1, 2013.
2. Andersen JC, Courson RW, Kleiner DM, McLoda TA. National Athletic Trainers' Association position statement: emergency planning in athletics. *J Athl Train*. 2002;37(1):99–104.
3. Almquist J, Valovich McLeod TC, Cavanna A, et al. Summary statement: appropriate medical care for the secondary school-aged athlete. *J Athl Train*. 2008;43(3):416–427.
4. Casa DJ, Anderson SA, Baker L, et al. The Inter-Association Task Force for Preventing Sudden Death in Collegiate Conditioning Sessions: best practices recommendations. *J Athl Train*. 2012;47(4):477–480.
5. Sawka MN, Burke LM, Eichner ER, et al. American College of Sports Medicine position stand: exercise and fluid replacement. *Med Sci Sports Exerc*. 2007;39(2):377–390.
6. Binkley HM, Beckett J, Casa DJ, et al. National Athletic Trainers' Association position statement: exertional heat illnesses. *J Athl Train*. 2002;37(3):329–343.
7. Armstrong LE, Casa DJ, Millard-Stafford M, et al. American College of Sports Medicine position stand: exertional heat illness during training and competition. *Med Sci Sports Exerc*. 2007;39(3):556–572.

8. Casa DJ, Guskiewicz KM, Anderson SA, et al. National Athletic Trainers' Association position statement: preventing sudden death in sports. *J Athl Train*. 2012;47(1):96–118.

9. Casa DJ, McDermott BP, Lee EC, et al. Cold water immersion: the gold standard for exertional heatstroke treatment. *Exerc Sport Sci Rev*. 2007;35(3):141–149.

10. Fox Medical Team. Heat stroke survivor. http://www.myfoxtwincities.com/story/17901802/fox-medical-team-heat-stroke-survivor. Published August 10, 2011. Accessed November 1, 2013.

11. Casa DJ, Csillan D, Armstrong, LE, et al. Preseason heat-acclimatization guidelines for secondary school athletics. *J Athl Train*. 2009;44(3):332–333.

12. Barrouquere B, Graves W. Details emerge in heat-stroke death of Kentucky high school football player. http://www.timesdispatch.com/news/details-emerge-in-heat-stroke-death-of-kentucky-high-school/article_39ac8c27-9369-59b6-9cfc-0e097d4e76bb.html?mode=jqm. Published January 24, 2009. Accessed November 1, 2013.

13. Caudell J. WCU football player collapses at practice, later dies. http://www.westerncarolinian.com/2.1669/wcu-football-player-collapses-at-practice-later-dies-1.118911#.UkWmwoaTiSo. Published July 17, 2009. Accessed November 1, 2013.

14. Task force recommendations on emergency preparedness and management of sudden cardiac arrest in high school and college athletic programs: a consensus statement. *J Athl Train*. 2007;42(1):143–158.

15. Limon, I. Ereck Plancher trial: three players say water and trainers at workout. http://www.naplesnews.com/news/2011/jun/28/ereck-plancher-trial-three-ucf-players-say-water-t/. Published June 28, 2011. Accessed November 1, 2013.

16. Finder, C. Former football player's concussion has altered his life. http://www.post-gazette.com/stories/sports/more-sports/former-football-players-concussion-has-altered-his-life-280132/. Published January 2, 2011. Accessed November 1, 2013.

17. Heck Jf, Clarke KS, Peterson TR, Torg JS, Weis MP. National Athletic Trainers' Association position statement: head-down contact and spearing in tackle football. *J Athl Train*. 2004;39(1):101–111.

18. Harmon KG, Drezner JA, Gammons M, et al. American Medical Society for Sports Medicine position statement: concussion in sport. *Br J Sports Med*. 2013;47(3):15–26.

19. McCrory P, Meeuwisse W, Johnston K, et al. Consensus statement on concussion in sport, 3rd International Conference on Concussion in Sport held in Zurich, November 2008. *Br J Sports Med*. 2009;43(suppl 1):i76–i90.

20. Report of the special presidential committee to investigate the January 2011 hospitalization of University of Iowa football players. Accessed February 7, 2014. http://www.asac.arkansas.gov/pdfs/reports/Rhabdomyolysis_-_University_of_Iowa_Board_of_Regents_Report.pdf

21. Witosky T. Iowa staff misused exercise that lead to rhabdo, experts say. http://hawkcentral.com/2011/03/28/iowa-staff-misused-exercise-that-led-to-rhabdo-experts-say/. Published March 28, 2011. Accessed November 1, 2013.

22. Jones T. Rhabdomyolysis laid low 6 athletes. http://www.dispatch.com/content/stories/sports/2013/03/09/illness-laid-low-6-athletes.html. Published March 9, 2013. Accessed November 1, 2013.

23. Drezner JA, Rogers KJ. Sudden cardiac arrest in intercollegiate athletes: detailed analysis and outcomes of resuscitation in nine cases. *Heart Rhythm*. 2006;3(7):755–759.

24. Casa DJ, Almquist J, Anderson SA, et al. The inter-association task force for preventing sudden death in secondary school athletics programs: best practices recommendations. *J Athl Train*. 2013;48(4):546–543.

Treatment Algorithm for Collapsed Athletes

Treatment Algorithm for Collapsed Athletes

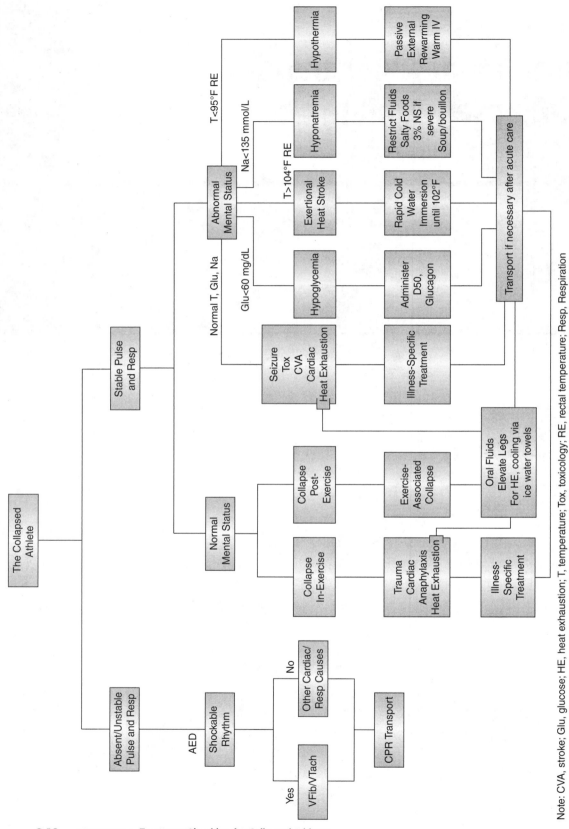

Note: CVA, stroke; Glu, glucose; HE, heat exhaustion; T, temperature; Tox, toxicology; RE, rectal temperature; Resp, Respiration

Source: Modified from Lawless C (Ed.), Malik S, Chiampas G, Roberts WO. Sports Cardiology Essentials. The Collapsed Athlete. Springer, 2011. With kind permission of Springer Science.

The Inter-Association Task Force for Preventing Sudden Death in Secondary School Athletics Programs: Best-Practices Recommendations

Douglas J. Casa, PhD, ATC, FNATA, FACSM (Chair)[*†]*; Jon Almquist, VATL, ATC*[*]*; Scott A. Anderson, ATC*[*]*; Lindsay Baker, PhD*[‡]*; Michael F. Bergeron, PhD, FACSM*[§]*; Brian Biagioli, EdD*[∥]*; Barry Boden, MD*[¶]*; Joel S. Brenner, MD, MPH, FAAP*[#]*; Michael Carroll, MEd, LAT, ATC*[*]*; Bob Colgate*[**]*; Larry Cooper, MS, LAT, ATC*[*]*; Ron Courson, PT, ATC, NREMT-I, CSCS*[*]*; David Csillan, MS, LAT, ATC*[*]*; Julie K. DeMartini, MA, ATC*[†]*; Jonathan A. Drezner, MD*[††]*; Tim Erickson, CAA*[‡‡]*; Michael S. Ferrara, PhD, ATC, FNATA*[*]*; Steven J. Fleck, PhD, CSCS, FNSCA, FACSM*[§§]*; Rob Franks, DO, FAOASM*[∥∥]*; Kevin M. Guskiewicz, PhD, ATC, FNATA, FACSM*[*]*; William R. Holcomb, PhD, LAT, ATC, CSCS*D, FNATA, FNSCA*[§§]*; Robert A. Huggins, MEd, ATC*[†]*; Rebecca M. Lopez, PhD, ATC, CSCS*[†]*; Thom Mayer, MD, FACEP*[¶¶]*; Patrick McHenry, MA, CSCS*D, RSCC*[§§]*; Jason P. Mihalik, PhD, CAT(C), ATC*[##]*; Francis G. O'Connor, MD, MPH, FACSM*[††]*; Kelly D. Pagnotta, MA, ATC, PES*[†]*; Riana R. Pryor, MS, ATC*[†]*; John Reynolds, MS, VATL, ATC*[*]*; Rebecca L. Stearns, PhD, ATC*[†]*; Verle Valentine, MD*[††]

The secondary school athletic population leads the nation in athletic-related deaths.[1–6] Given that many such deaths are avoidable through proper prevention, recognition, and treatment protocols, those involved with secondary school athletics can benefit from policy considerations regarding health and safety for participation in sport. The health and safety of secondary school athletes is paramount, but barriers that jeopardize the delivery of optimal safety and preventive measures remain prevalent across the secondary school athletic landscape. To date, these "best-practices" recommendations have been endorsed by the American College of Sports Medicine,

[*]National Athletic Trainers' Association; [†]Korey Stringer Institute; [‡]Gatorade Sports Science Institute; [§]American College of Sports Medicine; [∥]National Council on Strength and Fitness; [¶]American Orthopaedic Society for Sports Medicine; [#]American Academy of Pediatrics; [**]National Federation of State High School Associations; [††]American Medical Society for Sports Medicine; [‡‡]National Interscholastic Athletic Administrators Association; [§§]National Strength and Conditioning Association; [∥∥]American Osteopathic Academy of Sports Medicine; [¶¶]American College of Emergency Physicians; [##]Canadian Athletic Therapists Association

Source: Journal of Athletic Training 2013;48(4):546–553 doi: 10.4085/1062-6050-48.4.12 by the National Athletic Trainers' Association, Inc. www.natajournals.org. Reprinted by permission of *Journal of Athletic Training*.

American Medical Society for Sports Medicine, American Orthopaedic Society for Sports Medicine, American Osteopathic Academy of Sports Medicine, Canadian Athletic Therapists Association, Gatorade Sports Science Institute, Korey Stringer Institute, Matthew A. Gfeller Sport-Related Traumatic Brain Injury Research Center, National Athletic Trainers' Association, National Center for Catastrophic Sport Injury Research, National Council on Strength and Fitness, National Federation of State High School Associations, National Interscholastic Athletic Administrators Association, and National Strength and Conditioning Association.

This document provides a roadmap for policy considerations regarding health and safety concerns for secondary school athletes. Although these guidelines are not exhaustive for all conditions, these best practices address the leading causes of sudden death in this population (head and neck injuries, exertional heat stroke [EHS], sudden cardiac arrest [SCA], and exertional sickling). Further, we present information to address the infrastructure conditions and barriers that can introduce the most risk to athletes (lack of emergency action plans [EAPs], lack of medical staff, lack of emergency equipment [eg, defibrillators], poor heat acclimatization policies, and improper conditioning sessions).

The advent of increasing policy mandates and legislative efforts has resulted in a greater need to have a medical gatekeeper who can properly supervise the sports health of the secondary school athletes. This includes the policies, mandates, and laws that have been created to enhance the health and safety of these athletes. In addition, most of the deaths in secondary school sports can be avoided by providing appropriate prevention, recognition, and treatment strategies. Accordingly, supervisors of secondary school athletics programs would benefit greatly from having an athletic trainer (AT) who can guide these efforts. As James Roscoe Day said when chancellor of Syracuse University and after President Theodore Roosevelt mandated changes in collegiate football to decrease the number of deaths: "One human life is too big a price for all the games of the season." Day helped to overhaul the rules of collegiate football and form the National Collegiate Athletic Association because President Roosevelt provided this mandate, showing that smart implementation of policy changes and oversight can dramatically enhance the safety of sport participation. Therefore, the purpose of this consensus statement is to provide a similar benefit through recommendations and guidelines for best practices. Most deaths in sports are preventable; our charge is to meet this expectation.

Emergency Action Plans[7–16]

1. Each school should have an EAP, including specific details for each athletic facility where practice and competition occur, to ensure that appropriate strategies and site-specific procedures are invoked during a time of crisis. The EAP ideally is developed by school administrators in collaboration with coaches, school medical personnel (ATs, nurses, team and consulting physicians), and campus public safety officials and coordinated with the local emergency medical services (EMS) system.
2. The following components covering emergency communication and equipment should be included:
   a. Establish an efficient communication system to activate EMS at each athletic venue.
   b. Establish a communication system to alert on-site (school) responders to the emergency and its location.
   c. Post the EAP at each venue, including a list of emergency numbers, facility map with street address, and directions to guide EMS.
   d. Post the specific location of all emergency equipment.
   e. Strategically locate automated external defibrillators (AEDs) to allow immediate retrieval and use within 3 minutes (with 1 minute being ideal) of recognizing an emergency.
   f. Provide a readiness check of emergency equipment before each scheduled athletic activity.
   g. Maintain emergency equipment, including battery and lead replacement for AEDs, according to the manufacturers' guidelines and document the maintenance.
   h. Register each AED with the local EMS system and integrate it with the specific EAP.
3. All athletics staff who have contact with student-athletes and are associated with practices, competition, and strength-and-conditioning sessions, including coaches, strength-and-conditioning coaches (S&CCs), and administrators, should have the following:
   a. Current certification in first aid and cardiopulmonary resuscitation (CPR), including the use of an AED.

    b. Coaches also should be educated about factors contributing to sudden death and recognizing life-threatening situations.

    c. Coaches should be responsible for documenting competencies and continuing education specific to preventing sudden death in sport.

4. The EAP should be site specific and reviewed each sport season by all coaches, assistant coaches, and athletics and medical personnel in coordination with local EMS. The school-wide EAP should be rehearsed and reviewed at least once annually by all personnel involved with student-athletes and athletics programs. In addition, it should be reviewed any time the EAP is modified.

5. No scheduled athletic activity, including conditioning sessions, should occur until the school's athletic director or principal has confirmed that coaches and support staff are fully familiar with the EAP.

6. The EAP should be updated as needed if the athletic field or facility is altered (eg, by renovations) or its location changes permanently or temporarily.

Athletic Trainer Services

1. Athletic trainers are health care professionals who collaborate with physicians. The services ATs provide comprise prevention, emergency care, clinical diagnosis, therapeutic intervention, and rehabilitation of injuries and medical conditions.[17] The domains of athletic training include injury prevention, evaluation, immediate care, rehabilitation, and administration related to athletic injuries. A *state-regulated or certified AT* should be defined as one who

- has earned and currently holds national certification by the Board of Certification,
- currently holds state licensure in the state where employed, and
- is employed with the responsibility of coordinating or assisting with the implementation of the school's sports medicine program.

2. Related to emergency issues, the AT must be able to

- determine an athlete's readiness to participate via an appropriate preparticipation physical evaluation and, if necessary, consult with the supervising team physician or treating physician, or both;
- identify unsafe facilities or playing environments;
- properly select, fit, determine the function of, and maintain the athletic equipment;
- develop and implement an EAP;
- implement protocols for environmental conditions based on current recommendations;
- prevent, recognize, and treat emergency medical conditions; and
- develop and implement a comprehensive athletic health care administrative system.

3. The AT should be physically at the school and accessible for practices and competitive events as defined in the school's policies and procedures, with coverage decisions and priorities based on scientific data indicating the highest risk of catastrophic events, in consultation with the medical team and school administration.

4. Each AT employed by a secondary school in the United States should collaborate with a physician (medical doctor or doctor of osteopathic medicine only) who is licensed in the state and has an interest and expertise in sports medicine.

5. Ideally, the AT is employed directly by the school district. This increases the likelihood that emergency planning recommendations are developed as school-wide policies and ensures that relevant health and safety state laws and state athletic association policies are managed and enforced consistently.

6. The AT should conduct an annual safety education program for athletes, coaches, administrators, and parents focusing on athletic head and neck injury, cardiac, heat-related, respiratory, exertional sickling, and other emergencies and EAPs.

Conditioning Sessions and the S&CC

1. Athletes should acclimatize progressively to training demands and environmental conditions for optimal safety.

    a. These conditioning programs ideally are developed by an S&CC credentialed by an organization accredited by a recognized independent accreditation agency, but if the school does not have an S&CC, the basic principles of strength and conditioning need to be understood by all involved with conditioning programs. The S&CC should work cooperatively with medical staff (AT, supervising physician, or both) when developing transitional workout plans, particularly if the patient is recovering from an injury, if any uncertainty exists regarding the pace of exercise progression, or if the patient's medical history warrants it.

   b. Conditioning periods should be phased in gradually and progressively to encourage proper exercise acclimatization and to minimize the risk of adverse events.

   c. The first 7 to 10 days (at minimum, the first 4 separate-day workouts) of any new conditioning cycle (including but not limited to return to school after summer, winter, and spring breaks and return after an injury) are referred to as *transitional periods*.

   d. A progressive program of increasing volume, intensity, mode, and duration should be instituted for all transitional periods.

   e. Transitional periods should consist of an appropriate work-to-rest ratio for the sport. This is especially important during serial, intense activity. It is imperative to allow sufficient recovery during training sessions.

   f. A qualified coach or credentialed S&CC should be knowledgeable about and use acclimatization principles.

   g. Participation in summer workouts on school grounds under the supervision of a coach or an S&CC is preferable to unsupervised workouts elsewhere or workouts conducted by unqualified individuals.

   h. Training programs should be individualized. Some athletes will require a longer acclimatization process. An athlete at a different level of preparedness than his or her teammates (due to injury or time away from training) should use a training program tailored to his or her level of fitness or other medical needs.

2. New conditioning activities should be introduced gradually. Any new exercise or training drill introduced into a strength-and-conditioning program should be added in a deliberate, gradual fashion. This is particularly important during the early stages of a conditioning program.

3. Exercise and conditioning activities must not be used as punishment.

   a. Physical activity should not be used as retribution, for coercion, or as discipline for unsatisfactory athletic or academic performance or unacceptable behavior.

   b. No additional physical burden that may increase the risk of injury or sudden death should be placed on the athlete under punitive circumstances.

4. Proper education, experience, and credentialing of S&CCs should be ensured.

   a. Some coursework should be dedicated to the health and safety concerns of athletes, with a focus on preventing sudden death. This includes the prevention, recognition, and management of on-field emergencies.

   b. Continuing education requirements should ensure certified S&CCs engage in educational opportunities that provide applicable, up-to-date information regarding important health and safety topics, emergency procedures, and prevention of sudden death.

   c. All S&CCs should be required to pass a certification examination credentialed by an independent accreditation agency. Competency standards, ongoing assessment, and continuing education requirements should be documented clearly.

   d. All S&CCs should maintain certification in first aid and CPR, including the use of an AED.

Catastrophic Brain and Neck Injuries [12, 14, 18–20]

1. Any secondary school sponsoring contact or collision sports, including but not limited to baseball, basketball, diving, field hockey, football, gymnastics, ice hockey, lacrosse, pole vaulting, rugby, soccer, softball, water polo, and wrestling, should employ an AT.

2. When one is assessing suspected concussions, the following tests should be used as informational tools to aid in the clinical decision-making process of the health care professional:

   a. The third edition of the Sport Concussion Assessment Tool (SCAT3), which in part includes a Graded Symptom Checklist (GSC), the Standardized Assessment of Concussion (SAC), and the firm-surface conditions of the Balance Error Scoring System (BESS). If appropriate, the full BESS (including foam stances) should be completed; and

   b. If applicable, computerized neurocognitive testing.

3. The team physician and AT should consult, when necessary, neuropsychologists to help interpret the neurocognitive test findings when indicated.

4. Schools without ATs should not be performing points 2 and 3 without guidance or direct supervision from trained and experienced medical professionals.

5. An annual brain and spine safety education program should be conducted for all student-athletes and coaches and should include a discussion of the proper rules and safety measures to prevent dangerous and potentially catastrophic use of the head or helmet as a weapon.

6. Providing student-athletes with in-season behavior modification "check-ups" may prevent unnecessary head and neck injuries. This includes regular instruction and feedback regarding heads-up tackling technique and ensuring that athletes do not lead with the head during contact.

7. Physicians and ATs working in the secondary school setting should complete an education module focusing on updates in appropriate medical management and return to activity after brain (concussion) and neck injuries. An example includes the Centers for Disease Control and Prevention's "Proper Management of Cervical Spine Injuries" in *Heads Up to Clinicians: Addressing Concussion in Sports Among Kids and Teens*.[19]

8. The AT and school athletics officials should enforce the standard use of certified helmets and should educate athletes, coaches, and parents that helmets do not prevent concussions.

   a. The AT, in conjunction with the school's equipment manager or coaches, or both, should ensure helmets have appropriate manufacturer-specific corrosion-resistant hardware, are maintained regularly throughout the season and the helmets' lives, are reconditioned and recertified based on manufacturers' guidelines, and meet national certification standards.

   b. The AT, in conjunction with the school's equipment manager or coaches, or both, should ensure proper fitting of all helmets for all athletes.

9. A comprehensive medical-management plan for acute care of a potential cervical spine or brain injury (eg, an intracranial hemorrhage or diffuse cerebral edema) should be implemented. The plan should be initiated in the presence of unconsciousness or altered level of consciousness, bilateral neurologic findings or other substantial neurologic concerns, substantial midline spine pain with or without palpation, or obvious spinal column deformity. Cervical spine injury should be ruled out for all injured but conscious patients before moving them.
   If the AT suspects a head or neck injury, he or she should be prepared to do the following.

   a. Provide on-field and sideline medical management of head injury to address more serious, quickly deteriorating, and potentially life-threatening conditions;

   b. Stabilize the patient and activate the local EMS system in the event of a serious head or neck trauma;

   c. Provide rescue ventilations (eg, bag-valve-mouth resuscitation);

   d. Provide CPR and use an AED in case of cardiopulmonary collapse;

   e. Properly spine board an injured patient without compromising the cervical spine; on-field rescue training and spine-boarding practice should be conducted at least annually by the AT and other identified school staff who may assist in an emergency situation; and

   f. Immediately transfer the patient with assistance from local EMS to a medical facility equipped to manage traumatic head and neck injuries. Local EMS should be responsible for transporting the patient, and the AT and school officials should facilitate this process with a well-rehearsed EAP. Elevating the spine board to a 30° head-up position during transport may reduce intracranial pressure.

10. No athlete with a suspected concussion should be permitted to return to a practice, game, or activity on the same day.

   a. The school's AT or physician should evaluate a patient with a suspected concussion. When a trained medical professional is not present, the patient should be withheld from activity, and the coach, parent, or responsible adult—whoever is present at the time of the injury—should initiate a referral to the patient's primary care provider or emergency department for timely medical evaluation.

  b. Oral and written instructions for home care should be given to the patient and a responsible adult (eg, parent, legal guardian, or other responsible party).

  c. Before returning to participation, the patient must receive written release from a licensed medical professional trained and experienced in the evaluation and management of concussion, in accordance with the state's concussion law.

11. To prevent a premature return to participation and to avoid placing the patient at risk for a catastrophic brain injury, the AT and team or treating physician should work together to implement a supervised, graduated return-to-participation progression after a concussion. If the patient becomes symptomatic at any stage of the graduated return-to-participation progression, exercise should be ceased, and the patient should regress 1 step and immediately consult with the physician or AT in charge. The patient should progress no more than 1 step in a 24-hour period. A 6-step graduated return-to-participation progression follows:

- Exertion step 1: no activity until complete symptom resolution.
- Exertion step 2: light aerobic exercise for 20 minutes.
- Exertion step 3: sport-specific exercise, which may include interval aerobic exercise and body weight circuit.
- Exertion step 4: noncontact training drills, which may include repeated shuttle runs, plyometric workout, and noncontact sport-specific drills.
- Exertion step 5: limited, controlled, and gradual return to full-contact practice.
- Exertion step 6: full return to participation.

Exertional Heat Stroke[7,8,12,14,21,22]

1. Before the season begins, all teams should follow a heat acclimatization program that focuses on phasing in equipment use, intensity of exercise, duration of exercise, and total practice time. Specific guidelines should follow the 2009 preseason heat acclimatization guidelines for secondary school athletics[22] that adhere to the key points of a heat acclimatization program as defined by the National Federation of State High School Associations.[8]

2. Administrators, coaches, athletes, and parents must be educated about the common causes of EHS, wet bulb globe temperature (WBGT) and heat index guidelines, and predisposing factors.

  a. Intrinsic contributing risk factors include a history of exertional heat illnesses; insufficient heat acclimatization; low fitness; high percentage of body fat; substantial dehydration; current or recent fever or gastrointestinal illness; skin condition (eg, sunburn, skin rash); ingestion of certain medications (eg, antihistamines, diuretics, dopamine-reuptake inhibitors) or dietary supplements (eg, ephedra); motivation to push oneself/warrior mentality; and reluctance to report problems, issues, illness, etc.[a]

  b. Extrinsic contributing risk factors include intense or prolonged exercise with minimal breaks; high temperature, humidity, or sun exposure and exposure to heat and humidity in the preceding days; inappropriate work-to-rest ratios based on intensity, WBGT, clothing, equipment, fitness, and the athlete's medical condition; lack of education and awareness of exertional heat illnesses among coaches, athletes, and medical staff; no or inadequate emergency plan to identify and treat EHS; no access to shade during exercise or during rest breaks; limited duration and number of rest breaks; insufficient access to fluids before and during practice and rest breaks; and delay in recognition of early warning signs.[a]

3. Activities should be modified when environmental conditions are extreme. The WBGT should be used to determine these modifications, but specific WBGT thresholds for activity alterations may vary based on geographic location. Guidelines must dictate appropriate rest breaks, including dura-

---

[a] Portions of this document are adapted from Inter-Association Task Force on Exertional Heat Illnesses. Consensus statement. http://www.nata.org/sites/default/files/inter-association-task-force-exertional-heat-illness.pdf. Published 2003. Accessed April 10, 2013.

tion and total number, for practice sessions and should depend on session length and intensity of activity. Whereas WBGT is optimal for assessing the environmental stress, the heat index can provide an adequate reading if WBGT is not available.

4. Enough water or sports drinks must be available and placed at various stations around the practice field or sufficient breaks and a large central rehydration station should be provided to allow each player to drink quickly and freely throughout each practice and conditioning session.

5. The athlete's percentage of body mass loss must be limited to less than 2% in any session; weigh-ins are useful before and after each session and should be conducted under conditions of high heat and humidity. (Weigh-ins before and after practice sessions only account for water loss during the session and not the state in which the athlete arrived to the session. Athletes often arrive to practice 2% or more dehydrated.)

6. Exertional heat stroke should be suspected in any athlete who exhibits central nervous system dysfunction during intense exercise in the heat. The classic clinical diagnostic criterion is central nervous system dysfunction (eg, loss of consciousness, altered consciousness, personality change, staggering gait) combined with hyperthermia (>104°F–105°F [>40.0°C–40.6°C]) at the time of collapse.

7. When assessing body temperature in a patient suspected of having EHS, rectal temperature should be obtained by a medical professional. Other devices (eg, oral, axillary, temporal, tympanic) have been shown to be inaccurate for assessing body temperature when athletes have been participating in intense exercise in the heat.

8. When EHS is suspected, cold-water immersion or another cooling modality until cold-water immersion is ready should be implemented **before** transport by EMS.
   a. Active cooling should continue uninterrupted until the patient's core body temperature is less than 102°F (38.92°C).
   b. If a rectal temperature device is not available, cooling via cold-water immersion should be implemented for 15 minutes.
   c. Cold-water immersion should be implemented in a tub of cold water that is 45°F to 60°F (7.23°C to 15.57°C) with continuous stirring of the water.
   d. Examples of alternative cooling modalities to cold-water immersion (only if cold-water immersion is not available) include dousing with cold water, rotating wet ice towels over the entire body, and placing the patient under a cold shower.

9. All schools should have a cold-water immersion tub if a risk of EHS exists.
   a. All medical personnel and team coaches should have access to the tub for prompt treatment of patients with EHS.
   b. The tub should be set up on site for all high-risk activities, especially those performed during summer conditioning sessions and August and early September practices.
   c. The doctrine of "cool first and transport second" should be followed if appropriate medical professionals (medical doctor, doctor of osteopathic medicine, AT, or EMS) are on site when treating EHS.

10. All patients with EHS must be monitored thoroughly for appropriate return-to-participation considerations.
    a. A physician must clear the patient based on progress made during recovery, blood tests, and ability to tolerate gradual return to activity in the heat.
    b. The appropriate timeline for return to activity should be based on the specific case and advanced based on intermittent progress and re-evaluation.

Sudden Cardiac Arrest[2,12–16,18,20,23–25]

1. Athletes should undergo cardiovascular screening before participation in competitive athletics.
   1. The task force supports recommendations from the American Academy of Family Physicians et al[18] as the minimum standard for screening using a comprehensive personal history, family history, and physical examination.
   2. A resting 12-lead electrocardiogram (ECG) may be used in many preparticipation screening programs. An ECG may increase identification of athletes with cardiac conditions associated with sudden death. Questions and limitations regarding sensitivity and specificity, physician

infrastructure, and cost, however, preclude universal ECG screening for all athletes at this time. Proper physician education in ECG interpretation in athletes and appropriate cardiology resources for secondary evaluations when indicated are important.

2. An AED should be on site and readily available within 3 minutes (with 1 minute being ideal) for all organized athletic activities.

3. School staff, medical professionals, coaches, and athletes should be educated at least annually about the location, function, and use of AEDs.

4. Any athlete who has collapsed and is unresponsive should be assumed to be in SCA until proven otherwise or another cause of the collapse clearly is identified. Proper management of SCA includes the following.

   a. Prompt recognition of SCA
      1. Brief seizure-like activity is common in athletes with SCA. Therefore, assume "seizure equals SCA" until proven otherwise.
      2. Agonal respirations or intermittent gasps do not represent normal breathing.

   b. Early activation of the EMS system (ie, call 911). Call for additional rescuer assistance, as well.

   c. Early CPR beginning with chest compressions for a witnessed collapse. Chest compressions are provided at 100 per minute.

   d. Early defibrillation
      1. Immediate retrieval of the AED.
      2. Application as soon as possible for rhythm analysis and shock delivery if indicated.
      3. If no shock is recommended, a nonshockable SCA (ie, asystole or pulseless electrical activity) is still possible, and CPR and life-support measures should be continued until the patient becomes responsive or a noncardiac cause can be established clearly.
      4. If an athlete collapses with multiple bystanders present, EMS activation, initiation of chest compressions, and AED retrieval should happen concurrently.
      5. If only 1 rescuer is present, the rescuer should activate EMS and then retrieve and use an AED if known to be in close proximity. If no AED is known to be close, the rescuer should begin CPR and continue until additional help arrives.

   e. Transport of the patient with SCA to a hospital capable of advanced cardiac life support, as well as therapeutic cooling if possible, should be prioritized. Induced hypothermia (rapid cooling) in select cases (when cognitive function does not return on site or en route) for patients with SCA, including ventricular fibrillation arrest, has been shown to improve survival and decrease neurologic complications.

5. Athletes who have cardiovascular symptoms, such as exertional chest pain, exertional syncope or presyncope, palpitations, new or excessive shortness of breath, or exertional fatigue, should be evaluated by a physician and require medical clearance before returning to sport participation. Patients with an identified cardiac disorder, unexplained symptoms, or previous sudden death events should be cleared by a cardiologist before return to sport participation is considered.

6. The supervising physician for a school should discuss clearance decisions with appropriate consultants and parents to help make prudent clearance decisions.

7. Clearance for patients with cardiac disorders should be based on expert cardiology evaluation and should take into consideration the recommendations from the American College of Cardiology Foundation.[24]

8. The task force actively supports funding research and other initiatives that improve our collective knowledge about factors that contribute to sudden death in young athletes and that mitigate risk.

Exertional Sickling[9,12,14,26,27]

1. Efforts to obtain newborn screening results of sickle cell trait (SCT) status during the preparticipation physical evaluation are recommended.

2. In the absence of newborn screening results, SCT screening during the preparticipation physical evaluation should be considered for all athletes, especially if they are performing intense physical activity.
3. No patient who has SCT should be denied participation in sport.
4. All personnel overseeing athletic activity should be educated about the signs and symptoms of and the preventive and immediate treatment measures for an exertional sickling crisis, which some have termed *exertional collapse associated with SCT.*[9]
   a. All athletics personnel should be aware of which athletes have SCT in case an emergency arises.
   b. Signs and symptoms of exertional sickling include lower extremity or low back pain, "cramp" or "spasm," muscle weakness, fatigue, difficulty recovering from exercise, shortness of breath, or "slow" collapse (unlike cardiac collapse, which is instantaneous).
   c. Supplemental oxygen should be available for training and competitions at high altitude.
5. Simple precautions and modifications during exercise, such as modifying training intensity, monitoring environmental conditions, evaluating for acute illness, maintaining hydration, acclimatizing to heat, and adapting to recent or new exercise, can prevent complications from SCT.
   a. Patients with SCT should be allowed longer periods of rest and recovery between conditioning repetitions and possible exclusion from participation in performance tests that occur in early training (ie, transitional periods), such as mile runs and serial sprints.
   b. Work-rest cycles should be adjusted for environmental heat stress, and athlete hydration should be emphasized.
6. Athletes with signs or symptoms of exertional sickling should be removed immediately from participation and managed with rest, oxygen, hydration, and cooling.
7. A patient with exertional sickling collapse should be treated as having a medical emergency.
   a. Check vital signs and activate the EAP.
   b. Provide high-flow oxygen (15 L/min) with a non-rebreather face mask.
   c. Cool the patient if necessary.
   d. Activate EMS, attach an AED, start an intravenous line if feasible, and transport the patient to the hospital as soon as possible if the patient is obtunded or if his or her vital signs decline.
   e. Monitor the patient for metabolic complications, explosive rhabdomyolysis, and cardiac arrhythmias.

Next Steps

The health and safety of secondary school athletes are of paramount concern for health care professionals, organizations, administrators, coaches, parents, athletes, and other stakeholders. Issues and barriers that jeopardize the delivery of optimal safety and preventive measures at the secondary school level need to be addressed. One of the current challenges is that each state athletic association or legal system (or both) is tasked with developing and implementing its own safety standards. Therefore, guidelines, policies, and laws must be developed and implemented on a state-by-state basis. This is an arduous process requiring extensive resources, time, and effort that in many cases does not involve medical or health professionals who are best equipped to develop the policies. We hope these guidelines can provide a roadmap to safer sport participation for the secondary school athlete.

Disclaimer

The National Athletic Trainers' Association (NATA) and the Inter-Association Task Force for Preventing Sudden Death in Secondary School Athletics Programs advise individuals, schools, athletic training facilities, and institutions to carefully and independently consider each of the recommendations. The information contained in the statement is neither exhaustive nor exclusive to all circumstances or individuals. Variables such as institutional human resource guidelines, state or federal statutes, rules, or regulations, as well as regional environmental conditions, may impact the relevance and implementation of these recommendations. The NATA and the Inter-Association Task Force advise their members and others to carefully and independently consider each of the recommendations (including the applicability of same to any particular circumstance or individual). The foregoing statement should not be relied upon as an independent basis for care but rather as a resource available to NATA members or others. Moreover, no opinion is expressed herein regarding the quality of care that adheres to or differs from any of NATA's other statements. The NATA and the Inter-Association Task Force reserve the right to rescind or modify their statements at any time.

References

1. National Center for Catastrophic Sport Injury Research. http://www. unc.edu/depts/nccsi/. Accessed April 30, 2013.
2. Maron BJ, Doerer JJ, Haas TS, Tierney DM, Mueller FO. Sudden deaths in young competitive athletes: analysis of 1866 deaths in the United States, 1980–2006. *Circulation.* 2009;119(8):1085–1092.
3. Kerr ZY, Casa DJ, Marshall SW, Comstock RD. Epidemiology of exertional heat illness among U.S. high school athletes. *Am J Prev Med.* 2013;44(1):8–14.
4. Boden BP, Breit I, Beachler JA, Williams A, Mueller FO. Fatalities in high school and college football players. *Am J Sports Med.* 2013;41(5):1108–1116.
5. Grundstein AJ, Ramseyer C, Zhao F, et al. A retrospective analysis of American football hyperthermia deaths in the United States. *Int J Biometeorol.* 2012;56(1):11–20.
6. Meehan WP 3rd, Mannix R. A substantial proportion of life-threatening injuries are sport-related. *Pediatr Emerg Care.* 2013;29(5):624–627.
7. Council on Sports Medicine and Fitness, Council on School Health. Policy statement: climatic heat stress and exercising children and adolescents. *Pediatrics.* 2011;128(3):e741–e747.
8. National Federation of State High School Associations Sports Medicine Advisory Committee. Heat acclimatization and heat illness prevention position statement. Published 2012. http://www.nfhs.org/content.aspx?id¼5786. Accessed April 3, 2013.
9. O'Connor FG, Bergeron MF, Cantrell J, et al. ACSM and CHAMP Summit on Sickle Cell Trait: mitigating risks for warfighters and athletes. *Med Sci Sports Exerc.* 2012;44(11):2045–2056.
10. McCrory P, Meeuwisse WH, Aubry M, et al. Consensus statement on concussion in sport: the 4th International Conference on Concussion in Sport held in Zurich, November 2012. *Br J Sports Med.* 2013;47(5):250–258.
11. Andersen JC, Courson RW, Kleiner DM, McLoda TA. National Athletic Trainers' Association position statement: emergency planning in athletics. *J Athl Train.* 2002;37(1):99–104. http://www.nata.org/sites/default/files/EmergencyPlanninginAthletics. pdf. Accessed February 15, 2012.
12. Casa DJ. *Preventing Sudden Death in Sport and Physical Activity.* Burlington, MA: Jones & Bartlett Learning; 2012.
13. Drezner JA, Courson RW, Roberts WO, Mosesso VN, Link MS, Maron BJ. Inter-Association Task Force recommendations on emergency preparedness and management of sudden cardiac arrest in high school and college athletic programs: a consensus statement. *J Athl Train.* 2007;42(1):143–158.
14. Casa DJ, Guskiewicz KM, Anderson SA, et al. National Athletic Trainers' Association position statement: preventing sudden death in sport. *J Athl Train.* 2012;47(1):96–118.
15. Drezner JA, Rao AL, Heistand J, Bloomingdale MK, Harmon KG. Effectiveness of emergency response planning for sudden cardiac arrest in United States high schools with automated external defibrillators. *Circulation.* 2009;120(6):518–525.
16. Toresdahl BG, Harmon KG, Drezner JA. High school automated external defibrillator programs as markers of emergency preparedness for sudden cardiac arrest. *J Athl Train.* 2013;48(2):242–247.
17. Terminology: definition of athletic training. National Athletic Trainers' Association Web site. http://www.nata.org/athletic-training/terminology. Accessed May 22, 2013.
18. American Academy of Family Physicians, Academy of Pediatrics, American College of Sports Medicine, American Society for Sports Medicine, American Orthopaedic Society for Sports Medicine, and American Osteopathic Academy of Sports Medicine. *Preparticipation Physical Evaluation.* 4th ed. Elk Grove Village, IL: The American Academy of Pediatrics. Published 2010. http://www.aap.org/en-us/professional-resources/practice-support/ pages/Preparticipation-Physical-Evaluation-Forms. aspx. Accessed March 21, 2013.
19. Centers for Disease Control and Prevention. Proper management of cervical spine injuries. In: *Heads Up to Clinicians: Addressing Concussion in Sports Among Kids and Teens.* http:// preventingconcussions.org/. Accessed March 18, 2013.
20. Hazinski MF, Markenson D, Neish S, et al. Response to cardiac arrest and selected life-threatening medical emergencies: the medical emergency response plan for schools. A statement for healthcare providers, policymakers, school administrators, and community leaders. *Circulation.* 2004;109(2):278–291.
21. Armstrong LE, Casa DJ, et al. American College of Sports Medicine position stand: exertional heat illness during training and competition. *Med Sci Sports Exerc.* 2007;39(3):556–572.
22. Casa DJ, Csillan D; Inter-Association Task Force for Preseason Secondary School Athletics Participants. Preseason heat-acclimatization guidelines for secondary school athletes. *J Athl Train.* 2009;44(3):332–333.
23. Harmon KG, Asif IM, Klossner D, Drezner JA. Incidence of sudden cardiac death in National Collegiate Athletic Association athletes. *Circulation.* 2011;123(15):1594–1600.

24. American College of Cardiology Foundation. 36th Bethesda Conference: eligibility recommendations for competitive athletes with cardiovascular abnormalities. *J Am College Cardiol.* 2005;45(8):1313–1375.

25. Rittenberger J, Abella BS, Guyette FX. Postarrest cardiocerebral resuscitation: an evidence-based review. *EM Crit Care.* 2012;2(5):1–12. http://www.ebmedicine.net/topics.php?paction=showTopic& topic_id=341. Published October 2012. Accessed April 11, 2013.

26. Harmon KG, Drezner JA, Klossner D, Asif IM. Sickle cell trait associated with a RR of death of 37 times in National Collegiate Athletic Association football athletes: a database with 2 million athlete-years as the denominator. *Br J Sports Med.* 2012;46(5):325–330.

27. Christopher SA, Collins JL, Farrell MH. Effort required to contact primary care providers after newborn screening identifies sickle cell trait. *J Natl Med Assoc.* 2012;104(11–12):528–534.

Address correspondence to Douglas J. Casa, PhD, ATC, FNATA, FACSM, Korey Stringer Institute, Department of Kinesiology, University of Connecticut, 2095 Hillside Road, Box U-1110, Storrs, CT 06269-1110. Address e-mail to douglas.casa@uconn.edu.

The Inter-Association Task Force for Preventing Sudden Death in Collegiate Conditioning Sessions: Best Practices Recommendations

Douglas J. Casa, PhD, ATC, FNATA, FACSM (Chair)[*]; Scott A. Anderson, ATC[*]; Lindsay Baker, PhD[†]; Scott Bennett, MS, MSCC, SCCC, CSCS[*]D[‡]; Michael F. Bergeron, PhD, FACSM[§]; Declan Connolly, PhD, FACSM, CSCS[*]D[‡]; Ron Courson, PT, ATC, NREMT-I, CSCS[*]; Jonathan A. Drezner, MD[||]; E. Randy Eichner, MD[¶]; Boyd Epley, MEd, RSCC[*]E, FNSCA[#]; Steve Fleck, PhD, CSCS, FNSCA, FACSM[#]; Rob Franks, DO, FAOASM[**]; Kevin M. Guskiewicz, PhD, ATC, FNATA, FACSM[*]; Kimberly G. Harmon, MD[||]; Jay Hoffman, PhD, RSCC[*]D, FNSCA, FACSM[#]; Jolie C. Holschen, MD, FACEP[††]; Jon Jost, MS, RSCC[*]E[#]; Alan Kinniburgh, PhD[#]; David Klossner, PhD, ATC[‡‡], Rebecca M. Lopez, PhD, ATC, CSCS[*]; Gerard Martin, MS, RSCC[*]D[#]; Brendon P. McDermott, PhD, ATC[*]; Jason P. Mihalik, PhD, CAT(C), ATC[§§]; Tom Myslinski, MS, RSCC[#]; Kelly Pagnotta, MA, ATC, PES[||||]; Sourav Poddar, MD[‡‡]; George Rodgers, MD, PhD[‡]; Alan Russell, MS, ATC, PES, CES[¶¶]; Latrice Sales[‡‡]; David Sandler, RSCC[*]D[#]; Rebecca L. Stearns, PhD, ATC[||||]; Chuck Stiggins, EdD[‡]; Charlie Thompson, MS, ATC[*

© Giorgio Micheletti/ShutterStock, Inc.

In January 2012, the National Athletic Trainers' Association, along with the National Strength and Conditioning Association, convened a meeting in Colorado Springs, Colorado. Its purpose was to hold an interdisciplinary forum and gather input to address sudden death in collegiate conditioning sessions. Based on these discussions, a writing group drafted the following recommendations. To date, these best practices have been endorsed by the American College of Emergency Physicians, American College of Sports Medicine, American Medical Society for Sports Medicine, American Osteopathic Academy of Sports Medicine, Canadian

[*]National Athletic Trainers' Association; [†]Gatorade Sports Science Institute; [‡]Collegiate Strength and Conditioning Coaches Association; [§]American College of Sports Medicine; [||]American Medical Society for Sports Medicine; [¶]University of Oklahoma, Retired; [#]National Strength and Conditioning Association; [**]American Osteopathic Academy of Sports Medicine; [††]American College of Emergency Physicians; [‡‡]National Collegiate Athletic Association; [§§]Canadian Athletic Therapists' Association; [||||]Korey Stringer Institute; [¶¶]National Academy of Sports Medicine

Source: *Journal of Athletic Training* 2012;47(4):477–480 doi: 10.4085/1062-6050-47.4.08 by the National Athletic Trainers' Association, Inc. www.nata.org/journal-of-athletic-training. Reprinted by permission of *Journal of Athletic Training*.

Athletic Therapists' Association, Collegiate Strength and Conditioning Coaches Association, Gatorade Sports Science Institute, Korey Stringer Institute, National Academy of Sports Medicine, National Athletic Trainers' Association, and National Strength and Conditioning Association. Other reviewers and meeting participants are listed with the professional organizations they represent at the end of this article.

Maximizing strength and conditioning sessions has become fundamental to sport. The right combination of strength, speed, cardiorespiratory fitness, and other components of athletic capacity can complement skill and enhance performance for all athletes. A sound and effective training program that relies on scientific principles of exercise physiology and biomechanics intended to produce outcomes that are sensitive and specific to the sport should be the goals. Unfortunately, the athlete's development, health, and safety are sometimes overshadowed by a culture that values making athletes tough, instilling discipline, and focusing on success at all costs.

This ill-conceived philosophy has been a contributor to the alarming increase in collegiate athlete deaths and serious injuries during conditioning sessions. A total of 21 National Collegiate Athletic Association (NCAA) football players have died during conditioning workouts since 2000.[1] The 3 most common causes of the fatalities were (in order) exercise-related sudden death associated with sickle cell trait (SCT), exertional heat stroke, and cardiac conditions.[1] Seventy-five percent of the fatalities (n = 16) were Division I football players.

Also, the incidence of exertional rhabdomyolysis in collegiate athletes appears to be increasing. Excesses in strength training and conditioning—workouts that are too novel, too much, too soon, or too intense (or a combination of these)—have a strong connection to exertional rhabdomyolysis. Introducing full-intensity workouts too quickly is especially high risk: 11 of the 21 deaths occurred during day 1 or day 2 workouts.

Rule changes enacted in 2003 related to heat acclimatization procedures during August football practices have been extremely effective. In the NCAA Division I Football Bowl Subdivision, no player died from practicing or playing in a game between 2000 and 2011. However, conditioning workouts continue to be a catalyst for catastrophic outcomes. It is imperative that similar guidelines be implemented to improve the safety of conditioning sessions. This consensus statement provides specific conditioning recommendations with the intent of ending conditioning-related morbidity and deaths of collegiate athletes.

(1) Acclimatize Progressively for Utmost Safety

Conditioning periods should be phased in gradually and progressively to encourage proper exercise acclimatization and to minimize the risk of adverse effects on health. The first 7 to 10 days (at minimum, the first 4 separate-day workouts) of any new conditioning cycle (including but not limited to return in January, after spring break, return in summer, and return after an injury) are referred to as *transitional periods*. A written, progressive program of increasing volume, intensity, mode, and duration should be instituted for all transitional periods. These conditioning programs should be approved by a credentialed strength and conditioning coach ([S&CC] see following paragraphs). The S&CC should work cooperatively with medical staff (certified athletic trainer, team physician, or both) when developing transitional workout plans, particularly if the athlete is recovering from an injury or if any uncertainty exists regarding the pace of exercise progression.

Transitional periods should invoke an appropriate work- to-rest ratio for the sport. A 1:4 work-to-rest ratio (with greater rest permissible) when conducting serial activity of an intense nature, for example, is a good starting place to emphasize recovery.

A qualified S&CC is knowledgeable about and uses acclimatization principles. Participation in summer workouts on campus under the supervision of an S&CC is preferable to unsupervised workouts elsewhere or workouts conducted by unqualified individuals.

Training programs should be individualized. Some athletes will require a longer acclimatization process. An athlete at a different level of preparedness from his or her teammates (due to injury or time away from training) should use a training program tailored to his or her level.

(2) Introduce New Conditioning Activities Gradually

Any new exercise introduced into a strength and conditioning program should be added in a deliberate, gradual fashion by a qualified S&CC. This guideline is true for any aspect of the regimen but is particularly important during the early stages of a conditioning program.

(3) Do Not Use Exercise and Conditioning Activities as Punishment

Physical activity should not be used as retribution, for coercion, or as discipline for unsatisfactory athletic or academic performance or unacceptable behavior. No additional physical burden that would increase the risk of injury or sudden death should be placed on the athlete under any circumstance.

(4) Ensure Proper Education, Experience, and Credentialing of S&CCs

(A) Education. All S&CCs are required to obtain an undergraduate degree to sit for the examination and become credentialed. It is recommended that the degree be in exercise science or a related field of study.

The strength and conditioning profession is urged to establish an accredited educational curriculum at the collegiate level for entry-level programs. A suitable amount of coursework should be dedicated to the health and safety concerns of and challenges facing athletes, with a focus on preventing sudden death. This includes the prevention, recognition, and management of on-field emergencies. Continuing education requirements should ensure that certified S&CCs engage in educational opportunities that provide applicable, up-to-date information regarding important health and safety topics, emergency procedures, and preventing sudden death. Content should be reviewed annually, so that timely topics can be incorporated.

(B) Experience. Collegiate S&CCs should have adequate mentoring and experience to independently design and implement individual and team conditioning programs.

(C) Credentials. All S&CCs should be required to pass a certification examination credentialed by an independent accreditation agency. Competency standards, ongoing assessment, and continuing education requirements should be clearly documented.

All S&CCs should maintain certification in first aid, cardiopulmonary resuscitation (CPR), and use of an automated external defibrillator (AED).

(5) Provide Appropriate Medical Coverage

An S&CC should be present during all strength and conditioning sessions and be prepared to provide first aid as soon as an athlete shows signs of distress. The S&CC should be able to administer CPR, apply an AED, and activate the emergency action plan (EAP) if needed. An athletic trainer or team physician should be present during each high-risk collegiate conditioning session (eg, sprinting, timed sessions, mat drills, stations). For lower-risk conditioning sessions and the strength portion of a conditioning program, an S&CC should be present and an athletic trainer should be on campus and accessible to assist if a problem arises. The institution should determine the need for and level of medical coverage for conditioning sessions. Among the factors to be considered are squad size, type of athlete, time of year (eg, immediately postseason, off season, in season, summer), expected environmental conditions, and planned duration and intensity level of the workout.

(6) Develop and Practice EAPs

Strength and conditioning venues should have EAPs specific to the venue, sport, and circumstances.[2,3] The EAP should be developed by the sports medicine staff with the input of all concerned parties, approved by the head team physician, and most importantly, reviewed and rehearsed at least annually by all staff involved. A conditioning session should not take place if those supervising the session are not familiar with the EAP.

(7) Be Cognizant of Medical Conditions

The most prevalent medical conditions associated with sudden death during collegiate strength and conditioning sessions are atraumatic cardiac conditions, exertional collapse associated with SCT, exertional heat stroke, and asthma.[4–9] The designated medical supervisor must be familiar with the characteristics of exertional collapse and the differential diagnosis of the conditions listed earlier. Institutional, governing, and credentialing agencies for S&CCs, sport coaches, and sports medicine professionals should require ongoing continuing education covering these major health concerns.

The National Athletic Trainers' Association position statement[10] on preventing sudden death in sport is a recommended resource for recognition and treatment of these conditions. The likelihood of preventing problems is enhanced when S&CCs, sport coaches, and the medical staff are aware of the athlete's medical history, supplement use, medications, conditioning status, and acute illnesses, as well as other predisposing risk factors.

Key Points

(A) Exertional sickling and SCT-related concerns:

- Athletes should know their SCT status. Athletes who do not know their status should be encouraged to undergo testing and not invoke the waiver.
- The S&CCs, sport coaches, and medical staff should be aware of the SCT status of each athlete as they would be aware of any other medical condition that may predispose an athlete to exertional collapse and death.
- The supervising staff should know the common prevention, recognition, and treatment strategies for exertional collapse in those athletes with SCT.[10]
- Athletes tested for SCT should be made aware of the health implications of both positive and negative tests for SCT and be provided genetic counseling and education regarding the prevention and recognition of exertional sickling.

(B) Exertional heat stroke:

- An exertional heat-stroke cooling plan (using a cooling modality with proven effectiveness) should be developed for each venue.
- A heat-acclimatization plan should be in place for transitional-period practice sessions that take place in warm or hot environments.
- Appropriate work-to-rest ratios based on intensity of activity, environmental conditions, and individual factors should be implemented. These breaks allow the body to cool and provide ample time for rehydration.

All S&CCs, sport coaches, and medical staff should be well versed in common prevention, recognition, and treatment strategies.

(C) Cardiac conditions:

- Initial management of sudden cardiac arrest includes early activation of the emergency medical services system, early CPR, and early defibrillation.
- Sudden cardiac arrest of traumatic or atraumatic origin should be suspected in any collapsed and unresponsive athlete and an AED applied as soon as possible.
- A collapsed athlete experiencing seizures should be treated as having sudden cardiac arrest until proven otherwise.[11]
- Prompt resuscitation of young athletes with sudden cardiac arrest results in high survival rate.[10]

Exertional rhabdomyolysis should also be comprehensively addressed. This condition can have serious health ramifications, but it is easily prevented when basic precautions are followed.

(8) Administer Strength and Conditioning Programs

A strength and conditioning coach and a sports medicine staff member (athletic trainer or physician [or both]) should be part of the institution's athletics administration to encourage institutional ownership of the sports performance and sports medicine programs and effectively manage health- and safety-related concerns for the student-athlete. Ideally, a sport coach should not serve as the primary supervisor for an athletic health care provider or for an S&CC, nor should he or she have sole hiring or firing authority over those positions. The S&CC should work closely and cooperatively with the sports medicine staff. It is critical that S&CCs and athletic trainers have a harmonious, synergistic working relationship with open lines of communication.

A meeting should be held between the strength and conditioning staff and the sports medicine staff at the beginning of each semester and training season to discuss the health and safety concerns of at-risk athletes, including the sharing of pertinent medical information and conditions (eg, SCT status, asthma, diabetes, history of exertional heat illness) and applicable educational materials, including updates on sudden death risks and prevention strategies. The EAP should be reviewed and rehearsed to ensure proper assignment and execution of duties and responsibilities in the event the plan must be implemented.

(9) Partner With Recognized Professional Organizations

The key organizations responsible for athletes' safety during strength and conditioning sessions should formalize a partnership to periodically review these best practices. The organizations include relevant athletic, coaching, sports medicine, and strength and conditioning organizations.

(10) Provide Adequate Continuing Education for the Entire Coaching and Medical Teams

The task force strongly recommends that key professions—S&CCs, sport coaches, athletic trainers, and team physicians—adopt requirements for education and training and require individuals to demonstrate knowledge in the area of preventing sudden death in sport. Each reporting cycle should require a continuing education component on managing emergencies and preventing sudden death in athletes.

References

1. National Center for Catastrophic Sport Injury Research. http://www.unc.edu/depts/nccsi/. Accessed March 14, 2012.
2. Andersen JC, Courson RW, Kleiner DM, McLoda TA. National Athletic Trainers' Association position statement: emergency planning in athletics. *J Athl Train*. 2002;37(1):99–104. http://www.nata.org/sites/default/files/EmergencyPlanninginAthletics .pdf. Accessed February 15, 2012.
3. Hazinski MF, Markenson D, Neish S, et al. Response to cardiac arrest and selected life-threatening medical emergencies: the medical emergency response plan for schools. A statement for healthcare providers, policymakers, school administrators, and community leaders. *Circulation*. 2004;109(2):278–291.
4. Casa DJ. *Preventing Sudden Death in Sport and Physical Activity*. Burlington, MA: Jones & Bartlett Learning; 2012.
5. Maron BJ, Doerer JJ, Haas TS, Tierney DM, Mueller FO. Sudden deaths in young competitive athletes: analysis of 1866 deaths in the United States, 1980–2006. *Circulation*. 2009;119(8):1085–1092.
6. Harmon KG, Drezner JA, Klossner D, Asif IM. Sickle cell trait associated with a RR of death of 37 times in National Collegiate Athletic Association football athletes: a database with 2 million athlete-years as the denominator. *Br J Sports Med*. 2012;46(5):325–330.
7. Harmon KG, Asif IM, Klossner D, Drezner JA. Incidence of sudden cardiac death in National Collegiate Athletic Association athletes. *Circulation*. 2011;123(15):1594–1600.
8. Armstrong LE, Casa DJ, et al. American College of Sports Medicine position stand: exertional heat illness during training and competition. *Med Sci Sports Exerc*. 2007;39(3):556–572.
9. Drezner JA, Courson RW, Roberts WO, Mosesso VN, Link MS, Maron BJ. Inter-Association Task Force recommendations on emergency preparedness and management of sudden cardiac arrest in high school and college athletic programs: a consensus statement. *J Athl Train*. 2007;42(1):143–158.
10. Casa DJ, Guskiewicz KM, Anderson SA, et al. National Athletic Trainers' Association position statement: preventing sudden death in sport. *J Athl Train*. 2012;47(1):96–118. http://www.nata.org/sites/ default/files/Preventing-Sudden-Death-Position -Statement_2.pdf. Accessed February 15, 2012.
11. Drezner JA, Rao AL, Heistand J, Bloomingdale MK, Harmon KG. Effectiveness of emergency response planning for sudden cardiac arrest in United States high schools with automated external defibrillators. *Circulation*. 2009;120(6):518–525.

Additional task force participants were Julie Gilchrist, MD, of the Centers for Disease Control and Prevention; Peter Indelicato, MD, of the American Orthopaedic Society for Sports Medicine; Christine Lawless, MD, FACC, FACSM, CAQSM, and Reginald Washington, MD, of the American College of Cardiology Council on Sports and Exercise Cardiology; Bill Moreau, DC, DACBSP, CSCS, of the United States Olympic Committee; and Brian Robinson, MS, LAT, ATC, of the National Athletic Trainers' Association.

Thanks also to reviewers Jeffrey M. Anderson, MD, FACSM, and Robert L. Howard, MA, ATC.

Address correspondence to Douglas J. Casa, PhD, ATC, FNATA, FACSM (Chair), Korey Stringer Institute, Department of Kinesiology, University of Connecticut, 2095 Hillside Road, Box U-1110, Storrs, CT 06269-1110. Address e-mail to douglas.casa@ uconn.edu.

Preseason Heat-Acclimatization Guidelines for Secondary School Athletics

Douglas J. Casa, PhD, ATC, FNATA, FACSM; David Csillan, MS, LAT, ATC*;
Inter-Association Task Force for Preseason Secondary School Athletics
Participants: Lawrence E. Armstrong, PhD, FACSM[†]; Lindsay B. Baker, PhD[‡];
Michael F. Bergeron, PhD, FACSM[§]; Virginia M. Buchanan, JD[†];
Michael J. Carroll, MEd, LAT, ATC[||]; Michelle A. Cleary, PhD, LAT, ATC[||];
Edward R. Eichner, MD, FACSM[†]; Michael S. Ferrara, PhD, ATC, FNATA[||];
Tony D. Fitzpatrick, MA, LAT, ATC[||]; Jay R. Hoffman, PhD, FACSM, FNSCA[¶];
Robert W. Kenefick, PhD, FACSM[#]; David A. Klossner, PhD, ATC[||]; J. Chad Knight,
MSHA, MESS, ATC, OTC[||]; Stephanie A. Lennon, MS, NBCT, LAT, ATC[||]; Rebecca M.
Lopez, MS, ATC[||]; Matthew J. Matava, MD[**]; Francis G. O'Connor, MD, FACSM[††];
Bart C. Peterson, MSS, ATC[||]; Stephen G. Rice, MD, PhD, FACSM, FAAP[‡‡];
Brian K. Robinson, MS, LAT, ATC[||]; Robert J. Shriner, MS, LAT, ATC[||];
Michael S. West, MS, ATC[||]; Susan W. Yeargin, PhD, ATC[||]*

A proper heat-acclimatization plan in secondary school athletic programs is essential to minimize the risk of exertional heat illness during the preseason practice period. Gradually increasing athletes' exposure to the duration and intensity of physical activity and to the environment minimizes exertional heat-illness risk while improving athletic performance. Progressive acclimatization is especially important during the initial 3 to 5 days of summer practices. When an athlete undergoes a proper heat-acclimatization program, physiologic function, exercise heat tolerance, and exercise performance are all enhanced.[1-6] In contrast, athletes who are not exposed to a proper heat-acclimatization program face measurable increased risks for exertional heat illness.

*Co-Chairs; †Individual Representatives; ‡Gatorade Sports Science Institute; §American College of Sports Medicine; ||National Athletic Trainers' Association; ¶National Strength and Conditioning Association; #United States Army Research Institute of Environmental Medicine; **American Orthopaedic Society for Sports Medicine; ††American Medical Society for Sports Medicine; ‡‡American Academy of Pediatrics

Source: Journal of Athletic Training 2009;44(3):332–333 by the National Athletic Trainers' Association, Inc. www.nata.org /jat. Reprinted by permission of *Journal of Athletic Training*.

For these reasons, the Inter-Association Task Force for Preseason Secondary School Athletics, in conjunction with the National Athletic Trainers' Association's Secondary School Athletic Trainers' Committee, recommends that these "Preseason Heat-Acclimatization Guidelines for Secondary School Athletics" be implemented by all secondary school athletic programs. These guidelines should be used for all preseason conditioning, training, and practice activities in a warm or hot environment, whether these activities are conducted indoors or outdoors. When athletic programs implement these guidelines, the health and safety of the athletes are primary. However, the recommendations outlined here are only minimum standards, based on the best heat-acclimatization evidence available. Following these guidelines provides all secondary school athletes an opportunity to train safely and effectively during the preseason practice period.

Definitions

Before participating in the preseason practice period, all student-athletes should undergo a preparticipation medical examination administered by a physician (MD or DO) or as required/approved by state law. The examination can identify predisposing factors related to a number of safety concerns, including the identification of youths at particular risk for exertional heat illness.

The *heat-acclimatization period* is defined as the initial 14 consecutive days of preseason practice for all student-athletes. The goal of the acclimatization period is to enhance exercise heat tolerance and the ability to exercise safely and effectively in warm to hot conditions. This period should begin on the first day of practice or conditioning before the regular season. Any practices or conditioning conducted before this time should not be considered a part of the heat-acclimatization period. Regardless of the conditioning program and conditioning status leading up to the first formal practice, all student-athletes (including those who arrive at preseason practice after the first day of practice) should follow the 14-day heat-acclimatization plan. During the preseason heat-acclimatization period, if practice occurs on 6 consecutive days, student-athletes should have 1 day of complete rest (no conditioning, walk-throughs, practices, etc).

Days on which athletes do not practice due to a scheduled rest day, injury, or illness do not count toward the heat-acclimatization period. For example, an athlete who sits out the third and fourth days of practice during this time (eg, Wednesday and Thursday) will resume practice as if on day 3 of the heat-acclimatization period when returning to play on Friday.

A *practice* is defined as the period of time a participant engages in a coach-supervised, school-approved, sport- or conditioning-related physical activity. Each individual practice should last no more than 3 hours. Warm-up, stretching, and cool-down activities are included as part of the 3-hour practice time. Regardless of ambient temperature conditions, all conditioning and weight-room activities should be considered part of practice.

A *walk-through* is defined as a teaching opportunity with the athletes not wearing protective equipment (eg, helmets, shoulder pads, catcher's gear, shin guards) or using other sport-related equipment (eg, footballs, lacrosse sticks, blocking sleds, pitching machines, soccer balls, marker cones). The walk-through is not part of the 3-hour practice period, can last no more than 1 hour per day, and does not include conditioning or weight-room activities.

A *recovery period* is defined as the time between the end of 1 practice or walk-through and the beginning of the next practice or walk-through. During this time, athletes should rest in a cool environment, with no sport- or conditioning-related activity permitted (eg, speed or agility drills, strength training, conditioning, or walk-through). Treatment with the athletic trainer is permissible.

Recommendations for the 14-Day Heat-Acclimatization Period

1. Days 1 through 5 of the heat-acclimatization period consist of the first 5 days of formal practice. During this time, athletes may not participate in more than 1 practice per day.
2. If a practice is interrupted by inclement weather or heat restrictions, the practice should recommence once conditions are deemed safe. Total practice time should not exceed 3 hours in any 1 day.
3. A 1-hour maximum walk-through is permitted during days 1–5 of the heat-acclimatization period. However, a 3-hour recovery period should be inserted between the practice and walk-through (or vice versa).

4. During days 1–2 of the heat-acclimatization period, in sports requiring helmets or shoulder pads, a helmet should be the only protective equipment permitted (goalies, as in the case of field hockey and related sports, should *not* wear full protective gear or perform activities that would require protective equipment). During days 3–5, only helmets and shoulder pads should be worn. Beginning on day 6, all protective equipment may be worn and full contact may begin.

    a. Football only: On days 3–5, contact with blocking sleds and tackling dummies may be initiated.

    b. Full-contact sports: 100% live contact drills should begin no earlier than day 6.

5. Beginning no earlier than day 6 and continuing through day 14, double-practice days must be followed by a single-practice day. On single-practice days, 1 walk-through is permitted, separated from the practice by at least 3 hours of continuous rest. When a double-practice day is followed by a rest day, another double-practice day is permitted after the rest day.

6. On a double-practice day, neither practice should exceed 3 hours in duration, and student-athletes should not participate in more than 5 total hours of practice. Warm-up, stretching, cool-down, walk-through, conditioning, and weight-room activities are included as part of the practice time. The 2 practices should be separated by at least 3 continuous hours in a cool environment.

7. Because the risk of exertional heat illnesses during the preseason heat-acclimatization period is high, we strongly recommend that an athletic trainer be on site before, during, and after all practices.

References

1. American College of Sports Medicine, Armstrong LE, Casa DJ, et al. American College of Sports Medicine position stand: exertional heat illnesses during training and competition. *Med Sci Sports Exerc.* 2007;39(3):556–572.
2. Bergeron MF, McKeag DB, Casa DJ, et al. Youth football: heat stress and injury risk. *Med Sci Sports Exerc.* 2005;37(8):1421–1430.
3. Binkley HM, Beckett J, Casa DJ, Kleiner DM, Plummer PE. National Athletic Trainers' Association position statement: exertional heat illnesses. *J Athl Train.* 2002;37(3):329–343.
4. Casa DJ, Almquist J, Anderson S, et al. Inter-Association Task Force on Exertional Heat Illness consensus statement. *NATA News.* June 2003:24–29.
5. Department of the Army and Air Force. *Heat Stress Control and Casualty Management.* Washington, DC: Dept of the Army and Air Force; 2003. Technical bulletin MED 507/AFPAM 48-152 (I).
6. Wallace RF. *Risk Factors and Mortality in Relation to Heat Illness Severity.* Natick, MA: United States Army Research Institute Environmental Medicine; 2003. Technical report T-03/14.

Disclaimer

The National Athletic Trainers' Association (NATA) and the Inter-Association Task Force for Preseason Secondary School Athletics advise individuals, schools, athletic training facilities, and institutions to carefully and independently consider each of the recommendations. The information contained in the statement is neither exhaustive nor exclusive to all circumstances or individuals. Variables such as institutional human resource guidelines, state or federal statutes, rules, or regulations, as well as regional environmental conditions, may impact the relevance and implementation of these recommendations. The NATA and the Inter-Association Task Force advise their members and others to carefully and independently consider each of the recommendations (including the applicability of same to any particular circumstance or individual). The foregoing statement should not be relied upon as an independent basis for care but rather as a resource available to NATA members or others. Moreover, no opinion is expressed herein regarding the quality of care that adheres to or differs from any of NATA's other statements. The NATA and the Inter-Association Task Force reserve the right to rescind or modify their statements at any time.

GLOSSARY

© Giorgio Micheletti/ShutterStock, Inc.

accidental hypothermia   Hypothermia that occurs in natural settings.

acclimation   A complex series of adaptive responses to climatic changes that demonstrate improved response in multiple organs and systems; usually requires 10 to 14 days for responses to develop adequately. Acclimation occurs in response to experimentally induced changes in particular climatic factors. Used most often in research studies to refer to the artificial process of acclimatization that is induced via climate-controlled chambers.

acclimatization   Similar to acclimation, but occurring in a natural setting. Acclimatization is a complex series of adaptive responses occurring in multiple organs and systems; usually requires 10 to 14 days for responses to develop adequately. The body can acclimatize (to varying degrees) to hot, cold, high altitude, underwater, and air-polluted environments.

agreement   The meeting of the minds where there is an offer and acceptance. The terms need to be specific and understood by both parties.

airway access   Ability to expose and maintain breathing through an injured patient's airway.

airway lumen   The inner lining of the bronchial airways.

anaphylaxis   A life-threatening allergic reaction with symptoms that develop rapidly.

anterograde amnesia   Sometimes referred to as posttraumatic amnesia, it is characterized by difficulty remembering events immediately following an injury.

arginine vasopressin (AVP)   A hormone that limits production of urine by stimulating water reabsorption in the kidneys (also known as antidiuretic hormone or ADH).

arrhythmia   An abnormal heart rhythm.

arrhythmogenic right ventricular cardiomyopathy (ARVC)   Progressive fibro-fatty replacement of the right ventricular myocardium, causing wall thinning and right ventricular dilatation.

arterial pressure index (API)   A measure of arterial flow determined by dividing the systolic pressure of the lower extremity (cuff just above the ankle) by the systolic pressure of the upper extremity (brachial artery); acceptable level is greater than 0.90.

atherosclerotic plaque   Deposits of cholesterol and other cells in the walls of the arteries that cause blockages in the arteries.

automated external defibrillator (AED)   Computerized device that analyzes the heart rhythm, determines whether a shock is needed for a ventricular arrhythmia, charges to an appropriate shock dose, shocks a patient's heart, and uses audio and visual instructions to guide the rescuer.

axial load   A situation in which the neck is flexed between 20° and 30° and the head serves as a point of contact for an applied load.

blood sodium   The level of sodium measured within the blood, usually between 135–145 miliequivalents per liter of blood for healthy cell functioning.

blunt injury   A mechanism of lightning injury by which the lightning strike causes a concussive force creating blunt injuries such as ruptured tympanic membranes or violent muscular contractions that cause dislocations or fractures.

263

body temperature   Temperature of the internal organs or thermal core as measured by a valid device (i.e., rectal thermometer, gastrointestinal thermistor). Rectal temperature has been validated as an accurate tool for temperature assessment in exercising individuals and is the most common form used in heat stroke cases.

bronchoconstriction   Constriction of the airways.

capacity   This means that the contracting parties need to meet certain criteria. They need to be the right age (those under 18 can void many contracts), they cannot be drunk/under the influence of drugs, and they cannot be certified insane by the courts.

catastrophic cervical spinal cord injury   An injury in which a structural distortion of the cervical spinal column has occurred and is associated with actual or potential damage to the spinal cord.

catastrophic injury or illness   A sudden death or disability in which there is life-altering physical or mental impairment, or both.

cerebral concussion   A complex pathophysiologic process affecting the brain, induced by traumatic forces that result in a rapid but temporary onset of neurologic dysfunction; typically does not result in any structural brain injury that can be identified using traditional imaging techniques.

cold acclimatization   A complex series of beneficial adaptations made over 14 days that enhances heat production and minimizes heat loss while exposed to cold conditions.

cold stressor   Any intrinsic or extrinsic factor that encourages heat loss from the body.

cold water immersion (CWI)   Cooling via immersion in a tub of water with temperatures ranging from approximately 2° to 13°C (35°–55°F), with faster cooling occurring at lower temperatures and when the water is circulated. Often referred to as *ice-water immersion*.

commotio cordis   Nonpenetrating, blunt trauma to the chest, usually from a firm projectile such as a baseball, lacrosse ball, or hockey puck, that induces ventricular fibrillation and sudden cardiac arrest.

consideration   This is an exchange of value where both parties need to give something such as a waiver where one party gives another the right to participate in exchange for agreeing not to sue if injured through normal negligence.

contact injury   A mechanism of lightning injury by which the lightning strikes an object to which the victim is connected.

coronary artery disease (CAD)   Condition in which plaque builds up inside the coronary (heart) arteries.

deep vein thrombosis (DVT)   A blood clot that forms in a vein deep in the body, most typically in the lower extremity but also possible in the upper extremity.

dehydration   The process of water loss leading to hypohydration. Usually measured by body mass loss, urine color, urine osmolality, urine specific gravity, or serum osmolality (the gold standard).

diffuse brain injury   Brain injuries that result in widespread or global disruption of neurologic function and are not usually associated with macroscopically visible brain lesions except in the most severe cases. Structural diffuse brain injury (diffuse axonal injury) is the most severe type of diffuse injury because when axonal disruption occurs, it often results in disturbance of cognitive functions, such as concentration and memory.

direct fatality   A fatality resulting directly from participation in the fundamental skills of a sport.

direct injury   (1) An injury or fatality resulting from participation in the skills of a sport. (2) A mechanism of lightning injury by which the lightning strikes the person or object directly.

emergency action plan (EAP)   (1) A written document that defines the standard of care for the management of emergencies in athletics. (2) For a mass participation event, a written document that outlines event day policy well in advance of the event to reduce debates about critical decisions during the event and to establish protocols for emergency situations.

emergency management   Treatment of an acute injury or condition that poses a risk of sudden death.

epidural hematoma   A brain injury characterized by pooling of blood between the dura mater (outermost meningeal layer) and the skull.

epinephrine autoinjector   Intramuscular drug delivery system preloaded with a specific dosage of epinephrine for use during an emergency anaphylactic reaction.

equipment load   Amount of equipment that an athlete wears during practice or competition (protective or uniform motivated). In the case of exertional heat illnesses, increases in the amount of clothing or gear that an athlete wears will increase heat load and potentially the ability for an athlete to dissipate heat.

equipment removal   Skills executed in an emergency injury situation to remove protective equipment that interferes with the ability to effectively treat or immobilize a victim.

exacerbation   Worsening of a disease or condition.

exertional heat stroke (EHS)   A medical emergency involving life-threatening hyperthermia (rectal temperature > 40.0–40.5°C [104–105°F]) with concomitant central nervous system dysfunction; treatment involves cooling the body.

exertional sickling   A medical emergency that occurs when an athlete with sickle cell trait experiences the sickling of red blood cells.

explosive rhabdomyolysis   A potentially fatal condition involving the breakdown of skeletal muscle fibers, resulting in the release of muscle fiber contents into circulation.

first aid   Emergency treatment administered to an injured or sick person before professional medical care is available.

first responder   The first person present at the scene of a sudden illness or injury.

fluid overload   An excess of total body fluid volume (hypervolemia).

fulminant ischemic rhabdomyolysis   Rapid breakdown of muscle tissue because of decreased blood flow.

glucagon   A hormone produced by the pancreas that helps increase serum glucose level by stimulating glycogen release.

graded symptom checklist   Sometimes referred to as a postconcussion symptom scale, it is a symptom inventory scale used to evaluate both the number and severity of symptoms commonly associated with cerebral concussion and other forms of traumatic brain injury.

ground current   *See step voltage.*

heart attack (myocardial Infarction)   An injury of the muscle wall of the heart caused by a lack of oxygen, usually due to a blockage of the blood vessels on the surface of the heart. In some cases this can lead to sudden cardiac arrest and death.

high-altitude cerebral edema (HACE)   A condition that only manifests in high-altitude outdoor settings in which low oxygen levels trigger swelling of brain tissue.

high-altitude pulmonary edema (HAPE)   A condition that only manifests in high-altitude outdoor settings in which low oxygen levels trigger swelling of lung tissue, filling them with fluid.

hydration status Measurement of an individual's body water content (usually done via urine or blood sample) that can be used to indicate if an individual has a healthy, low, or high level of body water content. Either extreme (high or low levels) can have health and performance implications.

hypertrophic cardiomyopathy Pathologic hypertrophy (thickening) of the ventricular wall muscle.

hypoglycemia A low serum glucose level that affects physiologic function.

hypothermia Clinically defined as being when body temperature drops below 35°C (95°F) as a result of the human body losing more heat than it can produce. Central nervous system dysfunction is also present in this condition.

hypotonic Having a blood concentration less than that of normal blood.

immobilization The use of external stabilization devices such as extrication collars and a spine board with straps to secure an injured patient's body so that it will not move during transport or emergency treatment.

indirect fatality A fatality caused by systemic failure as a result of exertion while participating in a sports activity or by a complication that was secondary to a nonfatal injury; examples include cardiac failure and an asthma attack.

indirect injury An injury resulting from systemic failure secondary to exertion while participating in a sport.

insulin A hormone produced by the pancreas that helps glucose move into cells for use.

intensity of exercise The relative workload during a bout of exercise. This is largely individual, varying between athletes, and will change with exercise training.

keraunoparalysis A transient paralysis, extreme vasoconstriction, and sensory disturbance caused by a lightning strike.

legality This means that the subject matter of the contract has to be for a legal purpose.

lift and slide A transfer technique to a spine board for a potential spine-injured victim who is lying supine.

Marfan syndrome Inherited disorder of connective tissue that affects multiple organ systems, causing a progressive dilatation and weakness of the proximal aorta that can lead to rupture and sudden death.

metered dose inhaler A pressurized hand-held device that uses propellants to deliver medication to the lungs.

myocardial infarction (MI) The sudden loss of blood supply to heart muscle because of blockage in one or more coronary artery.

myoglobinuric renal failure Kidney failure from myoglobin (a by-product of muscle breakdown) in the urine.

myonecrosis The death of muscle cell fibers.

nebulizer A device used for delivering medication into the lungs during inhalation.

negligence Conduct that falls below the standards of behavior currently established by law for the purpose of protecting others against unreasonable risk or harm.

neutral alignment A situation in which the head and neck rest in an aligned position, as in the anatomic position.

Paget-Schroetter syndrome (PSS) A deep vein thrombosis occurring in the upper extremity without secondary cause (trauma).

peak flow meter   A hand-held device that is used to measure peak expiratory flow rate.

plaintiff   The party who initiates a lawsuit by filing a complaint with the clerk of the court against the defendant in a civil action.

pneumothorax (PTX)   Air that has leaked into the pleural space, either spontaneously or as a result of traumatic tears in the pleura following chest injury or iatrogenic/surgical procedures.

preparticipation exams (PPEs)   A formal requirement prior to participation in sports. PPEs must be conducted by a qualified health professional. They are usually performed once a year with the goal of identifying medical problems that may place an athlete at risk for injury or illness.

primary assumption of risk   Involves two participants engaged in sport where one participant's injuries have resulted from an accident because of the inherent nature of participation.

prodrome   An early indication or symptom of impending disease or illness.

pulmonary embolism (PE)   Complication of a venous thromboembolism (*see* deep vein thrombosis); a clot (embolus) breaks off and travels through the blood to the lung, impeding blood flow.

rectal temperature   Body temperature taken rectally. In most medical situations this involves a rectal probe inserted 10 centimeters past the anal sphincter. This has been validated as an accurate tool for temperature assessment in exercising individuals and is the most common form used in heat stroke cases.

retrograde amnesia   Difficulty remembering events immediately preceding (or leading up to) the injury.

second impact syndrome   A brain injury that occurs when an athlete sustains a second injury to the brain before the symptoms associated with an initial brain injury have fully cleared; may cause delayed catastrophic deterioration resulting in death or persistent vegetative state after a brain injury.

secondary assumption of risk   The duty owed by a coach or event administrator to participants.

shivering   A thermogenic response initiated by the autonomic nervous system in order to produce heat to combat cold stressors.

sickle cell trait (SCT)   A condition resulting from inheriting one gene for normal hemoglobin (A) and one gene for sickle hemoglobin (S). Strenuous exertion in those with SCT can cause red blood cells to sickle when they release their oxygen. This may then cause these cells to "logjam" in small blood vessels, which, as the athlete tries to continue exercising, may result in fulminant rhabdomyolysis.

side flash   A mechanism of lightning injury by which the lightning strikes a nearby object, then a portion of the strike side steps to a nearby person.

space available for the cord (SAC)   The natural space surrounding the spinal cord, where cerebral spinal fluid will freely circulate.

spirometry   A lung function test that measures the volume of air as a function of time.

standard of care   The manner in which an individual must act based on his or her training and education.

step voltage   A mechanism of lightning injury by which the lightning strikes the ground and radiates outward from the strike to affect those within the radiating current. Also known as *ground current*.

subdural hematoma   A brain injury characterized by accumulation of blood between the outermost (dura mater) and middle (arachnoid mater) meningeal layers.

sudden cardiac arrest   Sudden cardiac arrest (SCA) is an abrupt stop of the heartbeat, typically caused by an abnormal electrical signal from the bottom half of the heart. This is different from a heart attack (or myocardial infarction).

sudden cardiac death (SCD)   The sudden death of an individual during or within 1 hour after exercise as a result of a cardiovascular disorder.

symptomatic exertional hyponatremia (EH$_s$)   Sodium deficiency that involves a blood sodium concentration of less than 130 mEq·L^{-1} accompanied by typical symptoms (headache, nausea, vomiting, extreme weakness, etc.). This is the result of the replacement of sodium losses with hypotonic fluids, the loss of total body sodium, or both.

tetraplegia   Paralysis caused by illness or injury to a human that results in the partial or total loss of use of all of the individual's limbs and torso.

tort   A civil wrong or wrongful act that may be intentional or accidental from which injury occurs to another.

total body water   The water content of the human body, which includes water that is both within and outside cells.

trigger   Anything that introduces an allergen that can cause a potential anaphylactic reaction.

type 1 diabetes   An autoimmune illness that causes the pancreas to not produce adequate amounts of insulin, which causes inadequate regulation of blood glucose.

type 2 diabetes   A disease in which the pancreas produces large amounts of insulin; however, cells become less sensitive and resistant to it, which causes inadequate regulation of blood glucose.

upward leader   A mechanism of lightning injury by which the victim becomes a weak, incomplete part of the lightning channel attempting to complete the lightning channel to earth.

ventricular fibrillation (VF)   A lethal ventricular arrhythmia characterized by rapid ventricular depolarization leading to disorganized and unsynchronized contraction of the heart's ventricular muscle and inability to pump blood effectively.

wet bulb globe temperature (WBGT)   The most widely used heat stress index in industry and sports; may be used to assess the severity of hot environments. It is derived from a formula that incorporates the dry bulb, wet bulb, and black globe temperature. A measure of heat stress that incorporates air temperature, the water content of the air, and radiant heat from the sun.

INDEX

Note: Page numbers followed by *b*, *f* and *t* indicate material in boxes, figures and tables respectively.

atherosclerotic plaques, 45
athletic trainer, role of, 7–9, 220–221
atropine, inhaled, 163
automated external defibrillator (AED), 9, 33, 36–38,
      120, 208*t*, 209*t*
    accessing, sudden cardiac death, 10–11
    for commotio cordis, 58
    implementing, 11
AVP. *See* arginine vasopressin
axial load, 99, 100*f*

B
β-agonist, 159
    long-acting inhaled, 164
    short-acting, 163
beta-blockers, 159
blood clots, in deep veins of legs and lungs, 136–137
blood sodium, 170
blunt injury, 148
body, organs and systems of, 173
body temperature, 63
brain injuries
    assessment, on-field, 88–90, 90*t*
    background and occurrence, 85–86
    biomechanics, 87
    causes, 86–87
    cerebral concussion, 84
    definitions, 84–85
    evaluation, 88–90
    fatalities in football, 86*t*
    neurometabolic cascade, 84
    pathophysiology, 84
    physician referral checklist, 90*t*–91*t*
    player behavior, role of, 87
    preventing, 87
    previous injury, 87
    protective mechanisms of, 86–87
    recognition and management, 87–91
    recovery, 91–92
    return to play issues, 92, 92*t*
    signs and symptoms, 88–89, 89*t*
    statistics, 84
breastbone (sternal) fracture, 131
bronchoconstriction, 159, 163
Brugada syndrome, 34
"but for" test, 218

C
CAD. *See* coronary artery disease
Canadian Standards Association, 87
capacity, 216

cardiac arrest. *See also* sudden cardiac death
    preventing, 28*t*
    recognizing, 28*t*
    signs and symptoms, 26–27
    treatment for, 28*t*
cardiac collapse
    diagnosis of, 119–121
    settings and patterns of, 119
cardiac concussion. *See* commotio cordis
cardiac emergencies, athletic facilities for handling,
      46–47
cardiopulmonary resuscitation (CPR), 9, 33, 46, 120
cardiovascular disease risk factor, atherosclerotic, 47*t*
catastrophic cervical spinal cord injury. *See* spinal
      cord injury
catastrophic injuries or illnesses, 128. *See also*
      emergency action plan
    defined, 2, 203
    guidelines, 211–212, 212*f*
Centers for Disease Control (CDC), on
      concussion, 3, 12
central nervous system, manifestations of, 190*t*
cerebral concussion, 84
cerebrospinal fluid (CSF), 86, 89
cervical spinal cord injury. *See* spinal cord injury
chest injuries
    breastbone (sternal) fracture, 131
    lung (pulmonary) contusion, 130–131
    PTX and PM, 131–133
chest protectors, 57, 57*f*
clothing, 192
cold acclimatization, 193
cold diuresis, 188
cold stressors, 187
cold water immersion (CWI), 13, 73–76, 73*f*, 75*f*
cold-weather events, 192, 192*b*
commotio cordis, 35, 54
    clinical profile, 56
    emergency medical services to, 58
    experimental animal model, 56–57
    impact velocity, 56
    management, 58–59
    mechanism, causes, and recognition of, 54–57
    medical reports, 58–59
    occurrence, 54
    prevention, 57–58
    reducing, 58*t*
    survival, 58–59
comparative negligence rule, 220
computed tomography (CT) scanning, 133

signs and symptoms, 26–27
treatment for, 28*t*
heat exhaustion
preventing, 28*t*
recognizing, 28*t*
signs and symptoms, 26–27
treatment for, 28*t*
heat gain, 63, 64
heat loss, 63, 64, 188
heat stress response
factors affecting, 64–68
physiologic changes in, 64
heat stroke. *See* exertional heat stroke
heat syncope, overlap of signs and symptoms, 26–27
hematoma
epidural, 85
subdural, 84–85
high-altitude cerebral edema (HACE), 197
high-altitude pulmonary edema (HAPE), 197
histamines, 182
hockey, brain injuries in, 87
Hockey Equipment Certification Council, 87
hold harmless clause, 217
hydration status, 65, 67
hyperglycemia, 193
hyperthermia, 74*f*
hypertrophic cardiomyopathy, 33–34
hypoglycemia
defined, 193
management, 196–197
hypohydration, 63, 67
hypothermia
classification, 187*t*
defined, 186
management, 189–191
mechanisms and causes, 187–188
occurrence, 187
predisposing factors, 188–189
preventing, 188–189, 191*t*–192*t*
recognition, 189
recovery and return to play, 191
signs and symptoms, 190*t*
sports where it can occur, 186*t*
hypotonic fluid, 170, 173

I
ice hockey, 109
immobilization, 102, 105–106
immunity, government, 219
impact velocity, commotio cordis, 56
indemnity clause, 217

indirect fatalities
defined, 18, 19*f*
fall sports, 19–20, 20*t*
football, 18, 19*f*
spring sports, 22–24
winter sports, 21–22
indirect injury, 98
injury
mechanisms, 147–148
negligence, 218
insulin, 193
delivery, 194
insurance, 220
intensity of exercise, 67
intentional torts, 217
intracerebral hematoma, 85*t*
intrinsic risk factors
for exertional heat stroke, 69*t*
SCI, 100, 101*t*
ion channel disorders, 34–35
ipratropium bromide, 163

K
keraunoparalysis, 150
Kleinknecht v. Gettysburg College, 204
knee dislocations, 134–136

L
lacrosse, spinal cord injuries and equipment
removal, 109
late hypoglycemia, 196
legal concepts
contract law, 216–217
laws development, 215–216
real cases, 221–236
tort law, 217
defenses, 219–220
involved parties, status of, 218–219
negligence, elements of, 217–218, 217*t*
legality, 216
legislative bodies, 215
Lichtenberg figures, 151
lightning
causes, 144–145, 155–158
comparison of properties of electricity
and, 145*t*
educational tools, 149*b*
long-term complications of lightning
survivors, 151*b*
management, 150–151
mechanisms, 147–148

lightning (*cont.*)
  places that are not safe for waiting out a storm, 147*b*
  preventing, 148–150
  recognition, 150
  recovery from lightning strikes, 151–152
  return to play, 152
  weather-monitoring websites, 148, 148*t*
long QT syndrome, 34
lung (pulmonary) contusion, 130–131

M

magnesium sulfate, 163–164
Marfan syndrome, 34
mast cell stabilizers, 164
mediation clause, 216
medications, asthma and, 159
metered dose inhaler, 163
methacholine, 163
MI. *See* myocardial infarction
mild hypoglycemia, 196
ministerial acts, 219
myocardial infarction (MI), 32
myocarditis, 34
myoglobinuric renal failure, 117
myonecrosis, 121

N

National Athletic Trainers' Association (NATA), 3, 148, 176, 195, 203
  position statement, 107
  Preseason Heat Acclimatization Guidelines for Secondary School Athletics, 4*t*
  for preventing sudden death, 10, 11
National Center for Catastrophic Sport Injury Research, 98
National Collegiate Athletic Association (NCAA), 5, 17, 116, 148
  guidelines, 65
  and injury rate, 3
National Commotio Cordis Registry, cases in, 54–55, 55*f*
National Federation of State High School Associations (NFHS), 3, 5, 17
National Football League (NFL), policy changes, 3
National Lightning Safety Institute, 148*t*
National Oceanic and Atmospheric Administration (NOAA), 146, 148, 148*t*
National Operating Committee for Standards on Athletic Equipment, 87
National Spinal Cord Injury Statistical Center (NSCISC), 98
National Weather Service (NWS), 144, 148*t*

NCAA. *See* National Collegiate Athletic Association
nebulizer, 163
negligence, elements of, 217–218, 217*t*
neurologic exam, 136
neurometabolic cascade, 84
neutral alignment, 104
NFHS. *See* National Federation of State High School Associations
NFL. *See* National Football League
NOAA. *See* National Oceanic and Atmospheric Administration
noncompete clause (trade secrets), 216
nonfatal EHS cases, 69*f*
nonprofit immunity, 219
nonsteroidal anti-inflammatory drugs (NSAIDs), 159, 175
NSCISC. *See* National Spinal Cord Injury Statistical Center
nutrition, 193
NWS. *See* National Weather Service

O

oral steroids, 164
organs, abdominal, 129*t*
overhydration, signs and symptoms of, 175

P

PA injuries. *See* popliteal artery injuries
Paget-Schroetter syndrome (PSS), 136
PE. *See* pulmonary embolism
peak flow meters, 164
peroneal nerve injuries, 135
plaintiff, 217
pneumomediastinum (PM), 131–133
pneumothorax (PTX), 131–133
policy development, for risk of injury, 1, 2
popliteal artery (PA) injuries, 134
posttraumatic amnesia. *See* anterograde amnesia
preparticipation exams (PPEs), 11
primary assumption of risk, 219
prodrome, 120
proximate cause, negligence, 218
PSS. *See* Paget-Schroetter syndrome
PTX. *See* pneumothorax
pulmonary contusion, 130–131
pulmonary embolism (PE), 136

Q

quadrants, abdominal, 129*t*

R

radiation, 63, 64
rectal temperature, 13, 14, 71, 72